GOLF
IN THE MAKING

GOLF
IN THE MAKING

BY IAN T. HENDERSON
AND DAVID I. STIRK

REVISED EDITION

Sean Arnold
London Mayfair

First edition 1979
Second revised edition 1982
Reprinted 1986
Reprinted 1990
Reprinted 1994

Published by
Sean Arnold
Golf & Polo Antiques
Grays Antique Market
58 Davies Street
London W1Y 1AR
Tel.: 071 409 7358
Fax.: 071 499 5890

ISBN 0 9516078 0 4

Designed by Charlton/Szyszkowski

Made and printed in Great Britain
by The Bath Press, Avon

Contents

List of Illustrations

Chapter 9

Foreword

As a result of years of research, dedication and experience, David Stirk and Ian Henderson wrote *Golf in the Making*. By the compilation of this fine volume, they have made available to collectors and historians throughout the world, a history of golf yet to be surpassed. I feel a deep sense of gratitude to Mr David Stirk and Mrs Henderson for allowing me to publish this outstanding book.

Sean Arnold

Sean Arnold is a name synonymous with the art of collecting golf antiques and memorabilia.

An art it surely is. There are so many pitfalls for the novice collector, and indeed, the experienced collectors are still known to make an 'unwise buy.'

Should anyone, on reading this book, have any questions, please contact Sean Arnold direct.

If you are able to visit his gallery in London's Mayfair, you can be assured of a warm welcome, a wonderful selection of golfing antiques, and professional advice.

Introduction

This book is not about great golfers but about the men who made and developed the clubs and the balls and helped create the game we know today.

It came about as a result of the authors, each with a collection of old golf clubs, meeting by chance at Westward Ho! where Ian Henderson's clubs were being restored. It provided the opportunity of studying a combined range of antique long-headed clubs, the names of whose makers we knew, though that was the extent of our knowledge. It was then that we decided to find out more for ourselves, and we soon came to appreciate that the answers must lie in Scottish archives which apparently had never been systematically examined.

This was the challenge which George Gibb, our Research Editor, Dr Audrey Paterson and James Robb, all connected with Edinburgh University and each an expert in their own field, took on. They started work in 1976 examining census records, valuation rolls (i.e. rating records), birth and death registers, the various early trade directories such as *Slaters, Pigot, Fife Trade Directory* and the *Edinburgh Post Office Directory*, together with all the early golf magazines and golf manuals such as *Forgans Annual, Frys Magazine, Golf, Golf Illustrated, Golf Monthly*, etc. Many collections of clubs and balls have been examined and the clubs measured. The enquiry extended to the golfing centres of Aberdeen, Carnoustie, St Andrews, the Fife coast, Edinburgh, Leith, Musselburgh and North Berwick on the East coast and Glasgow and Prestwick on the West. The results of the research include a card index containing some 500 entries and a wealth of information taking us back to the sixteenth century and continually inviting further research.

We discovered that as far back as 1864 Admiral Bethune, a member of the Royal and Ancient, suggested that the Club should collect historic golf items. In 1866 the first *Golfer's Yearbook* had an advertisement on the back page which announced that a Museum had been opened in the Union Club House and appealed for contributions for the collection. In England, Harry B. Wood was the first to interest himself in the subject and in 1910 his book *Golfing Curios and the Like* was published. This illustrated part of his collection, which is still intact at the North Manchester Club, and also contained the first bibliography of the game. In his Preface he said that he hoped someone would find his book useful in completing the 'History and archaeology of the Royal and Ancient game' and he went on to say 'that as yet there does not exist any standard work dealing exhaustively and thoroughly with the History of the Game'. In 1968, J. S. F. Murdoch (Chairman of the Golf Collectors' Society) published *The Library of Golf* and so completed one part of Harry Wood's objective, for he was the first to produce a bibliography of all books relating to golf. It was complete up till 1968, and was an outstanding piece of original research.

Mr Murdoch records that from the appearance of Mathison's *The Goff* in 1743 until 1889 only thirty books exclusively devoted to golf were published and only eighteen of these books were sold publicly.

From 1890–1900, when golf came into fashion, forty-eight books were published including the first biography of a golfer, the first book describing famous courses, the first golfing novel, the first American book on the game, the first book on the subject written by a woman and the first book by a working professional. An examination of all these early books has revealed how few references there were to club- and ballmakers and that Harry B. Wood was unable to tell us much about his collection. It was not in fact until the *History of Golf in Britain* was published that chapters on 'The development of implements – clubs and balls' appeared and provided a limited review of the subject.

Apart from the examination of so many old records, the opportunity has been taken to bring the story of the origins of golf up to date – a subject which has always attracted golf historians.

Much interesting research has been undertaken by the Dutch golf historian Steven van Hengel into Dutch records and the Dutch golfing pictures, backed by the discovery of irons, clubs and a wooden golf-ball in Amsterdam and published privately in a treatise *Early Golf*. In Britain clubs and a ball for playing jeu de mail have also come to light, replicas have been made and we now have a far better insight into the game which was so similar to golf in style of swing.

We believe that by extracting the golfing element in many crowded Dutch landscapes, our artist Roger Morris has for the first time shown the prominent part played by golf in Holland up to the time when it died out early in the eighteenth century, just as the Scots were taking the decisive step of forming the first golfing societies.

To anyone interested in the history of the game, the thirty years preceding World War I are particularly important. They saw the beginning of the craze for the game of golf and its spread throughout the world and particularly the USA. Clubs and balls were changed dramatically, and hundreds of new ideas were patented; we hope that we have fulfilled our mission in recording not only what happened but who the pioneers were who should be remembered.

This book contains a considerable amount of information which has never been published before, and it is hoped that a knowledge of the past may interest many a golfer in his idle moment, and perhaps bring to light some long-lost golfing treasures of the past and more information hitherto unrecorded. Perhaps it may also inspire Clubs to preserve their own antiquities and maybe honour their past professionals by exhibiting their photographs, their playing records and (if they can be found) a few of the clubs they played with and in some cases made.

The opportunity has been taken in this revised edition to include a Supplement, prepared in the light of information which has come to light since the first publication, and an index.

Acknowledgements

We are deeply grateful to the large number of people who have contributed to gathering the information on which this book is based. We wish to thank the members of the Golf Collectors' Society, their Chairman Joe Murdoch, Bob Kuntz and Jim Nolan (especially for his loan of books), Archie Baird (for his loan of illustrations) and in particular Sheila Baird, Steven van Hengel, Harry Langton and Bob Grant for their contributions included in the book.

We would like to thank: The Captains, Secretaries and Committees of the following Golf Clubs for permission to examine their collections and obtain illustrations: The Royal & Ancient (St Andrews), Baberton, the Honourable Company of Edinburgh Golfers, King James VI (Perth), Prestwick, Prestwick St Nicholas, Royal Musselburgh, Royal Troon (Dr L. A. Hardie), Budleigh Salterton, Old Manchester, Royal Blackheath, Saunton Golf Club, Royal St George's; and North Manchester Golf Club (the home of the Wood Collection) for details of their records.

The following museums: the British Museum (Mr J. F. Russell), the Scottish National Museum, Edinburgh (Mr S. Maxwell), the Spalding Collection (Miss C. Young and Mr J. Boyd, Curator), and in America the US Golf Association Museum, Far Hills, New Jersey (Miss J. Seagle).

The following libraries: City of Edinburgh District Council Library (Mr A. Shearman), North East Fife Library, St Andrews (Mr. A. Rodden), Royal Society of Arts (Mr D. Goddard), the Signet Library, Edinburgh and the Hampshire County Reference Library (Mr McGrave).

The Army & Navy Stores, Mr R. E. Hadingham of Slazengers Ltd, Mr D. F. P. Sharrock of British Tyre & Rubber Co., Mr A. D. Edwards of Accles & Pollock, Mr E. C. Millard and Mr H. Letters of the Ben Sayers Co., Mr R. and Mr T. D. Ovenstone and Mr D. Spittal of George Nicoll of Leven, Fife.

Mr L. J. W. Bailey and Mr S. G. Ball (formerly of Dunlop Ltd), Mr George Colville of Inveresk, Mr Edward Davies of Northam, Master Clubmaker, Mr Patric Dickinson, Miss Mina Forgan of St Andrews, Mr George Gibson (son of the late William Gibson of Kinghorn, Fife), Mr Jack Gibson (son of the late Charles Gibson of Westward Ho!), Mr J. W. D. Goodban, OBE, Secretary of Saunton Golf Club (in particular for the loan of books), Mevrow E. M. van Henkelom-Ife (daughter of A. J. Ife of The Hague, Holland), Mrs McEwan of St Andrews, Mrs Doris Porter of Jersey (granddaughter of Willie Park Jr.), Mr Robert Simpson of Carnoustie and Mrs J. Walker of Troon (granddaughter of Willie Fernie).

For permission to reproduce illustrations from other publications we thank: *Golf Illustrated* and *Golf Monthly*; Hutchinson Publishing Group Ltd for the subjects appearing on pages 203–209 taken from the *Book of Golf and Golfers* ed. by Horace Hutchinson and for the subject appearing on page 207 taken from *Taylor on Golf* by J. H. Taylor; Methuen & Co Ltd for the subjects appearing on pages 206 and 205 taken from *Advanced Golf* by James Braid and *The Complete Golfer* by Harry Vardon respectively. Thanks are also due to Hutchinson Publishing Group Ltd for permission to include the chapter on Practical Club-making by J. H. Taylor from the *Book of Golf and Golfers* ed. by Horace Hutchinson.

Our thanks are especially due to our research team in Edinburgh – Mr George Gibb, Research Editor, Dr Audrey Paterson and Mr James Robb, for the splendid and painstaking task they completed. To Mr Roger Morris (for his excellent sketches), to Mr Ralph Arnott, without whose advice and help the compilation of the patents section would never have been achieved, and to Dr A. J. Newton, MB BS for his expert photography.

We wish also to thank Mr John Taylor of Lund Humphries Publishers Ltd for his invaluable help as consultant publisher and Charlton/Szyszkowski for their ingenious book design.

Finally, we thank our respective wives for all their help and encouragement extending over three years, Mrs Veronica Balman for secretarial help and Mrs Patricia Rawson who has seen the whole script through to its final completion.

Chapter 1
The Origins of Golf

That golf is an ancient game is undeniable but its origins and its relationship with other games which involved striking a ball with some form of club have so far not been resolved – and maybe never will be. Although Victorian romantics wrote imaginary tales about shepherds hitting round stones with sticks, tales which have been ridiculed and discounted by those who adhere to a more 'scientific' and factual approach to such matters, the latter are guilty of equal romance as they try to fit facts into their own preconceived theories concerning how and where it all began. As the object of this book is to trace the development of golf clubs and balls, it may well prove worth while to examine the subject from this angle which is at least a factual approach.

It has been natural for man to exercise his prowess in many ways, one of which is to play with a round object such as a ball. The attraction of a ball is, perhaps, that it can move in any direction and skill is required to make it move in one direction only. If anyone doubts this inherent human characteristic let him consider the many ways in which man has disported himself at ball games. The ball may be hit with a stick, or a racquet, or a bat, or a foot or a hand. The stick may be a golf club, hockey stick, polo stick, billiard cue, cricket bat, baseball bat, and so on. Altogether, there are an enormous number of ball games played throughout the world. What we are searching for in this medley is someone who is equipped with a club and is standing sideways on to a ball, which he proposes to strike. There are two illustrations which offer the kind of evidence we are seeking, one taken from Gloucester Cathedral *c*.1350 and one from South America *c*.1835. Each case must be accepted as a coincidence since there is no idea what form of game is being played and all that can usefully be deduced is that from early times in various parts of the world this was a form of activity that attracted adherents – call it what you will.

There are, however, a number of pastimes possibly related to golf which it is worth examining.

Left: Sketch of the stained-glass roundel from the Battle of Crecy window in Gloucester Cathedral, *c*. 1350.

Right: An Araucanian Indian boy from Chile, taken from an illustration in *The Zoology of the Voyage of HMS Beagle* which is concerned with Charles Darwin's exploration of South America, *c*. 1835.

Paganica or cambuca

It is known that the Romans played a game called paganica using a leather ball stuffed with flock and that in England in the fourteenth century a similar game using a wooden ball was played, called cambuca. In neither case do we know anything about the clubs used to hit the balls.[1]

Pall mall – jeu de mail – or pele mele

This is the game which by all descriptions closely resembled golf. It was originally played in Italy and was then taken up by the French. It came to England at the beginning of the seventeenth century and in 1717 a Monsieur Lauthier wrote a small treatise on how to play the game together with the rules. (There are two translations, one, in part, by H. B. Wood in *Golfing Curios and the Like*, and the other by Andrew Lang of St Andrews, both published in 1910.) The main principles for playing the game are set out in Appendix 1 on page 314. These show what a remarkable similarity the style of play had to the golf swing and for those who are interested it should be read in conjunction with Kincaid's treatise of 1687 (see Appendix 1 on page 323) on how to play golf.

A sketch of jeu de mail (pall mall) being played in the eighteenth century, taken from Lauthier's *Treatise* (Paris, 1717).

[1]Forcellini's *Dictionary* and Martial VII XXXII, 7 Calendar of Close Rolls (Record Office), p.534–5, Rymers Foedera, VI, p.417, column 2.

Lauthier describes the rules for playing pall mall in a court which had a prepared surface and boundaries. From the illustrations and from the clubs in the British Museum, we know that it was necessary to loft the ball through an iron hoop or hoops, the finish of the game being through a 'passe' or hoop. The game was apparently quite complicated and required the necessary maintenance and administration to keep a court in being. It is not known when the original course in Pall Mall, St James's, London, was established, but Charles I was certainly playing the game c.1629. After the Restoration of Charles II to the throne in 1660, the course in what is still today known as Pall Mall was turned into the road running from St James's Palace to Trafalgar Square and a new course was made in what is still called The Mall, which runs from Trafalgar Square to Buckingham Palace.

The game of jeu de mail went out of fashion in the early eighteenth century, leaving, however, a continuing interest, particularly in Southern France, in jeu de mail 'à la chicane' – in other words a game to be played in open country, and particularly along roads, to a definite target. Here the resemblance to golf becomes even more marked and the use of a club with one end lofted was clearly already adapted to the crude form of course.
A description of 'Golf in France' is given in *Historical Gossip about Golf and Golfers* (Edinburgh 1863). This states:

'The game is played along the bye-roads, in the neighbourhood of the town, sometimes with high banks on each side, sometimes ditches, at other places level, with the fields sometimes lined with hedges, but usually quite open. The surface of the ground is very variable ... The goals are not very long, averaging perhaps half a mile. At the end of each is placed a touchstone, as it is called, which the players have to strike before the match is won, and he who can do it in the least number of strokes wins.'

Extract from Faithorne and Newcourt's map, surveyed in 1643–7, published in 1658.

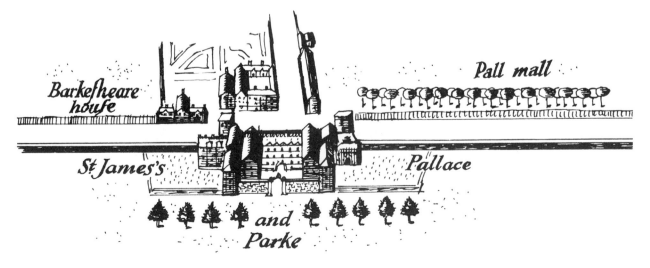

3

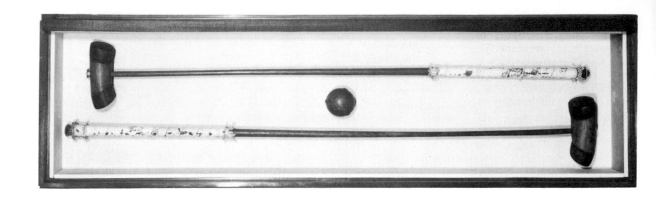

Above and right: A pair of pall mall clubs and a wooden ball which came from a house, No. 68 Pall Mall, and were presented in 1854 to the British Museum by Mr. P. Vulliamy whose family are known to have lived in Pall Mall since 1760. The longer club measures $46\frac{1}{2}$ in. (weight 720 gms) – the shaft being whippy and warped. The shorter club measures $43\frac{1}{2}$ in. (weight 715 gms) and is in good condition. The shafts were probably made of ash. The longer club has the maker's name 'Latour' impressed on it and it was customary to make them at that time from evergreen oak. The measurement of the base of the clubhead is approximately $5\frac{1}{2}$– 6 in. and the diameter of the face is $2\frac{1}{8}$ in. – the face being bound by iron rings to assist in preserving the striking face. One face of each club has approximately $15°$ of loft whereas the other face has a slight loft of $5°$. The shafts were fixed straight through the clubhead and apparently glued – there is no evidence of any holding pegs. The handles were a single layer of white leather, 14 in. long. The ball was made of boxwood and is $2\frac{9}{16}$ in. in diameter and weighs 160 gms. Reproduced by courtesy of the Trustees of the British Museum.

[2]See also *Golf Illustrated*, May 1909 for an illustrated article on the game then still being played in the South of France.

It is hard to see how this game of jeu de mail[2] could have influenced the development of golf, although it is apparent that the method of fixing the clubhead to the shaft was superior to the method by which all early wooden golf clubs had their heads bound to the shaft by what became known as the 'scared-head principle'. It was not until late in the nineteenth century that the practice of inserting the shaft through the socket-head of the club was introduced. It is ironic that in the 1890s mallet-headed clubs were introduced and that in 1897 a little booklet *Golf on a New Principle: Iron Clubs Superseded* by L. Everage introduced his 'cross-head' clubs which performed quite well and were even used in the championships. There was nothing new about the principle, but

A game of jeu de mail (pall mall) by
Paul Bril (painted in Rome, 1624).
Clearly an imaginary scene. The
game played in open country as
opposed to a court was called 'à la
chicane'. Reproduced by courtesy
of the Minneapolis Institute of
Arts.

Enlargement of the righthand
bottom corner of Bril's painting –
the 'shop' of a club and ballmaker
showing a variety of types of clubs
and balls. Hanging from the tree
are jeu de mail (pall mall) clubs.

Sir George Alexander, the distinguished actor, playing with a mallet-headed club before they were barred (*Golf Monthly*, November 1911).

mallet-headed clubs came under the Royal and Ancient ban in 1909, and the illustration above shows the end in Britain of what might have become a revival of an old principle.

Chole and soule

The game of chole was played in Flanders from a very early time and is still played, though not commonly, today. A very similar game called soule was played in Northern France. The clubs had rigid shafts and iron heads which were sometimes spoon-shaped. The game made use of one beechwood ball and was something of a team game. One group hit the ball toward the target, which might be a stone or tree or stake or doorway, and might be as far away as twelve miles. The first group were allowed three shots toward the target and the opposing group were then allowed one shot in the opposite direction – the 'de chole' – or, indeed, in any direction so that they might make difficulties for their opponents.

Print by Jan Luyken (1649–1712). A player with the ball teed up in the snow; clearly the game is not being played on ice.

6

The Dutch 'long game' – 'spel metten kolve' Early golf in Holland

The history of club and ball games in Holland has been much enriched by the admirable researches of the Dutch golf historian van Hengel the results of which have been published in his *Early Golf* (1972).

The main obstacle to research for British authors in the past has been the language problem and van Hengel is the first who has been able to investigate Dutch national and local archives, picture galleries, old maps, prints and private collections. He also records the sudden and inexplicable end of Dutch golf, which he terms 'spel metten kolve'. With the exception of one course at Loenen this game ceased and all evidence of play disappeared at the beginning of the eighteenth century. In its place appeared 'Kolf' or 'Het Kolven', a short-distance and often indoor game which might be termed 'mini-golf', using heavier rigid clubs and larger balls. This game in turn was to lose its popularity, although still played, when the Scottish version of golf arrived at The Hague in 1890.

Van Hengel has traced the beginnings of golf in Holland back to 1296, to the village of Loenen, which had four holes for the playing of golf, and where the game continued until as late as 1830. He cites numerous records of the playing of the game during the fourteenth century and in 1501 there appears the first well-known picture of the game in a Flemish Book of Hours, now in the British Museum.

Sketch after a Flemish Book of Hours.

Golf was played in Dutch city streets and churchyards, and there were numerous edicts against such play with the object of driving the players outside the city or on to the city ramparts. From the end of the sixteenth century until the game faded out, there is an illustrated record which is unique in the annals of any sport.

The first European landscape artist proper did not appear until the beginning of the sixteenth century. Until then religious painting, portraiture and classical allegory had held sway and landscape was only an incidental aspect of such paintings. Even the art of the Greeks and Romans carved and represented men and horses, herds and beasts and all kinds of living things, but as Ruskin said 'not so much as the outline of a mountain', and much the same thing applied to medieval art. By the end of the sixteenth century Dutch and Flemish artists were to sketch and paint in dozens of landscapes a remarkable record of life in Holland, and life in Holland included a

7

The Shock of Recognition

Sketches of golfers extracted from
seventeenth-century Dutch
landscapes

Scene on the ice near Dordrecht
(one of the principal ports for the
Scottish trade), Jan van Goyen
(1596–1656).

'Winter Sports o
Aernout van de

'Kilted figures playing golf',
Adriaen van de Velde (1668).

'Frozen River Scene', Aernou
foreground, and other games i
'refreshment' sledg

From a painting by Van der Neer.

'Skating Scene

a Frozen Canal',
Neer (1603–77).

'Golf on the Ice', Hendrick
Avercamp (1585–1634).

a Frozen Canal',
Neer (1603–77).

From a painting by Esaius van de
Velde (1591–1630). There appears
to be a hole in the ice.

van der Neer. A 'four-ball' in the
progress in the background. Note the
(or nineteenth hole).

Hendrick Avercamp.

'The Castle of Muiden in Winter',
Jan Beerstraaten (1622–66).

Left: Early seventeenth-century club fragments and a wooden ball with a modern ball for comparison. when excavating for the City of Amsterdam underground railway system, the municipal rubbish dump (used between 1565–1650) outside the city ramparts was crossed and amongst a number of other objects were more than a dozen heads of golf clubs, some with pieces of broken shafts in the heads. The clubheads were apparently shafted with hazel, the maker looking for a straight hazel shaft with one branch. The branch was cut back to about $1\frac{1}{2}$ in. and the clubhead was then cast around it, ensuring a firm joining of head and shaft. The metal used was mainly lead. No example of a seventeenth-century wooden club has so far been found. The wooden ball $c.1590$ (centre) is made of beechwood, again excavated in Amsterdam and belonging to Mr van Hengel. It has a diameter of 2 in. and weighs 85 gms. This type of ball is believed to have been in use until well into the 1600s. The leather-covered ball (right) is an enlarged version of the white leather-covered ball from the Master Slijper portrait opposite (diameter approximately 2 in.) and looks exactly like the 'feathery' ball used in Scotland.

game of golf – until it disappeared from the scene in the early 1700s.

In many a crowded scene – on ice or on land – tiny figures can be seen away in the distance, club in hand. There are more prominent figures, unmistakably playing the game, even a couple of Scotsmen in kilts, as well as children posing with clubs and balls. Here was recorded what then must have been a national pastime, at a period in Dutch history when the populace were continually at war. Artistic licence there was in many an overcrowded scene, but here were pioneers in landscape art recording contemporary circumstances to the best of their ability and in scene after scene they included golfers, because undoubtedly they were part of the scene.

In 1971 an exhibition of paintings was held at the Tate Gallery, London, half of which were Dutch landscapes of the seventeenth century and the other half landscapes by British artists such as Constable, Turner and Paul Sandby, who so greatly admired and were influenced by the Dutch masters of landscape. The exhibition was entitled 'The Shock of Recognition' and was intended to convey what this confrontation with the Old Masters of the Low Countries meant to the first British landscape painters.

With the help of van Hengel a selection of sketches and pictures – all of them featuring golf clubs and balls which can also be found in a far greater number of pictures – has been made which should also be entitled 'The Shock of Recognition'. They are reproduced here. They alone provide unmistakable evidence that the Dutch were playing an earlier game of golf with enthusiasm in the environment which Holland provided at that time: but in addition to the pictures, there are the early seventeenth-century clubheads and balls which have come to light. The map of Holland shows where golf was played $c.1650$ and gives the population figures. The map of Scotland shows similar figures and is supported by the first Scots pictures which are of a much later date.

Golf in progress, supported by the necessary refreshment. Hendrick Avercamp.

Left: Master Slijper. Taken from a life-size painting at the age of seven in 1612. The club is for a grown-up player. There are other pictures of children with clubs and balls and it is suggested that they were used in an endeavour to hold their attention whilst posing for their picture. Artist unknown.

Right: Taken from a painting by an unknown artist (Flemish) this is reputed to be Henry Frederick, eldest son of James VI/I in 1595 at the age of two. The original has been referred to as the 'Holdenby House' (near Rugby, England) portrait.

Left: Portrait of a child by Jan Anthonisz van Ravesteyn, 1626.

Right: Portrait of a boy-golfer by Albert Cuyp, 1650.

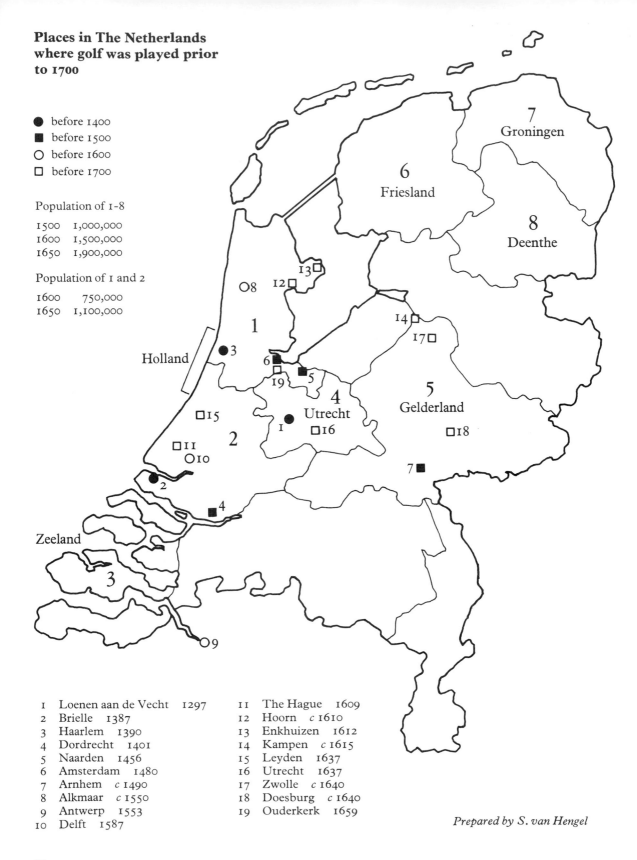

**Places in The Netherlands
where golf was played prior
to 1700**

● before 1400
■ before 1500
○ before 1600
□ before 1700

Population of 1–8

1500	1,000,000
1600	1,500,000
1650	1,900,000

Population of 1 and 2

| 1600 | 750,000 |
| 1650 | 1,100,000 |

Holland

7
Groningen

6
Friesland

8
Deenthe

○8   □12   □13

1

●3

6   □14
□17
19   ■5

4   5
Utrecht   Gelderland
1   □16

□15

2   □18

□11
○10

●2   ■7

■4

Zeeland

3

○9

1	Loenen aan de Vecht	1297		11	The Hague	1609
2	Brielle	1387		12	Hoorn	c 1610
3	Haarlem	1390		13	Enkhuizen	1612
4	Dordrecht	1401		14	Kampen	c 1615
5	Naarden	1456		15	Leyden	1637
6	Amsterdam	1480		16	Utrecht	1637
7	Arnhem	c 1490		17	Zwolle	c 1640
8	Alkmaar	c 1550		18	Doesburg	c 1640
9	Antwerp	1553		19	Ouderkerk	1659
10	Delft	1587				

Prepared by S. van Hengel

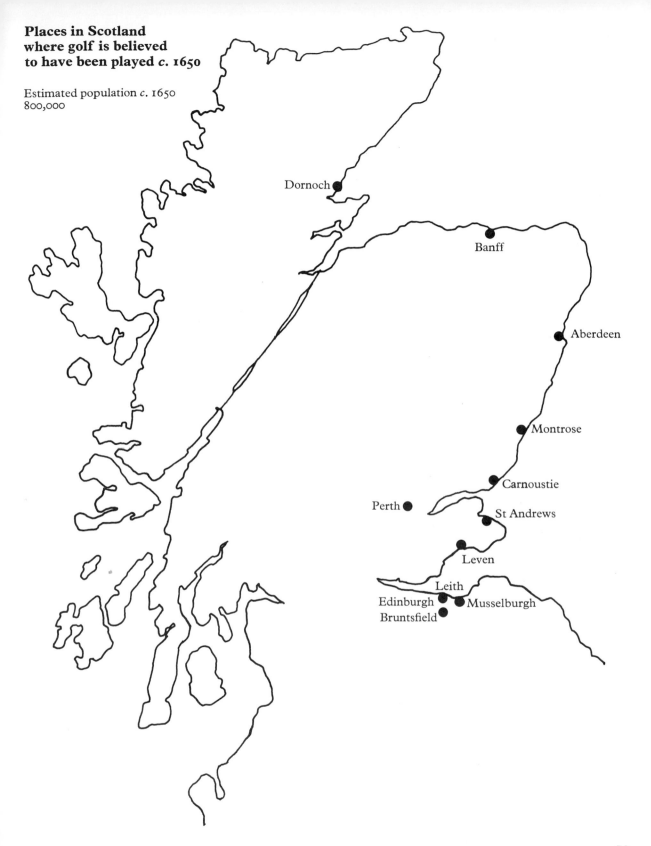

**Places in Scotland
where golf is believed
to have been played *c.* 1650**

Estimated population *c.* 1650
800,000

Dornoch

Banff

Aberdeen

Montrose

Carnoustie

Perth

St Andrews

Leven

Leith

Edinburgh

Musselburgh

Bruntsfield

Golfers taken from a 'View of Bruntsfield Links looking towards Edinburgh Castle' by Paul Sandby R.A., dated 1746. He was one of the earliest English watercolour artists and this is probably one of the first pictures of Scottish golfers. Reproduced by courtesy of the Trustees of the British Museum.

Sketch: 'William Inglis on Leith Links' by David Allan. He was Captain of the Hon. Company of Edinburgh Golfers from 1782–84. Another celebrated portrait of the time is that of William St Clair of Roslin which is shown on page 198.

Sketch: 'Alexander 1st Lord Macdonald (1745–1795)' by Jeremiah Davidson. The club is clearly an adult's as it is far too large for the child.

14

Golf in Scotland

In the fifteenth and sixteenth centuries there were close ties between Scotland and Holland based particularly on the export of wool through the Scottish East Coast ports and for the most part in Dutch ships. In those days sailing ships had not acquired the art of tacking 'against the wind' and in winter in the absence of favourable weather conditions, ships' crews could find themselves stranded for months on end on a foreign shore.

It is against this background of a poor community providing raw materials for a far more civilised society on the Continent, that we must look for the origins of the Scots' subsequent devotion to the game of golf.

It is necessary to emphasise, of course, that not only Scotland but the whole of Britain was a poor community prior to the Industrial Revolution. It is worth quoting Samuel Smiles, the industrial biographer, in his preface to the *Lives of the Engineers* Vol.1: 1862:

'. . . But it may possibly excite the reader's surprise to learn how modern England is in all that relates to skilled industry, which appears to have been among the very youngest outgrowths of our national life.

Most of the Continental nations had a long start of us in art, in science, in mechanics, in navigation, and in engineering. Not many centuries since, Italy, Spain, France, and Holland looked down contemptuously on the poor but proud islanders, contending with nature for a subsistence amidst their fogs and their mists. Though surrounded by the sea, we had scarcely any navy until within the last three hundred years. Even our fisheries were so unproductive, that our markets were supplied by the Dutch, who sold us the herrings caught upon our own coasts. England was then regarded principally as a magazine for the supply of raw materials, which were carried away in foreign ships and partly returned to us in manufactures worked up by foreign artisans. We grew wool for Flanders, as America grows cotton for England now. Even the little manufactured at home was sent to the Low Countries to be dyed.

Most of our modern branches of industry were begun by foreigners, many of whom were driven by religious persecution to seek an asylum in England. Our first cloth-workers, silk-weavers, and lace-makers were French and Flemish refugees. The brothers Elers, Dutchmen, began the pottery manufacture; Spillman, a German, erected the first paper-mill at Dartford; and Boomen, a Dutchman, brought the first coach into England . . .'

Early Scottish records have again been examined, this time with particular reference to clubs and balls and those who made them, but the overall result remains disappointing. There is no clue as to the type of ball, no description of the clubs, but, thanks to Kincaid's *Diary* in 1687, there is an account of how to play and there is Paul Sandby's landscape of Bruntsfield links in 1746 with golfers playing.

There are, however, many references to the playing of the game and restrictions (religious and otherwise), and the principal events and information relating to clubs and balls may be noted as follows:

1424   James I forbids the playing of football – because of the need for archery practice. This date is noted because 'Gouf' is not mentioned (Parliament I, Cap.17)

1457   James II (Parl.14, Cap.64) ⎫ Three Acts of Parliament continuing

1470   James III (Parl.6, Cap.44) ⎬ the discouragement of football, but

1491   James IV (Parl.3, Cap.32) ⎭ 'Gouff' is now included.

1501   *Treaty of Glasgow.* Signed in Glasgow Cathedral this brings peace between England and Scotland; as a result James IV in due course started to play himself and the long association of the Stuart Kings of Scotland and England with golf begins. This is confirmed by accounts of the Lord High Treasurers of Scotland (1503–1506: Purchases of clubs and balls at Perth).

1554   There is a reference to a dispute between the cordiners (cobblers) of the Canongate and the cordiners and gouff ball makers of North Leith, and amongst the latter are the names of John and William Patersone – a name which is to appear again at the end of the next century. The inference from this entry is that cobblers were then stitching leather balls – but we do not know what they were filled with. (See Appendix IV: *The Chronicle of the Royal Burgess Golfing Society* 1735–1935.)

1566   First printed reference to the game of golf. Folio xl and xli. 'Futball and golf be utterly cryit downe and not to be uset . . .'. Printed by Robert Lekprerek.

1567   Mary Queen of Scots was charged with playing golf and pall mall at Seton House, East Lothian, a few days after the murder of her husband, Darnley (*Inventories of Mary Queen of Scots,* Preface p.lxx, 1863). She is believed to have brought the idea of jeu de mail from France.

1585   Letter from James Dickson, servitor to the Master of Orkney, from Kirkwall to Andrew Martin asking for one dozen 'commoun golf ballis'. *The Correspondence of Sir Patrick Warn,* 1882, p.341.

1603   William Mayne, although he appears to have been appointed Royal Warrant Holder for Clubmaking . . . no other record relating to him appears describing him as a clubmaker (Registrum Secreti Sigilli Lib. lxxiij 234).

1614   Earl of Caithness, writing from the siege of Kirkwall: 'Cannon balls of the besiegers were broken like golf balls and cloven in two halves'. The suggestion is that the reference is to wooden balls.

1616   John Muir of Leith convicted of abusing Francis Hay by striking him with a golf club. Fined £50 Scots. Records of the Burgh of Edinburgh 1606/26.

1618   5th August at Salisbury, England. The grant of a monopoly to James Melvill in favour of William Berwick and his associate for the sale of golf balls for twenty-one years. Around this time James I had started granting monopolies as a means of raising money for the Crown and from the fact that there is no reference in the records either to Melvill or Berwick as golf ballmakers, it seems clear that they obtained the grant as a money-making proposition and that it would be unwise to read too much into the wording of the document. The events of 1629 (below) show Melvill as quartermaster of the Earl of Moreton's Regiment – a private army of dubious reputation where he appears in character. (Registrum Secreti Sigilli Lib. lxxxvij 169.) See Appendix 2 on page 315.

1628/9　*Memoirs of the Marquis of Montrose*, Mark Napier, Edinburgh. T. G. Stevenson 1856, gives account of golfing expenses at St Andrews, Leith and Montrose for the young Lord Montrose.

1627　James Pett, recorded as clubmaker of St Andrews.

1629　A complaint by William and Thomas Dicksoun 'makers of Gowffe ballis in Leith' is given in Appendix 3 on page 316.

1632　Thomas Catto killed by a golf ball in Kelso Churchyard. (Justiciary Cases, 1624–1650.)

1637　April 21st John Dickson 'maker of golf balls' married Barbara Kennedie. This is noted because the description 'golf club' and 'golf ball' maker begins to appear.

1640/42　Charles I plays golf at Newcastle while a prisoner of the Scots. (*Local records of Northumberland* by John Sykes, Newcastle 1833). Charles I is playing at Leith when he has news of the Irish rebellion (see *Transactions of Society of Antiquaries of Scotland*, p.504).

1642　Aberdeen Town Council gives licence to John Dickson of Leith (probably the same man who was married in 1637) to make golf balls.

1643　Signature of Andrew Dickson 'ballmaker' to Solemn League and Covenant signed at St Andrews.

1669　Sale of a shop at foot of Leith Wynd to George Watson, ballmaker (Records of Burgh Edinburgh 1665–1669).

1681/2　Somewhere around this date is the legendary match between James, Duke of York (later James II), then resident at Holyrood, and one John Paterson, against two English nobles, whom they defeated – a boy Andrew Dickson acting as forecaddy. The winning of this match was said to have resulted in Paterson being given a sum of money by the Duke with which he built a residence, No.77 Canongate, and also a coat of arms and the motto 'Far and Sure'. Clark in *Golf: A Royal and Ancient Game* illustrates this house and the tablet on it bearing the coat-armorial but he states that there are several different stories connected with this achievement. A match may have taken place but, if it did, it is surprising that the date and the amount of any wager were not recorded. A John Paterson certainly owned property at Leith but the Canongate land story has never been confirmed from any records. John Paterson appears in records at this time as a ballmaker and cordiner, and Andrew Dickson subsequently became a ballmaker. No grant of a coat of arms can be traced and maybe this was a joke dreamed up some fifty years after the alleged event. It would have been satisfactory to have linked up the earlier Patersons (from 1554) and the Dicksons (from 1629) of Leith, because both families appear to have had a long association with golf and with Leith, and the Dicksons can at any rate be traced down to 1787 by which time they had become clubmakers. 77 Canongate has been demolished but a plaque may still be seen on the wall of a nearby house.

1687/8   Thomas Kincaid's *Diary* taken from *An Edinburgh Diary*, 27th volume of the Old Edinburgh Club. See Chapter 7 where extracts are quoted giving a description of how to swing a club.

1735   Order for clubs and balls to Andrew Bailey, Bruntsfield.

1743   Shipment of clubs and balls from Leith to Charleston, South Carolina, USA. See Appendix 2 on page 316.

1743   Thomas Mathison's poem 'The Goff'. The first description and indeed mention of the making of a feathery ball (see page 43).

1746   Watercolour by Paul Sandby of Bruntsfield Links showing golfers playing.

These Scottish notes are as much as can usefully be compiled and really tell us little. The exception is Kincaid's *Diary* of 1687 which explains how to swing the club but tells nothing about the game itself, the course and how far those playing hit their shots. It can possibly be deduced that the 'commoun ball' was a wooden ball, and once there is a mention of cordiners (1564) as 'gouff ball makers', at a time when leather balls were being made. The problem is what they were originally filled with – flock, wool or feathers – and it is not until 1743 that there is a clear description. No examples of balls or documented clubs have survived either and perhaps the most memorable legacy of the first 200 years of golf in Scotland is that it was played by the Stuart Kings of Scotland and the United Kingdom, and thus acquired the title of the 'Royal and Ancient' game. The lack of any early picture is emphasised by the examples shown, all dated late in the history of the game.

Conclusion

Opposite:
Alexander McKellar known as the 'Cock o' the Green' who died *c*.1813. The sketch for this print was made by Kay 1803 who went especially out to the links at Bruntsfield, Edinburgh. It was published in Kay's *Portraits* (Edinburgh: Hugh Paton 1838). McKellar's story is told in R. Clark's *A Royal and Ancient Game*. It appears that he became completely obsessed with the game, playing all day and every day except Sunday, leaving his wife to run a small tavern in the New town. Strangely he never became a member of a golfing society.

Perhaps the evidence can now be summarised, leaving aside any theories as to who was responsible for starting the game. The Dutch were playing a similar game from *c*.1300–*c*.1725, when it faded out as did jeu de mail. This has been attributed to a decline in 'manly' sports in the eighteenth century. They left copious pictorial evidence of their game. Perhaps further research will ultimately turn up a description of how the game was played in Holland. Happily for us when the Dutch were turning to mini-golf (Het Kolven) the Scots were taking decisive steps to establish the game on a more permanent footing with the first golfing societies, which were the foundation of Golf Clubs, through which the game was to be spread throughout the world.

Finally there is the question of the relationship between the environment in which the game was played and its objective of directing a ball with the fewest number of strokes into a hole or to hit a post. Games played on ice in winter months over considerable distances, to posts, sometimes elaborately decorated, feature in many landscapes and must have been fun. A post instead of a hole was the only practical answer on ice. Some of the posts were decorated and were liable to be stolen, thus leaving a hole in the

By the la' Harry
This shall not go for Nothing

COCK OF THE GREEN.

ice – see the sketch on page 9 with players playing to a hole in the ice. The concept of a hole was undoubtedly known to the Dutch whereas in Scotland there has never been a suggestion that anything else was ever used. As for the environment in which golf was played, the Dutch in medieval times and later were addicted to playing in the city streets and constant efforts were made to drive them outside or onto the city ramparts. Their countryside at that time had no natural links ideally suited for the purpose. As for Scotland, the seaside links were ideal, but inland courses such as Perth and Bruntsfield could not be used at all in high summer because of the long grass. The game was thus only played in spring, autumn and winter when the grazing animals (cows and sheep) had cropped the grass. In the absence of links, ice provided a satisfactory fairway.

From the evidence so far produced it is difficult to avoid the conclusion that the Dutch played a significant part in the establishment of the game in Scotland, where it remained confined to the East Coast until the nineteenth century.

Chapter 2
The Growth of the Game of Golf

The formation of Golf Clubs and Societies

From earliest times golf was played in the east of Scotland by people of all classes on public waste land, some being called 'links'. Anyone with a couple of clubs and a ball could amuse themselves, there were no rules, but gradually they came to play over a recognised series of holes. For the more affluent there were challenge matches and wagers and the day's golf was always followed by eating and drinking at a nearby tavern. By the beginning of the eighteenth century the game was attracting influential and well-to-do Edinburgh citizens more and more to the golf courses at Bruntsfield and Leith and in 1735 at Bruntsfield a Society was formed for the purpose of meeting together, arranging matches and wagers, and dining. The golfers of Leith had a slightly different idea which was that, if they could persuade the Town Council of Edinburgh to donate them a prize, it would give official recognition to Leith Links which were owned by the Council. They apparently got the idea from the Royal Company of Archers who were given a Silver Arrow in 1709 and shot for it annually on those same links.

A Silver Club was presented by the Town Council in 1744 for annual competition and along with it went a set of rules to govern the competition:

'It being represented that Several Gentlemen of Honour, Skilful in the Ancient and Healthful Exercise of the Golf, had from time to time Applied to Several Members of Council for a Silver Club to be annually played for on the Links of Leith, at Such time, and upon Such conditions as the Magistrates and Council should think proper: And it being reported That the Gentlemen Golfers had drawn up a Scroll, at the Desire of the Magistrates, of such Articles and Conditions as to them seemed most Expedient as proper Regulations to be Observed by the Gentlemen who Should Yearly offer to play for the said Silver Club which were produced and read in Council.'

The winner of the competition had the privilege of appending 'a gold or silver piece to the prize' and furthermore of being captain for the following year. The expense of what became a silver-coated ball was not always appreciated. The silver club is itself interesting – as being a model of a contemporary putter – $5\frac{1}{2}$ inches long, just an inch deep in the face – a design which would have remained in fashion until wooden putters declined in popularity 150 years later. It was not until 1800 that the Society was eventually incorporated as 'The Honourable Company of Edinburgh Golfers'. They succeeded in obtaining two further clubs from the Edinburgh Council in 1811 and 1879. Thus the first societies were formed and the first rules of golf appear (see Appendix 1 on page 316). The Gentlemen of Fife invited 'The Gentlemen Golfers of Leith' to join them in forming the St Andrews Society in 1754, later to become the Royal and Ancient Golf Club of St Andrews. The early Societies often kept exemplary minutes of their meetings. A member of a Society was expected to play golf, wear the uniform expected of him

Portrait of 'Old Alick' – The hole-maker to the Royal Blackheath Golf Club by G. Allen, c.1835. 'Alick' Robertson, born 1756, died 1840, ended his days as a caddy and latterly hole-maker to the Club. In addition to the iron club that he is holding in his right hand, he also has a type of net for recovering golf balls from ponds and ditches on the course. Reproduced by courtesy of the Royal Blackheath Golf Club.

[3] See Bibliography on page 331.

and attend the dinners so closely associated with the game. Matches were arranged, betting took place and the records were faithfully kept. From time to time there are references to changes in the rules of the game, but we look in vain for references to the state of the game itself. Yet later on, the state and care of the green resulted in the appointment of the keepers of the green, who combined their work with making clubs, playing with members and were in fact the first professionals.

By the middle of the eighteenth century there was a 'Golf House' at Bruntsfield which was a tavern not owned by golfers, but by Thomas Comb who was also a clubmaker (see Chapter 5, page 119). At Leith c.1767 the Gentlemen Golfers put up and furnished a 'Golf House' at a cost of £760. It was run as a tavern, let to a tenant for £40 p.a. and the Society members had a locker-room and dining-room of their own. The money was put up by twenty-two members who therefore owned it, which caused difficulties later on when the enterprise foundered.

Thus some seven Societies or Clubs were formed in the eighteenth century and a further ten in the first half of the nineteenth century. The impression is that golf Societies were still struggling to exist and this tends to be confirmed by the handful of clubmakers whose names appear in the records – the Cossars (father and son), the McEwans, Philp and Jackson of Perth being the best known. Meanwhile, the increasing disadvantages of playing golf at Bruntsfield and Leith prompted more and more Edinburgh citizens to use the seaside links at Musselburgh, which were only a few miles further out of the city and offered superior golfing conditions. In 1847 McEwan the clubmaker moved to Musselburgh whilst still remaining represented at Bruntsfield. Gourlay the ballmaker also moved. Musselburgh was to become the home of golf for some years until the rise of St Andrews ended in its final eclipse in the 1890s and the leading Clubs left to found their own courses.

Few if any owned or controlled the links on which they played. Some of them even ceased to exist for a time, until some enthusiast had the initiative to start up again. The arrival of the gutta percha ball in 1848 did make it possible for more people to play golf but it appears doubtful if it had the immediate effect on golf that has been claimed. The first *Golfer's Manual* by 'A Keen Hand' was published in 1857 and was followed by the *Golfer's Year Book* in 1866 by Robert Howie Smith and in 1880 by the *Golfer's Handbook* by R. Forgan. [3] These recorded the growth of Clubs from eighteen in 1857, thirty-six in 1866 to fifty-nine in 1880. These lists have been analysed and are set out on pages 41 and 42. In many cases they give the dates when Clubs claim to have been founded but they are not necessarily historically accurate. For many years prior to the formation of the actual Society or Club, groups of people met regularly and played golf together without any form of organisation. To use a modern word, 'incorporation' came about when the first prizes were presented for competition, e.g. the original silver clubs,

A sketch of probably the earliest hole cutter still surviving.

[4]See *A History of Golf* by Robert Browning, London 1955, Chapter VI (1743–1787).
[5]See *Reminiscences of Golf on St Andrews Links* by James Balfour, Edinburgh 1887, p.49.
[6]See Chapter 8 on Patents.

and it was necessary to prescribe rules for the playing of the game and to cover the competition.[4]

In 1880 few Clubs or Societies owned their own courses. The greens were only then being separated from the teeing ground and the number of holes required to constitute a golf course had not been standardised. The Royal and Ancient Golf Club had issued new rules for its members on 5th May 1858 and in Rule I had stated 'one round of the Links or 18 Holes is reckoned a match unless otherwise stipulated'. At that time other courses had anything from five to twelve holes, but by the 1870s more courses had eighteen holes and a round of golf was being accepted as consisting of 18 holes, which meant that a 6 hole course was played three times and a 9 hole course twice.

As to the size of the hole, apart from mention of the use of flower pots, no reference has been found as to how it came to be accepted as $4\frac{1}{4}$ inches in diameter. Horace Hutchinson in his article 'Old Memories of Westward Ho!' in *The Midland Golfer* 1914 reports on 'an enormous piece of extravagance' when Westward Ho! sent to Scotland for a hole cutter. He goes on to say that previous to that the mode had been to cut the holes with an ancient dinner-knife or clasp-knife and that a gallipot was held on the ground to give a circle round which the knife could incise the turf. Probably the earliest hole cutter still surviving is that belonging to the Collection of the Royal Musselburgh Club, and, according to the Club Minutes of 13th March 1829, the Hon Secretary was authorised to pay Mr R. Gay's account 'for the instrument for forming the holes the sum of £1'. This strongly-made piece of equipment made a hole $4\frac{1}{4}$ inches in diameter which is the diameter of the hole used throughout the world today. Mr Harry B. Wood (author of *Golfing Curios and the Like*) recovered it and presented it to the Club *c.*1910 and recorded in his book that the modern 'screw' came in around 1850. St Andrews finally decided in 1894 that the size of hole was to be $4\frac{1}{4}$ inches diameter and not less than 4 inches deep. We are left wondering if this Musselburgh tool was the grand-daddy of them all and whether $4\frac{1}{4}$ inches was then considered just a handy size, remembering that there was no limitation then on the size of a golf ball.

The location of the hole in the days before there was a defined green must have presented problems to the players: but when was the idea of marking the hole with a stick and a flag on the end of it introduced? We know, for instance, that Allan Robertson, the famous professional, happened to be holding the stick at the 'high hole' coming home at St Andrews when Sir Hope Grant holed in one and his opponent James Balfour missed following suit by a foot.[5] This must have been in the 1850s because Robertson died in 1859, but it does not appear to have been general practice to use sticks surmounted by flags until a later date and may be coincidental with the size of the hole becoming standardised and the metal cup being adopted to receive the flagstick.[6] At Westward Ho!, for instance, although Tom Morris came to lay out the course, he certainly did not bring the idea with him to mark the holes with a flagstick. The site of the hole was indicated by a feather of a rook or gull stuck in the ground at its edge.[7]

In America the St Andrews Club at Yonkers first used inverted wicker liquor containers and these were developed as an alternative to flags as markers.

There were few purpose-built Clubhouses and the game was still being played with those elegant long-headed wooden clubs, carried loose by a caddy. The 1880 census consisted of fifty-nine clubs whose total membership numbered just under 5000, although the golfing societies at St Andrews were somehow left out. In any case, there were a number of players who belonged to several Clubs and the membership of the Royal and Ancient Golf Club was largely non-resident. There were certainly many players who did not belong to any Club and the numbers had increased quite sharply in the 1870s. This is confirmed by the increased number of clubmakers appearing in the records.

'Stymied', Reprinted by Master James Walker and His Co Partners in the Ancient City of Dublin.

[7]'Old Memories of Westward Ho!' by H. G. Hutchinson in *The Midland Golfer* 1914.

24

Golf was cheap to play. The maximum subscription quoted was £3.3.0; McEwan was despatching clubs south to Manchester for 3s 6d each in 1857; the gutta percha balls which had just come in cost 1s 0d and the caddies 3d or 6d a round at the most. Eating and drinking must have cost more than the golf, to say nothing of the wagers won or lost. Perhaps that may even be the case today though the cost of playing the game itself is no longer cheap.

Included in the details of Clubs are their competitions and prizes and a list of the recent winners – obviously one of the attractions of the game which was helped by the development of the system of handicaps. The game is unique in that a weak player can be enabled to play a stronger on equal terms and no other game has succeeded to such an extent in matching strong and weak. A further development which did a great deal to publicise the game was the start of the competition for the Championship Belt in 1860, thereafter held annually at Prestwick, and finally won outright by Tom Morris, Jr. in 1870. This led to the start of the present Open Championship in 1872 and the Amateur Championship in 1885. Few books were written about golf prior to 1890, but local and other newspapers were beginning to take notice of the golfing world of those early days. Championships and the winning of competitions provided news which attracted readers, and local papers started publishing the results of Club competitions in their area.

Although golf was played all the year round on the seaside links, on the inland courses such as Perth and Bruntsfield it was confined to two spring months, three autumn months and such play as they could get in the winter. This was entirely because of the growth of the long grass which on the common lands belonged to the 'cow feeders'. It was only as a result of the growing popularity of the game that arrangements were finally made to maintain a useable fairway in the summer months. Until the advent of suitable grass-cutting machinery this was achieved by using sheep and other grazing animals.

Players at St Andrews in the 1860s.

One problem which is never mentioned and which today never even crosses our minds concerns the way in which golfers made their way to the course. If they lived near, there was no problem since they walked. Otherwise it was a question of horse transport and traps, carriages and ponies. Yet there is never a mention of the horse or carriage park or even a sketch of the scene. Later on the bicycle became another popular method of getting to the course, although it was the railway that became a prime method of transport.

Referring again to the list of Clubs there is already mention of access by railway, and as early as 1850 the line reached St Andrews – providentially almost at the same moment as the gutta percha ball. The development of the city as a resort, which involved the building of hotels, had already started, with golf as the main attraction, although it still took over three hours to get there from Edinburgh. The Industrial Revolution in Britain eventually brought wealth, a degree of leisure and regular holidays to a new class of people who demanded somewhere to go on holiday and something to do when they got there. Railways helped to provide the answer; as they spread out so towns began to grow and people lived further from their work. As the railways reached the seaside, so people flocked there. The population of seaside resorts began to grow. Piers were built and the resorts set out to attract visitors. One of the new seaside attractions was golf, but it also became established in urban communities. If golf, as in many places in Scotland, was already established when the railway arrived, the result was an influx of new players and overcrowding. At Musselburgh, for instance, just eight miles from Edinburgh and already accommodating several different Clubs there were only 9 holes, and there was apparently always an undignified rush from the station to secure a place from the starter, with many a dark insinuation that he had been squared.

Below left:
H.R.H. the Prince of Wales (at Oxford) 1912.

Below right:
Teeing off a club's length from the hole. Edinburgh 1860.

The railway was, indeed, to play a vital part in the later expansion of golf, not only in Britain but particularly in the USA and in other parts of the world. In the early days many of the railway tracks ran alongside the course and were a hazard from which the ball had to be played, until local rules were brought in, together with the 'out of bounds' rule.

Louis Wain, the Victorian artist who drew cats as humans, catches the spirit of the age in 'Holed Out' as does the cartoon below, reproduced by permission of Punch.

THE GOLF STREAM.—Flows along the eastern coast of Scotland during the summer and autumn.
(Vide Report of British Association—Section V.).

The great golf craze

Scottish exiles had played golf at Blackheath according to tradition from 1608 although there is a lack of documentary evidence supporting this exact date. Play obviously continued there for many years without the actual formation of a Society or Club. In 1766 Mr Henry Foot presented a silver driver to 'The Honourable Company of Golfers at Blackheath' and in accordance with Browning's earlier dictum, he gives this as the date of the foundation of the first Golf Club outside Scotland. The Blackheath Club was to play a significant part in spreading the game in England and overseas. Westward Ho! was formed in 1864, the oldest English Club still playing on its original course; it received active support from Blackheath who also helped Royal Calcutta in India, re-established in 1874. The membership of three English Clubs in 1880 is significant:

Royal Liverpool (1869) 519 members
London Scottish (Wimbledon) (1865) 340 members
Westward Ho! (1864) 277 members

The Scots were also active in Manchester in 1819, playing at Kersal Moor. They and their archives are still intact today, although they lost their course at Kersal Moor in 1960. New Clubs were soon to appear on the Lancashire coast.

There were three requirements necessary to enable the game to spread:

(1) The availability of ground for a course.
(2) The availability of clubs and balls to play with.
(3) Someone to look after the course, the golf equipment and to teach people how to play the game.

The term 'links' came to be associated with the special qualities of seaside courses in Scotland – such as Dornoch, Montrose, Carnoustie, St Andrews, Elie, Musselburgh, Gullane, North Berwick and Prestwick, as opposed to inland 'courses' such as those at Edinburgh and Perth.

The natural qualities available for the creation of golf courses in certain seaside areas have allowed golf to be enjoyed in unique conditions which are without parallel anywhere else, which is the reason why people come from all over the world to play on them today. The creation of inland courses making use of most unsuitable terrain presented a challenge which could not properly be met until a new race of experts in laying-out courses had appeared. The only people who knew anything about the game were the Scots, and so Tom Morris in 1864, travelling all the way, we assume by train, to Westward Ho!, laid out the first purely English course. The search for sites for courses followed two directions, first to find somewhere to play golf near the big cities and towns for those who were seeking recreation within reach of their homes and second to fill the demand of seaside and other holiday resorts so that their visitors might be entertained.

'The Green Man', Blackheath. Following the loss of the original Club House about 1730, The Green Man was used by the Blackheath Golf Club, mainly for dining and for storing the Club's casks of whisky and claret. For the main competitions and medal days, a tent was erected close by The Green Man. In 1843 the Club acquired a temporary Club House at No.3, College Place, Royal Hill, and in 1869 a permanent Club House was purchased. The Club continued to use The Green Man for dining. Reproduced by courtesy of the Royal Blackheath Golf Club.

'Medal day at Blackheath 1875',
Reproduced by courtesy of the
Royal Blackheath Golf Club.

Right:
The Knuckle Club Medal
(reproduced by courtesy of the
Royal Blackheath Golf Club) dates
from 1792 and was played for
annually by the Knuckle Club
Members until 1825, when the
Knuckle Club was disbanded and
it was agreed to transfer the medal
to the Blackheath Golf Club. It
continued to be played for annually
at their Spring Meeting and it then
became known as the Spring
Medal. It was first won by a Mr W.
A. Cunningham with a score of 114
strokes. Every winner's name since
1793 has been engraved on the gold
leaves inside the medal, which is
believed to be the oldest trophy in
golf and the origin of Medal play as
we know it today.

Right:
The Loretto House Golf Club
Medal 1854. Loretto School is
adjacent to Musselburgh golf
course.

In the second half of the nineteenth century only a few of the well-known golfers were qualified by their upbringing to organise and carry out the laying-out of golf courses and there were many who had no qualification at all. Willie Park, Jr. was the first to write about the laying-out of a golf course in his book *The Game of Golf* (1896) and he it was who laid the foundation of what was to become known as golf-course architecture. At the time golf courses were often laid out in a stereotyped fashion, often on most unsuitable terrain and without the aid of any mechanical devices. The arrival of the rubber-cored ball in the early 1900s meant that all courses had to be lengthened, and the golf-course architect became a recognised profession in itself, with such well-known names as Colt, Abercromby, Fowler, Croome, Mackenzie, Hutchinson and Simpson coming into their own. There is now an ample bibliography on the subject.

Aided by a revolution in the art of making clubs and balls, by professionals such as Tom Morris, W. Park, Jr. and Tom Dunn, who laid out new courses, and by the growing number of people who wanted to become golf professionals and greenkeepers, the scene was set for the introduction of golf to those seeking leisure all over the world. The golf manuals endeavoured to record the growing number of Clubs and the following figures have been taken from the early annuals and later the *Golf Annual*:

Two cartoons reproduced by permission of *Punch*. That on the left suggests that a golf course was a better proposition than an unprofitable farm.

Growth of Clubs and Societies in the UK

1800	1850	1860	1870	1880	1890	1900	1905	1910
7	17	25	34	60	387	2330	2899	4135

A POSER.—" Farmers always grumbling ? Well, supposin' your pigs were down wi' th' fever, an' your sheep had got th' influenza, if your crops were drownded in eighteen inches o' water, an' your rent were overdue—what would you do ? "
" I ? I'd give it up and start a golf club ! "

" Mummy, what's that man for ? "

These figures are for Clubs and Societies and not for the number of courses in existence at the time, and include Ladies Clubs, etc. The number of new courses was almost certainly considerably less than the number of Clubs and Societies. Nevertheless from 1880 onwards there was a dramatic increase in the number of new courses.

The ladies and the formation of Ladies' Clubs
Women played golf from an early date but a Ladies' Golf Club was not formed until 1868. An occasional reference to ladies playing golf occurs in early records. For example, one of the indictments against Mary Queen of Scots at her trial was that she played at golf in Seton Fields on the day after the death of the Earl of Darnley. Another early account is taken from *Statistical Account of Scotland, Vol.I* (Edinburgh 1791–9) written in the eighteenth century concerning Musselburgh. 'The golf, so long a favourite and peculiar exercise of the Scots is much in use here. Children are trained to it in their early days . . .' The account goes on to say that 'Musselburgh needs to guard her precious field in which every burgess has a right to play'. It continues: 'When speaking of a young woman, reported to be on the point of marriage, "Hout", they will say "How can she keep a man who can hardly maintain herself?" As they do the work of men

Ladies' Golf at Westward Ho!, 1873.

and their strength and activity is equal to their work, their
amusements are also of a masculine kind. On holidays they
frequently play at golf; and on Shrove Tuesday there is a standing
match at football between the married and the unmarried women in
which the former are always the victors.' Miss Amy Pascoe writing
on Ladies' Golf (Horace Hutchinson's *Book of Golf and Golfers*
1899, p.223) says that in 1810, the ladies of Musselburgh played in a
golf competition for a new Barcelona handkerchief and a new fish
creel and shawl.

Apart from such sporadic references, little is said about ladies'
golf until the formation of the first Ladies' Club at Westward Ho!
on 8th June 1868. Known as the Westward Ho! and North Devon
Ladies' Club, it had forty-seven full members (ladies) and twenty-
three associate members who were all men. This Club had its own
9-hole course on Northam Burrows, close to, but separate from, the
main (men's) course. It also had its own professional, the brother of
the steward at Royal North Devon. The professional Andrews, only,
was allowed to teach the ladies: the men's club professional was
forbidden to do this.

Play was at first confined to 'every other Saturday between 1st
May and 31st October'. Some of the holes were seventy to eighty
yards long. It was decreed by the Club that no club should be used
on the course other than a wooden putter. A picture of the ladies at
play 'Ladies' Golf 1873' shows that the sport was genteel to a
degree and it was clearly more important not to show an ankle than to
execute a full swing. It also shows that their 'club house' was a
marquee. Nor did the dress, decorative as it was, suggest that a
complete golf stroke was physically possible.

Nevertheless, they took their golf seriously and J. Benet of the
Royal Blackheath Golf Club gave a Golf Challenge Medal that was
played for from September 1868. It seems likely that the golf
played by the working ladies of Musselburgh was much more
like the real thing. It was in England that ladies' golf made its early
debut as a complete game. The London Scottish Ladies' Club was
founded in 1872, and play was on Wimbledon Common. In 1890 it
was re-formed as the Wimbledon Ladies' Club. It was this Club that,
in 1893, promulgated the formation of the English Ladies' Golf
Union, which was formed in that year and in the same year the first
English Ladies' Championship was played over 9 holes at Lytham
and St Annes Golf Club.

It is clear that men did not approve of women playing golf and
this remained a stumbling block to women's golf in the early days.
Willie Park in *The Game of Golf* 1896 graciously acknowledged that
women play golf (some quite well!), but goes no further than that.
Sir W. G. Simpson in *Art of Golf* 1887, does not deign to mention
them. In the *History of the St Nicholas Golf Club* by W. Galbraith
1950 (p.104) he says that a few clubs gave facilities for ladies in the
second half of the nineteenth century but they were restricted
purely to putting. He mentions the St Andrews putting course and
also that the Glasgow Club admitted ladies for putting in 1871 but

withdrew the privilege in 1883. The Elie and Earlsferry Ladies' Club was formed in 1884: they were allowed no club house and their right to play on the men's course was somewhat uncertain.

The ladies were not to be denied and, in 1899, Horace Hutchinson's *Book of Golf and Golfers* has a section on Ladies' Golf, written by Miss Amy Pascoe (Chapter VII p.223). Horace Hutchinson was perhaps more sympathetic towards ladies' golf and their aspirations because he was a member of Westward Ho! where ladies' golfing efforts had received sympathy and help from the early days. At all events, Miss Pascoe says that there were one hundred and twenty-eight Ladies' Clubs in the UK at this time, nearly all instituted since 1880. She also talks of ladies playing golf in America (at Shinnecock Hills), in Baghdad, in New Zealand and in Algiers.

Clearly there was a golf explosion in the feminine world in the 1880s. The introduction of the Ladies' Championship in 1893 altered the concept, in men's minds, of ladies' golf and of their ability to play on a full-length course. The ladies required golf clubs and balls and the club- and ballmakers made them. The Lady Golfers' Club in London has a very fine and comprehensive collection of clubs and balls – at present on exhibition in Oxford Street, by courtesy of Colgate-Palmolive.

The spread of golf overseas

This is not the place to chronicle the first appearance of golf in various parts of the world, where, prior to the last quarter of the nineteenth century, it often arrived as a result of the enthusiasm of a handful of Scotsmen, often flourished for a while, came to a halt and was then re-started by some later enthusiasts.[8] If organised golf was to be established it became essential to engage a professional from Britain, which was how Pau in France, formed in 1866, engaged one of the first professionals to go abroad in 1869 – 'General' Lloyd – with the result that it became the first organised Club in Europe.

Canada
The Scots in Canada formed Clubs at Montreal (1873), Quebec (1874), Toronto (1876), Ottawa (1876), and Niagara (1882). Some years before the game started in the USA, it was the Royal Montreal Club, with just twenty-five members, who engaged the first professional golfer to appear in North America. Strangely enough, it was the comparatively new golfing centre of Hoylake who produced W. F. Davis. He became professional to the Royal Montreal Club and from their records there is an interesting account of his engagement, which is worth recounting. Arriving early in April 1881, he received wages of $5 or just over £1 a week plus all he could make from selling balls and clubs and repairing them. He got 11 cents for playing or teaching over the 9-hole course and had to return a third of that to the Club – and his playing ability was confirmed by his certifying that he averaged 86 strokes a round in playing Hoylake. The agreement also provided that he should keep the green in order as well as the putting holes – in other words the

[8]The start of golf in various Dominions and other countries throughout the world is for the most part covered by *Shell International Encyclopaedia of Golf*, Donald Steel and Peter Ryde, Ebury Press and Pelham Books Ltd, London.

fairways and the green. His time was his own, running the shop and teaching or playing with members, but from 1.30 pm each day onwards his time was to be given entirely for the benefit of the Club.

He obviously did not like greenkeeping and when the Club complained to him about the state of the course and that he should take a pride in it, Davis pointed out that at Hoylake a man was paid for doing the manual work. The Captain of the Club explained the position as follows:

> 'You must understand that his position there and yours here are very different. He has a Club of 500 members to attend to, with a green made for twenty years. Our Club of 25 members required compared with the other Club, little time, and one principal object in getting you here was that our new and rough green might be made as like the long made greens as can be done.'

Montreal therefore parted company with their first professional but in 1889 he was back again selling golf equipment and giving lessons. In 1893 he helped lay out 9 holes and was engaged as clubmaker and instructor to the Newport Golf Club near Boston, one of the five founder Clubs of the US Golf Association, so that he must have made good in the end.

The arrival of golf in the USA
The start of organised golf has been well recorded by such books as the first book on golf by an American *Golf in America – A Practical Manual* by J. P. Lee (Dodd Mead and Co. 1895), *Scotland's Gift – Golf* by C. B. Macdonald (Scribner, New York 1928) and *Fifty Years of American Golf* by H. B. Martin (Dodd Mead and Co. 1936).

It has been generally accepted that the first organised golf of the new era was played by what became the St Andrews Club at Yonkers in 1888, organised by John Reid, often regarded as the father of US golf. There is old documentary evidence of the Dutch playing golf in New York when it was a Dutch colony and from the pictorial evidence of their enthusiasm for 'Spel metten kolve' it would be surprising if they did not play there.

Recent research into the Port of Leith records has disclosed a large shipment of 96 clubs and 432 balls to Charleston, South Carolina, in 1743. This was at a time when the first Societies or Clubs were being formed in Scotland. In due course the South Carolina Golf Club was formed (in 1786), followed by the Savannah Golf Club in 1795 – the only surviving evidence of which is the invitation to a Miss Eliza Johnston to a Ball to be given by members of the Club on 20 December 1811 (see Appendix 2 on page 316).

It is now possible that further shipments may be traced from Leith and we shall know who was responsible for placing an advertisement in the *Rivington Royal Gazette*, New York, on 21st April 1779 offering 'excellent Clubs and Caledonian balls for sale'.

The establishment of the Shinnecock Hills Golf Club in 1891 can be studied in detail. This was the first incorporated Club in the USA and possessed a handsome architect-designed Club House. Shortly afterwards a 9-hole course exclusive to the ladies was added. At the time they thought they were the first to lay out a course in America only to find that St Andrews at Yonkers had preceded them.

The start of golf at Boston is also intriguing because it involves a young lady from Pau arriving to stay with a Mr Arthur Hunnewell with a set of clubs and balls. She proceeded to demonstrate how the game of golf was played and as a result a 7-hole course was laid out in the grounds of the house using 5 inch flower pots as holes. The ultimate result was the Country Club course at Brookline, Mass., but unfortunately the young lady from Pau is denied her place in history because no one remembers her name.

The greatest achievement in these early years was the creation of what was ultimately called the US Golf Association. The original five Clubs which formed it were:

The St Andrews Golf Club of Yonkers on Hudson.
The Shinnecock Hills Golf Club of Southampton, L.I.
The Country Club of Brookline, Mass.
The Newport Golf Club of Newport, R.I.
The Chicago Golf Club of Chicago, Ill.

The formation of this Association is of importance in a consideration of how it became possible to organise the game of golf so that today it is played under universally accepted rules. The Americans at an early stage recognised the need for a guiding spirit to ensure the orderly development of the game, the observance of the same rules, and the organisation of championships and international matches. Thus on 22 December 1894 the Amateur Golf Association of the USA was formed by the five Clubs listed above. Later it changed its name to the American Golf Association and finally to its present title of the US Golf Association. It is not generally appreciated that it was not until 1896 that the Royal and Ancient Golf Club finally agreed to become the authority in Britain and established its 'Rules of Golf Committee', and not until 1920 that it undertook the responsibility of organising the British Championships. No one can read the history of how the USGA and the R & A established common ground to observe basically the same rules for golf, without being impressed by Charles B. Macdonald, whose book *Scotland's Gift – Golf* covers every aspect of the game from 1872, when he was a student at St Andrews and learnt the game, until 1928 when his book was published. He was a remarkable man, with a reputation for being a difficult character; but he was passionately devoted to the game and to the maintenance of its traditions. He fought and succeeded in keeping the game intact on both sides of the Atlantic, when the Americans might so easily have gone their own way. The result is that today the game is played in ever-increasing numbers all over the world, with the same rules and equipment, and this did not happen by accident.

Macdonald's grandfather lived at St Andrews and he was sent there from the USA at the age of sixteen to attend the University. There he learnt his golf and soon became a good player. He played with all the leading players at St Andrews and became friendly with young Tom Morris (as he was to become friendly later with Bobby Jones – the other great player of his era). Luckily his work took him regularly to Britain, during what he termed the Dark Ages before golf reached America. He therefore maintained his links with St Andrews and particularly with Hoylake. He was in a unique position when golf took hold in America to play a leading part in promoting the game, in forming the US Golf Association and in maintaining the links with St Andrews. He laid out the National Golf Club links at Southampton, L. I., every hole of which was a copy of a well-known hole on a British course – and he probably rated this as one of his greatest achievements. Nevertheless, he has left a classic account of the growth of every aspect of the game, of how difficult it was to persuade some of his friends to try it and of how the very rich tried it but were not prepared to back it financially, suspecting that it was a fad that might well disappear overnight.

Charles B. Macdonald, the first official winner of the American amateur title, in 1895.

How the game was developed in America

The first requirement to establish the game in America was to provide courses on which the game could be played. Although the early courses were laid out by men such as Willie Dunn and other immigrant professionals, the story of Tom Bendelow, a Scotsman who was taken out of the composing room of the *New York Herald* by Spaldings and made their course consultant, is worth telling. H. B. Martin in *Fifty Years of American Golf* states that the only recommendation Tom had was a Scottish accent, but that was sufficient to convince everyone that he knew all about the game of golf. From his Chicago base shortly after 1895 he started laying out courses by the dozen, chiefly in the Middle West, and by the time he died in the 1930s he is believed to have laid out more than 600 courses. His procedure when laying out the course at Brook, Indiana, has been described as follows:

'Bendelow came to town early in the morning by appointment. He inspected the ground selected, and complimented the town officials, or the interested parties, on the character of the terrain. Then he proceeded to get busy. Tom's system was unique, but quite satisfactory. First, he would pick out an appropriate spot for the first tee and put down a stake, then he would pace off 100 yards and stake out a cross bunker and plant another stake. Stepping off another 100 yards or so he would put down his third stake, which marked the location of a pit or a cop bunker or a mound which was built in the shape of a chocolate drop, these drops being arranged in groups.

'Another stake located the green, which could be built round or square according to one's taste. The same process was used for all the holes, although some were made very short. On each unit of nine holes there was always one long hole and two very short ones. Few clubs found it necessary to keep Bendelow longer than one day, as this was supposed to be all the time required, and besides the charge was only $25. Bendelow always left instructions to guide the builder and in leaving he never failed to impress it upon the promoters that there were wonderful possibilities in the layout, and that when completed according to the prescription it would be one of the sportiest courses in the country.'

Bearing in mind that all concerned in those days were learning an entirely new game, and all were beginners, Bendelow's efforts did have the merit of an inexpensive start for many communities, even if few of his many courses survived for long. In any case, the professionals who came out all thought that they could also lay out golf courses, but their job was in any case about to be taken over by recognised golf-course architects, such as Donald J. Ross who came over from Scotland in 1899, and who subsequently laid out over 250 courses and remodelled countless others.

Willie Dunn Jr. (1865–1952)

The Smith family of golfers, immigrants to the USA from Carnoustie, Scotland.

The influx of professionals

The game in America could never have been expanded so quickly if it had not attracted hundreds of young men from Britain to better themselves, and a knowledge of golf was often the only asset which they carried overseas. Their most important job was to teach others how to play and it must be conceded that they were remarkably successful in producing home-bred championship winners and many players of the highest class within twenty years of the game having started in the United States. The Scots were naturally in the forefront of the invasion, and as seen in the case of T. Bendelow a Scottish accent brought with it an undisputed respect for their assumed knowledge of the game. It is worth noting that two English golfing centres – Westward Ho! (Club formed 1864) and Hoylake (Club formed 1866) – were by then producing young men whose knowledge of the game also qualified them to emigrate. (Note that W. F. Davis of Hoylake was the first professional to go to North America). The Scots brought the full St Andrews swing with them, in which the club was taken far back round the neck and this was accepted as the orthodox style. Hoylake, however, had developed a three-quarter swing considered to be far more accurate, and so new theories of how to play were soon introduced.

H. B. Martin devotes a chapter of his book (*Fifty Years of American Golf*) to the story of these immigrants, and, as he says, they came singly, they came in pairs and they came collectively – entire families embarking in one ship. He goes on to mention such families as the Smiths and Maidens, both from Carnoustie, whose pupils collected no less than twenty-eight national Championships. The story of the men who left Scotland, and to a lesser extent England, is one that has never been written and hopefully someone will undertake a task which would be of rewarding interest to many.

A reliable source of equipment for playing the game was the final requirement to establish it in America and at first it was supplied entirely from Scotland. The overseas demand, added to that from England, resulted in the inevitable demise of the craftsmen and the mechanisation of the clubmaking processes. Hickory for shafts was already in general use and was imported from the Tennessee Hickory belt in America. Before long persimmon and dogwood, also from America, were being used and the Americans found themselves with the raw materials for wooden-clubmaking and were not slow in setting up factories for this purpose. Only cleek (or iron) heads came to be imported and they were shafted by the professionals in America. The Dunn family were not only early immigrants but set up in the golf equipment business and their catalogue of prices is shown on page 107. John Duncan Dunn was to join the Bridgeport Gun & Implement Company (BGI) as a manager and there produced an American version of the Dunn 'all in one piece driver'. Slazengers were there in New York as equipment suppliers, as was Willie Park. Later on Taylor and Cann (J. H. Taylor was winner of the Open Championship five times) set up a factory in New Jersey, as a counterpart to the one they had at Richmond, London.

THE ENGLISH WIFE

THE AMERICAN HUSBAND

Three cartoons, reproduced by permission of *Punch*.

LINK(S)ED SWEETNESS

The Real Caddie (*audibly*).   " This club is going to ruin—
allowing all these ladies to join !"
Miss Sharp.   " They evidently can't get gentlemen !"

The manufacturers' field was soon to be entered by A. G. Spalding who started making clubs in 1894 and balls in 1898, by Crawford, McGregor and Canby of Dayton, Ohio (founded in 1829 as shoe-last makers) who started in the club business in 1896, together with BGI, who had entered the market when J. D. Dunn joined them, as mentioned above. The possession of raw materials, their scientific approach and the promotion of their products was to prove irresistible and it was not to be many years before the American manufacturers completely dominated the market for golf equipment. The subject is discussed in Chapter 4.

Finally, a word should be said about the standard of Club House accommodation which was expected in North America. In Britain in the nineteenth century there was a tradition of gentlemen's social Clubs in the cities. In America in the early 1880s on the other hand the Country Club idea was being introduced. When it arrived, golf became an additional attraction. The new Club Houses which were put up were in many cases erected to a high standard, and what originally started as a Golf Club later acquired other facilities. The ladies, too, appear not to have tolerated being pushed into the background – and the Morris County G.C., N.Y. for instance, was formed as a Ladies' Club with gentlemen as associate members. Perhaps the *Punch* cartoons on page 39 illustrate the point being made at the time.

The Club in Britain, whether social or golf, was mainly a male preserve, whereas the American ladies, from the very beginning, refused to be excluded from the activities of their Clubs.

Dates of foundation of leading Golf Clubs

Club	Founded	Membership 1866	1881 (Golf Annual)	Entrance Fee	Annual Subscription	
Aberdeen	1815	46	178	3 gns.	10/–	
Aberlady (Luffness)	1867		250			
Airdrie	1877		34		10/6	
Alnmouth	1869		94		10/–	
Arbroath	1877		60			
Ardeer	1880					
Ballantrae	1877		46		3/6	
Banff	1871					Boyndie Links
Bath	1880		60		20/–	
Broughty Ferry	1878		28		2/6	See Monifieth
Burntisland	1867		40	5/–	4/–	5 holes. Reinstituted
Cambridge University	1876		44		30/–	Coldham Common
Cambelton (Kintyre GC)	1876		40			
Carnoustie & Tay GC	1850	29	45		1/–	
Caledonian Union	1848	68				
Crail	1786	Dormant	30		2/6	Sauchope Links & Balcomie Links
East Neuk	1873		40	1/–	2/–	
Cullen	1878				2/6	
Cupar	1855	28	42	7/6	5/–	
Dalkeith	1880		34			
Dornoch	1878					
Dunbar	1857	50		30/–	10/6	
Dunbar Ladies	1873			10/–	1/–	
Dundee Dalhousie	1868		256	3 gns.	10/–	Plays at Carnoustie
Dirleton Castle	1854		30		2/6	
Edinburgh						
Bruntsfield	1761	55	125	3 gns.	10/–	
Bruntsfield Allied Golfing Club		34				
Burgess	1735	56	126	3 gns.	30/–	
Warrender GC	1858	57				Played on Musselburgh Links
Hon. Company of Edinburgh Golfers	1744	245	Not stated			
Merchiston GC	1860	37				
St Leonards	1857	26				
Earlsferry & Elie	1858	75	50	4/–	2/–	
Elie – Golf House	1875	75	100+			Using Earlsferry Links
Felixstowe	1880				10/6	Noted. 2½ hrs. from London by rail
Glasgow			200+			Alexandra Park
Royal Blackheath (London)	1608	92	117	5 gns.	3 gns.	
East Lothian GC (Gullane)	1859	30				
Haddington	1865					
North Berwick	c.1836	54	Not stated			
Hawick	1877		50		10/–	23 holes played for competitions
Tantallon GC	1853	33	Not stated			
Lanark	1851	48		1 gn.	5/–	
Kirkaldy						
Raith Golf Club	1877		60		10/6	
Wemyss GC	1857	50	Not stated			

Club	Founded	Membership 1866 (Golf Annual)	1881	Entrance Fee	Annual Subscription	
Ladybank	1879		30	1 gn.	10/6	
Leith						
Seafield	1878		60			
Thistle	1815	65	120	2 gns.	£1.5.0	
Leven						
Leven	1847	81	40			
Thistle	1860		50	1/–	1/6	
Innerleven (Dubbieside)	1820	72	100	1 gn.	10/–	
Royal Liverpool (Hoylake)	1869		519	2 gns.	30/–	
London Scottish	1865		340	6 gns.	2 gns.	
Manchester	1817	15				Kersal Moor course
Monifieth	1856		80	3/–	1/6	
Panmure	1845	139	Not stated			
Montrose		25	100	2 gns.	£1.0.0	
Montrose (Royal Albert GC)	1810					
Victoria GC	1862		60	10/–	5/–	Union, Mercantile, Mechanic and Star
Musselburgh						
Royal Musselburgh	1774		Not stated			
Royal Musselburgh Ladies	1872		Not stated			
Perth						
Royal Perth Golfing Society	1842	140	193	10 gns.	2 gns.	
King James VI	1858	51	60		15/–	
Perth Artisan GC	1879		30	2/–	2/–	Play at North Inch 12 holes
Prestwick						
Prestwick GC	1851	90	240	£10	£1.10.0	
St Nicholas GC	1851	71	112	10/–	£1	
Stirling GC	1869		80	10/–	10/–	
*Troon GC	1878		100			
Westward Ho!	1864	71	277	1 gn.	2/6	

*Members from Glasgow, Edinburgh, Kilmarnock and Ayr. 'There is a good Club House, boxed to accommodate upwards of 150 members, having a lavatory, with a supply of very fine spring water. There is also a supply of fluid on the establishment of another kind not derived naturally from mother earth.'

Clubs omitted

Club	Founded	Membership 1866	1881		
Royal & Ancient GC, St Andrews	1754	704	Not stated	⎫	
St Andrews GC	1843	110	Not stated	⎬ From 1866 Annual only	
Thistle GC	1865	46	Not stated		
University GC	1855	53	Not stated	⎭	

Chapter 3
The Golf Ball

The great development in the game of golf can be directly attributed to the wonderful strides made in perfecting the ball and making it a more pleasant game to play. Today's golfer has little idea of the marvels of ingenuity that have gone into producing a ball which gives unquestioned satisfaction and at a price which is only a fraction of the price of a new club. The first golf ball was probably made of beechwood, its successor was a leather ball filled with wool, flock or feathers and this was followed by the introduction of rubber and the gutta and composition gutty balls and finally the present corewound balls.

The ball has dictated changes in the design of clubs and the links and courses on which the game is played. We are indebted to the late John Stuart Martin of the USA for writing *The Curious History of the Golf Ball: Mankind's Most Fascinating Sphere* published by Horizon Press, New York, 1968, and for producing the first and so far only work of reference on the golf ball. In his acknowledgement he says '. . . A work like this, especially on the first go-round, must inevitably fall short of perfection . . . there will always be room for additions, corrections, clarifications . . .'. It is in this spirit that we add the result of our research into various records and archives in an endeavour to distinguish legend from fact.

We have already seen in Chapter 1 the illustrations of a wooden ball *c.*1600 and a leather ball *c.*1612, both Dutch. The latter looks remarkably like the feathery ball later used in Scotland. The Dutch were also known to use a leather-covered ball filled with wool or flock and called a 'sajet'. Balls were also stuffed with hair.

Van Hengel tells us that the game of 'Kaatsen' (hand tennis) is a sport that goes further back than the earliest references to golf and is still popular in Friesland today. A leather ball filled with feathers was, and still is, used, having a diameter of approximately 1·6 inches and weighing $\frac{3}{4}$ ounce (22 grams) or half the weight of a modern golf ball. The Royal Netherlands Kaats Association has at present an annual consumption of 3,000 featheries. What is apparent is that the Dutch had a knowledge of how to make a feathery ball from early times.

Early Scottish records are sparse in even mentioning balls used for golf and if a wooden ball was first used followed by a feathery, this must remain a matter for conjecture. It was not until 1743 that in a famous poem 'The Goff' by Thomas Mathison there is a description of the making of a ball and the first mention of feathers:

> '. . . the work of Bobson; who with matchless art
> Shapes the firm hide, connecting every part,
> Then in a socket sets the well-stitched void
> And thro' the eyelet drives the downy tide;
> Crowds urging crowds the forceful brogue impels,
> The feathers harden and the Leather swells; . . .'

How rightly he describes it as a 'matchless art'. It may have been perfected a long time before the poem appeared, and this brilliant innovation was to remain in use for another hundred years.

The tools required for making a feathery ball can be seen in the Royal and Ancient Museum and elsewhere. It was made from tanned leather – sometimes bull's hide, sometimes horse. The leather was cut in two, three or four lobes, fanned out from a common centre like the petals of a flower. The sewing was done with a needle, the seams to be into the inner edge so that the pouch could be reversed at the finish when the final stitches were put in and pulled tight, a $\frac{1}{4}$ inch slit being left in one flap of the leather through which to poke the feathers.

The feathers most commonly used were those from the breast of a goose, boiled to make them limp and malleable, though chicken feathers were also used. The maker started the operation by poking the feathers through the slit with a wooden stuffing wedge. Then he applied what was called the 'brogue', an iron rod 16–20 inches long, tapered to a blunt point and set at the top into a wooden cross-piece, to which the ballmaker applied pressure by placing it under his arm. When the brogue could fill the ball no more, a small awl forced in the last few feathers before the slit was sewn up. Calipers were used for determining the correct size. The leather having been soaked in warm alum water before the operation started and having had wet feathers inserted, when the ball dried out on completion, the leather shrank and the feathers expanded. The dual pressure of a shrinking cover and expanding core produced a hard ball.

The making of a golf ball was a slow process and only three or four could be made in a day. The price was therefore high and ranged between 2s 6d and 4s 0d throughout the duration of the feathery-ball period. There have been a number of references which state that the balls were egg-shaped, but all those which have survived are now as hard as nails and round. A few have their maker's name stamped on them, but with use this soon disappeared and those named balls which have survived were either new or had been little used.

In appearance the feathery was not unlike the modern fives ball and from all accounts it played well in dry weather, provided it was not mis-hit, particularly by iron clubs. Once it got wet it deteriorated rapidly and wheezed through the air when struck. In good conditions it was quite capable of being struck between 150–200 yards.[1] Amazingly, until after World War I there was no limit whatever on the size of a golf ball. You could have any size you liked. The feathery balls were numbered in size from 25–33 dram weight with the most popular being 26–28. The largest ball known to have been made is a 33 by T. Alexander of Musselburgh and this can be seen in the Honourable Company of Edinburgh Golfers' Collection at Muirfield. A tiny feathery ball together with a particularly large one just under 2 in. in diameter is also in the Burgess Company's Collection at Barnton, Edinburgh. One of the attributes of the feathery as against the subsequent gutta ball was the ability of the leather to take paint and in October 1688 Thomas Kincaid of Edinburgh's diary records 'collured a golve ball with white lead'.

[1] The longest drive with a feathery is credited to Samuel Messieux, a French-Swiss teacher of immense muscular power, at St Andrews. According to W. Dalrymple, writing in *Golf Monthly* September 1911, he drove a teed ball from the Hole o' Cross Green into the Hell bunker, a distance of about 360 yards. The wind and ground were favourable. Old Tom Morris more than once confirmed his belief in the truth of this himself.

The ballmaking craft involved a long apprenticeship. Tom Morris was apprenticed to Allan Robertson for four years. It would also appear to have been a more remunerative and steadier craft than that of clubmaking. We note that well-known names like the Dunn twins, Tom Morris, etc., were apprenticed to ballmakers and subsequently became clubmakers.[2,3]

It has been frequently stated that the ballmakers generally died young as a result of the dust from the feathers affecting their lungs. Generally speaking, from the records of ballmakers they do not appear to have achieved longevity, but they probably fared no better nor worse than the rest of the community.

Allan Robertson

[2]This is confirmed by the census of Scottish Summary Statistics at Register House, Edinburgh, where in 1831 one clubmaker and four ballmakers were listed and in 1841 two clubmakers and ten ballmakers.
[3]There is another reference to the golf ballmaking business in *The New Statistical Account of Scotland* (Vol.IX pp.476–477) report on the Parish of St Andrews, Fife in 1838. 'The manufacture of golf balls has long been carried on here, to a considerable extent. Above 10,000 are made annually. Nearly one-half of the produce is required for the use of the cultivators of the amusement in St Andrews. A market for the remainder is found in other places. Some have been sent as far as Calcutta and Madras.' Clearly St Andrews has established a reputation over a considerable period for making golf balls.

The early ballmakers

Allan See Allan Robertson.

Alexander, Thomas (1803–1841). Musselburgh ballmaker

The Dickson (Dicksoun) family See clubmakers' entry. William & Thomas Dickson (Dicksoun) were ballmakers in 1629. John Dickson of Leith licensed to make golf balls by Aberdeen Town Council in 1642. Andrew Dickson (1665–1729) of Leith – relationship not yet traced – was also a ballmaker, but a son and a grandson were both clubmakers, also at Leith.

Cosgrove, Alex (1821–1867) of Musselburgh.

Duncan, T. (c.1722) ballmaker at St Andrews.

The Gourlay family (Edinburgh and Musselburgh) (See page 47)

Gressick (Gressock), David (1821–1871) Musselburgh. At one time ballmaker to the Royal Perth Golfing Society who paid him £4 per annum. He made feathery balls. An example is in USGA Golf House, New Jersey, and he was still making gutta balls in 1861 (census). By then he was back at Musselburgh 'resident at Mrs Taylor's lodging house', Mill Hill.

Marshall, David of Leith. No birth and death dates known, but resided at 19 Meadow Place, Edinburgh 1815–22; then at Leith 1822–30 with an entry in the Edinburgh POD for 1830 and *Pigot's Directory* 1825–6. Marked examples of his feathery balls are known.

Melvill, James, and Berwick, William & Associates Although granted a monopoly for twenty-one years to make and sell golf balls (see letter dated August 1618), there is no trace of any of these names as golf ballmakers. Melvill and his syndicate acquired the monopoly as a money-making proposition, and in attempting to enforce it in 1628 against the Dicksons of Leith, landed himself in trouble, the Court pronouncing that it had never been ratified (see Chapter 1).

Miln, George (c.1753) of St Andrews. See also Henry Miln, clubmaker.

The Paterson family Cordiners (shoemakers) and golf ballmakers. Appear in records between 1565–c.1680.

Potts, Thomas (1825–1860) Recorded as a ballmaker at Perth. His father was a fishing-rod maker. He was also at one time in the employ of the Royal Perth Golfing Society and made feathery balls.

Ramsay, John (1822–   ) of Musselburgh, appears in 1841 Census as a feathery ballmaker and would then have been aged nineteen. Nothing more is known.

Robertson, James was a ballmaker at Leith. No birth or death dates known. He witnessed baptism of David, son of Simon Cossar, clubmaker, in 1788, where his occupation was given as ballmaker and he appears in Edinburgh POD at intervals 1800–1818.

Robertson, George ballmaker, lived at Wrights Houses, Bruntsfield Links. *Pigot's Directory* 1825–26, but in 1831 he is at Mill Hill, Musselburgh.

Robertson, William of Leith. Ballmaker. Death of child aged twenty months recorded in 1789.

The Robertson family of St Andrews. They were making golf balls at St Andrews from the first half of the eighteenth century – with six Robertsons, brothers – Andrew (d.1733), John (d.1754), David, Alexander (he married Penelope Miln – possibly the daughter of George Miln, ballmaker), William and Patrick. At least four or five generations of the family continued as ballmakers ending up with the most famous of them all, Allan Robertson (1815–1859), one of the great St Andrews players, who bitterly opposed the introduction of the gutta ball. His father, David Robertson, died in 1836 (he had at one time been McEwan's the clubmaker's agent in St Andrews). The inventory of his estate reported by his son totalled £92, the household furniture including twenty-three club boxes, forty clubs and £2 worth of golf-balls. Surprisingly his son, Allan, only left £91. With so many of the Robertson family having been engaged in making feathery golf balls, it is possible that the Leith Robertsons were in fact related. Allan Robertson stamped his golf balls 'ALLAN'. There is a feathery so stamped in a private collection and a gutta, random hammered and also stamped 'ALLAN', in the Wood Collection at North Manchester.

Russal, Charles ballmaker at St Andrews (d.1735).

Sharp, John Dates unknown, but he is recorded as being employed and succeeding David Gressick as ballmaker to the Royal Perth Golfing Society in the 1850s, for which he only received 2 gns. as against £4 per annum paid to his predecessor.

Stewart, Thomas (1816–   ) of Musselburgh, ballmaker. There is evidence that he made and stamped his own feathery balls. In 1861 Census he was a widower, also residing at Mrs Taylor's lodging house, Mill Hill, Musselburgh.

Tod, John (c.1730) of St Andrews. Ballmaker.

The Gourlay Family

Although Douglas Gourlay is chronicled as arriving at Bruntsfield as a ballmaker, *c.*1780, there have been unchecked references to the family being connected with golfing in even earlier times. A glance at the family tree shows the connection by marriage with the McEwan and Dunn families. They achieved in the nineteenth century an unrivalled reputation as feathery ballmakers. They also moved down to Musselburgh in the 1840s when McEwans the clubmakers set up there. John (1815–1869) and William (1813–1844) were in partnership as J. & W. Gourlay until the latter died in 1844. Thereafter John Gourlay accepted the arrival of the gutta ball and started making them with success. Examples of feathery balls marked J. & W. Gourlay and J. Gourlay, are to be seen together with the latter's early gutta balls.

John Gourlay

The Gourlay Family

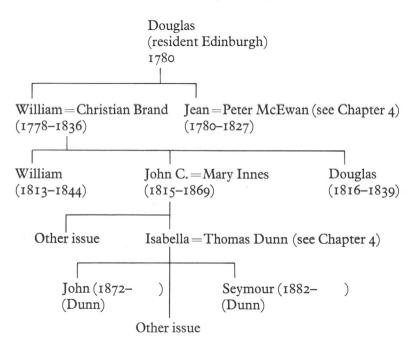

Douglas
(resident Edinburgh)
1780

William = Christian Brand   Jean = Peter McEwan (see Chapter 4)
(1778–1836)   (1780–1827)

William   John C. = Mary Innes   Douglas
(1813–1844)   (1815–1869)   (1816–1839)

Other issue   Isabella = Thomas Dunn (see Chapter 4)

John (1872–   )   Seymour (1882–   )
(Dunn)   (Dunn)

Other issue

The arrival of rubber

Probably the most important development in the history of golf was the use of rubber in the making of a ball.

'Caoutchouc', called in this country elastic gum or rubber, is said to mean 'weeping wood' and it was used by Charles de la Condamine who brought some of it back to France in 1736 after he had finished surveying along the Equator in Brazil. Joseph Priestley, the Unitarian minister and chemist, called it india rubber and discovered that it rubbed out pencil marks. Whilst the French kept the name 'Caoutchouc' the British found it difficult to pronounce and it came to be referred to just as rubber. The main source of supply was Brazil. Incidentally in the sixteenth century early explorers had reported seeing South American natives playing with balls which bounced.

By the end of the eighteenth century the waterproofing qualities of rubber were already known, and by the 1820s Hancock and Macintosh were waterproofing textiles and the 'macintosh' was born. By the 1830s rubber balls were certainly being made and in 1833 Queen Victoria gave her dog 'Dash' three rubber balls as a Christmas present (Elizabeth Longford *Queen Victoria – Born to Succeed*, diary for January 1833).

In 1838 Hancock and Charles Goodyear of the USA working independently discovered how to harden rubber by the vulcanisation process and later it was discovered that if sulphur was added then vulcanite or ebonite could be made. In 1844 T. Forster, a London rubber manufacturer, described in UK Patent 10,002 the making of rubber balls and dolls' limbs by moulds and vulcanisation.

It is conceivable that by the 1840s someone had tried to make an india rubber ball to play golf with, but found it unsatisfactory.

Then in 1843 an entirely different 'gum' called gutta percha (a Malayan phrase meaning 'tree sap') appeared on the scene. Mr William Montgomerie (1797–1856), a surgeon to the East India Company, noticed in his travels in Malaya that the handles of daggers, knives, whips and hoes were made of a hard substance which, however, could be softened by immersion in hot water. He therefore sent various specimens to London, stating the uses to which the material might be put, including the making of medical vessels. He received the gold medal of the Society for the Encouragement of Arts Manufactures and Commerce in June 1845 for his work, in spite of the fact that Dr Jose d'Almeida had also sent specimens of gutta percha to the Royal Asiatic Society in 1843. Some of Mr Montgomerie's specimens were later shown at the Great Exhibition of 1851.[4]

The milky juice of the gutta percha tree – sometimes fifty to one hundred years old – was unfortunately obtained not by making incisions in the tree, but by cutting it down, stripping off the bark and collecting the milk from cavities in the tree trunk in coconut shells. The yield of a tree was said not to exceed 30 lbs and furthermore was contaminated by sawdust, bark and dirt. The milk soon dried in the open air. Forests were decimated to obtain a small yield of gutta percha.[5]

[4]See *Journal of the Society of Arts,* Vol. XLVI (1897–8) 'Gutta Percha Lecture I' by Dr Eugene Obach.
[5]Information from the German magazine *Aus der Natur* 1862 (Caoutchouc and Gutta Percha).

The evolution of the golf ball from feathery to gutta percha.

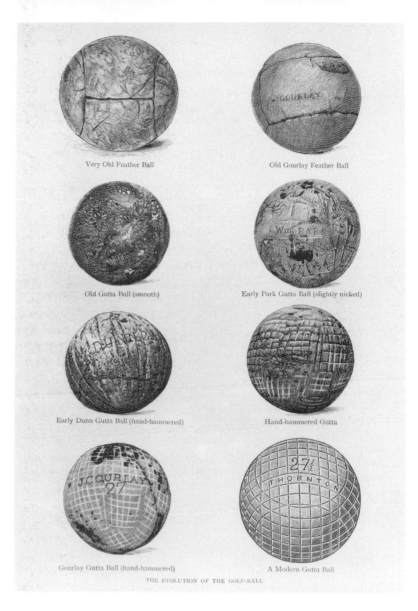

Very Old Feather Ball

Old Gourlay Feather Ball

Old Gutta Ball (smooth)

Early Park Gutta Ball (slightly nicked)

Early Dunn Gutta Ball (hand-hammered)

Hand-hammered Gutta

Gourlay Gutta Ball (hand-hammered)

A Modern Gutta Ball

THE EVOLUTION OF THE GOLF-BALL

The first appearance of the gutta percha ball

The gutta percha ball is referred to as a 'gutta' because it was made entirely of that substance and in order to distinguish it from the composite ball first introduced in the 1870s and referred to thereafter as the 'gutty'.

Blackheath
The new balls first appeared in 1848 and in James Balfour's *Reminiscences of Golf at St Andrews Links*, Edinburgh 1887, p.17, there is the following reference:

'About the beginning of the year 1848 balls were made of Gutta Percha. I remember the commencement perfectly. My brother-in-law Admiral Maitland Dougal played a doubles match at

Blackheath with the late Sir Ralph Anstruther and William Adam of Blair Adam and another friend with gutta percha balls on a very wet day. They afterwards dined together at Sir Charles Adams' at Greenwich Hospital and Sir Ralph said after dinner "A most curious thing – here is a golf ball of gutta-percha; Maitland and I have played with it all day in the rain and it flies better at the end of the day than it did at the beginning". Maitland came to Edinburgh immediately after and told me of this. We at once wrote to London for some of these balls and went to Musselburgh to try them. Gourlay the ball maker had heard of them and followed us on round . . . He was alarmed.'

Blackheath looks as logical a place as any for trying out gutta percha as a material for making golf balls. We know from the Blackheath Club records that there were members of the Club who were City merchants connected with the Far East. They would almost certainly have known about the importation of gutta percha and its qualities, and they could easily have obtained samples. Just down the road from Blackheath at Woolwich was the rubber works of S. W. Silver, the City tropical kit outfitters, who by 1852 had moved to the opposite bank of the River Thames and founded Silvertown – future home of the India Rubber Works and Telegraph Company. Over thirty years later in the 1880s they did make golf balls, the first of the Silvertown range appearing, followed by the famous Silver King. There is no reason to assume that the company were in any way involved in those early guttas; all that can be said with certainty is that Blackheath had access to knowledge as to what could be made from the raw material gutta percha.

Musselburgh
The gutta ball was also being used at Musselburgh in 1848 by James Balfour and his brother-in-law, Admiral Maitland Dougal, who had first obtained them in London. There was also a Mr William Smith (1814–1903), an inventive clockmaker. He moved to Musselburgh in 1846 and shortly after his arrival made some smooth balls from sheet gutta percha with the aid of a wooden mould and played with them with his friends – according to an interview with him recorded in *Golf Illustrated*, 22.2.1901. He later moved to Glasgow, leaving his mould with a Mr Goodsir (1798–1853), a grocer and spirit dealer of Newbiggin who made and sold balls in his shop until his death in 1853. Balls made by John Paterson of Edinburgh were also said to be on sale in the Race Stand. Willie Dunn, the well-known Musselburgh professional and a trained feathery ballmaker, was sent some sheet gutta percha by Sir Thomas Moncrieff (then of Blackheath) to make up balls. Musselburgh at this period was the centre of golf in Scotland, and although no exact dates are mentioned there is ample evidence that by 1848 gutta percha balls were being introduced from several sources.

The introduction of the new ball was also recorded in a splendid song 'In Praise of Gutta Percha' by W. Graham of Edinburgh, sung at a meeting of the Innerleven Golf Club, Fife, on 1st September 1848. It is set out in full in Appendix 1 on page 317. In the first verse it confirms 1848 as the date of introduction of the new ball

> '. . . I sing – the change brought round this year
>   By balls of Gutta percha!'

It acknowledges its early faults:

> '. . . Some purse-proud billies haw and hum,
>   And Say ye're douf at fleein'.
> But let them try ye fairly out . . .'

This refers to its tendency to duck in flight but after the smooth ball had been hacked and used the tendency disappeared and the song ends as follows:

> 'But Noo that a' your praise is spent,
> Ye'll listen to a friend's comment,
> And kindlier tak on the paint –
> Then ye wad be perfection.
> And sure some scientific loon
> On golfing will bestow a boon
> And gie ye a cosmetic soon,
> And brighten your complexion.'

The early guttas refused to take on paint and those that have survived are black or brown in colour. They must have been most difficult to find.

The 'invention' of the gutta ball

Although from time to time there was discussion as to when and where the gutta was first used, no one was too worried as to who was the first person to make one. Then in November 1900 W. Dalrymple of Leven, well-known as a writer on golf matters, made a brief claim in *Golf Illustrated* that the Rev. Dr R. Paterson of St Andrews had 'invented' the ball as early as 1845. A few months later (*Golf Illustrated* 22.2.1901) a lengthy article, which appeared in the same magazine, sponsored W. Smith the clockmaker of Musselburgh, who was still alive, as the inventor *c.*1846–7. It was not followed up in *Golf Illustrated* until 24.1.1902 when the Rev. J. G. McPherson of St Andrews recounted the life story of the Rev. Dr Paterson in romantic detail as a result of correspondence he had had with him the previous year. Any claim his half brother, John Paterson, who did make balls in Edinburgh, might have had was specifically dismissed. The now famous Hindoo Statue packed with 'chunks and chips' of gutta percha on its arrival in St Andrews, is introduced

Siva and Parveti (photograph by courtesy of Dundee City District Museums and Art Galleries Department). This is not a statue but a high-relief group containing two figures, Siva and his wife Parveti. This couple have an important place in Hindu Mythology – Siva being also Vishnu while Parveti is the famous goddess Kali in another aspect. An entry appears in the 'St Andrews Literary and Philosophical Society's Museum' of 'Hindoe Idol, Shiva and Parbottu his wife, donated by the Rev. James Paterson, taken from a Kineu temple in a town called Clyrabad'.

for the first time. The story tells how he ultimately made the packing material into a ball and painted it white, and how early one April morning in 1845 at St Andrews he played it – without claiming success and with no witness. The Rev. Dr Paterson was described as formerly President of the Ladies College, Binghampton, New York, and details were given of his education at Edinburgh University, the names of five of his tutors and how he decided to become a clergyman and emigrate, saying:

> 'I quit St Andrews for a louder call,
> And left to golfers all I had – a ball'

This then was the story which, without a moment's hesitation, was accepted, repeated and improved upon to such effect that the 'Rev. Dr' was declared the inventor of the gutta percha ball. It is only fair to add that certain well-known writers have never recognised this story.

The Patersons were not a St Andrews family – they came from Lauder, south of Edinburgh, and became closely interlinked with the Forgans (see Forgan family tree in Chapter 4). The Paterson name was carried through as a Christian name in the Forgan family. John Paterson (1777–1843) a merchant and turner, had three sons by three wives. John (born 1802) was a turner who lived at various addresses in Edinburgh before emigrating (c.1850) to join his cousin, John Ellis, a locomotive manufacturer in Cincinnatti, USA. He did make early guttas and tried to sell them, not very successfully, in Melville Fletcher's (a relative) bookshop in St Andrews, the Grand-Stand in Musselburgh and at a toy shop (Steels) in David Street, Edinburgh. The second son, by his second wife, was the Rev. James Paterson (1807–54), educated at St Andrews, who spent his life as a missionary in India and sent back the Hindoo 'Statue'. The third son, by the third wife, was Robert Paterson, born in 1829, who was therefore only sixteen in 1845. Robert A. Paterson has proved an elusive figure. We have the record of his birth in 1829, but so far he has not appeared in any other Scottish records, nor was he a student either at St Andrews or Edinburgh Universities (where he does not appear in the student lists of the five professors mentioned).

The only reference found is at Binghampton, New York State. It appears that an institution for the education of young ladies called Dean College was founded there in 1872 by a Mr Dean Smith, his wife and daughter, and that Robert Paterson was a teacher. He married the daughter and when Mr Smith died in 1877, he became President, his wife being described as Principal. The enterprise foundered and his last appearance was in the Directory of Binghampton in 1879–80 where he is described as Rev. Robert A. Paterson, A.M., President of Binghampton College. We still do not do not know where he was educated, qualified as a teacher, became 'Reverend' (the Rev. Doctor is not a recognised title) or where and when he died.

Previously the magazines *Golf* and *The Golfer* of 1895[6] mentioned his efforts to try to get old Tom Morris to visit the USA. *The Golfer* specifically stated that 'Dr. Paterson's brother was the inventor of the gutta percha ball and his description is most interesting of the disdainful manner in which what is now universally used was at first received'. In 1895, therefore, he was not claiming to be the inventor but by 1902 he had achieved immortal fame thanks to the Rev. J. G. McPherson. His life still remains a mystery. Rev. J. G. McPherson had previously written *Golf and Golfers – Past and Present*[7] and various golf articles, and had been a great champion of Allan Robertson, but Bernard Darwin, the well-known golf writer, had this to say about him:

'He had been about the best of the amateurs and had held the amateur record of 80, a fact that he never let his readers forget. He had given up golf young and retired to his quiet manse, to emerge years later as a man with a mission. This was to proclaim Allan Robertson as the greatest of all golfers and golf in the

[6] *The Golfer* 22.11.1895; *Golf* 9.8.1895.
[7] *Golf and Golfers – Past and Present* by Rev. J. G. McPherson (Edinburgh – Wm. Blackwood 1891).

53

eighties as a decadent game played on the mere wreck of what had once been a noble course.' [St Andrews]

In Tulloch's *Life of Tom Morris*, the author also has a tilt at the Rev. J. McPherson for championing Allan Robertson as the greatest of all golfers, in spite of his well-known reluctance to play anyone who might defeat him. The Rev. McPherson had clearly undertaken another mission, which was to establish a sixteen year old boy as the inventor of the gutta ball (see also Murdoch, J., *Library of Golf*, p.145). The verdict of *Golf Illustrated* (1.3.1901) was that no one person can be credited with its adoption and it is likely that independently, and at different times, the idea was tried out. Even though the 'Rev. Dr.' Paterson's claim did not appear until a year later, there seems no reason to dispute their original verdict.

The demise of the feathery ball

The fate of the feathery was indeed sealed by the adoption of the gutta ball, to the dismay of those who had spent years as apprentices learning their craft, and who now found, as they thought, their livelihood at stake. It must have been a bitter blow and Allan Robertson at St Andrews, eminent golfer and last of six generations of ballmakers, did everything he could to fight the new arrival. He is said to have seen it first at Innerleven in 1848 and derided its qualities (quite rightly at the time). He is then said to have bought up all the gutta balls he could at St Andrews and burnt them. Finally, having sworn Tom Morris (who had been apprenticed to him as a ballmaker and was employed by him) never to play with one, he parted company with him when he learnt that he had in fact used one. Tulloch's *Life of Tom Morris* states that the incident arose because Morris was 'stint' of balls, i.e. he had run out and had to borrow one from his opponent Mr Campbell of Saddell. (He then goes on to comment that a caddy usually expected to take out at least six balls on behalf of the player he was carrying for. This really does explain the high cost of golf because players, particularly at St Andrews where the whins were bad, obviously lost a number of golf balls. These were searched for diligently by boys – good ones being resold at 8*d* and downwards according to their condition.) Tom Morris was then engaged by the newly formed Prestwick Club and moved there in 1851. Douglas Gourlay had more sense and as soon as he realised the potential of the new ball, he promptly fulfilled a standing order for featheries and reduced his stock by sending six dozen to Sir David Baird.

Contrary to legend, the feathery ball was not immediately 'dead as a dodo' but the strongest reason for using the gutta ball related to the golfer's pocket. It could be made and sold for 1*s* 0*d* against 2*s* 6*d* – 4*s* 0*d* for the feathery, although Clubs often bought in bulk for as little as 24*s* 0*d* a dozen. Nobody at the time recorded any opinion as to whether the feathery, on a dry day, performed as well as the gutta or how it felt in comparison off the clubheads. Among the few records on the changeover are the Royal Burgess Club's minutes of 24 July 1852 authorising gutta percha balls as prizes instead of 'Gourlays'. The Honourable Company of Edinburgh Golfers attached a feathery ball which had been covered with silver each year to the silver club awarded to the winner of their annual Competition for the Silver Club. It was not until 1865 that they changed from using featheries and used a gutta ball. There is no evidence, however, that they were still in use at that date except for this purpose.

Apart from the price, the feathery ball may have been a pleasanter ball to hit in good conditions than a gutta, for those who could afford it. As we shall see, later on, when the rubber-core ball arrived, it was so superior to the gutta or gutty that price became immaterial.

The making of a gutta

The early descriptions of making a ball made it all sound fairly simple, but there must be some doubt as to the quality of the balls that were first produced. In those early days gutta percha arrived full of impurities of all kinds, such as sawdust or dirt and it has been discovered in recent efforts to make a gutta that it must have been difficult to get the ball to bind properly. Here is a description taken from a *Golf Illustrated* article of 27.12.1907.

'At first the gutta-percha was in the form of sheet, which was cut up in pieces, and when softened in hot water was drawn out in the form of a ribbon and wound up into a ball and pressed with the hand on a smooth board; then it was heated again and pressed until it was as solid as possible, and as there were no moulds at that time, the ball was rounded in the hands, and after some practice, a good ball maker could make them very round indeed. Then they were dropped into cold water to harden, and had to be constantly moved in the water to keep them round, for if they were left still in the water, the part that was above the surface would be swelled out of shape. The golf balls were made in this manner for some years.'

('Golf Ball Making in St Andrews Fifty Years Ago' by James Paterson Forgan (1839–1923), Robert Forgan's younger brother, who had weak feet and could not stand at the bench to learn to be a clubmaker and contented himself with ballmaking.)

A gutta ball, and the mould used to make it.

Home-made gutta, and the sheet gutta percha in the background from which it was made.

The authors decided to make a gutta ball and not without difficulty obtained sheet gutta percha from Malaya. It did not cut easily, even with surgical scissors. Strips were eventually made and immersed in hot water – but not boiled, for nobody had mentioned that – and from time to time they were taken out, stretched 'in the form of ribbon' as instructed above and an endeavour made to wind them into a ball. The strips however did not fuse easily and the potential ball unwound itself. After more heating and more winding it was decided to use an early smooth-type iron mould and this was successful. When taken from the mould the ball bounced freely – the following day when cool (and helped by a short period in the refrigerator – not available in the 1840s) it had lost its bounce. The use of the mould helped considerably and the final result, subject to a period for maturing, was satisfactory. The significance of Horace Hutchinson's advice in 1892 'Have your balls made of good gutta percha, by a good maker' is now appreciated. Perhaps the making of *good* gutta balls was not after all as simple as has been made out.

The early gutta would not fly properly until it was discovered that the more it was played and hacked, the better it flew. It was first claimed that the ball would last for ever and that all that was needed was to put it into warm water and roll the marks out, thus creating the original disadvantage of a smooth ball. Before long it became the practice to hack the new balls in random style in order to make them fly properly by providing a primitive form of mesh. Robert Forgan of St Andrews claimed to have been the first to hand-hammer balls to a regular pattern. The ball was placed in a half mould and a skilful workman could complete the job in $2\frac{1}{2}$ minutes – the ball being turned and struck by a sharp-faced hammer. Later on, the enormous significance of cover markings on the ball will be appreciated.

Golf balls: (left to right) Dunlop Maxfli *c.*1922; Rubber-cored Springvale Hawk *c.*1907; Cestrian gutty, *c.*1900.

A further discovery was that it was necessary to leave finished balls to mature; this requirement lasted throughout the gutta and the gutty era for reasons which are not entirely clear. The illustration below shows a box of Silvertown golf balls with 'thoroughly seasoned' printed prominently on the front. The Army & Navy Stores Catalogue of 1900 offered 'unpainted Golf Balls for Seasoning' at 6d discount a dozen – 10s 6d against 11s 0d and for quantities in excess of 6 dozen, 1s 0d discount per dozen. Two reasons have been advanced as to why balls needed to be matured – the first being to dry out any water content and the second to allow the paint to dry. Early gutties would not take paint at all well and furthermore the painting tended to obliterate the hand-hammered markings. It is probable that if balls were painted white, and were then kept while they matured, they tended to yellow.

The new balls were soon made up to the comparable sizes of the feathery (26, 27, 28, 29, 30) but were smaller in size. There has been some uncertainty as to what these sizes meant in weight terms, and as a result of articles and discussion in the April 1914 issue of *Golf Monthly*, it was stated that dram weight was used for featheries and also for guttas up to around 1880. Thereafter Troy weights were used and the sizes were then expressed as dwt. – pennyweights – so that a $32\frac{1}{2}$ approximated to the weight of today's ball. Before mechanisation the gutta ballmakers must have used scales to determine the weights of the balls which they made. No examples of such scales have yet been discovered.

The first 'floaters' for use on courses where the ball might be lost in the water were made by placing a piece of cork in the centre as a core, although guttas would in fact just keep afloat on their own. H. T. Peter in his *Reminiscences* (1890) states that he and his brother used to insert a piece of lead in the centre, believing that they

Silvertown golf ball box.

putted more accurately and flew better against the wind. He also stated that 'other players used to lead their balls by rolling them when warm in lead filings, but as these were on the surface they fell out when struck and gave the ball a very unsightly appearance. I played with unpainted balls under the impression that they flew better but there was the drawback that they were difficult to find.' Recently a ball was found at the bottom of a rabbit hole at Gullane, Midlothian and an x-ray revealed the presence of metal.

The further development of the golf ball

Following the introduction of the gutta golf ball, it was possible for anybody to make these balls who could obtain the raw material, which later came in rope form and was easy to cut off into chunks suitable for making a ball. This obviated the necessity of cutting the strips from sheet gutta percha, winding them and making them fuse together. The first moulds in general use were made of wood or iron and produced smooth balls, and there were probably different sizes for the various weights of ball. They were then hand-hammered, painted and left to mature for some considerable time and in some cases the maker's name was put on. We know from an example that Allan Robertson continued to use his trade name of 'ALLAN' as used in the days he made featheries. The use of moulds which impressed mesh or other markings did not come into practice until much later, probably in the 1870s when the machine-made balls began to appear. By the 1880s the 'Home Golf Ball Kit' could be bought which consisted of a mould, a supply of paint and a drying rack. Painting remained a real problem until improved paints appeared which adhered better to the ball.

No patent for the original gutta ball appears to have been applied for. In 1858 Charles Cowper (UK Patent No.2288) describes the vulcanising process for india rubber and gutta percha, including the use of moulds, and in 1860 Nicolson H. (UK Patent No. 1478) describes a ball for cricket, golf, etc., which has a centre core bound by cotton or twine and covered with gutta percha (or leather if it is to be a cricket ball). It is not known whether golf balls were ever made from this patent but it is doubtful.

The development of a 'composite' gutta ball followed which we shall refer to as the 'gutty' as opposed to the 'gutta ball'. The dictionary meaning of composite is 'made up of distinct parts or elements' and the patents we are about to refer to bring in for the first time another substance or substances to be combined with gutta percha.

In August 1876 (UK Patent No.3428) there was the first patent taken out relating specifically to a golf ball by a Capt. Duncan Stewart RN of St Andrews, who has never been recognised as the considerable pioneer he was. He made a composite ball combining gutta percha with ground cork, metal filings and a suitable solvent – which sold well but unfortunately its name has not been established.

This ball was, sadly for him, only a second best for in 1871 he had started making a ball of wound rubber thread enclosed in a cover of gutta percha. This was the principle on which the world-beating rubber core-wound Haskell ball was made thirty years later, and it was Capt. Stewart's evidence in the great Haskell patent infringement case of 1905, which made a vital contribution to the verdict that there was no novelty in Haskell's idea. Stewart of St Andrews had made the first core-wound ball and then the first composite gutty and he deserves his niche in the history of the golf ball.

The following extract is taken from Mr Justice Buckley's summing up of Duncan Stewart's evidence in 1905:

'. . . I find the facts to be as follows. Captain Stewart was an enthusiast, continually experimenting in the making of golf balls. He made many kinds. Amongst them was a ball of wound rubber thread enclosed in a cover of gutta-percha. He made these from about 1871 to as late as 1879. In the course of those years he arrived at what he considered to be a satisfactory ball. In his view it was the best ball he made, or knew. He played with it himself; he gave it to friends; he sold it often to Mitchell-Innes; when a fellow-golfer was not willing to accept a ball as a present he would take a shilling for it. He sent some to Tom Morris, and to Thornton for sale, and some of them were sold. He disclosed the construction of the ball to Mitchell-Innes, and his impression is that he told others, but he is not sure. He kept the construction of it a secret from professionals, and did not want any who were golf ball makers to know it. He regarded it as a secret of importance and did not want to disclose it to any one in the trade or professionally engaged in golf. Notwithstanding that he had arrived at this which he thought was, and continued to make, because it was a satisfactory ball, he could not sell it commercially; it had no click, and, according to the sentiment of the day, golf without a click was not golf, but a waste of time. So he went on with his composition ball which he was able to sell, and when he took out his Patent in 1876 it was for the composition ball. The wound rubber thread ball was in his view the best ball to play, but the composition ball was the best ball to sell. His manufacture therefore continued principally to be of the composition ball, but he made, and used to give to others to use, and, to the extent I have stated, sold to others for use, the wound rubber thread ball. He did so to the extent of many dozens. In 1879 he left St Andrews and went to live at Campbeltown. He was captain of the golf club there, and played occasionally, but, in substance, from the time he left St Andrews in 1879 his enthusiasm was over, whether for making golf balls or playing golf, and after 1879 he never made a rubber wound ball.'

The year following Stewart's patent, in 1877, William Currie of the Caledonian Rubber Works, Edinburgh, took out UK Patent No.4838. It was also for a composite ball to be made of a mixture of rubber, ground cork, leather, etc., which was moulded and vulcanised. In order to indent the surface of the ball the mould was lined with canvas which adhered to the surface of the ball and was later removed. This ball was the famous 'Eclipse' and heralded the arrival of the manufacturer in the golf equipment field. It was successful for quite a time but as the advertisement in the 1887 *Golfing Annual* shows, the Caledonian Rubber Works were by then having their troubles over manufacture. It is also amusing to see how they sneaked a Victorian sponsorship from the Amateur Champion, Horace Hutchinson, 'in all round merit the Eclipse is quite as good as the Gutta' (Note the use of gutta at this time – to distinguish it from the gutty or composition ball).

THE "ECLIPSE" GOLF BALL.
(CURRIE'S PATENT.)

THESE have quite superseded the old gutta-percha balls. They are almost inde-structible, no club or iron will hack them, they fly beautifully, and retain their per-fectly round shape; they can be driven further than the gutta-percha ball, and are quite true on the putting-green.

EXTRACT FROM "THE FIELD," 23RD JULY, 1881. —" We have thoroughly tested the specimens sent, and were agreeably surprised to find how near they came to the high estimate put upon them by the Patentee. Most assuredly they do not get hacked; not only did we play for four hours with the one ball, but for nearly two minutes afterwards we hammered away at it with our niblick, and no trace of hacking could be found. A better driving ball, too, we never struck; but the very elasticity which constituted its excellence in that particular at first rendered it somewhat un-certain in the short or putting game, especially where the green was a bit rough. That drawback, on our calling attention to it, the Patentee has remedied, and a fresh trial has convinced us that the remedy is effectual. As to the alterations effected by change of temperature, we cannot, in this tropical weather, speak from ex-perience; but every Golfer knows that during intense frost the gutta-percha balls occasionally split, and these we are assured will not."

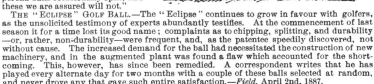

THE "ECLIPSE" GOLF BALL.—The "Eclipse" continues to grow in favour with golfers, as the unsolicited testimony of experts abundantly testifies. At the commencement of last season it for a time lost its good name; complaints as to chipping, splitting, and durability —or, rather, non-durability—were frequent, and, as the patentee speedily discovered, not without cause. The increased demand for the ball had necessitated the construction of new machinery, and in the augmented plant was found a flaw which accounted for the short-coming. This, however, has since been remedied. A correspondent writes that he has played every alternate day for two months with a couple of these balls selected at random, and never drove any that gave such entire satisfaction.—*Field*, April 2nd, 1887.

Messrs. Currie, of the Caledonian Rubber Works, Edinburgh, are the patentees of the "Eclipse" Golf Ball, which, since they first introduced it, has been greatly improved in flying qualities. No less authority than Mr. Horace Hutchinson, the amateur champion, has pronounced the opinion that in its all round merit, the "Eclipse" is quite as good as the Gutta Ball. There can be no doubt about the "Eclipse" being the better ball to play with against the wind; it also retains its roundness, a great desideratum in putting, and is the most economical ball of the two.—The *Newcastle Daily Journal*, April 14th, 1887.

To be had from all Indiarubber Depots and Golf Club Makers.

PATENTEES AND SOLE MAKERS,
WILLIAM CURRIE & CO.,
Caledonian Rubber Works, Dalry Road, Edinburgh.
[1]

Advertisement for the 'Eclipse' golf ball.

The following year the India Rubber Gutta Percha & Telegraph Works Co. Ltd (the Silvertown company), once at Woolwich, and now at Silvertown, London, produced a new composite ball, much harder than anything that had been produced before. It was called the 'Silvertown No.4', the forerunner of many generations of famous balls including the 'Silver King'. Silvertown did not take out a patent but William Currie in February 1888 charged them with infringement of his patent for the 'Eclipse'. Not surprisingly no more was heard from him for the balls were totally different.

In the 1892 edition of *Badminton,* Horace Hutchinson, the Editor, compares:

1   The Silvertown – harder, slightly longer flight, somewhat harder to control in high wind. Good ball for weak driver and it rises quickly in the air. It is not a good ball against the wind but it is a good friend to the clubmaker for it is liable to break the heads of wooden clubs.

2   The Eclipse – is the very opposite to the Silvertown. It is a soft india rubber ball and goes off the club with the silence of a thief in the night. Good ball in wind, easier to keep straight but will not rise quickly from the club. Nevertheless it is going fast out of fashion.

3   Final advice. Have your balls made of good gutta percha, by a good maker . . . Keep them for *six months* before playing with them!

Nevertheless, the arrival of the Silvertown added to the influence already bearing on the design of wooden clubs as referred to in Chapter 5. The old long-headed wooden clubs were on their way out and the faces of the wooden clubs were being protected by vulcanite, leather, etc., from the effect of hitting the new gutty. According to the Silvertown records, rubber golf balls at that time were vulcanised in a tank of molten sulphur and on one occasion a ball was left unnoticed at the bottom of the tank and when recovered at the end of the week had hardened into ebonite. Manufacturers had therefore found out how to obtain the ultimate degree of hardness, but it was also accompanied by a brittle quality and the ball tended to shatter. The ruling at the time in such a case was that another ball was put down where the largest piece of the old one lay (without penalty) – there was comment at the time that the largest piece always appeared to finish on the fairway.

During the 1890s there was a rush of ideas in the form of patent applications. Attention was now being paid to markings. Willie Park Jr. of Musselburgh, for instance, registered his diamond mesh mark in October 1890 (UK Patent No.16,862) and in 1896 took out a patent for another which he called the Royal. It had flat hexagonal panels which were meant to slow the ball upon the putting green. This was a truly remarkable ball, one of which can be seen in the Wood Collection, North Manchester. The number of rubber manufacturers manufacturing golf balls was growing and they were being offered for sale through the professionals and through sports-equipment shops in big cities. The necessity for the professional to make his own golf balls was being removed and he could better spend his time retailing manufacturers' balls than making gutta balls which were about to become obsolete, although the gutty was to survive for some years.

The advent of the Haskell rubber-cored ball from the USA

At the turn of the century the gutta ball was giving way to the ever-improving composite gutty, when out of the blue came a ball which did more to stimulate the game than any other development before or since. The solid golf balls in use had to be hit in the middle of the club and hard 'tops' for instance could jar the hands quite severely. This new ball, however, gave immense pleasure to most golfers because it went further and if you mis-hit it, then it still performed far better. Unlike the original gutta ball, which encouraged more golfers by being so cheap compared to the feathery, this ball was so good that players were quite prepared to pay a hefty premium to get one in the early days. Later on the best balls cost up to 2s 6d each, which was a lot when clubs cost no more than 4s 0d to 5s 0d each.

This new ball from America was made by the Goodrich Tyre & Rubber Co. of Akron, Ohio, and called the 'Haskell'. The principle behind the construction of the new ball was to wind elastic thread or tape round itself to form the main core of the ball and then to put on a gutta percha cover to hold it in place. To start with, the balls were wound by hand and were not successful – just as early British experiments had failed. It was the mechanisation of the winding process, using an inner core on which to start the process, which completely changed its prospects and produced the modern golf ball. Most of today's golfers have little idea of the make-up of the golf ball and the marvel of ingenuity that has gone into producing it by winding hundreds of feet of elastic thread onto a core. The reason is the tough cover which is now used and which stands up to terrible treatment. In the early days of the rubber core, one 'hack' and the ends of the rubber thread were out and the entrails of the ball laid bare, to the delight of all small boys who had anything to do with the game. They could extract hundreds of feet of elastic thread from discarded balls and later on investigate the centre core as well. What a tremendous idea it was! Without it, there would still be the solid ball, no doubt performing better and better, but lacking that magical 'click' (a promotional word used at the time) which provided universal satisfaction. There is no doubt about what is owed to the rubber-cored ball and to all those associated in developing it, a debt of gratitude for the greatest single invention in the history of golf.

Nevertheless the Haskell did not come in overnight and in top-class golf it had its disadvantages. It was harder to control on and around the greens and became known as the 'bounding Billy'. When it first appeared in Britain in 1901, it was received with considerable suspicion, conferring an unfair advantage on the player who used it (and presumably won) as against someone who did not, or in the early days, was unable to get hold of one. John S. Martin states that this is how the expression that 'someone was a bounder' arose, implying that it was not sporting to use a 'bounding Billy' when playing against those who had not got one.

In the USA it was a limited success in 1900. In the UK in 1902 Sandy Herd using a Haskell won his only Open Championship at Hoylake by one stroke from Vardon and Braid. Imported Haskells were so scarce that up to £1·50 ($7.50) was being paid for them and at the last moment Herd decided to play one. He used the same ball for four rounds and when he finished, it was in such a state that its entrails of rubber thread were showing. That tiny margin of one stroke nevertheless was something of a triumph. In the 1904 British Amateur Championship, Britain's longest hitter, Ted Blackwell, played a gutty and was beaten in the Final by Walter Travis of the USA using a Haskell although it was on the putting green that he really won the match. It was by now definitely in the ascendant, but here again, as with the gutty and feathery fifty years earlier, the Haskell did not sweep all before it immediately.

The late Francis Ouimet, the famous American amateur who won the US Open Championship in 1913 at the age of twenty, beating the great British players Vardon, Ray and Braid, in his book *A Game of Golf* (Hutchinson & Co. 1932) has this to say of the early Haskells and the Kempshall Flyer. 'I have seen both of these crack open and become unfit for play on the first or second shot. If the golfer topped one of them, it was the finish. They just would not last at all. Then came the Spalding Wizard, like the first two it could not stand up to punishment. British made balls put in an appearance and they were easily destroyed.'

Ouimet goes on to tell us of the little-known story of the Goodrich Company who had produced the Haskell 'Pneumatic' ball – a rubber cover or shell into which air was compressed, introduced around 1906. It apparently caught the fancy of golfers at the time but it had to be hit powerfully in order to get it along and players in 1906 were new to the game and did not have the necessary hitting powers. It tended to explode in flight or in caddie bags and he says 'Golfers had many interesting experiences with the Pneumatic'. In 1907 Goodrich produced an improved ball called the 'Silk Pneumatic' which had woven silken strands inside the cover to strengthen it, similar in structure to motor tyre fabric. This performed better but there was always the danger that something would happen. Alex Campbell, a professional playing in the 1907 USA Open Championship at Philadelphia Cricket Club, had a fine chance to win until, reaching the edge of a green in two strokes, he took four more to hole out from about twenty feet – his ball had lost its compression.

Captain Nelson Zambra (one-time Secretary at Hayling Island GC and born in 1881) confirms from his own experience in the UK that the early Haskell core-wound balls were far from satisfactory except in so far as length of shot was concerned. They seldom lasted a round without the cover being cut through, and the gutty was still far more satisfactory and controllable around and on the green and also for use at short holes. Many players carried a gutty for use at short holes only.

There was a long fight to retain the use of the gutty for championship and other important events. The final nail was not put into the coffin of the gutty until a great contest was held on 2nd April 1914 at Sandy Lodge, London, when the 'Great Triumvirate' (as they were known), Vardon, Braid and Taylor, together with George Duncan played a four-ball match turn and turn about: the Gutty *v.* Rubber-Core Ball. This contest was promoted by *Golf Illustrated,* together with a long-driving contest the previous day which was won by the Haskell as expected. From reading the account of the matches, these men could play brilliantly with the gutty; really it was *length* which finally mattered and this was confirmed by the driving match. It was not until 1914 that *Golf Illustrated* in its leader by Harold Hilton said 'The Gutty has passed away for ever'.

The invention of the Haskell and the greatest legal action in the history of golf

Just as the development of the gutta and gutty golf ball was never chronicled, neither was that of the rubber-cored ball, nor the details of how it was invented. We are indebted to John S. Martin for telling us who Coburn Haskell was, for he has often been wrongly described. He was born in 1868, and went to Harvard though he did not graduate. In 1892 he went to Cleveland where among other things he became involved in a bicycle-manufacturing business and came to meet Bertram Work of the B. F. Goodrich rubber plant at Akron, Ohio, who supplied him with bicycle tyres. In 1895 he married Mary Gertrude Hanna of the wealthy Hanna Mining Company family and ultimately joined the Board. He was involved as an entrepreneur in various industrial enterprises. Martin states that his main hobbies were horses, shooting and books, beside golf. He died in 1922, aged fifty-four.

It was from the combined work of Coburn Haskell of Cleveland and Bertram G. Work of Akron, Ohio, that the idea of winding an elastic thread round a core and covering it with a gutta percha cover arose in 1898. Martin records three different versions of how the idea came about but there is no authentic first-hand account. Haskell provided the inspiration and enthusiasm plus his own rather unusual name to give to the ball. He is unlikely to have known of similar earlier ideas in Britain, but without Mr Work and the Goodrich employees there would have been no ball. Many people have just assumed that Haskell invented the ball – he may have had an idea, but he played little part in making it.

In the first place, Martin pays tribute to Emmett R. Junkins of Goodrich who himself hand-wound the first balls to be covered and tested and then taught some girls how to proceed. At the behest of the Goodrich Co., John Gammeter invented the first automatic golf ball winding machine and in April 1900 was granted a US Patent which he assigned to his employers. Its success depended on a core or centre on which to wind the elastic thread and it was this machine which mechanised the process and made the Haskell ball possible. It was the most memorable invention in the history of golf but it is the name Haskell which is remembered and few people have ever heard of Gammeter. Without him the hand-wound balls of the Goodrich Company could not have succeeded. The early Haskells before mass-production was introduced were not a great success; although marked in a similar way to gutties, they exhibited the same tendency to duck and dart as smooth guttas had done when they first came out. The problem was solved when the new ball was given a bramble pattern cover, and when, according to tradition, one of the Foulis brothers at Wheaton, Chicago, accidentally put an improved Agrippa Bramble cover onto a Haskell ball. The letter below from Eliphalet W. Cramer to C. B. Macdonald dated Chicago, 18 July 1927 with a different version of the same incident – from *Scotland's Gift – Golf* by C. B. Macdonald, (Charles Scribner & Sons, New York, 1928) – appears to have some relevance.

'My dear Charles:

'The credit of the remade Haskell ball is primarily due to you who gave me the hint as to what was the matter with the original Haskell ball. It seems in the old days, so you told me, when they played with the gutta ball that the experience was, after they had been nicked a bit, the flight was longer. My experience with the Haskell was that it would go a certain distance and then duck, so I took one of these into the shop and had David Foulis put it in an Agrippa mould. It, of course, came out black, and just as I was about to try the effect James Foulis came across with a driver in his hand. I asked him to try this ball and see if he could hit it. He took his full swing, and then an explosion of holy oaths ending up with "What is it?" I then told him what we had done and asked him to keep it a secret for a time and make me a dozen of them. This he did and I found, of course, the length of my drive tremendously improved. The first one I worked it on was your own dear self, and I said to you one day: 'Charley, my game is improving and I will play you a game for a box of balls at the same odds that you are giving' – you had always been winning heretofore. The first ball I drove was beyond yours and I remember distinctly you saying, "You have improved". At the second hole the same thing happened and you went and looked at the ball. It seemed all right to you and I said nothing. When we finished the game, and I for the first time had won, I told you what we had done and I ordered a dozen balls made for you and I think also for Jim Whigham. You were both going to some tournament, perhaps it was Newport.

'At the time of my discovery I told the Foulis brothers to buy up all the Haskell balls they could get and remold them, which they did. Haskell finally got on to it and tried to stop them, but, of course, they were perfectly within their rights and nothing was done to prevent them. The Foulis brothers made quite a bit of money.

Yours sincerely,
"LIPH"'

Bertram G. Work and Coburn Haskell, in that order were granted USA Patent No.622834 in 1898, Gammeter's Patent following in 1900 as already mentioned. The patent was opposed on the grounds of 'prior user' for the manufacture of a baseball, but the objection was over-ruled. The leading golf ball companies in the USA, Kempshall, N.J. (and its British affiliated St Mungo of Glasgow), Spalding and the Worthington Golf Ball Company all took out licences to manufacture. In Britain the Silvertown Co. also took out a licence. Under the name Boult A. J., UK Patent No.17,554 of 1898 and UK Patent No.4165 of 1900 were taken out in Britain to cover the Haskell and Gammeter patents respectively.

Almost immediately in Britain there were a number of infringements of patent and the Haskell Golf Ball Co. Ltd. decided that it had to proceed against a British manufacturer and win. In the most celebrated legal golf case of all time they sued Hutchison Main & Co of Glasgow, manufacturers of the Springvale range of core-wound balls, named Eagle, Hawk and Kite. On the face of it, they should have won their case, but they did not, even though they took it through the Appeal Court to the House of Lords. The case failed on the issue of novelty, or prior user of the idea; the defendant's two chief witnesses, of many, were Captain Duncan Stewart RN (already referred to earlier) and Willie Fernie of Troon. The latter had made a few core-wound balls in 1892 and had passed the idea on to his brother George who in 1904 was attempting to patent his method of manufacture and was also advising the defendants on how to make them. Another witness was a marvellous old lady from Derby called Mrs Hickinbottom who made substantial numbers of children's balls, costing $\frac{1}{2}d$ to $1d$ each and made by using elastic-thread oddments, winding them round a core and then dipping them in rubber solution to coat them. She was summoned to London and sat beside the judge demonstrating how she made the balls and dipping them in her rubber brew that smelt abominably. This was clearly a most entertaining trial and Horace Hutchinson gives a light-hearted account of it in his *Fifty Years of Golf* (1919).

The plaintiffs had replied to the defence of 'no novelty' by pleading 'abandoned user' of an idea – which is the same as saying that their ideas never came to anything. Perfectly true, but of no avail. It was the mechanical ingenuity of Gammeter's machine which produced a totally new concept of a golf ball – yet somehow something went wrong with that case.

The result in Britain was that the field was open to everyone, but the patent was good in the USA where royalties had to be paid. As described in Chapter 8 further stimulus was given to the registration of patents to evolve even more exciting new balls: there were, between 1902 and 1905, ninety-seven patents in the UK and forty-one in the USA and a hot pace was maintained right up to World War I.

Still further improvements to the golf ball

There were now a number of areas in which the original Haskell ball could be improved upon. The first concerned the toughness of the cover of the ball, because for many years one good hack with an iron club could cut through the cover and make it useless. It was an expensive ball to play with. Second, there was the mesh or design for the cover marking; and William Taylor of Leicester in UK Patent No.18,668 of 1905 brought out the idea of dimple markings on golf balls and a short description of his object was as follows:

> 'To improve the flight of a golf ball, the surface of a covered or solid ball is formed with a number of shallow isolated cavities which are substantially circular in plan and evenly distributed . . . as applied to cored balls the structure is stated to be adapted to increase the tensile strength of the core.'

Sketches of new developments for balls and cover markings, taken from *Frys* magazine 1911–12.

A BALL WITH FOUR STEEL BALLS FIXED IN A PLAIN RUBBER CENTRE SURROUNDED BY RUBBER THREAD WOUND UNDER TENSION AND COVERED WITH COMPOSITION.

A BALL WITH FOUR LOOSE STEEL BALLS ROLLING FREELY IN A CELLULOID RACE WITH WOUND RUBBER THREAD AND COMPOSITION OUTSIDE. AN EXTREME IN ORIGINALITY.

A RUBBER CORED BALL WITH MERCURY IN THE MIDDLE. CLAIMED FOR THIS AND THE LAST THAT THEY "LIKED THE HOLE."

THE PNEUMATIC. AN AMERICAN BALL OF COMPRESSED AIR WITH COMPOSITION COVER.

A BALL WITH A CENTRE OF WATER SURROUNDED BY A RUBBER CORE AND COVERED WITH COMPOSITION.

THE SAME WITH CENTRE OF JELLY OR SOFT SOAP, A VERY POPULAR BALL FOR A TIME AND STILL IN USE.

THE "DIMPLE" MARKING.

THE "STUD" MARKING.

THE "ZOME" MARKING.

This idea was immediately taken up in particular by Spaldings who produced their Black & White, Glory and finally the Red Dot, with dimples or recessed markings instead of the bramble pattern, which in fact was reversed. After many years of aerodynamic research this is the design principle which has won through to the present day and Taylor is the man who should be remembered for this particular contribution to the design of the modern golf ball.

Another area which offered opportunities for a further advance in the performance of the ball was the core on which the elastic thread was wound. As Chapter 8 (Patents) shows, all sorts of ideas were tried out involving materials as diverse as rubber, cork, metal and celluloid. Frank H. Mingay of Scotland in UK Patent No.20,905 of 1905 conceived the idea of a liquid core or centre as follows: 'Balls – the cores of golf balls are formed of a bag of elastic material filled with an incompressible fluid, such as water, glycerine, treacle, which has no detrimental action on the bag . . .'. The liquid centre had come to stay and offered a further improvement in the ball's performance, which was also added to by a fourth factor – even tighter winding of the elastic thread. This was to be a feature of the Dunlop balls when they entered the golf ball field in 1911. All these improvements on both sides of the Atlantic are dealt with in J. S. Martin's book *The Curious History of the Golf Ball* already referred to.

Sketches showing the development of the golf ball from the solid gutta up to 1911 (taken from *Frys* magazine 1911–12).

THE PLAIN SOLID GUTTA PERCHA BALL WITH SCRATCHED OR HAMMERED SURFACE. THIS DISPLACED THE FEATHER BALL.

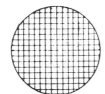

THE GUTTA PERCHA BALL, WITH CUT LINE MARKING; POPULAR FOR A PERIOD.

THE GUTTA PERCHA BALL WITH BRAMBLE MARKING. THIS WAS THE LAST OF THE HOMOGENEOUS BALLS.

THE FIRST RUBBER-CORED BALL (THE "HASKELL") WITH CORE OF RUBBER THREAD WOUND UNDER TENSION AND COVER OF GUTTA PERCHA. FIRST USED IN BRITAIN IN 1902.

BRITISH IMPROVEMENT ON THE HASKELL, WITH LARGER CORE AND SOLID CENTRE.

FURTHER IMPROVEMENT; CORE AGAIN LARGER AND THE COVER MUCH THINNER.

STILL LARGER CORE AND "EGGSHELL" COVER.

A NEW DEPARTURE. DIAMETER OF BALL REDUCED FROM $1\frac{11}{16}$ INCH TO $1\frac{5}{8}$, WEIGHT IN PROPORTION.

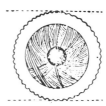

BALL OF NORMAL SIZE BUT MUCH HEAVIER THAN BEFORE. FIRST BALL TO SINK IN WATER.

THE 1911 BALL, SMALL SIZE ($1\frac{5}{8}''$) AGAIN AND MUCH HEAVIER THAN BEFORE; SINKS IN WATER.

The solid gutta or gutty required a degree of accuracy in striking the ball and one effect of the Haskell was to reduce the skill required to play golf well. This is discussed elsewhere. The new type of ball had a further effect, for the drive could be anything between 25 and 30 yards longer. As a result, all courses had sooner or later to be lengthened. The short holes were not affected, but the long holes were turned overnight from par *fives* to par *fours*. This was to become an expensive business, but no doubt was useful grist to the mill of the new profession of golf architects.

By the turn of the century the golf ball market had become extremely competitive and we have recorded the names of many of the balls and their makers from this period. This information can be verified in golf magazine advertisements or elsewhere in print or in collections. There is no suggestion that this list is anywhere near complete and there was indeed a development which complicates matters. The large-volume manufacturers were prepared to make not only their own brand of balls but also to make balls for other people and put their name on them. Golf ball making had by now completely left the professional's shop, apart from the re-mould trade. The professional collected old balls and sent them off to be re-covered and these were sold at inexpensive prices. A considerable trade was done in re-moulds and many of the advertisements offered a re-mould service. There are also some splendid claims about the performance of new balls. World War I whittled down the competition until only the big names survived, but promotion of the name still lives on.

Before World War I there was still no limit to the size of golf balls and as they were being improved and being hit further and further, a strong movement started in favour of a uniform and standard ball. Great controversy raged in the golfing periodicals of the time and it was alleged that the future of the game was being endangered. Happily, not long after World War I was over, the British and American authorities did agree on a standard ball and although subsequently the Americans opted for a larger ball, there are now only two standard sizes in use worldwide today – the slightly larger US ball and the British.

Finally, a word on the cost of balls in comparison to that of clubs.

		Balls	*Clubs*
Prior to 1850	The feathery	2s 0d–4s 0d	Wood clubs around 4s 0d
1850–80	The gutta	1s 0d or less	Woods around 4s 0d
1880–1904	The gutty	1s 0d or less	Irons 3s 6d woods 5s 0d
1905–1914	The core-wound ball	1s 0d–2s 6d	Irons 3s 6d woods 5s 0d
1920–39	Top-class balls	2s 6d	Irons £1 woods £1.10s 6d
1978	Top-class balls	12s 0d (or 60p)	Clubs £8–£15

The most striking thing about this table is the price golfers – many of whom must have been beginners – were prepared to pay for the core-wound ball (which would not last long anyway) when it first came in, compared to club prices which were ludicrously cheap. Now the pendulum has swung the other way, and either we are paying too little for our balls or far too much for our clubs, with the added requirement that we have to carry a matched set of up to a dozen clubs or more. Let us at any rate salute all those who have contributed to that marvel of ingenuity – the modern golf ball.

The alphabetical list of balls on pages 84–89 carries the name of the manufacturer if known and is preceded on pages 72–83 by a list of the manufacturers together with any notes about them which may be of interest. The list of balls' names has been compiled from advertisements, other written material or where examples of balls have been seen. It cannot be complete and once manufacturers started producing for other people and putting their names on the ball, no accurate attribution is possible. Where it is known for certain that a ball is a gutta, gutty or core-wound it has been noted, but where there is no note and the ball is dated prior to 1903–4 from the advertisement it appears in, then it is likely to be a 'gutta' or 'gutty' and is unlikely to be core-wound. A further clue is the price – the rubber-cored always being more expensive. The page opposite shows golf balls offered for sale in June 1903 by the well-known retailer, Benetfink of London, where the rubber-cored are designated and are nearly double the price of gutties. (See below, for comparison of weights). A glance at Chapter 8 on Patents (ball section) will show what infinite varieties of internal composition a golf ball might possess – and indeed some advertisements are explicit in revealing all.

The early guttas made by the Gourlays, Robertson, McEwans, Parks and Dunns are now collectors' pieces. However, as the number of professionals making their own balls increased, the chance of keeping track of them disappeared.

This list should be regarded as a partial record of those who made balls in the 64 years between 1850–1914, which saw the change from feathery to rubber-core. Coming forward another sixty-four years – to 1978 – we find that apart from better quality, there has been no change in the principle of construction. A separate list on pages 90–92 indicates balls obtainable in the USA pre-1914 (researched from advertisements in American golf magazines of the period) and their manufacturers. The following table shows the wide difference in weight between the different makes of ball (taken from *Golf Monthly* April, 1914). The comparable weight of today's British ball is $32\frac{1}{2}$dwt.

Domino Dimple $1\frac{3}{4}$ oz $= 34$ dwt.
Dunlop V. Black Spot $1\frac{5}{8}$oz $= 32\frac{1}{2}$ dwt.
White Flyer – Blue Spot $1\frac{5}{8}$ oz $= 32\frac{1}{2}$ dwt.
White Flyer – Green Spot $1\frac{1}{2}$ oz $= 30$ dwt.
Silvertown Mesh $1\frac{1}{2}$ oz $= 30$ dwt.
Silvertown Pal $1\frac{3}{8}$ oz $= 27\frac{1}{2}$ dwt.
Silvertown Challenger $1\frac{3}{8}$ oz $= 27\frac{1}{2}$ dwt.

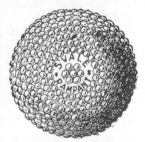
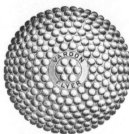

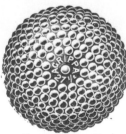

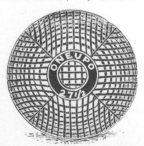

Adams Golf Ball Co
64 Broad Street, Birmingham
Adams A.1 (*Golf Monthly* Nov. 1913)

Alan Herbert & Greening
38 Dover Street, London w
38 Red Dot   } 2/– ea. *Golf Ill.*
38 Green Dot } 17.12.09

Agrippa Golf Ball Co
Coventry
Agrippa 11/– doz. *Golfing Annual* 1898

Anderson, Anderson & Anderson Ltd
37 Queen Victoria St, London
Varsity *Golfing Annual* 1898

Army & Navy Stores
Victoria Street, London
A & NCSL Furlong 11/– doz. 1900
A & NCSL Driver
A & NCSL No.1 21/– doz. 1910
A & NCSL No.2 11/– doz.

Auchterlonie, Willie
St Andrews
'Auchterlonie Flyer' *Golf Ill.* 20.3.03
'Ortogo' – Singer (Patent No. 15856 – 1902) *Golf Ill.* 19.6.03

Avon Rubber Co
Melksham, Wilts
Avon 2/– ea.
Avon Rifled 2/– ea.

F. H. Ayres
111 Aldersgate, London. Sports equipment manufacturers
International *Golfing Annual* 1893
Supreme *Golf Ill.* 21.6.07
Olympic *Golf Ill.* 30.6.11
Vaile

Beldam
Harlequin

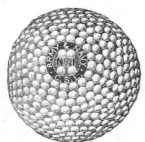

Benetfink
Cheapside, London EC. Large scale retailers

Bettoruss Ltd
35 & 36 Rathbone Place, Oxford Street, London W
Bettoruss 2/– ea. *Golf Ill*. 26.4.12
Joyce 1/3 ea. *Golf Ill*. 26.4.12

Bird & Etherington
Earlsfield, London SW
Wee Bird 2/6 ea. *Golf Ill*. 26.6.14
The Bird 2/6 ea. *Golf Monthly*, Nov. 1913
The Birdeth 2/– ea. *Golf Monthly*, Nov. 1913

F. A. Bryne
The Elect Works, Birmingham
09 Elect *Golf Ill*. 2.4.09

Capon Heaton & Co Ltd
Stirchley, Birmingham
Yellow Ring *Golf Monthly*, Oct. 1913
Green Ring 2/– ea. ⎫
Black Ring 2/– ea. ⎪ *Golf Ill*.
Red Ring 2/– ea. ⎬ 27.2.14
Blue Ring 2/– ea. ⎪
Sunbeam 1/– ea. ⎭

Clan Golf Club Co
(Thistle Trade Mark)
'Clan' brand of gutta percha balls
Golf Annual 1893

J. & D. Clark
Edinburgh
One of the largest makers of gutta balls who failed to bring out a rubber-cored ball (Edinburgh POD 1895; *Slaters* 1895 & 1900)
The Musselburgh *Golf Ill*. 12.1.1900

Clydesdale Rubber Co
Glasgow
'C' *Golf Annual* 1894

J. P. Cochrane (1863–1928)
Murano Works, Albert Street, Edinburgh
An extremely active ball manufacturer in Edinburgh (Edinburgh POD 1905 & 1914)
Cochrane Challenger (bramble) 2/– ea. *Golf Ill*. 12.2.04
New Ace 1901

The BENETFINK "BEST BALL"

These three pictures show the manner of making the Benetfink "Best" Ball. The inner core is hand-wound with the finest Para rubber tape to a diameter of ¾", after which it is automatically wound to 1½" with the very best rubber thread.

Get the new Benetfink Golf Ball, No. 20, just published, post free.

The outer cover is so tough as to render the ball practically indestructible, and has at the same time wonderful resilience. Our "Best" Ball is guaranteed not to crack, and the paint is guaranteed not to chip off in play.

Price 19/6 per dozen, post free.
Sample ball 1/7½, post free.

BENETFINK & CO., Ltd., CHEAPSIDE, E.C.

New Pro (1901)
Star Challenger 1907
Yellow Dot
Ace 'Gelatine Centre' *Golf Ill*. 4.1.07
Challenger 2/– ea. *Golfing Annual* 1908
R & A Challenger 2/6 ea. *Golf Ill*. 19.6.14
26½ Challenger 2/– ea. *Golf Ill*. 5.4.12
Challenger King 2/6 ea.
Profs Ball – Red Dot 1901
Floating Challenger 2/– ea. *Golf Ill*. 12.12.13

The Success of the
R & A CHALLENGER
(*Royal & Ancient*)

HAS BEEN WON ON QUALITY, AND NOT ON ADVERTISED PERFORMANCES OF EMINENT PLAYERS.

When the 'R & A' was introduced, golfers were quick to appreciate the fact that this was a ball absolutely perfect in every detail of design and construction.

Small. Medium Weight. Patent and Bramble Marking.

2/6   2/6

Every Ball critically examined before being sent out

J. P. COCHRANE & CO., Edinburgh, London, Carnoustie.

Regina 1/6 ea. *Golf Monthly*, Mar. 1913

Wm. Currie & Co

(founded by Wm Currie, 1840–1928)
Caledonian Rubber Works
Edinburgh
In 1871 census 100 men employed at Viewpoint Place, Edinburgh. It is not known whether they produced any other ball than the Eclipse which was popular for some years. (See illustration, page 60)

Dunn of London

W. Dunn Sen. made guttas while at Blackheath. Some of them were marketed in Scotland.

Dunlop Rubber Co

Birmingham
The Dunlop Rubber Co first entered the golf ballmaking industry in 1908 and really came to the fore after World War I with its famous Maxfli ball.
Junior ⎱ *Golf Ill.* 25.6.09
Orange Spot ⎰
No.29 1912 (Women Golfers' Museum)
No.31
'V'
New Dunlop 2/– ea. ⎱ *Golf*
The Manor 1/3 ea. ⎰ *Monthly*
Manor Junior 1/3 ea. ⎱ April 1914
Nimble 1/– ea. ⎰

Edina Golf Ball Manufacturing Co Ltd

174 Easter Road, Edinburgh
Homer 2/– ea. ⎱
Silkor 2/– ea. ⎰ *Golf Ill.* 3.5.07
Dux 1/3 ea. ⎰
Ensign 1/6 ea. ⎱ *Golfing*
Knock Out 1/– ea. ⎰ *Annual 1908*
Red Ensign 1/6 ea. ⎰

R. Forgan & Son

St Andrews
They made early guttas, see page 56.
Forgan ⎱ *Golf Ill.* 28.11.02
Acleva ⎰

Geipel & Lange

Vulcan Works, St Thomas Street, London SE
Pneumatic Golf Ball 24/– doz.
Golf Ill. 14.4.05

County Chemical Co

Birmingham
De Luxe 2/6 ea. ⎱
Popular 1/6 ea. ⎰ *Golf Ill.* 20.6.13
Bob 1/– ea. ⎰
Stella 1/– ea. *Golf Ill.* 10.2.11
Comet *Golf Monthly*, Mar. 1911
Special 2/– ea. *Golf Monthly*, Oct. 1913
'Chemico' Triumph 2/– ea. *Golf Monthly*, April 1914

Craigpark Electric Cable Co

Express 2/– ea. *Golf Ill.* 6.3.08
Craigpark 1/6 ea. ⎱
Craigpark Special 2/– ea. ⎰ *Golf Ill.* 19.3.09
Climax 1/3 ea. ⎰
Mono 1/– ea. *Golf Ill.* 3.10.13
White Flyer 2/6 ea. *Golf Ill.* 10.4.14

Crombie & Smith

Leith
Cromith *Golf Monthly*, July 1912
Dormy *Golf Monthly*, July 1912

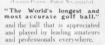
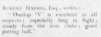

Golf Balls Ltd
Hammersmith
Black Star 2/– ea. *Golf Ill.* 6.3.08
Red Dot 2/– ea. *Golf Ill.* 16.7.09

B. F. Goodrich Co
7 Snow Hill, London
The British subsidiary of the US company which developed the original Haskell.
'Regular' Haskell *Golf Ill.* 16.12.04
'No.10' 24/– doz. *Golf Ill.* 16.12.04 (rubber-cored)
Tournament 1/3 ea. *Golf Ill.* 7.6.07
Haskell Royal 2/– ea. *Golf Ill.* 19.2.09

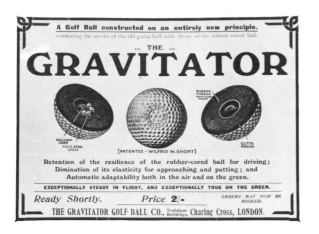

Gravitator Golf Ball Co
Trafalgar Buildings, Charing Cross, London
Wilfred Short, who took out various patents, was associated with this company.
The Gravitator 2/– ea. *Golf Ill.* 7.6.07
The Gravitator Flyer *Golf Ill.* 17.12.09

Gutta Percha Co
Wharf Road, City Road, London EC
Special A1 1/6 ea. *Golf* 17.2.93
Alpha ⎱
A1 Black ⎰ *Golf* 1.7.98
Eureka ⎰

J. B. Halley
Tom Tit 1/9 ea. *Golf Monthly*, Sep. 1911
Halley's Ball *Golf Monthly*, June 1912
Made Gutties and core-wound balls under the name Ocobo. *Golf Monthly*, April 1914

Harlequin Ball & Sports Co
Ascot
Dot & Dash
Red Spot
Super Harlequin

The Helsby Co
(British Insulated & Helsby Cables), Helsby, Nr. Warrington
Red Dot 2/– ea. ⎱ *Golf Ill.*
New Green Dot 2/– ea. ⎰ 24.9.09
The 'Mersey' 2/– ea. *Golf Ill.* 5.4.12
Link 2/– ea. *Golf Monthly*, August 1913

W. T. Henley
Telegraph Works, London EC
See also Scottish India Rubber Co. and advert. in *Golf* 1896 for 'Melfort' ball.
Why Not 2/– ea. *Golf Ill.* 5.5.11
Henco Recessed & Meshed

Alexander Henry
Edinburgh
He was a gun and rifle maker who patented and sold 'Henry's Rifled Ball' (rubber-cored).
Rifled Ball *Golf Ill.* 9.10.03 (rubber-cored)

Alex. Herd
Fixby Hall, Huddersfield
Fixby *Golf* 15.4.98

Ramsay Hunter
Hunter (gutta) *Golf* 26.8.92

Hutchison Main & Co
Glasgow (Springvale golf balls)
They fought the great legal case against Haskell. They were taken over by the North British Rubber Co. in 1912.
Rampart 20/– doz. rubber-cored ⎱
Springvale 14/– doz. rubber-cored ⎰ *Golf Ill.* 19.6.03
Springvale Eagle 2/– ea. rubber-cored ⎱
Springvale Kite 2/– ea. rubber-cored ⎰ *Golf Ill.* 19.5.05
Springvale Hawk 1/– ea. rubber-cored ⎰
Golden Kite ⎰

Hyde Imperial Rubber Co
Woodley, Cheshire
Woodley Flier *Golf* 15.4.98

Improved Golf Ball Co Ltd
Limehouse, London
Jellicore 2/– ea. ⎱
White Star 2/– ea. ⎰
White Vulcan 1/8 ea. ⎰ *Golf Ill.* 4.1.07
Elastine 1/3 ea. ⎰
I.G.B. 1/– ea. ⎰
Arcadia (Harry B. Wood Collection)
They were represented in St Andrews by H. M. Singer, said at one time to have been a butler. He was associated with W. Auchterlonie

Alexander Henry

Frank A. Johnson
29 Paternoster Row, London
A retailer of clubs who had a factory for a short time but was unlikely to have made golf balls.
Pin 2/6 ea.
Tee 2/– ea. } *Golf Ill.* 9.7.09
Snipe 1/3 ea. *Golf Ill.* 30.4.09

THE PAL is made in two weights—floating and non-floating, light and heavy. The floating Pal is distinguished by a red dot and the heavy by a blue dot. Both are of the highest half-crown quality but both are sold at 2/-.

From a Pencil Drawing by J. Newman.

METROPOLITAN GOLF BALL CO. (Josiah Newman, Proprietor)
Avenue Chambers, Southampton Row, LONDON, E.C.
TELEGRAMS—"METGOBAL, LONDON." TELEPHONE—REGENT 3900.

R. Lehmann & Co Ltd
Monument Street, London EC
Zenith 2/6 ea. *Golf Ill.* 22.3.12
Bogey
Zenith Orb

Leith Golf Ball Co
19 South Fort Street, Leith
Persevere

Leyland & Birmingham Rubber Co Ltd
Leyland Flier 24/– doz. } *Golf Ill.*
Leyland Birco 1/3 ea. } 19.6.08

Donald Loune & Co
London
Farsure Meteor *Golf Ill.* 27.10.05
Loune's Special *Golf Ill.* 19.9.02

Lunn & Co
Balfour golf balls 1890

M. McDaid
Edinburgh
(See patent 11,656 of 1903 for golf ball winding machine)
Iris
Pimpernel 2/– ea. *Golf Monthly*, Sep. 1911
Scarlet Runner 2/– ea. *Golf Monthly*, Aug. 1914
The Radio 2/– ea. *Golf Monthly*, Sep. 1911
The Active 1/3 ea. *Golf Monthly*, Aug. 1914
Corona 2/– ea. *Golf Monthly*, July 1911
Eaglet 1/– ea. *Golf Monthly*, Aug. 1914

Martin McDaid Ltd
Pilrig, Edinburgh
This business was taken over by the Scottish Golf Ball Manufacturing Co. in 1911. (*Note*: Still advertising under its own name Aug. 1914.)

Martins
Birmingham
Martins Tube Core Golf Ball *Golf Ill.* 14.7.05
Zodiac 2/– ea. *Golf Ill.* 11.6.09
Marzo 1/6 ea. *Golf Ill.* 10.4.08
Hex
Pearl Zodiac
Zome *Golf Ill.* 10.4.08
Pluto 1/– ea. *Golf Monthly*, Nov. 1913

Metropolitan Golf Ball Co
Southampton Row, London WC
Pal 2/– ea. *Golf Ill.* 2.9.13
Opal 2/– ea. *Golf Ill.* 17.4.14

The Midland Rubber Co Ltd

Ryland Street, Birmingham
The Aero 2/– ea.
Ajax 1/6 ea. *Golf Ill.* 26.4.12
'M' Recessed 2/– ea. *Golf Ill.*
17.10.13
Aero 'M' 2/– ea.
Aero Small recessed
pattern 2/– ea.   } *Golf Ill.*
Aero Bramble 2/– ea.   } 27.2.14
Ajax Bramble 1/6 ea.
'Nimble' Bob 1/– ea.

Miller & Taylor

Glasgow
The Little Model 2/– ea. *Golf
  Monthly*, Sep. 1911
Black Spot } *Golf Monthly*, Oct.
Green Spot } 1913
Superior Brown Spot *Golf Ill.*
  29.5.14

The North British Rubber Co Ltd

Castle Mills, Edinburgh
They took over the business of
Hutchison & Main Ltd of Glasgow
in 1912 and continued to use their
trade names.
Chick 2/6 ea.
The Clincher 2/– ea.
The Diamond Chick   } *Golf Ill.*
1/6 ea.   } 10.6.13
The New Hawk 1/3 ea.
The Osprey 1/– ea.
Big Chick
Hi Spot   } 1912 advert.
N.B. Twin Dot
The New Kite *Golf Monthly*, July
1912
Bramble Chick 2/– ea. *Golf
Monthly*, April 1914
Dimple Chick 2/– ea. *Golf Monthly*,
April 1914

The 'Orme' Co

93 Chancery Lane, London
'Orme' 1/3 ea. *Golf Ill.* 1.8.13

A. & D. Padon

13 St Andrews Square, Edinburgh
Allaway *Golfing Annual 1904*

The Parks

W. Park Sr.
W. Park Jr.
Wm. Park Sr. made and sold guttas stamped 'WM. PARK' from the 1860s onwards. W. Park Jr. was active in designing cover markings in the 1890s and marketed 'The Royal' in 1896.
Dispatch
Times

Alex Patrick

Leven, Fife
The Honour *Golf Monthly*, Nov. 1911

Peter Paxton

See also Chapter 4 (Clubmakers). He came from a golfing family and was apprenticed as a clubmaker in Musselburgh but preferred making clubs and balls to playing as a professional. Invented in 1892 a machine for turning out 2,000–3,000 golf balls a week of red or black gutta.

Distant 10/6 doz.
Perfection 10/6 doz. } *Golf* 3.7.96
Agrippa 11/– doz.
Re-made 6/– doz.
Bramble
Sirdar
English } guttas – *Golf* 17.6.92
Perfection
Furzedown } *Golf* 24.6.98
Gladstone

Redfern's Rubber Works Ltd

Hyde, Nr. Manchester
Mercury 2/6 ea.
Favourite 2/– ea. } *Golf Ill.* 12.4.12
Wonder 1/6 ea.
O.K. 1/3 ea.

Jas. H. Roger

11 Kent Road, Glasgow
The Jonny *Golf Monthly* June 1912
(Ball made under Mingay Patent No. 20,905 of 1905; Roger Patent 3641 of 1907 – liquid core)

Rubastic Ltd

Southall, Middlesex
Chancellor 2/– ea.
General 1/6 ea. } *Golf Ill.*
Commodore 2/6 ea. } 4.7.13
Skipper 1/– ea.
Dictator 1/9 ea. *Golf Monthly*, June 1913
White Prince 1/3 ea.

St Andrew Golf Co Ltd

35 Pitt Street, Glasgow
Scottish King 2/– ea.

St Mungo Golf Ball Co

Glasgow
Originally described as the British associate of Eleazer Kempshall who had followed Goodrich and Spalding in making golf balls in the USA and taken a licence to manufacture under the Haskell Patent. Kempshall (see also Chapter 8 – Patents) took out over a hundred USA and British patents in an endeavour to incorporate celluloid into a golf ball. This was not successful and St Mungo, the biggest Scottish

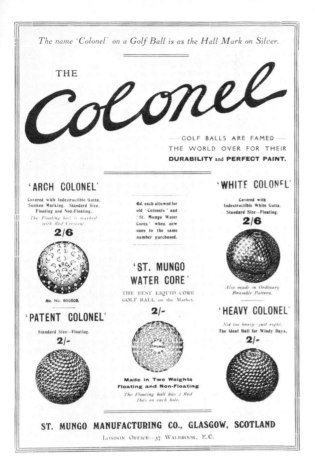

manufacturer, bought out
Kempshall in Newark, New Jersey,
USA, in 1910, and proceeded to
build a large new plant there. They
disappeared in the Great
Depression of the 1930s but prior
to World War I they were in the
forefront of the golf ball market
and their range of 'Colonel' balls is
still remembered.

One Up ⎫
Fife   ⎬ *Golfing Annual 1900*
Karifar ⎭
Kempshall Flyer 2/– ea. ⎫ *Golf Ill.*
Kempshall League   ⎬ 19.6.03
New St Mungo *Golfing Annual
1901*
Scotch Haskell 24/– doz. *Golf Ill.*
17.6.04
Arlington Kempshall *Golf Ill.*
3.6.04
Colonel 2/– ea. *Golf Ill.* 7.7.05
Oswald *Golf Ill.* 9.4.09
Patent Colonel 2/– ea. *Golf Ill.* 9.7.09
White Colonel 2/6 ea. *Golf Ill.*
15.4.10

The Judge *Golf Ill.* 22.4.10
Corporal 1/– ea. ⎫ *Golfing Annual*
Captain 1/3 ea. ⎬ *1906*
Admiral 1/6 ea. *Golfing Annual
1907*
Arch Colonel 2/6 ea. – see Scottish
India Rubber Co, 1899 – *Golf
Ill* 12.12.13
Heavy Colonel 2/– ea. – see Scottish
India Rubber Co, 1899 – *Golf Ill.*
10.4.14
Water Core 2/– ea. *Golf Ill.*
12.12.13
Plus Colonel 2/6 ea. *Golf Ill.*
26.6.14

Scottish India Rubber Co
Glasgow
A subsidiary of W. T. Henley's
Telegraph Works Co Ltd, 27
Martins Lane, Cannon St,
London.
  Advert *Golf* 1896
  Melfort   ⎫
  Scottish 10/6 doz. ⎬ *Golfing
  Jim   ⎭ Annual 1894*

Henley ⎫
Maxim ⎬ *Golfing Annual 1896*
Victor *Golfing Annual 1895*

Scottish Manufacturing Golf Ball Co Ltd
(See McDaid)
The Lunar   ⎫ *Golf Monthly*
Conqueror 2/– ea. ⎬ Sep. 1912
D.D. (diamond dent)
New Victor
Student
King Conqueror *Golf Monthly*,
Nov. 1913

Silvertown Co
London
The 'India Rubber Works and
Telegraph Co. Ltd.' was old
established and did not enter the
golf ball market until 1888 using
the name Silvertown, the location
of its rubber works on the Thames
near London. (The 'India Rubber

Works and Telegraph Co. Ltd.'
later became the 'India Rubber &
Gutta Percha Co.' then 'British
Goodrich' and finally the 'British
Tyre & Rubber Co. Ltd.') The
Silvertown No.4 – a really hard
'gutty' – was a great success but it
was not until 1911/12 that the
famous Silver King was launched
and was to remain popular for
many years. It issued what has now
become a collector's item entitled
the 'Cavalcade of Golf' – to
celebrate 50 years of golf ball
making.

Silvertown No.4 1888
Silvertown No.5 1898
Silvertown Bramble 1900
New Silvertown 11/– doz. *Golf Ill.*
12.2.04
Silviator
Silvertown No.9 1906
Lynx
Silvertown Snippet
Pentland *Golf Ill.* 17.12.09
Granton
Silver King Black Dot mesh 1913
Stoughton.

Slazenger & Sons

See Chapter 4. Slazengers have the
proud record of being the oldest
manufacturer of golf balls still in
business – Mr H. Hilton having
won the Open Championship in
1892 at Muirfield with a Slazenger
ball. The illustration 'Slazengers'
Golf Balls' is from the catalogue of
1904 and is particularly interesting
because there is not a rubber-cored
ball included. This indicates that it
was by no means in general use
then. The endorsement for the
'Slazenger' ball should also be
noted. Mr Horace Hutchinson is
recommending it when he won the
Kashmir Cup. It will be recalled
(p.60) that *c*.1890 he was
endorsing the 'Eclipse' ball!

Boodie 13/6 doz.
'L.P.H.' 12/– doz.   'Slazenger'
Slazenger 17/6 doz.   1904
Truflite 12/– doz.   catalogue
Xpres (floater)
12/– doz.

A. G. Spalding & Bros

317 & 318 High Holborn, London
They were the dominant
ballmakers in the USA at the turn

of the century and it was they who sponsored the great Harry Vardon to undertake his famous exhibition tour of the USA in 1900. He played with the Vardon Flyer ball which was also sponsored by them. They also eventually took out a Haskell licence for the rubber-cored ball which they were compelled to do for balls made and sold in the USA.

Spalding White *Golf Ill.* 12.5.05

Spalding White with black dot 24/– doz.
Spalding White with red dot 24/– doz.
Spalding Wizard 22/6 doz.
Spalding Bob 12/– doz. } *Golf Ill.* 16.8.07

The Dimple 30/– doz.
Spalding – Black & White 24/– doz.
Birds Eye 24/– doz. } *Golf Ill.* 14.5.09

Black Cross 24/– doz. *Golf Ill.* 26.2.09

Spalding black & white dimple 30/– doz. } *Golf Ill.* 25.2.10

Spalding red & black dot 24/– doz.
Spalding red & black dimple 30/– doz. } *Golf Ill.* 25.2.10

Spalding Blue Circle 20/– doz. *Golf Ill.* 15.4.10
Midget Dimple 2/6 ea. *Golf Ill.* 19.4.12
Domino Dimple 2/6 ea. *Golf Ill.* 26.4.12
Midget – Women Golfers' Museum
Topflite
Nimble
Glory 2/6 ea. *Golf Monthly*, Jan. 1914
Corker 2/6 ea. }
Cinch 1/6 ea. } *Golf Monthly*, April 1914
Vardon Flyer and Black Clinker

Telegraph Manufacturing Co Ltd
Helsby, Warrington
Helsby – gutta *Golf* 12.8.98

Thornton & Co
1892
78 Princes Street, Edinburgh

A prominent retailer and supplier of balls.
Thornton (gutta) *c.*1896
The Match (gutta) 11/– doz. *Golf* 1896
Flying Scotsman

Unio Golf Ball Co
15 Margaret Street, Glasgow
Little Traveller 2/– ea.
Royal 1/6 ea.
Traveller 2/– ea.
Field 1/3 ea.
New Success 1/– ea. } *Golf Monthly*, Nov. 1911

Wood Milne Ltd
Preston, Lancs
Lady 2/– ea.
Green Dot
Kiddy } *Golf Ill.* 17.11.11
Wood Milne Special 2/– ea. *Golf Ill.* 24.2.11
White Chief 2/– ea. *Golf Ill.* 26.6.14
Club 1/3 ea.
Eclipse 1/3 ea. } *Golf Monthly*, Oct. 1913

Wisden
Rocket 8/– doz. *Golf Ill.* 19.6.03

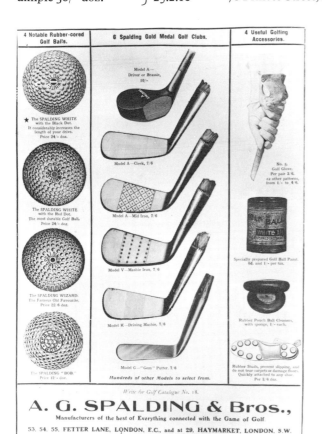

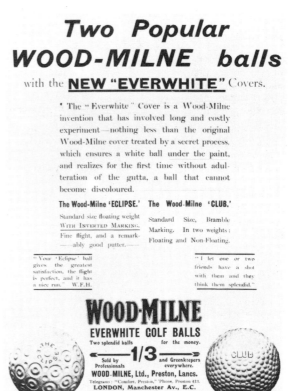

Alphabetical list of
golf balls pre-1914

*Manufacturers not known

Ace	J. P. Cochrane
Acleva	R. Forgan & Son
*Acme	
Active	M. McDaid, Edinburgh
Adams A1	Adams, Birmingham
Admiral	St Mungo Golf Co
Aero and Aero Bramble	Midland Rubber Co
Aero 'M' and Aero 'M' small recessed	Midland Rubber Co
Agrippa	Agrippa Golf Ball Co
Ajax and Ajax Bramble	Midland Rubber Co
A1 Black	Gutta Percha Co (sold by Wm. Millar, 40 Finsbury Circus)
'Allan' 25½	Allan Robertson 1856/9 (Wood Collection)
Allaway	A. & D. Padon, Edinburgh
Alpha	Gutta Percha Co.
Arcadia	Improved Golf Ball Co (Wood Collection)
Arch Colonel	St Mungo Golf Ball Co (Scottish India Rubber Co)
*Argus 27½	1907 (Wood Collection)
Arlington	St Mungo Golf Ball Co
Army & Navy No.1	Army & Navy Stores
C.S.L. No.2	Army & Navy Stores
Ascot	Harlequin Ball & Sports Co
Auchterlonie Flyer	Willie Auchterlonie
Avon	Avon Rubber Co
Avon Rifled	Avon Rubber Co
Balfour	Lunn & Co
*Baylan	(Wood Collection)
Best	Benetfink
Bettoruss	Bettoruss Ltd
*Be-Up	Rubber core c.1904 Women Golfers' Museum
*Be-Up Dimple	Rubber core c.1904 Women Golfers' Museum
Big Chick	North British Rubber Co
Bird	Bird & Etherington
Birdeth	Bird & Etherington
Birds Eye	Spalding
Black Cross	Spalding
Black Ring	Capon Heaton Co
Black Star	Golf Balls Ltd, Hammersmith
Black & White	Spalding
Black & White Dimple	Spalding
Black Vardon Clinker	Spalding (Wood Collection)
Blue Circle	Spalding
Blue Ring	Capon Heaton Co
Bob	Spalding
Bob	County Chemico Co
Bogey	R. Lehmann & Co
Boodie	Slazenger
Bramble	Peter Paxton
Bramble Chick	North British Rubber Co
*Bullet	
'C'	Clydesdale Rubber Co.
Captain	St Mungo Golf Ball Co
*Cestrian	(Wood Collection)
Challenger	J. P. Cochrane
26½ Challenger	J. P. Cochrane

R. & A. Challenger	J. P. Cochrane
Challenger King	J. P. Cochrane
Chancellor	Rubastic Ltd
Chick	North British Rubber Co
Cinch	Spalding
Clan	Clan Golf Club Co
Climax	Craigpark Electric Cable Co
Clincher	North British Rubber Co
Club	Wood Milne Club
Cochrane (Bramble) Challenger	J. P. Cochrane
Colonel	St Mungo Golf Ball Co
Comet	County Chemical Co
Commodore	Rubastic Ltd
Conqueror	Scottish Manufacturing Golf Ball Co.
Corker	Spalding
Corona	M. McDaid, Edinburgh
Corporal	St Mungo Golf Ball Co
Craigpark	Craigpark Electric Cable Co (1891 Wood Collection)
Craigpark Special	Craigpark Electric Cable Co
Cromith	Crombie & Smith
D.D.	Scottish Manufacturing Golf Ball Co
De Luxe	County Chemical Co
Diamond Chick	North British Rubber Co
Dictator	Rubastic Ltd
Dimple	Spalding
Dimple Chick	North British Rubber Co
Dispatch	W. Park
Distant	Peter Paxton
Domino Dimple	Spalding
Dormy	Crombie & Smith
Dot & Dash	Harlequin Ball & Sports Co
Driver	Army & Navy Stores
Dux	Edina Golf Ball Manufacturing Co
Dunn	Wm. Dunn of London (Blackheath)
Eagle	Hutchison Main & Co.
Eaglet	M. McDaid, Edinburgh
Eclipse	Wood Milne Ltd
Eclipse	Wm. Currie & Co (c.1880 Wood Collection – patent impressed)
Elastine	Improved Golf Ball Co
* Endura	
English	Peter Paxton
Ensign	Edina Golf Ball Co
Eureka	Gutta Percha Co (sold by Wm. Millar, 40 Finsbury Circus (1895 Wood Collection)
Express	Craigpark Electric Cable Co
* Falcon	
Farsure Meteor	Donald Loune & Co
Favourite	Redfern's Rubber Works Ltd
Field	Unio Golf Ball Co
Fife	St Mungo Golf Ball Co (Women Golfer's Museum)
Fixby	Alex Herd (Huddersfield)
Floating Challenger	J. P. Cochrane
* Flyandput	(Wood Collection)
Flying Scotsman	Thornton & Co, Edinburgh (Wood Collection)
Forgan	R. Forgan & Son
Furzedown	Peter Paxton
Furlong	Army & Navy Stores

General	Rubastic Ltd
⋆ Gipsy	
Gladstone	Peter Paxton
⋆ Globe	
Glory	Spalding
Golden Kite	Hutchison Main & Co
Granton	Silvertown Co
Gravitator	Gravitator Golf Ball Co
Gravitator Flyer	Gravitator Golf Ball Co
Green Dot	Wood Milne Ltd
38 Green Dot	Alan Herbert & Greening
Green Ring	Capon Heaton Co
Halley's Ball	J. B. Halley
Harlequin	Beldam
Haskell Royal	B. F. Goodrich Co
⋆ Haskin's 27½	From Hoylake 1897 (Wood Collection)
Hawk	Hutchison Main & Co
Heavy Colonel	St Mungo Golf Ball Co
Helsby	Telegraph Manufacturing Co Ltd (1896 Wood Collection)
Henco	W. T. Henley
Henley	Scottish India Rubber Co
Hex	Martins, Birmingham
Hi Spot	North British Rubber Co
Homer	Edina Golf Ball Co
Honour	Alex Patrick
Hunter	Ramsay Hunter (professional at St George GC Sandwich)
I.G.B.	Improved Golf Ball Co
International	Sold through F. H. Ayres
Iris	M. McDaid, Edinburgh
Jellicore	Improved Golf Ball Co
Jim	Scottish India Rubber Co
Jonny	Jas. H. Roger
Joyce	Bettoruss Ltd
Judge	St Mungo Golf Ball Co
Junior	Dunlop Rubber Co
Karifar	St Mungo Golf Ball Co
Kempshall Flyer	St Mungo Golf Ball Co
Kempshall League	St Mungo Golf Ball Co
Kiddy	Wood Milne Ltd
King Conqueror	Scottish Manufacturing Golf Ball Co
Kite	Hutchison Main & Co (Women Golfers' Museum 1904)
Knock Out	Edina Golf Ball Co
L.P.H.	Slazenger
Lady	Wood Milne Ltd
Leyland Birco	Leyland & Birmingham Rubber Co
Leyland Flier	Leyland & Birmingham Rubber Co
Link	Helsby Co
⋆ Lion	Women Golfers' Museum 1904
Little Model	Miller & Taylor, Glasgow
Little Traveller	Unio Golf Ball Co
Lounes Special	Donald Loune & Co
Lunar	Scottish Manufacturing Golf Ball Co
Lynx	Silvertown

'M' Recessed	Midland Rubber Co
Manor	Dunlop Rubber Co
Manor Junior	Dunlop Rubber Co
*Maponite	
Marzo	Martins, Birmingham
Match	Thornton, Edinburgh
Mauser	1900 (Wood Collection)
Maxim	Scottish India Rubber Co
Melfort	Scottish India Rubber Co
Mercury	Redfern's Rubber Works Ltd
Mersey	Helsby Co
Midget	Spalding
Midget Dimple	Spalding
*Mitchell	(Wood Collection 1896)
Mono	Craigpark Electric Cable Co
Musselburgh	J. & D. Clark, Edinburgh
N.B. Twin Dot	North British Rubber Co
New Ace	J. P. Cochrane
New Dunlop	Dunlop Rubber Co
New Green Dot	Helsby Co
New Hawk	North British Rubber Co
New Kite	North British Rubber Co
New Pro	J. P. Cochrane
*New Scarlet Sikh	
New St Mungo	St Mungo Golf Ball Co
New Silvertown	Silvertown
New Success	Unio Golf Ball Co
New Victor	Scottish Manufacturing Golf Ball Co
Nimble	Spalding
Nimble	Dunlop Rubber Co
Nimble Bob	Midland Rubber Co
No.09 Elect	F. A. Byrne, Birmingham
10	B. P. Goodrich Co
29	Dunlop Rubber Co
31	Dunlop Rubber Co
O.K.	Redferns Rubber Works Ltd
Ocobo	J. B. Halley
*Olympic	Sold through F. H. Ayres, London
One Up	St Mungo Golf Ball Co
Opal	Metropolitan Ball Co.
*Opresto	Women Golfers' Museum 1906
Orange Spot	Dunlop Rubber Co
Orme	The Orme Co
Ortogo – Singer	Willie Auchterlonie
Osprey	North British Rubber Co
Oswald	St Mungo Golf Ball Co
Pal	Metropolitan Ball Co
Park W	W. Park Sr.
Patent Colonel	St Mungo Golf Ball Co
Pearl Zodiac	Martins, Birmingham
Pentland	Silvertown Co
Perfection	Peter Paxton
Persevere	Leith Golf Ball Co
*Phoenix $27\frac{1}{2}$	(Wood Collection)
Pimpernel	M. McDaid, Edinburgh
Pin	Frank A. Johnson
Plus Colonel	St Mungo Golf Ball Co

Pluto	Martins, Birmingham
Pneumatic	Geipel & Lange (see also Wood Collection)
Popular	County Chemical Co
*Professional	(Gamage's Advertisement)
Profs Ball	J. P. Cochrane
*Pulford 27½	Hoylake (Wood Collection)
Rampart	Hutchison Main & Co
The Radio	M. McDaid, Edinburgh
38 Red Dot	Alan Herbert & Greening
Red Dot	Helsby Co
Red Dot	Golf Balls Ltd, Hammersmith
Red & Black Dot	Spalding
„ „ Dimple	Spalding
Red Ensign	Edina Golf Ball Man. Co Ltd
Red Ring	Capon Heaton Co
Red Spot	Harlequin Ball & Sports Co
Regina	J. P. Cochrane
Rifled ball	Alex Henry (Wood Collection 1902)
Rocket	Wisden
*Rompo	
Regular Haskell	B. F. Goodrich Co
Royal	W. Park's Hexagonal Patent 1896 (Wood Collection)
Royal	Unio Golf Ball Co
*S.27½	(Wood Collection)
Scarlet Runner	M. McDaid, Edinburgh
Scottish	Scottish India Rubber Co
Scotch Haskell	St Mungo Golf Ball Co (Wood Collection)
Scottish King	St Andrews Golf Co Ltd, Glasgow
*Siemens	(Wood Collection)
Silkor	Edina Golf Ball Man. Co Ltd
Silver King Black Dot	Silvertown Co
Silvertown (Nos.4, 5, 9 and Bramble)	Silvertown Co
Silvertown Snippet	(Wood Collection 1889) Silvertown Co
Silviator	Silvertown Co
Sirdar	Peter Paxton
Skipper	Rubastic Ltd
Slazenger	(Wood Collection) Slazenger
Snipe	Frank A. Johnson
Special	County Chemical Co
Special A1	Gutta Percha Co
*Special Argus	(Wood Collection)
Springvale	Hutchison Main & Co
Star Challenger	J. P. Cochrane
Stella	County Chemical Co
Stoughton	Silvertown (Wood Collection c.1903)
Student	Scottish Manufacturing Golf Ball Co
*The Sturrock	c.1895 (Wood Collection)
Sunbeam	Capon Heaton Co
Superior 'Brown, Green & Black spots'	Miller & Taylor, Glasgow
Super Harlequin	Harlequin Ball & Sports Co
Supreme	Sold through F. H. Ayres Ltd
Tee	Frank A. Johnson
Thornton	Thornton, Edinburgh
Times	W. Park
Tom Tit	J. B. Halley
Topflite	Spalding

Tournament	B. F. Goodrich
Traveller	Unio Golf Ball Co
Triumph (Chemico)	County Chemical Co
Truflite	Slazenger
Tube Core	Martins, Birmingham
* Unique	(Wood Collection)
V	Dunlop Rubber Co
Vaile	Sold through F. H. Ayres
Vardon Flyer & Black Clinker	Spalding (Wood Collection 1899)
Varsity	Anderson, Anderson & Anderson
Victor	Scottish India Rubber Co
* Viper	
Water Core	St Mungo Golf Ball Co
Wee Bird	Baird & Etherington
White	Spalding
White with black dot	Spalding
White with red dot	Spalding
White Chief	Wood Milne Ltd
White Colonel	St Mungo Golf Ball Co
White Flyer	Craigpark Electric Cable Co
* White Heather	
* White Imp	
White Prince	Rubastic Ltd
White Star	Improved Golf Ball Co
White Vulcan	Improved Golf Ball Co
Wizard	Spalding
Wonder	Redfern's Rubber Works
Wood Milne Special	Wood Milne Ltd
Woodley Flier	Hyde Imp. Rubber Co (Wood Collection 1896)
Why Not	W. T. Henley
Xpress	Slazenger
Yellow Dot	J. P. Cochrane
Yellow Ring	Capon Heaton Co
Zenith	R. Lehmann & Co
Zenith Orb	R. Lehmann & Co
Zodiac	Martins, Birmingham
Zome	Martins, Birmingham

US golf ball manufacturers pre-1914

Bridgeport Gun and Implement Co. (B.G.I.)
Champion Flyer (1902)

Davidson Rubber Co, Boston

Dunn, W.
Stars and Stripes (1899)

Goodrich Haskell
Bantam (1912)
Bunny (1911)
Comet (1912)
Final (1913)
Haskell (1898/99)
Haskell mesh (1902)
Jack Rabbit (1911)
Meteor (1912)
Moose (1912)
Stag (1912)
Streak (1909)
Whiz (Haskell – purple ring) (1908)

Goodyear
Arrow (pneumatic) (1902)

Kempshall
Gold Crescent (1909)
Kempshall Flyer (1906)
Non Skid (1909)
Six pole Bramble (1909)

Lee & Underhill
White & Black Diamond (1909)

Slazenger
Green Cross (1913)
Red Cross (1909)

Spalding
Baby (1899)
Black & White (1909)
Dimple (1908)
Domino Dimple (1912)
Glory (1907)
Glory Dimple (1914)
Spalding Bramble (1901)
    Red Dot ⎫
    Blue Dot ⎬ (1908)
    White Dot ⎭
    Practice (1898–99)
    White (1907)
Wizard (1903)
Vardon Flyer (1901)

St Mungo Golf Ball Co
Arch Colonel (1912)
The Colonel (1910)
Colonel 26½ (1911)
Colonel 27, 29 and 31 (1914)
Colonel Click (1910)
Crescent Colonel (1912)
Floater (1912)
Green Star Colonel (1912)
Little Crescent Colonel (1910)
Major (1912)
Patent Colonel (1909)
Red Star Colonel (1912)
Water Core (1911)
White Colonel (1911)
Heavy Colonel

Stoughton Rubber Co, Boston

Trianon Mills

Worthington
Ace (1914)
Crown (1914)
Deuce (1914)
Diamond A (1914)
Diamond King (1911)
Diamond Ring
Diamond Stud
Queen B
King B (1914)
Scotty (1913)
Standard (1903)
Trey (1914)
Worthington White (1909)

Wright Ditson, Boston
Eagle (1911)
Green Circle (1909)
Wright-Ditson Selected (1898/9)

UK Exporters

Agrippa Golf Ball Co, Coventry
Agrippa (1899)

Anderson, Anderson & Anderson, London
Anderson (1898)
Anderson White (1898)
Varsity (1898–99)
Varsity White (1898–99)

J. & D. Clark, Edinburgh
Musselburgh (1898)

Dunlop Rubber Co
Dunlop 4 (1909)
Junior (1910)
Orange Spot (1910)

Gutta Percha Co
A1 Black (1898)
Eureka (1898)

J. B. Halley
Ocobo (1898)

Hyde Imperial Rubber Co
Woodley Flyer (1896–1902)

Martin's Birmingham
Zodiac (1910)

Silvertown
Silvertown (1912)

Alphabetical list of golf balls obtainable in the USA pre–1914

A1 Black	1898	UK Gutta Percha Co
Ace	1914	Worthington
Agrippa	1899	UK Agrippa Golf Ball Co, Coventry
Anderson	1898	UK Anderson, Anderson & Anderson, London
Anderson White	1898	UK Anderson, Anderson & Anderson, London
Arch Colonel	1912	UK St Mungo Golf Ball Co
Arrow (pneumatic)	1902	Goodyear
Baby	1899	Spalding
Bantam	1912	Goodrich
Black & White	1909	Spalding
Bunny	1911	Goodrich
Champion Flyer	1902	BGI
The Colonel	1910	UK St Mungo Golf Ball Co
Colonel 26½	1911	UK St Mungo Golf Ball Co
Colonel 27, 29 and 31	1914	UK St Mungo Golf Ball Co
Colonel Click	1910	UK St Mungo Golf Ball Co
Comet	1912	Goodrich
Crescent Colonel	1912	UK St Mungo Golf Ball Co
Crown	1914	Worthington
Deuce	1914	Worthington
Diamond A	1914	Worthington
Diamond King, Ring, Stud	1911	Worthington
Dimple	1908	Spalding
Domino Dimple	1912	Spalding
Dunlop 4	1909	UK Dunlop
Eagle	1911	Wright-Ditson
Eureka	1898	UK Gutta Percha Co
Final	1913	Goodrich
Floater	1912	UK St Mungo Golf Ball Co
Glory	1907	Spalding
Glory Dimple	1914	Spalding
Gold Crescent	1909	Kempshall
Green Circle	1909	Wright-Ditson
Green Cross	1913	Slazenger
Green Star Colonel	1912	UK St Mungo Golf Ball Co
Haskell	1898/99	Goodrich
Haskell mesh	1902	Goodrich
Heavy Colonel		UK St Mungo Golf Ball Co
Jack Rabbit	1911	Goodrich
Junior	1910	UK Dunlop
Kempshall Flyer	1906	Kempshall
King B and Queen B	1914	Worthington
Little Crescent Colonel	1910	UK St Mungo Golf Ball Co
Major	1912	UK St Mungo Golf Ball Co
Meteor	1912	Goodrich

Moose	1912	Goodrich
Musselburgh	1898	UK J. & D. Clark, Edinburgh
Non Skid	1909	Kempshall
Ocobo	1898	UK J. B. Halley
Orange Spot	1910	UK Dunlop
Patent Colonel	1909	UK St Mungo Golf Ball Co
Red Cross	1909	Slazenger
Red Star Colonel	1912	UK St Mungo Golf Ball Co
Scotty	1913	Worthington
Silvertown	1912	UK Silvertown
Six pole Bramble	1909	Kempshall
Spalding Bramble	1901	Spalding
Spalding Red Dot	1908	Spalding
Blue Dot		
White Dot		
Spalding Practice	1898–99	Spalding
Spalding White	1907	Spalding
Stag	1912	Goodrich
Standard	1903	Worthington
Stars & Stripes	1899	Willie Dunn
Streak	1909	Goodrich
Trey	1914	Worthington
Vardon Flyer	1901	Spalding
Varsity	1898–99	UK Anderson, Anderson & Anderson
Varsity White	1898–99	UK Anderson, Anderson & Anderson
Water Core	1911	UK St Mungo Golf Ball Co
White & Black Diamond	1909	Lee & Underhill
White Colonel	1911	UK St Mungo Golf Ball Co
Whiz (Haskell – purple ring)	1908	Goodrich
Wizard	1903	Spalding
Woodley Flyer	1896–1902	UK Hyde Imperial Rubber Co
Worthington White	1909	Worthington
Wright-Ditson Selected	1898/9	Wright-Ditson
Zodiac	1910	UK Martins Birmingham

Chapter 4
The Clubmakers

The first record relating to the purchase of 'golf clubbes' concerns James IV of Scotland in 1502. They were bought at Perth from the 'bower' or bowmaker, then a considerable craft and one which possessed the tools for making the clubhead and shaft for what must at that time have been a primitive implement. It has always been assumed that as the bow declined in importance and gunpowder and guns made their appearance, it was the bowmakers who first took to making clubs. This assumption remains to be proved. Apart from William Mayne, described as a 'bower burgess' and referred to below, the only other reference we have so far found is to William Fergie (1856–1924) of Archers Hall, 'Bowmaker to the Queens Bodyguard for Scotland, golf club and ball maker' in the Edinburgh P.O.D. from 1894–1914. Apart from the old clubs at Blackheath, the Royal and Ancient and at Troon Clubs there are no documentary examples of sixteenth- or early seventeenth-century clubs to be seen today.

At the beginning of the seventeenth century the game was of sufficient importance for the first Royal warrant holder, William Mayne (1603), Bower Burgess of Edinburgh, to be appointed Clubmaker to the King – James I of England and VI of Scotland. In 1628 we have a brief mention of James Pett of St Andrews as a clubmaker supplying clubs to the Duke of Montrose. We also know that the Dickson family of Leith were in business from the beginning of the seventeenth century as club- and ballmakers until John Dickson a clubmaker died there in 1787, when he was almost certainly followed, at the end of the century, by Simon Cossar.

By the first half of the eighteenth century there are records of George and Henry Miln, ball- and clubmakers respectively at St Andrews, and David Dick, but thereafter and until the arrival of Hugh Philp in the next century only ballmakers are recorded. In Edinburgh there was Andrew Bailey at Bruntsfield – found as a result of a letter dated 20.6.1735, giving him an order for nine clubs and some balls to be ordered from St Andrews:

Ardoch 20th June 1735

Dear Sir,

. . . 'I hear Bachup is ready to sail. I want some gouff clubs and balls with him. Will you take the trouble any forenoon or afternoon you are at leisure to take a walk to Bruntisfield Links and call at Andrew Bailey's Clubmaker. He's well acquainted with me and knows what sort of clubs fit my play. Tell him to provide me in nine clubs viz three play clubs, three scrapers, one of which a half scraper or spoon and three putting clubs, with two dozen best St Andrews balls and order them to be shipped for me aboard of Bachup. Please do this commission for me and pay Bailey for the clubs and balls: and send Bachup's receipt . . .'

Bruntsfield must have had a succession of clubmakers. There was Thomas Comb, clearly an important figure, a clubmaker and the owner of the tavern 'Foxtoun', which acted as clubhouse. It would be nice to know more about him, whom he succeeded and whether he was in turn responsible for securing the services of James McEwan from Stirling in 1770.

Finally, Leith emerges, according to the records, with resident club- and ballmakers for well over two hundred years, from 1600 to the beginning of the exodus to Musselburgh *c.*1830. The Dicksons are there from the beginning right up until 1787 and the death of John Dickson, and there are other names such as the two Clephanes, relatives of the tavern keeper – Lucky Clephane. A Robert Neilson is recorded, indicating that there may have been room for more than one clubmaker. Subsequent references in later years have mentioned Leith as the 'metropolis of golf' (see *Old Leith at Leisure* by J. S. Marshall (Edina Press, Edinburgh, 1976) but it is probably more accurate to say that Edinburgh with its two centres, Bruntsfield and Leith, within a few miles of each other, was not only the capital city but understandably the 'metropolis of golf'.

The first half of the nineteenth century ushered in the gutta ball and Musselburgh, which, for a comparatively short time in the long history of golf, was a hive of activity. By the 1870s it had reached its peak. Of the fairly numerous records of club- and ballmakers (both feathery and gutta) who lived there it is difficult to be certain who worked for whom, who were just assistants, and who might have made clubs on their own account.

We are left wondering today how many wooden clubs there are left in museums and private collections which never even hit a gutta ball. Known examples are those of Cossar, Philp, the earlier McEwans and Jackson of Perth. Those that were used later on with a gutta (apart from putters) show signs of it – some with replacement hickory shafts and others with a leather inset let into the face of the club to protect if from the harder gutta ball (see also Chapter 5).

The second half of the century witnessed the great expansion of golf and a vast number of long-headed hooked-nose clubs were

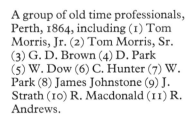

A group of old time professionals, Perth, 1864, including (1) Tom Morris, Jr. (2) Tom Morris, Sr. (3) G. D. Brown (4) D. Park (5) W. Dow (6) C. Hunter (7) W. Park (8) James Johnstone (9) J. Strath (10) R. Macdonald (11) R. Andrews.

produced by an increasing number of craftsmen. By the end of the 1880s a combination of circumstances produced a shorter clubhead, and all at once, apart from wooden putters, long-headed wooden clubs were obsolete. Now we love and admire the shape of these old clubs, seek to find out more about the people who made them and try to fathom exactly when they were made.

When the flood of golfing enthusiasm swept across the country the craftsmen could not keep pace with the demand and as J. H. Taylor (*Taylor on Golf*, Hutchinson & Co. 1902) wrote:

'up to this time the craft of making golf-clubs and balls had been for many years confined to a few golfing families in Scotland, and when the expansion came theirs was the right by usage and custom, the art had been passed from father to son, none enjoyed a less disputed claim to control an industry than they.'

These families were the Forgans (coupled with Philp), the McEwans, the Morrises of St Andrews, the Parks and Dunns of Musselburgh and the Patricks of Leven. For the reasons just given, their story and genealogy are told separately (and the Gourlay family, noted in Chapter 3, should be mentioned for its links with the McEwans and the Dunns).

By 1890 St Andrews had become the undisputed centre of the game which was rapidly being established throughout the world and the local records show this, indicating the number of men registered as clubmakers. The vast majority were by now employed by others in the trade and not on their own account. Those who emigrated and departed to spread the game throughout the world, and particularly in the USA, go unrecorded. St Andrews had become the Home of Golf and the Royal & Ancient its ruling body. By then, however, business enterprise had already cast its long shadow over the scene and there are included in the checklist of clubmakers such names as Slazenger, Ayres, the Army & Navy Stores and Grays of Cambridge, and, most significantly of all, perhaps, the future American giant – Spaldings. The craftsmen clubmakers now included a host of golf professionals spread throughout the land, whose work had been made considerably easier by receiving clubheads and shafts already machined down to easily workable shapes. They were still craftsmen though some were more talented than others, and they achieved reputations accordingly.

This chapter includes:

1   A history of the six leading clubmaking families and their respective family trees.
2   A checklist of the prominent clubmakers, but excluding the growing list of club professionals from 1880 onwards, except where special circumstances justify their inclusion.
3   A full list of all those who described themselves as clubmakers in the early records.
4   A history of early American clubmakers.

Hugh Philp and the Forgans of St Andrews

Hugh Philp (1782–1856) was born at Cameron, Fife, the son of Thomas Philp, an agricultural labourer. In the 1831 and 1841 census of St Andrews he is entered as a 'wright', which the dictionary describes as a maker or builder (e.g. a cartwright, wheelwright, etc.). In 1812 he began repairing golf clubs, and progressed to making them, so that by 1819 he was appointed clubmaker to the Society of St Andrews (later the Royal & Ancient), The Society had paid £2 2s p.a. to McEwans of Bruntsfield to send a representative to attend their Spring and Autumn meetings and in 1827 they cancelled this contract. (David Robertson, the famous Allan Robertson's father, was the McEwan agent in St Andrews at the time.) It seems doubtful whether clubmaking was his full-time occupation as he still described himself as 'wright' in the 1831 and 1841 census. He was, however, to establish a unique reputation as a clubmaker, and everyone wished to have the satisfaction of owning his clubs, particularly putters. This reputation was such that it even attracted the attention of at least two forgers, who put his name on their clubs in order to sell them. He left £782 when he died in 1856.

He used thorn, apple and pear wood for his heads and ash for the shafts, and it was said that he would spend hours polishing his heads to give them a fine finish. Thomas Peter (*Golfing Reminiscences* by H. T. Peter 1890) who first went to St Andrews in 1837 describes him then:

> 'Hugh was a dry haired man [whatever that may mean] rather gruff to strangers but quite the reverse to those who knew him, with a fund of dry caustic humour, but with all a kind heart.'

In 1845 Philp took on James Wilson as an assistant but the latter left him in 1852 when Philp brought in his nephew, Robert Forgan, with what must have been the obvious intention of handing over his business to him. Wilson was an excellent clubmaker and although he subsequently set up on his own account it must be reckoned that he had made clubs which bear the Philp stamp. The relationship between Philp and Robert Forgan remained in some doubt until recently a putter turned up marked " $\frac{\text{Philp}}{\text{Forgan}}$ ". We believe that this was the likely mark used on clubheads made between 1852 and 1856 when Philp died and that Forgan thereafter used his own name. In a trade catalogue of the late 1930s H. Philp was still credited as being the founder of the firm.

Philp clubs from the earliest days have been 'collectable' and, as a result, many have been preserved. There are large numbers distributed among numerous Golf Clubs and collections. There are many in the Spalding Collection and a particularly large and fine selection in the Museum of National Antiquities in Edinburgh.

Robert Forgan (1824–1900) came of a Fife family, his father being the harbour-master at Pittenween and his grandfather a farmer at Lathocar in Fife. Both these men married into successive generations of the Paterson family of Lauder whose story has been told in Chapter 3 dealing with the golf ball. Robert Forgan started life as a joiner. To complete the family story, Robert married Elizabeth, the daughter of the harbour-master of St Andrews, James Berwick, and James Berwick's sister married Hugh Philp. This is how Robert came to be chosen to take over his uncle's business. He continued the business on the death of his uncle in 1856 with one assistant, his young brother James, who later left him and went to reside at Anstruther as a golf ballmaker. He supplied his brother at St Andrews until he later returned there to work in the firm. Robert Forgan has always been credited as being the first to hand-hammer guttas to a regular pattern. He was also said to have inserted the pegs securing the 'bone' on a clubhead at a slant, as opposed to driving them in straight. He was too a pioneer in the use of hickory for shafts and as the business grew in later years paid personal attention to the buying of his raw materials. To make sure that the actual timber he had selected was delivered to him, he had a special hammer made with a stamp 'R. Forgan' on it, so that he could make sure the material he had selected was actually delivered.

When Tom Morris set up his clubmaking business alongside his own, he also bought his timber for him, thus no doubt obtaining the advantage of better prices for bulk purchasing. In 1863 he was appointed clubmaker to the Prince of Wales and from then onwards the Prince of Wales feathers were impressed on clubheads below the maker's name. Thereafter the presence of the Prince of Wales feathers mark denotes that it must have been made after 1863. In 1881 he took his son, T. B. Forgan, then aged twenty-eight into partnership and to celebrate the event there is a photograph of the staff and their names: R. Forgan; Conacher; G. Brown; Wm. Anderson; T. Baptie; J. Forgan; D. Anderson; T. B. Forgan. This is reproduced on page 98 (top) along with two other photographs. By 1895, as the second illustration shows, the staff had grown to 37, and the third photograph shows the staff in 1937. Here in 1895 are well-known names, such as Auchterlonie and Anderson, who learned their trade with Forgan before later setting up on their own.

The following are details from a letter from Robert Forgan (sending a copy of the 1895 photograph to his niece Mary Esther Uprichard in Australia) dated 29th March 1895. It relates that his son Jim (James Paterson Forgan) is in Chicago and Vice President of one of the largest banks in America, earns the equivalent of £3000 a year salary and will soon have £5000, if spared. A younger brother of his, David, is cashier or second man in a large bank in Minneapolis. 'He succeeded Jim in the Bank but as he was rather young they have a figure head above him. David does all the work and has one thousand pounds a year of salary.' He has this to say about his business: 'We employ about 50 men and apprentices (this included 3 clerks). We half make the clubs in the saw mill by machinery. There has been a great boom in Golf these three or four

The staff in 1895

1 J. Cuthbert	14 Crosthwaite	26 D. Brown
2 D. Blyth	15 R. Forgan	27 J. Anderson
3 J. Hutton	16 Yeoman	28 J. McGregor
4 G. Grieve	17 W. Auchterlonie	29 J. Gatherum
5 J. Stewart	18 J. Smart	30 J. Fowles
6 J. Govan	19 D. Grieve	31 W. Annal
7 A. Steven	20 J. Forgan	32 Gatherum
8 J. Thomson	21 A. Clark	33 W. Murray
9 Kay	22 F. Herd	34 P. Black
10 Thos. Baptie	23 H. Turpie	35 G. Braid
11 G. Brown	24 W. Robertson	36 W. Chisholm
12 D. Auchterlonie	25 R. Mason	37 T. B. Forgan
13 W. Braid		

years back.' The sons of Robert Forgan referred to in the letter were James Forgan who founded the National City Bank of Chicago and subsequently became Vice-Chairman of the National Bank of the Republic and D. R. Forgan who claimed to be the first man to swing a golf club in the State of Minnesota. Subsequently they must have founded their own bank since the name Forgan only disappeared from the Chicago banking world in the 1960s.

The Philp/Forgan/Paterson Families

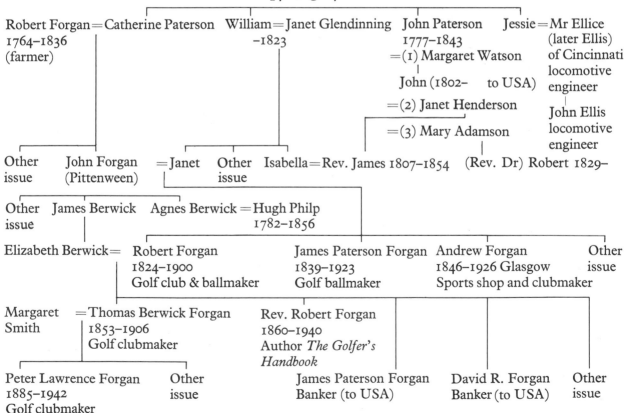

Another son, the Rev. Robert Forgan (1860–1940) was a fine golfer and while at St Andrews University published the first volume of *The Golfer's Handbook* 1881 (cost 1s 6d). This ran on until the sixth edition under the name of Forgan's *The Golfer's Manual* in 1897. At the turn of the century Forgans was the largest manufacturer of golfing equipment in St Andrews and they had mechanised their production. They did not make their own cleekheads although they shafted them. As they took over Spence & Gourlay, the cleekmakers, in 1920, it is possible that for some years previously they had been getting their supply from them. Particularly noteworthy among early iron clubs with the name 'Forgan' on them are those which appear to have been made using some form of bronze, thus avoiding rust. The changeover from the long-headed woods to the shorter bulger-type appears to have taken place around 1887, although wooden putters continued to be produced for some years after that.

There are many examples of Forgan clubs in a large number of Golf Clubs and collections. Apart from the Spalding Collection at Dundee there are some fine examples in the Museum of National Antiquities in Edinburgh. Forgan clubs by whichever Forgan are characterised by fine workmanship, are beautifully finished and well-balanced. The Forgans may well be named master craftsmen.

Andrew Forgan (1846–1926) A younger brother of Robert Forgan, he may well have had some training in the family business before he appears as greenkeeper to the Royal Perth Golfing Society c.1878. His predecessor in the 1860s was Watty McDonald who, it was reported, was paid 6s 0d per week and who should '. . . at all times be liable to be put off work for unsuitable weather etc.' So it is not surprising that around 1882 Andrew Forgan moved to Glasgow, setting up with a golf shop and as a clubmaker, retiring c.1911. His clubs were marked 'A. Forgan'.

The McEwans

J McEWAN.

The McEwan stamp

James McEwan (1747–1800)
Peter McEwan (1781–1836)
Douglas McEwan (1809–1886)
Peter McEwan (1834–1895)
In 1896 the magazine *Golf* published three articles on 'The History of the McEwans' whilst stating that the earlier books of the firm no longer existed and they were unable to quote the earlier dates of birth and death of the family. The founder of the business was James McEwan, said to have been a joiner or cartwright by trade. He came from Stirling to Edinburgh in 1770 although there is no evidence as to where he was born. He took up residence at Wrights Houses, a small cluster of houses adjacent to Bruntsfield Links. In 1775 he obtained his burgess ticket to the City of Edinburgh which is still in existence.

According to Douglas McEwan (1869–1929), who is quoted in these magazine articles of 1896, he was at that time in possession of a short spoon stamped with a thistle with 'J. McEWAN' underneath.

Peter McEwan (1781–1836)

All James McEwan clubs were so stamped, but when he died the 'J.' was struck off the old stamp and thereafter the stamp 'MCEWAN' by itself was used throughout the history of the firm.

By 1780 Douglas Gourlay, a feathery-ballmaker, had arrived at Bruntsfield. He was also to live in Wrights Houses and shared a single-storey building or shed with James McEwan. Thus they were able to offer a complete service to golfers, there being no reference to a ballmaker resident at Bruntsfield at that time. Gourlay, and his sons after him, were to build up a high reputation for their balls (see Chapter 3). Jean, the daughter of Douglas, became the bride of Peter McEwan in 1802 (see family tree) and their eldest son, James, was apprenticed to Gourlays before becoming a clubmaker. Sadly Peter and James McEwan both died on the same day in April 1836. Fifty years later another daughter of the house was to marry Tom Dunn, whose father had also been apprenticed to the Gourlays.

It appears that at the turn of the nineteenth century McEwans were supplying the other golfing centres of Aberdeen, Montrose, St Andrews, Perth and Blackheath (in London) with clubs. In St Andrews, their agent was David Robertson the ballmaker (the father of the celebrated Allan Robertson) and they were paid £2 2s. annually by the Royal & Ancient Society to send a representative to attend their Spring and Autumn meetings until 1827, by which time there was a resident clubmaker in St Andrews – Hugh Philp.

As golf at Leith and Bruntsfield became increasingly difficult the golf societies moved out to play at Musselburgh, and the McEwans first opened a branch there in 1847, which was soon to become their main establishment.

Premises of D. McEwan & Son, Musselburgh Links, c. 1890

MR. McEWAN'S PREMISES AT BRUNTSFIELD LINKS, EDINBURGH.

D. McEwan's premises at
Bruntsfield Links, Edinburgh

Below:
Peter McEwan (1834–1895)

Right:
D. McEwan (1869–1921)

Opposite is an account for clubs supplied to the Old Manchester Club in 1857, as an example of the type of business they were doing and what they were charging for their clubs. With the amount of work that went into the making of a wooden club by hand 3s 6d was indeed a modest sum.

It is some comment on the profitability of the business that Douglas McEwan's estate when he died in 1886 was worth only £800 net. In the 1851 Census Douglas McEwan is registered as employing one assistant. By 1871 his son, Peter McEwan, who described himself as a master clubmaker, was employing three men and two boys.

As the demand for clubs increased in the 1880s, the McEwans remained wedded to their craft and when finally mechanisation came in they refused to follow the trend. However, the design of their clubs, which had remained virtually unchanged throughout, did give way to the short-headed 'bulger' type woods in the 1880s.

Peter McEwan had five sons and in 1892 he suddenly accepted an appointment at the age of fifty-eight at Formby Golf Club, in Lancashire. With his son William he left his eldest son Douglas to run the business at Musselburgh, and two other sons left – one to neighbouring Birkdale and another to the Fixby Club, Huddersfield. Four years later he died suddenly and in 1897 the firm at Musselburgh closed down. This closure was attributed to the failure of an American importer to meet its obligations although trade notices for D. McEwan & Sons continued to appear until well after 1897.

In May 1898 they were advertising the opening of a Branch at Gullane 'where a well-selected stock of golfing articles will be held'. This must have been run by Douglas McEwan. There are many examples of McEwan clubs to be seen in museums and Golf Clubs. A fine mint set of woods won as a prize in 1859 is in the Honourable Company of Edinburgh Golfers' Collection at Muirfield. There are clearly problems in dating McEwan clubs, especially with so little change in design over a long period. A study of the family tree also shows how difficult it is to attribute a club to any one member of the family without some corroborating evidence.

Bought of Douglas McEwan, Clubmaker

1857
July 14 W. A. Park, Esq.

,,	3 Clubs	3/6	10. 6.
,,	2 do heads	2/–	4. 0.
			14. 6.

,,	J. A. Bannerman, Esq.		
,,	3 Clubs	3/6	10. 6.
,,	1 Iron	5/–	5. 0.
,,	1 Clubhead & 1 Ironshaft	2/– & 1/6	3. 6.
			19. 0.

,,	John Pendred, Esq.		
,,	5 Clubs, lefthanded	4/–	£1. 0. 0.
,,	1 Iron ,,	5/6	5. 6.
			£1. 5. 6.
			£2. 19. 0.
,,	Packing Box	3/0	3. 0.
			£3. 2. 0.

Received Payment
Douglas McEwan

With thanks

The McEwan Family
(Bruntsfield & Musselburgh)

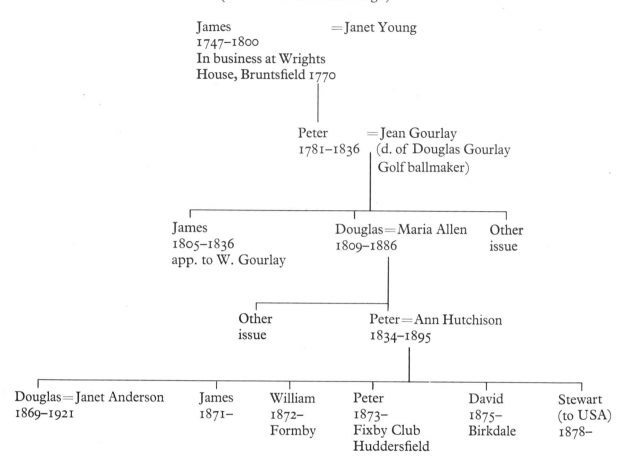

James   = Janet Young
1747–1800
In business at Wrights
House, Bruntsfield 1770

Peter   = Jean Gourlay
1781–1836   (d. of Douglas Gourlay
             Golf ballmaker)

James   Douglas = Maria Allen   Other
1805–1836   1809–1886   issue
app. to W. Gourlay

Other   Peter = Ann Hutchison
issue   1834–1895

Douglas = Janet Anderson   James   William   Peter   David   Stewart
1869–1921   1871–   1872–   1873–   1875–   (to USA)
                          Formby   Fixby Club   Birkdale   1878–
                              Huddersfield

Comment
It will be noted that Peter McEwan was only nineteen when his
father died in 1800. He therefore had to take over the business,
scarcely having served his apprenticeship. By the late 1820s the firm
had three working members for a period but from 1836 onwards
Douglas must have been on his own until his son Peter was old
enough to play a part in the business in the early 1850s. Thereafter
it became D. McEwan & Son.

The Dunns

Jamie (1821–1871)
William Sr. (1821–1878)
Thomas (1849–1902)
William Jr. (1865–1952)
John Duncan (1872–   )
Seymour (1882–   )
The Dunn family story starts with the twin brothers, Willie and
Jamie, born in 1821 at Musselburgh, the sons of a plasterer. They
were both apprenticed to the firm of W. & J. Gourlay as ballmakers

at Bruntsfield, Edinburgh for five years. Together they achieved fame as golfers in a number of celebrated challenge matches for wagers. At the age of thirty in 1851 Willie was appointed 'Keeper of the Green' at Blackheath where he stayed for fourteen years, being joined by his brother Jamie in 1854. Willie was then getting 17s 6d a week and Jamie 7s 0d.

Willie Dunn, before leaving Musselburgh, was making early guttas. He had been trained as a feathery ballmaker but after moving to Blackheath certainly established a ballmaking business – Dunn of London. It says something for his reputation that in the late 1850s they were being ordered from Edinburgh by the Royal Burgess Society (see Chapter 3). The Dunns must have made many clubs whilst at Blackheath.

Jamie Dunn did not marry until late in life and had no children, but Willie had two sons – Tom (1849–1902) and Willie Jr. (1865–1952) who was born while the family were at Blackheath. They were both to carry on the golfing enterprise shown by their father in going to Blackheath and were to take full advantage of the coming boom in golf.

In 1865 Willie Dunn Sr. moved back from Blackheath to Leith, where in 1869 he became 'Club and Ballmaker and Custodian of the Green' to the Leith Thistle Golf Club. In 1871 he moved to Musselburgh and set up a clubmaking business, eventually moving to North Berwick. In the meantime his eldest son Tom had in 1870 married Isabella Gourlay of the ballmaking family to whom his

Below:
Willie Dunn, Sr.

Right:
Jamie Dunn

father had been apprenticed. Tom Dunn moved south and became professional at Wimbledon (London Scottish Club) where he enlarged the course from 7 to 18 holes leaving there in 1881 when the club split up following disputes. His young brother Willie Dunn Jr. became his clubmaker apprentice there in 1878. He then returned to North Berwick to spend eight years as greenkeeper and clubmaker and numbered A. J. Balfour and W. E. Gladstone among his golf pupils. Finding that he could not make any money by combining the job of greenkeeper and clubmaker, he went to Tooting Bec in 1889. In 1894 he laid out a course at Bournemouth and made that town his future base for starting a most active business as one of the early golf course architects, especially of inland courses. Before he died at the early age of fifty-two he had laid out some 137 courses.

Willie Dunn, Jr., Champion of America 1894

Tom Dunn

Tom Dunn had a stereotyped approach to the layout of each hole: a ditch and a bunker to be carried by the tee shot and another by the second shot. At the time this seems to have satisfied a large number of customers. He had also become involved in the supply of golf requisites, and his two sons, John and Seymour, were to play an important role with their uncle William Dunn Jr. in opening up the game in the USA. Willie Dunn Jr. was a professional at Westward Ho! (1886–1888), then laid out and superintended the Chingford course in London before going to Biarritz, France, in 1887 for six years. There he met W. E. Vanderbilt who engaged him to go the USA and lay out the course at Shinnecock Bay, Long Island, where a Club was established and in 1892 the first Club House in the USA was built, exclusively devoted to golf. It was to have two courses – one for gentlemen and another one for the ladies. Willie always intended to return to France which he considered offered good prospects for the expansion of the game. In 1894, however, he won the first unofficial championship of the USA. The following year he was runner-up by which time it had become the first official championship, and by then there was no going back to France. He also was in demand as a golf-course architect. He laid out the Ardsley Course, N.Y., USA, in 1896 and in 1897 his nephew, John Duncan Dunn, had set up business there in conjunction with Tom Dunn & Son (presumably the youngest one – Seymour) of Bournemouth and Ardsley Casino, Dobbs Ferry, New York. The idea would appear to have been to establish a golf equipment business based on Dobbs Ferry, N.Y., and Bournemouth respectively. In 1897 there was an advertisement for 'John D. Dunn, Golf Club and Ball Manufacturer, Dobbs Ferry, New York. Lessons given. John D. Dunn has laid down extensive plant for manufacturing golf requisites in this country. Wood is seasoned . . .'

Taken from *Golf on a new Principle* by L. Everage, Simpkin Marshall 1897

Agents for
  'Crossheads'
  Dunn's Patent Driver $4
  Mashy Iron $2
  Toy clubs   50 cents
  Balls remade – if gutta is good $1 per doz.
  Club covers. Canvas. Ball pocket
  Shoulder strap & umbrella attachment $3
  —ditto— all leather $6
  Travelling cases $12
  —ditto— leather $18
  Initialling – per letter   25 cents
  Flags for holes – enamelled $2
  India rubber tees   25 cents
  Gloves $1
  Tee markers   50 cents
  Ball cleaners $1

It will be noticed that 'Dunn's Patent Driver' is advertised. This was his UK Patent No.14039 of 1894 (known as the 'all in one-piece' driver). It 'relates to wooden clubs and consists in forming the head and shaft in one piece, the head being bent by steaming in the usual way. Leather fitted into face of club if desired. Split hickory with kid grips.' (An example of this club can be seen in the North Berwick Museum). An advertisement claimed 'this club adds almost 20 yards to the drive and is almost indestructible'.

Willie Dunn and his nephew John Duncan Dunn were both of an inventive turn of mind and took out patents both in the UK and the USA covering developments relating to clubs and requisites, of which the above is the most interesting. Its commercial success was, however, limited.

Examples of clubs marked 'W. DUNN' and 'JAS. DUNN' clearly belong to the pre-1880 era, whereas examples of 'T. DUNN' clubs of the long-headed type must be of a period between 1875 and the change of design in *c.*1887. Willie Jr. could only have produced comparatively few of this type of club with his name on them before the changeover in style occurred.

The Dunn Family (Musselburgh)

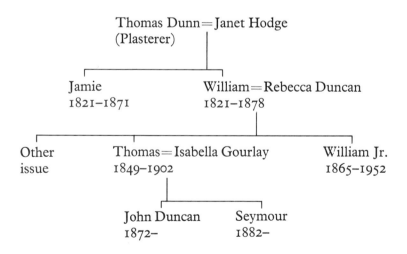

Thomas Dunn = Janet Hodge
(Plasterer)

Jamie
1821–1871

William = Rebecca Duncan
1821–1878

Other issue

Thomas = Isabella Gourlay
1849–1902

William Jr.
1865–1952

John Duncan
1872–

Seymour
1882–

The Patricks

John Patrick (1820–1866)
Alexander Patrick (1845–1932)
The business of clubmaking by the Patricks was established in 1847 at Leven, Fife, but, as will be seen in the family tree, John Patrick (1820–1866), the founder, was described as 'Cabinet maker and

clubmaker' and it is doubtful whether he ever made a living by
clubmaking alone. He died leaving £112. Alexander Patrick
(1845–1932), his eldest son, lived to the ripe old age of eighty-seven
and succeeded to the business at the age of twenty-one in 1866. He
moved to premises in Branch Street, Leven, later moving to a
works and shop adjacent to the last green at Leven Golf Club. The
firm was advertising itself in the *Golf Annual* of 1888 as the second
oldest family business, which is only true if you ignore the
continuance of Hugh Philp's business at St Andrews by Robert
Forgan.

Alexander Patrick's three brothers were all clubmakers, and so
were the third generation sons of John Patrick (1851–1916). A John
Patrick was professional at East Rink, Dunbar, appearing in *Slaters*
1889; a John Patrick was appointed clubmaker at Tuxedo Park,
New York, in 1895. Alex Patrick (1878–1920) was probably his
brother described in a trade advert. in *Golf* of 16.10.91 as of 'Leven
and Wimbledon Surrey'. These subsequent generations were unable
to carry on the business after World War I by which time, although
still trading as 'A. Patrick', it had passed into other hands. The
Patricks were, however, large and successful clubmakers for a long
period.

The Patrick Family (Leven)

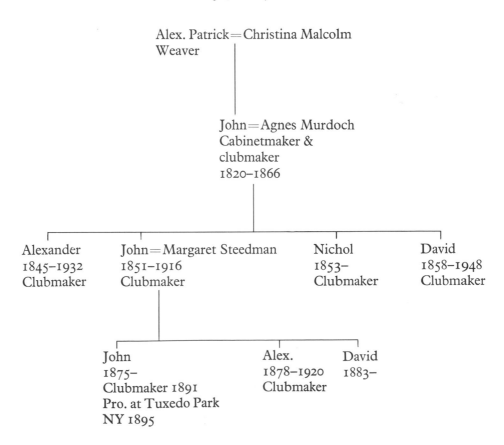

Alex. Patrick═Christina Malcolm
Weaver

John═Agnes Murdoch
Cabinetmaker &
clubmaker
1820–1866

Alexander   John═Margaret Steedman   Nichol   David
1845–1932   1851–1916   1853–   1858–1948
Clubmaker   Clubmaker   Clubmaker   Clubmaker

John   Alex.   David
1875–   1878–1920   1883–
Clubmaker 1891   Clubmaker
Pro. at Tuxedo Park
NY 1895

The Parks (of Musselburgh)

William Park Sr. (1834–1903)
Mungo Park (1839–1904)
William Park Jr. (1864–1925)

One cannot help wondering how a farmer, James Park, could have produced three sons, one of whom, David, became a golf ballmaker in the gutta era, and the other two, 'old' Willie and Mungo, both became Open Champions and clubmakers. In fact, all three started life as golf ballmakers. Old Willie won the Championship in 1860, 1863, 1866, and 1875 and Mungo in 1874, and if the latter had not spent a good deal of his early life at sea, he might have been even better known as a golfer.

'Old Willie' Park first appears in the trade directory as a club- and ballmaker in 1870 at Musselburgh and by the time Willie Jr. had won his two Championships in 1887 and 1889 it is likely that he had

Two pictures of Willie Park, Sr.

taken his son into partnership and 'W. Park & Son' appeared. Willie Park Jr. must have learnt all about clubmaking at an early age for in 1880 at the age of sixteen he was off to Ryton, Northumberland, as assistant greenkeeper-professional to his uncle Mungo, and stayed there until 1884, before returning to Musselburgh, where he was no doubt required to help with the growing demand on clubmakers and the change of design of clubs. Willie Jr. showed considerable ability at an early age as a designer of both woods and cleeks and in his book *The Game of Golf* states that he developed the 'bulger' driver with its shortened, slightly convex head in 1884 and that he played with it in the Open Championship of 1885. In 1890 he took out a Patent for the first diamond-mesh pattern for a golf ball (No.16,862 of 1890) followed in 1896 by No.11,761, a unique design which he named the Royal.

Perhaps his most successful design was his wry-necked putter (UK Patent No.20,914 of 1894) which remained popular for many years – the heads at one time being made by Winton of Montrose and later by Bishop & Hendry of Edinburgh, carrying the Bishop's mitre mark.

With the boom in golf developing, he first opened a retail shop in Edinburgh, built up the manufacturing part of the clubmaking business at Musselburgh where he is said to have employed eighty men and by 1901 had set up in Cannon Street, London, with a wholesale and retail warehouse, whilst his younger brother Mungo (1877–1960) had opened a branch in New York. Mungo later went to the Argentine and established the San Andres Course.

His chief activity was, however, the laying-out of new golf courses and he advertised his services in the early 1900s as a golf course architect – 'Grounds surveyed and Reports made, Courses laid out and made by contract'. He must have been a busy and successful man, for he went to North America and the Continent besides laying-out a number of well-known courses in the UK. It was at Huntercombe in Oxfordshire that he eventually came to grief, with one of the first projects of combining a golf course with a housing development (which he started in 1901), an idea which was to become popular elsewhere. This speculation was before its time, the motor-car was not yet available for ease of access and Huntercombe had no adjacent rail facility. The project failed shortly after World War I.

Sir Guy Campbell (*History of Golf*, p.108) says that 'It was only when Willie Park entered the lists that the foundation stone of golf architecture was laid'. Not only did he write about the subject in his book *The Game of Golf* as early as 1896, but it is now supported by an ample bibliography. Park is an interesting character. We have a portrait of him at the time he won his first Championship in 1887:

'Willie is a tall strapping young fellow of about 6 ft. in height and 24 years of age. He is in business as a club- and ballmaker in his native town of Musselburgh where he is held in high esteem for his exemplary conduct and for his rigid adherence to those temperance principles, the neglect of which has brought so many of his brother professionals to grief.'

He followed in his father's footsteps and after he had won his second championship he pursued a policy of issuing challenges to play anyone for £100. In 1890 he played Andrew Kirkaldy of St Andrews over 144 holes or eight rounds over four different courses. Although in this case he was beaten, an event such as this attracted considerable attention and when the final round was played at St Andrews, the match attracted some 3,000 spectators. As a form of public-relations exercise, the wager matches maintained Park in the public eye and although he did not win another Open Championship, it must have been an effective form of advertising the Park name in the golfing world. In 1896 he published his book *The Game of Golf*. This was the first book to be published by a professional golfer, and after a short description of the game, of the clubs and balls used, he proceeded to describe how to play the 'Game of Golf' – hence its title. In 1920 he published another book, *The Art of Putting* (J. & J. Gray, Edinburgh), one of the few ever to have been written on the subject. Park always held the opinon that 'The man who can putt is a match for anyone' and this is the heading for his opening chapter. Even though the greens of today bear no comparison to those of earlier days it still makes interesting reading. One of his favourite wooden putters, 'Old Pawky' made by Mungo Park, is in the Woking Golf Club Collection.

The Park family made an outstanding contribution to golf in those hectic boom years and Willie Park Jr. appears as a dominant figure of those days – as a top-class golfer, a leading golf course architect, and, as 'W. Park & Son, Champion Golfers 1860, 1863, 1866, 1876, 1887, 1889'. He should have made a fortune but he did not.

Wm. Park Sr. and Mungo both made long-headed clubs, using their own stamps – Wm. Park and M. Park. It is doubtful whether Wm. Park Jr. ever made long-headed clubs under his own stamp. It is also doubtful whether he ever stamped his own clubs with W. Park & Son, although he advertised the name as such. He actually used a variety of stamps such as Wm. Park, Wm. Park Maker Musselburgh and Wm. Park Patent Compressed (for some of his woods).

Willie Park, Jr., Champion
Golfer 1887

Advertisement for 'The "Pikup"
Club', W. Park & Son 1910

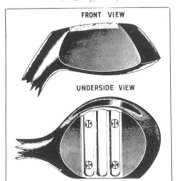

The *Very Latest Improvement in Golf Clubs.*

The "PIKUP"

(Regd. 552861.)

FRONT VIEW

UNDERSIDE VIEW

By using this club bad lies
lose their terror.   A ball
can be picked out of a bad
lie with the greatest of
ease.

**Makes a weak player
—strong,**

**and a strong player
—stronger.**

**Drivers,
Brassies,
Baffies,**

8/6

EACH.

W. PARK & SON,

CHAMPION GOLFERS
1860 1863 1866 1875 1887 1889.

**115, Cannon Street, London,
28a, South Frederick St., Edinburgh,
and Musselburgh.**

GOLF COURSES LAID OUT AND CONTRACTED FOR.

TELEPHONE: 4331 CENTRAL.

The Park Family (Musselburgh)

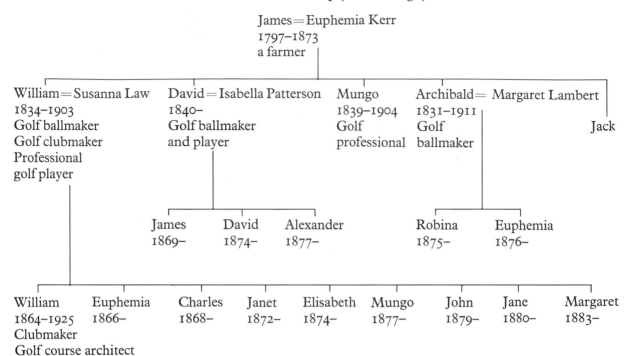

```
                          James = Euphemia Kerr
                          1797–1873
                          a farmer

William = Susanna Law    David = Isabella Patterson   Mungo      Archibald = Margaret Lambert
1834–1903               1840–                         1839–1904  1831–1911
Golf ballmaker          Golf ballmaker               Golf       Golf                        Jack
Golf clubmaker          and player                   professional ballmaker
Professional
golf player
                  James    David    Alexander          Robina    Euphemia
                  1869–    1874–    1877–              1875–     1876–

William      Euphemia   Charles   Janet    Elisabeth  Mungo    John     Jane     Margaret
1864–1925    1866–      1868–     1872–    1874–      1877–    1879–    1880–    1883–
Clubmaker
Golf course architect
```

The Morris Family

(old) *Tom Morris Sr* (1821–1906)
(young) *Tom Morris Jr* (1851–1875)
J. O. F. Morris (–1906) sons
George Morris (brother of Tom Sr.) (–1888)
Jack Morris (son of George)
T. Hunter (son-in-law
of Prestwick)

'Old Tom' Morris, the son of a hand-loom weaver according to the 1841 Census, was and still is probably the greatest of all St Andrews historical figures. He is the only one of the great golfing families to have had a biography written of him. (W. W. Tulloch, D.D. *The Life of Tom Morris*, T. Werner Laurie, London 1908). The book itself contains a lengthy record of all Tom's numerous challenge and other matches and triumphs in the Open Championship. It tells also of Tom Morris beating Allan Robertson in 1853 and of the latter's great reluctance to repeat the match or to respond to any challenge which he did not think he could win. It also records Tom Morris's great weakness as a golfer – he was an extremely bad 'holer out' of short putts, although he was quite capable of holing the longer ones.

W. W. Tulloch went to live in St Andrews in 1854 at the age of eight and therefore had a personal knowledge of him for a considerable period of his life. Unfortunately, in common with so much contemporary golf literature of the time, the book contains hardly a word about clubmaking. Yet Tom Morris's golf business still survives today on its original site, bearing his name although

Old Tom in later life

'Young Tom' and 'Old Tom'
Morris, *c.* 1873

clubs are no longer manufactured there, and there is still a family connection interested in it.

According to Tulloch, old Tom was apprenticed to the famous Allan Robertson, last of a long line of ballmakers and pre-eminent golfer, for four years, and also five years thereafter as a journeyman. He became an outstanding golfer at an early age and, having served his time as apprentice and journeyman, stayed on making golf balls. He was in demand as a professional player. He also learnt to make clubs at this time. No date is mentioned but in 1848–9 he quarrelled and parted company with Allan because he played with a gutta ball, having been foresworn not to do so. He was then aged twenty-seven or twenty-eight and must have spent at least a couple of years as player, club- and ballmaker at St Andrews before being offered and accepting the new post of 'Keeper of the Green' at Prestwick where he was to remain from 1851–64. He then returned to St Andrews to take up a similar position. This period of his life has been dealt with in some detail because it has never been clear where he acquired his skill as a clubmaker.

Tom Morris won the Championship Belt in 1861, '62, '64 and '67, when he was already aged forty. His son, Tom Morris Jr., won it outright by winning three times in succession – in 1868, '69, '70. There was no contest in 1871 and the first Open Championship proper was held in 1872. This was again won by young Tom. He was to die in 1875 following the tragic death of his young wife, at the age of twenty-four, much lamented as the finest golfer of his day.

'Old Tom' Morris set up his clubmaking business in 1867 and by 1871 he is reported to have employed three men and one boy. He subsequently entered into an arrangement with Robert Forgan for his supply of raw materials for clubheads and shafts. No doubt his two sons – Young Tom and Jamie (J. O. F. Morris) were brought up in the business of clubmaking but the former made few clubs. After the early death of Young Tom, Jamie appeared in many St Andrews

challenge matches, dying in the same year as his father – 1906.
'Old Tom' Morris's golf business was undoubtedly successful and
turned out fine clubs such as may be seen in many museums and
collections. He should have been reasonably well off, what with years
of challenge matches, laying-out a number of golf courses, a job at
the Royal & Ancient and his own business. In 1896 the Royal &
Ancient initiated the Tom Morris Testimonial which raised £1240 –
and was designed to give him £100 a year – although he did not
retire as greenkeeper until 1903. If he had lived a hundred years
later he would have been a rich man, after such a distinguished
career, but in the absence of any evidence to the contrary, his
financial rewards appear to have been modest.

Of the other members of the family, George Morris went to
Carnoustie as a clubmaker but the last twenty-five years of his life
were spent in the employment of Dr Robert Chambers of W. & R.
Chambers Publishers, Edinburgh. George designed the first nine
holes at Hoylake and his son Jack Morris was subsequently
professional at Hoylake for the record span of sixty years (1869–
1929). He must have made many clubs under his own name. 'Old
Tom's' daughter married Tom Hunter of Prestwick and when he
died, she came to keep house for her father in St Andrews.

Conclusion

These six families produced the bulk of the long-headed wooden
clubs which became obsolete in the late 1880s. They divide into two
categories – The Morrises, Parks and Dunns were all outstanding
golfers, took part in many challenge matches against each other and
also made money by making clubs, balls and equipment and by
laying-out golf courses. It was their golfing prowess which promoted
their trade. The McEwans, Forgans and Patricks were craftsmen
pure and simple. The McEwans never had the will to enter the new
mechanical age, and it was only the Forgans who came through to
establish an outstanding business which only finally succumbed
after World War II. Golf had become so popular and world-wide
that it became the target for big business. Yet the clubs which these
families made will remain as the only memorials to the outstanding
part they played in expanding the game nearly a hundred years ago.

Alphabetical list of clubmakers — List A
c.1600–1914

Allan, John (1848–c.1900–05)
Prestwick
Appointed professional to
Westward Ho! and North Devon
Golf Club 1867 and remained there
until 1886. He returned to
Prestwick in 1887 and became
professional to the St Nicholas
Golf Club, Prestwick. He made
sturdy, useful clubs. Ref.
'Prestwick St. Nicholas Golf Club
1851–1951' W. Galbraith pub.
1950.

Allan, James and Mathew
Brothers of John Allan and also
born at Prestwick.

Anderson, D. & Sons
5 Ellice Place, St Andrews
Appear in *Slaters* at intervals
1893–1915. **David Anderson**
(1847–1912) founded this firm – his
father being 'Old Da' (1821–1901)
a well known St Andrews
character, feathery ballmaker and
greenkeeper at St Andrews. His
elder brother was Jamie Anderson
who also had his own firm. David
Anderson had as a basis for his
work force five sons (see articles
Golf Illustrated 17.7.03 and
19.2.04) and the firm appeared in
Slaters (1893, 1900, '03, '07, '11,
'15). A picture of the workshop in
1904 shows a work force of twelve
including no doubt the family.
They had a good export business,
re-covered golf balls and were then
marketing 'Excelsior' and
'Triumph' putters and a 'New
Pitcher'.

Anderson, James (1842–1905),
brother to David Anderson. Eldest
son of 'Old Da' and Open
Champion 1877, '78, '79. Appears

in *Slaters* 1878 and as Anderson J.
& Sons, 122 Market Street, St
Andrews (*Slaters* 1893) and
undoubtedly made long-headed
clubs in St Andrews marked 'J.
ANDERSON'. It is doubtful if he
was ever in partnership with his
brother David, although he appears
in the *Fife Directory* of 1893–94 at
his address of 5 Ellice Place. He
later went to Ardeer and Perth, but
died aged sixty-three in Dysart
Combination Poor House, Perth.

Anderson, James (1878–   ),
the son of Jamie Anderson, the
Open Champion, was apprenticed
to Forgans and appears in the 1895
illustration (see page 98). Around
1910 he left and set up in
partnership with **David Blythe**
(1860–1913) as **Anderson &
Blythe** 8 Golf Place, St Andrews
The firm appears in the 1910
Valuation Roll and advertised
regularly in *Golf Monthly* and in
the 1912 *Golfer's Handbook*. They
made 'Invincible' drivers.

Anderson, R. & Sons
67 Princes Street, Edinburgh
Anderson, Roderick (1843–1915)
Anderson, Robert (1846–1917)
Edinburgh & Leith P.O.D.
1892–1905 *Slaters* 1893
'Fishing-tackle makers' who
entered the golf club market as
'patentees of the Anderson golf
clubs'. Robert Anderson's patent
No.3794 of 1891 was the first to
pass the shaft through a shortened
neck right through to the sole of a
wooden club – splicing also
securing the shaft. This
development has stood the test of
time down to the present day.
Clubheads had 'Anderson & Son,
Princes St. EDINBURGH –
Patentees' stamped on them. See
Chapter 8 for other patents
including centre-shafted iron club.
There is an interesting driver in the
Spalding Collection with a
greenheart shaft and fishing-rod
handle. The firm went bankrupt
before World War One.

Army & Navy Stores Ltd
Victoria Street, London SW1
This was an early form of

co-operative society for the Army
and Navy. It issued a mail-order
catalogue as early as the 1870s
which went out to Service depots all
over the Empire. Their first golf
entry related only to the offer of
Eclipse golf balls. By 1890 they
were carrying Forgan's range of
clubs, but so great was the demand
that they decided to manufacture
themselves using 'experienced
Scottish workmen'. This is how
James Braid came to work there
from Elie in 1893, having been
persuaded to join him by Ralph
Smith, another clubmaker from
Elie. Extracts from the 1890, 1900
and 1910 catalogues are referred to
in various parts of the book and
have afforded good illustrations of
the development of clubs. It is
worth commenting that in 1910
they were offering the 'B.S.D. Set'
of long-headed spoons, 'somewhat a
copy of the old-fashioned spoons –
and will delight the old school of
golfers'. These cost 7s 6d against
the approximate 5s 0d for the
ordinary wooden club.

Auchterlonie, D. & W.
David (1865–   )
William (1873–1963) was
apprenticed to R. Forgan & Sons
and won the Open Championship
of 1893. They originally set up
business with A. W. Crosthwaite as
Auchterlonie & Crosthwaite in
1892 (*Golfing Annual 1893*), but in
1894 Crosthwaite dropped out and
in a review of the business in *Golf
Illustrated* (26.7.01) the firm of
D. & W. Auchterlonie was quoted
as employing sixteen workmen,
having been founded in 1894.
W. Auchterlonie was professional
to the Royal & Ancient, becoming
an Honorary Member and
Honorary Curator of their Museum.

F. H. Ayres
Ayres & Smith Ltd (Est. 1810)
111 Aldersgate St, London EC
Made golf clubs and equipment –
see also cleekmakers.

Bailey, Andrew
Bruntsfield Links
Letter dated 20.6.1735 ordering
nine clubs and two dozen
St Andrews golf balls (see p.93).

Ballantyne, William (1793–1845)
and
Ballantyne, William Jnr (Son) (1826–1851)
Recorded in *Pigot* as residing at
Golf House, Leith, from 1818 to
1834 during which time the
Edinburgh Almanack of 1821
(p.267) describes him as clubmaker
to the Edinburgh Company of
Golfers and the Thistle Golf Club.
He moved to Musselburgh in 1834
when the Edinburgh Company of
Golfers moved there and remained
there until his death in 1845.
(*Pigot* and P.O.D.).

Beveridge, J. (1852–1899)
Born in St Andrews and learned
trade in Tom Morris's shop. 1881
Census at West Links, North
Berwick, and later at Royal Isle of
Wight Club before emigrating to
the USA. 1894 to 1899 clubmaker
to the Shinnecock Hills Golf Club,
Long Island. A rare set of wooden
clubs made by him is in the
possession of Hankley Common
Golf Club, Surrey.

Braid, James (1870–1950)
Elie
Open Champion 1901, '05, '06, '08,
'10. He was a joiner by trade and in
1893 was persuaded by Ralph
Smith, a clubmaker from Elie who
worked at the Army & Navy Stores
in London to join him, as he was by
then already a good golfer. He left
there after two years, going to
Romford in Essex and in 1904
joined Walton Heath Golf Club
where he remained for the rest of
his life. He kept a staff of
clubmakers but never attempted to
enter the larger retail field.

Buchanan, John & Co
John Buchanan (1862–   )
Edinburgh, Glasgow and
Musselburgh
They were fishing-rod makers, who
according to *Golf* (6.1.91), Vol.III
started making shafts in Edinburgh

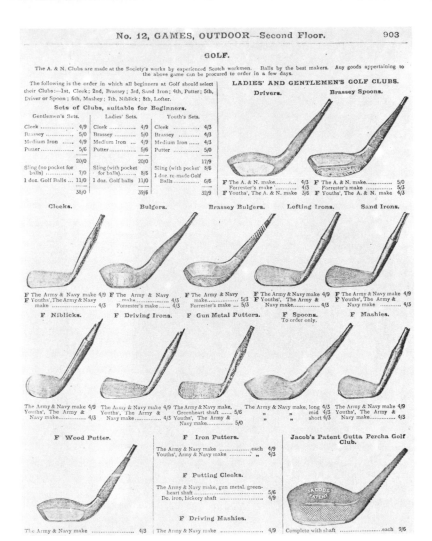

Army & Navy Stores Catalogue, 1900. Note 'scared-head' wooden clubs and a niblick track-iron style.

in 1878 and patented machinery for
turning and tapering hickory
shafts, of which they produced at
that time some 30,000 a year. They
were reputed to have made
clubheads also, and were described
as 'club and ballmakers'. It seems
likely that they marketed golf
equipment and unlikely that they
actually made clubs, but it is
possible that they did market
equipment under their own name.
No trade entries appear after 1899.

Butchart, John (1854–   )
11 Panmure Terrace, Carnoustie,
appears in the 1891 Census and

the 1910 Forfarshire Valuation
Roll. He made long-headed clubs
bearing the Butchart name, of
which a few appear in collections
that have been examined. Two of
his sons achieved distinction:

Butchart, Cuthbert Strachan (1876–   )
who became professional at West
Hill, Brookwood, Surrey, and
Butchart, Charles S. (1876–   )
who according to *Nisbet* 1906
established a golf club factory at 71
Archway Road, London N. He also
became a golf course architect and
in 1914 was professional to the

Berlin Golf Club and was interned with other British professionals when war broke out.

Campbell, Colin ( )
Recorded at Leith 1817–30 and in *Pigot* 1825–26.

Cann & Taylor
J. H. Taylor and George Cann both came from Westward Ho! in North Devon and both served an apprenticeship as clubmakers to Charles Gibson, master clubmaker from Musselburgh. Taylor, destined to become five times British Open Champion, was interested in playing golf but not in the making of clubs, and Cann, who had no great skill in playing, became a great clubmaker.

When J. H. Taylor went to Winchester in 1891 (from where he won his first Open Championship in 1894), they set up a small golf club factory, and later opened a factory at East Sheen, Richmond, Surrey. In 1902 Cann & Taylor also set up at Astbury Park, New Jersey, USA, and in the January 1902 issue of *Golf Illustrated* there is an account of George Cann's visit to the UK to buy more plant for the American factory. The US enterprise was probably not successful, for by 1912 only the Richmond factory was being advertised and this continued in business for many years making finished clubs and clubheads.

Clephane, John and Clephane, David
Both mentioned as clubmakers in Leith Records 1725–50. 'Lucky' John Clephane's tavern in the Kirkgate, Leith, was where the Honourable Company of Edinburgh Golfers dined after the day's play before their Golf House was built. John Clephane was known as a formidable golfer. It is likely that clubmaking by members of the Clephane family took place.

Collins, Richard (1852–)
Leith Trade Entry 1875–82. Professional at Ryton-on-Tyne – *Nisbet* 1906.

Collons
Long-headed clubs bearing this stamp have been seen, but no maker of this name has been identified.

Coltart, F. (1882–)
Professional at James VI Club, Moncrieffe Course, Perth, and a shop at Jay Street. Appears in *Slaters* 1900, 1903 and *Nisbet* 1906 and is said to have gone to the USA in 1910. His brother Sandy built a workshop near the Club House.

Comb, Thomas (*c.*1770)
Bruntsfield
He was to acquire the 'great house with the court, bowling-green and garden called Foxtoun' which was the 'Golf hall' of the earlier days and the meeting place of early Burgess members (see *The Chronicle of the Royal Burgess Golfing Society of Edinburgh 1735–1935*, pp.15, 74).

Cossar, Simon (1766–1811)
First appears as a clubmaker at Golf House, Leith, in the Edinburgh P.O.D. of 1794 and again in 1810. He died on 31 December 1811 and 'is buried in the Tailors Ground one pace South West from Euphan Tods Headstone'. He was a celebrated clubmaker in his day and there are specimens in the Royal & Ancient Collection.

Cossar, David (1788–1816)
Son of Simon Cossar, described as a clubmaker. It is reasonable to suppose that he carried on his father's business. He was 'buried 2 paces West by South from Euphan Tod's headstone'.

Crowley, James (1860–1937)
Elie and Earlsferry
One of the three rival clubmakers at Elie in the 1880s – the others being A. H. Scott and G. Forrester – he is described in *Slaters* 1893 and 1896 as a 'Golf Implement Maker' which is a description also used by Forrester, the exact meaning of which is not clear. In 1911 he departed for Glasgow.

Currie, Thomas (1878–)
Emigrated to Pittsburgh, Pa. Appears in *Slaters* 1903, '07, '11, and '15. *Nisbet* 1906. Professional at Dornoch, formerly at Dunbar. See also *Golfer's Handbook* 1912, advert. and photo.

Dalgleish, Joseph (1860–)
Nisbet 1906. Professional at Nairn. Mentioned in *Golf Illustrated* (17.8.1900) as an experienced clubmaker. Club (driver) in Spalding Collection.

Davidson, Robert (1801–1875)
Newwynd, The Links, Montrose
Slaters 1852 and 1867.

Day, W. D. (1837–)
Golf ball- and clubmaker. In 1881 resident at Bruntsfield Club House, but in 1892 is at Links Place, Musselburgh, and in 1889 and 1896 is in *Slaters*. Has example of club in Spalding Collection.

Denholm, David (–1820)
Officer and clubmaker to the Burgess Company, Edinburgh, 1809–20. *Edinburgh Almanack* 1814.

Dick, David (–1731)
St Andrews
Clubmaker.

The Dickson Family of Leith
Further research might reveal interesting details of this family and their relationships which are at present not known. Thomas and William Dickson – club and ballmakers at Leith – were raided by Melvill in 1628 for failing to pay their dues to him in accordance with his alleged monopoly. Melvill however was bound over for his assault in the sum of £5 and a surety of £100 (Scots) and the Dicksons are said to have challenged his Letter saying that it was never ratified. This challenge was successful (Register of Privy Council, Scotland, 2nd Series. Volume III, A.D.1629–30, p.174.) See Chapter 1, appendix 3.

John Dickson (1678–1729)

John (1710–1755)   James (1713–1740)

John (1735–1787) Buried in Bakers ground '6 paces South from the middle of the Bakers window'. Leith Church.

John Dickson, ballmaker, was appointed by Aberdeen Town Council to make 'gouff' balls in 1642. **Andrew Dickson** (1665–1753) was a ballmaker and a reputed forecaddy to James II when Duke of York and resident in Edinburgh, c.1682. We then get the family tree as shown above, all being described as clubmakers. We also read in 'The Goff' by Thomas Mathison 1743 'of finest ash . . . the work of Dickson who in Letha dwells and in the art of making clubs excels'. This would likely be John Dickson (1710–1755). It is clear that the Dickson family were makers of golf clubs and balls from at least the 1620s until 1787. See also *Golf*, Jan. 31, 1896, article on Dickson family.

Dickson, J. & A.
Golf clubmakers at 8 Braid Road, Edinburgh, first appearing in *Slaters* 1893 and in the directories up until 1914. We know of **Alexander Dickson** (1861–1926) but have no dates for J. Dickson. The authors have a long-headed wood, stamped 'Dickson' but shafted by J. & A. Dickson; evidently they may have been in business some time before they appeared for the first time in *Slaters*. It would be interesting to know where they learnt their clubmaking. A cleek stamped 'John Dickson' in the Spalding Collection was made by Gibson of Kinghorn.

Dow, Robert (Bob) (1832–1909)
There is a reference to him as a clubmaker of Montrose when he was Keeper of the Green to the Royal Albert Club, Montrose. Later he was golf clubhouse keeper at Dundee. He made long-headed clubs and often took part in challenge matches.

The Dunn Family (see p.104)

Fergie, William (1856–1924)
1894 P.O.D. Archers Hall. 'Bowmaker to the Queens Bodyguard for Scotland, golf club and ballmaker', he appears in the P.O.D. up until 1914. *Golf* 1890 reported that Canadian hickory, specially imported for him for bows, was well adapted for club-shafts and that during the previous three years he had turned his attention to clubmaking. He was one of the only two exhibitors of golf equipment at the International Exhibition, Edinburgh, 1891.

Ferguson, Robert (1846–1915)
Musselburgh
Open Champion 1880, '81, '82, tied 1883 and lost play off. Appeared in *Slaters* 1889 as a golf club and ballmaker, but after a severe illness retired from active play and became greenkeeper at Musselburgh, and later, a regular caddie there.

Fernie, William (1858–1924)
One of five brothers – the others being Tom, George, Harry, and Eddie.
Won the Open Championship in 1883 (after a tie with Bob Ferguson) and became greenkeeper, clubmaker and professional at Dumfries and then at Felixstowe (1884) before going to Ardeer and ending up at Troon, where he appears in *Slaters* from 1896–1915. See Chapter 3 for the part his brother George and he played in early Haskell-type golf ball experiments. He had a reputation as a fine clubmaker and must have made long-headed clubs. Tom Fernie was the first professional to Aldeburgh, Suffolk, founded in 1883.

The Forgan Family (see p.96)

Forrester, George (1847–1930)
Earlsferry and Elie, Fife
Made long-headed clubs and appears as a clubmaker in *Slaters* 1889, but in 1893 is described as a 'Golf Implement Maker' in *Slaters* and the *Fife Directory* until 1915, becoming 'George Forrester & Son' in 1903. Volume IV of *Golf* (1.4.92) reports a 'patent' bull-dog bulger driver. There is also a wry-neck putter by him in the Wood Collection, Manchester. There were three 'shops' at Elie occupied by Crowley, Forrester, and Scott, and Forrester's shop was eventually taken over by Thomas Reekie (1880–1958).

Gibson, Charles (1864–1937)
Musselburgh
His family were not golfers. He became interested in clubmaking at an early age and was apprenticed to Willie Dunn Sr. at North Berwick. In 1888 he was appointed professional and clubmaker to the Royal North Devon Golf Club and remained there until his death in 1937. He was a master clubmaker and trained his four sons and a large number of apprentices, many of whom became in their time well known clubmakers in the USA, Far East, Egypt and the Continent of Europe. His clubs are finely made and well-proportioned. He made three miniature golf clubs and they were placed in Queen Mary's Dolls' House at Windsor Castle.

Grieg, Alexander
Leith
Golf club and ballmaker of 18 Duke Street, Leith. First entry in *Edinburgh General Directory* 1866 and he was a resident there until 1872.

Hood, Thomas (1843–1909)
Musselburgh
His father was a joiner. Listed in 1881 Census as a clubmaker. 1882 *Slaters* at Mill Hill, Musselburgh, but moved to 2a Braid Road, Morningside, Edinburgh – Edinburgh P.O.D. 1894, '95. Died in an asylum. He was a well-known

Top:
G. Forrester of Elie, and advertisement
Below:
C. Gibson of Westward Ho!, and advertisement

clubmaker and examples of his long-headed clubs exist in several collections including the Royal & Ancient.

Hunter, Charles (1837–1921)
Born at Prestwick and succeeded Tom Morris in 1864. Went to Royal Blackheath (1866–68) but returned to Prestwick on the death of Andrew Strath in 1868 and remained there until his death in 1921.

Hutchison, J. H. (1847–1912)
North Berwick
1881 Census – Golf clubmaker. *Slaters* 1896, 1900, '03, and '07.

Ife, A. J. (1870–1927)
Hayling Island, Hants
In 1904 he was the first professional at The Hague Golf Club and remained there until he died. Up to World War I he made all his own golf clubs, both woods and irons. The woods are marked 'A. J. Ife' and the irons are stamped 'A. J. Ife Maker'. Some of his clubs may be seen in the Rye Golf Club Collection.

Jackson, John (1805–1878)
63 South Street, Perth
'Wright' and golf clubmaker. *Pigot* 1825–6. Appears in Perth Directory at various addresses in Perth from 1837–1872 and had a shop in Northport, Perth. He must be regarded as one of the master clubmakers whose clubs were beautifully finished and finely made. Examples may be seen in the Collection of King James VI Club at Perth and in the Spalding Collection.

Kirk, Robert Jr. (1845–1886)
Professional at Blackheath (1864–66) and returned to St Andrews. There is a fine set of his long-headed clubs which he made for the Club and displayed with miniature woods, cleeks and balls at Blackheath.

Lang, Bennet (1849–1913)
Northport, Perth
Slaters 1900, '03, and '07. Collection of his long-headed clubs

in the King James VI Club, Perth. He was a specialist in hand-made wooden clubs which were made to measure to suit each individual client, said to have been of excellent quality. He was, also, a roving craftsman locksmith and a violinist, and apparently quite an entertaining character.

Lloyd, Joseph (   )
Came from Hoylake where he was nicknamed the 'General'. He was professional to Pau Golf Club (Southern France) – founded in 1856. He is reported as a first-class player, taking a great interest in golf and giving excellent lessons, and was said to turn out and repair clubs to everyone's satisfaction (*Golf* 3.10.1890). He later went to Cleveland, USA. There is a club in the Spalding Collection.

McDonald, Walter (1836–   )
Clubmaker at 14 Charlotte Street, Perth – *Slaters* 1867, and shop at 7 Northport, *Slaters* 1882 and McDonald's Scottish Directory 1884. Originally trained in St Andrews *c*.1863. 'Watty' McDonald was said to have been a fine craftsman. Was a part-time greenkeeper on North Inch Course. He was a keen professional competitor. Examples of his clubs are in the King James VI Club, Perth.

The McEwan Family (see p.100)

McGregor, John (1862–   )
St Andrews Valuation Roll 1890, 1910, '11. Clubmaker. Appears in Forgans' staff photograph of 1895.

Manderson, Alexander (1813–1891)
Dunbar
Master joiner, 1 High Street, Dunbar. Census 1881, *Slaters* 1882 as club- and ballmaker.

Mayne, William
Edinburgh
First Royal Warrant holder, issued by Privy Seal of Scotland, 4 April 1603.

Miln, Henry (d.1755)
Clubmaker – St Andrews, See also George Miln – ballmaker (p.46).

Mills aluminium clubs – see Standard Golf Co.

The Morris Family (see p.114)

Munro, Alexander (1796–1847)
Aberdeen
Golf club and fishing-rod maker at Union Street. Appears in 1841 Census as fishing-rod maker. Not born in Aberdeenshire. The Bon Accord Directory Aberdeen 1842–3. 118/20 King Street (shop) fishing-rod and tackle maker. See reference to L. Sandison.

Neilson, Robert (1719–1767)
Clubmaker at Leith. A son, **Alexander** (1752–   ) also a clubmaker to whom a son, **John,** was born in 1784. No other reference has so far been found to this family of clubmakers.

The Park Family (see p.110)

The Patrick Family (see p.108)

Paxton, Peter (1859–   )
Musselburgh
Apprenticed to Tom Hood, Musselburgh, and was coached by David Park (Willie Park Sr.'s brother). He succeeded his brother John as golf professional and clubmaker at the Worcestershire Golf Club, Malvern, around 1880 and in 1887 went to Royal Eastbourne (ref. *Golf*, Vol. III, 1891 – he is said to have preferred club and ballmaking to professional playing of golf). He was a fine clubmaker and of an inventive turn of mind. He developed square-socketed clubs and in 1892 perfected a machine for making golf balls which could turn out 2,000–3,000 per week made of red or black gutta. *Golf* (25.8.1893) reports that he is leaving Royal Eastbourne taking with him four skilled workmen and a large stock of finely made clubs and balls and that 'he is now branding his clubheads with a crown being favoured with the Royal Patronage' of the Duke and

Duchess of York. *Golf* (27.2.1899, p.378) reports him inventing a combined club cover and portable stand for carrying and supporting golf clubs during play.

Paxton, James B. (1874–   )
Musselburgh and Guernsey
Nisbet 1906 reports him making fibre-faced clubs for rubber-cored balls.

Pett, James (*c.*1627)
St Andrews
Supplied clubs to the Marquis of Montrose.

Philp, Hugh (1782–1856)
See Philp-Forgan Family (see p.96)

Sandison, Ludovic (1825–1884)
Appears in the Aberdeen P.O.D. for 1848 as a fishing tackle maker at 118 King Street, Aberdeen, with a shop at 120 King Street. Later on in the same directory he is listed as a turner and clubmaker. The addresses above are the same as those previously occupied by A. Munro and he must therefore have taken over his business, which accounts for the names

SANDISON
LATE A. MUNRO
ABERDEEN

both appearing on the club in the Royal Blackheath Collection, which must have been made by him. The authors have a club, stamped SANDISON. The shaft is of uniform width – probably ash and never had a grip on it.

Sayers, Ben (1857–1924)
North Berwick
One of the most colourful characters in the hey-day of the Victorian and Edwardian era at North Berwick, when it became the most fashionable golfing resort in Britain. He was born in Leith, was only 5ft 3in and affectionately always known as 'the Wee Yin'. He was originally trained as an acrobat. He thought nothing of turning a cartwheel on the green to celebrate the holing of a putt. He was apprenticed at Musselburgh and eventually became professional

Top: Ben Sayers and son
Below: Ben Sayers, bunkered at North Berwick, 1895

at North Berwick, having become an outstanding golfer who played in every Open Championship from 1880 until 1923 without ever winning it.

He first went into the manufacture of golf balls, buying his moulds from Davie Strath of North Berwick and in *Slaters* 1889 he is still described as a golf ballmaker. He achieved renown as an ideal teacher of golf in society circles and was in demand in Monte Carlo and the USA. This stimulated the demand for his clubs, all of which were then made to order. His son Ben Jr., who was born in 1884 (also a professional golfer), joined him in opening a factory in High Street, North Berwick. This factory was only abandoned in recent years in favour of the modern plant on the outskirts of the town. The name Ben Sayers still flourishes today over a hundred years after he made his first clubs. He may have developed the popular Dreadnought driver named after Admiral Sir 'Jackie' Fisher's famous flagship *Dreadnought* prior to World War I, but there are others who claimed it – e.g. C. Gibson and J. White. His early clubs may have added distinction from possession by his many distinguished customers.

Scott, A. H. (1875–   )
Elie and Earlsferry
Was a most successful clubmaker of the new school. He first appears in *Slaters* in 1896 continuing to do so until World War I, and was appointed golf clubmaker to King George V in 1911, an appointment he secured as a result of the Duchess of Connaught's patronage. He was among the first to have a mechanised workshop run by power from a 10 h.p. engine with a copying lathe capable of turning out forty clubheads an hour. Beech was on the decline and being replaced by stonewood, persimmon and dogwood which required better machinery to fabricate it (see *Centenary History – The Golf House Club, Elie* – Alasdair Drysdale, 1975). Originally Scott was one of

the three rival clubmakers at Elie – the others being J. Crowley and G. Forrester.

Simpson, Robert (1862–1923)
Carnoustie
Simpson, Archie (1866–   )
The well-known six golfing Simpson brothers originally came from Elie and with the exception of David were professional golfers – Jack Simpson winning the Open Championship in 1884, and Archie twice being runner-up. It was Robert who established himself with a substantial workshop in Carnoustie and who first appears in the Dundee Trade Directory of 1885/6 – although he may well have been in business prior to this. In

1893 Robert and Archie Simpson were apparently together, but in 1896 he is listed in *Slaters* on his own and remains there up till 1915, employing twenty to twenty-five men. Examples of his clubs are in the Spalding Collection, including the 'bulger' – a club which he developed for Henry Lamb – with the head 4in. long made with a yellow thorn head. Robert revolutionised clubmaking in Carnoustie and was a master of his craft.

Slazenger & Sons Catalogue (1904)

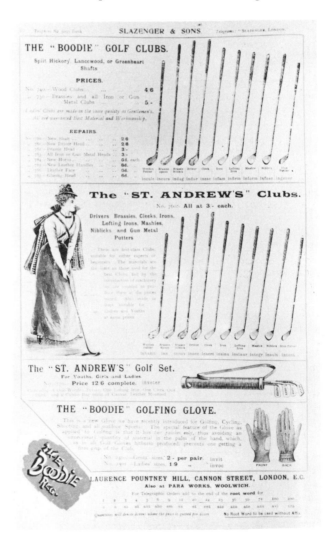

124

Slazengers Ltd

First registered 1881 as a company. Appear in this list as manufacturers of clubs and balls from before the turn of the century and, today, as a subsidiary of Dunlop Ltd, remains a household name for sports equipment. In the early 1870s the three brothers of the Moss Family were india rubber manufacturers and merchants in Manchester, particularly in the rainwear trade.

Sphairistike, or lawn tennis, having been patented by Major W. C. Wingfield in 1874 and having caught on, attracted the brothers to start making racquets and balls for this new game. For some reason they then decided to change their name and that of the firm to Slazenger, and transferred it in 1878 to London. By the 1890s they were engaged in making golf clubs and balls and Mr H. H. Hilton won the Open Championship with a Slazenger ball in 1892. At the turn of the century they were established in New York advertising that they had the largest stock of golf equipment on sale in America. In 1901 and 1902 Frank Slazenger of New York took out two patents relating to the screwing of the shaft into the clubhead and A. E. L. Slazenger registered it in the UK – No.1675 of 1901. In 1896 they were one of the first to give Crawford, McGregor and Canby of Dayton, Ohio, a bulk order for persimmon clubheads, which they presumably shipped to the UK.

A. G. Spalding & Bros

Founded 1878 at Rockford, Illinois, USA. Factory at Fetter Lane, London and later Putney, London (see US Clubmakers).

The Standard Golf Company

Was formed by Sir William Mills (1856–1932). Sir William came of an old Sunderland ship-building family and early in life spent a considerable amount of his time inventing machinery which would minimise labour or lessen danger to life: this included the Mills Patent for instantaneous engaging and disengaging gear for ships boats,

which was adopted worldwide. In the late 1890s he established one of the first, if not the first, aluminium plant for the production of aluminium alloy castings – at the Atlas Works, Bonnersfield, Sunderland. Thus it came about that, besides the many other things he was engaged in, he started producing aluminium golf clubs. He took out his first UK Patent (No.13,545) in 1896 with USA cover as well (No.572,436) in the same year, and this was for a club 'made of a framework of aluminium or other metal filled in by wood or other suitable material'. This idea was followed in 1900 by UK Patent No.20,915 – 'The heads of clubs, ordinarily composed of wood, are made of aluminium or other suitable material'.

Working in aluminium he proceeded to make exact models of fine older putters, the 'Braids Mills' models being bestsellers for many years (*Golf Illustrated* article 16.10.03 'one now to be seen in every bag'). The range was extended to the equivalent of the old baffys and spoons and you could have a matched set with simply the loft of the club varying. They were an instant success in the Amateur Championship of 1901 and the professionals immediately feared that aluminium clubs would replace irons, because they were said to be easier to play with and did less damage to the turf – it being unnecessary to take a divot.

Among the interesting clubs in the illustration is that which could

be used either left-handed or right-handed. *Golf Illustrated* noted in 1903 that 'many players carry a left-handed club in their set for use in emergencies' and this club was therefore the ideal answer.

Mills undoubtedly employed excellent craftsmen in wood in making the moulds for the aluminium castings, and the clubs were also believed to have been shafted in hickory by them. There were a number of imitators of his clubs.

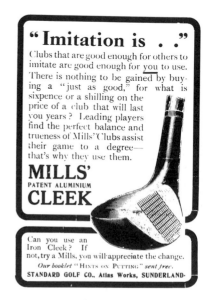

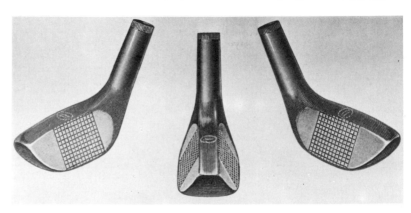

Mills' dual-purpose club (1903).

The Strath family – three brothers all born in St Andrews.
Andrew Strath (1836–1868)
He succeeded Tom Morris at Prestwick in 1864 as Keeper of the Green, winning the Championship on his home green in 1865, but died in 1868. Entry in *Slaters* 1867.
David Strath (1840–1879)
Was Keeper of the Green at North Berwick 1876–78 when for health reasons he went to Australia and died there immediately he arrived. He was the only golfer who could offer serious opposition to Young Tom Morris (Badminton Library *Golf* 1892 edit).
George Strath (   )
First professional at Troon 1881–87 and subsequently emigrated to the USA, being one of the earliest to do so.
All three brothers made clubs in the long-headed era but examples are not often seen.

Taylor, J. H. (1871–1963)
Northam, Devon
Open Champion 1894, '95, 1900, '09, '13, and see Cann & Taylor.

Vardon, Harry (b. 1870 at Granville, Jersey; d. 1937 at Totteridge, Herts.)
Vardon took up golf, having been advised to lead an outdoor life, following an early diagnosis for TB which dogged him during his career, and which he successfully overcame. He was winner of the British Open in 1896, '98, '99, 1903, '11, and 1914 and the US Open in 1900. He was professional at Ripon, Yorkshire in 1890, at Ganton from 1896 to 1903, and at Totteridge, Hertfordshire for the remainder of his life. The greatest golfer of his era and a great stylist, he popularised but did not invent the Vardon grip. In 1900 he began a year's tour in the USA playing a great many matches and appearing in stores giving demonstrations. This was as the result of J. W. Spalding coming to England, seeing Vardon play and signing him up to sponsor Spalding clubs and balls and make the US tour. This tour aroused considerable interest in golf which was still in its early stages in the USA.

He possessed diverse golfing talents, and, tired of giving his members at Totteridge an impossible number of strokes and beating them, he obtained a left-handed set of clubs and giving them the same number of strokes, still beat them.

His 'shop' at Totteridge employed six to eight men and they turned out large numbers of clubs under his occasional supervision.

White, Jack (1873–1949)
North Berwick
A nephew of Ben Sayers, he came from North Berwick and was for twenty-five years professional at Sunningdale and a well-known clubmaker. He won the Open in 1904 being the first man with a score of under 300.

Wilson, James (1803–1866)
St Andrews
Became Philp's assistant in 1845 but left him in 1852 when Philp brought in his nephew, Robert Forgan, with what must have been the intention of handing over his business to him. Wilson then set up on his own account and by all accounts was an excellent clubmaker. It must be noted that he may have been responsible for many clubs which bear the Philp stamp. He married Jane Auchterlonie.

List of all clubmakers whose names have appeared in the records —List B

Adam, John
Leven. Fife Directory 1866.

Adams, David
Glasgow. *Slaters* 1911.

Aitken, Alexander (1865–1944)
Edinburgh/Gullane. *Slaters* 1893,
'96, 1900, '03, '07. Edinburgh &
Leith P.O.D. trade entry 1892–96.
Appears in 1912 *Golfer's Handbook*
as clubmaker at Gullane.

Alexander, Charles
Carnoustie. Forfarshire Valuation
Roll 1914.

Allan, John (1848–)
See List A.

Allan, James & Mathew
See List A.

Allan, Thomas
Glasgow. *Slaters* 1911.

Anderson, D. & Sons
See List A.

Anderson, J.
Musselburgh. 1903 Handbook.

Anderson, James (1842–1905)
See List A.

Anderson, James (1878–)
See List A.

Anderson & Blythe
See List A.

Anderson, R. & Sons
See List A.

Army & Navy Stores Ltd.
See List A.

Auchterlonie, D. & W.
See List A.

Auld, Robert (1872–1939)
North Berwick. Voters Roll 1897–
1904.

**Ayres, F. H. (Ayres & Smith
Ltd)**
See List A.

Bailey, Andrew
See List A.

Bain, Colin (1863–1925)
Edinburgh. *Slaters* 1905.
Edinburgh Trade Directory 1911.
P.O.D. 1895, 1914.

Ballantyne, William (1793–1845)
See List A.

Ballantyne, William (1826–1851)
See List A.

Baptie, Thomas (1861–)
St Andrews. Voters Roll 1892,
1899. One of Forgan's employees.

Beck, James (1844–)
Leith. Born in England. Census
Leith 1881. Later said to be
'residing in Cape Town', S. Africa.

Beveridge, J. (1852–1899)
See List A.

Binnie, William
Kinghorn, Fife. *Slaters* 1903, 07,
11.

Bissett, Andrew (1861–1917)
North Berwick 1901–1914. *Slaters*
1911, 15.

Black, John
Carnoustie. Forfarshire Valuation
Roll 1905, 14.

Black, William
Carnoustie. *Slaters* 1911.

Boon, Neil
Prestwick. 1881 Census.

Braid, James (1870–1950)
See List A.

Braid, William
St Andrews 1895–97.

Brand, Charles (1849–1922)
Carnoustie. *Slaters* 1900, '03, '07,

'11, '15. Keeper of Caledonia Golf
Club House. Trade Directory 1890,
'92.

Brown, Alexander
Musselburgh. *Slaters* 1882.
McDonald's Scottish Directory
1884. Premises Racecourse
Grandstand, Musselburgh.

Brown, Daniel (1869–)
Musselburgh. *Slaters* 1911.

Brown, George
St Andrews. Voters Roll 1892–97
then 1910/11.

Brown, George Daniel
St Andrews. *Slaters* 1867.
Westwoods Parochial Directory for
Fife & Kinross 1862.

Brown, William
St Andrews/Earlsferry. Earlsferry
Voters Roll 1900/09.

Buchanan & Co, Edinburgh
See List A.

Buchanan, John (1862–)
See List A.

Butchart, Charles S. (1876–)
See List A.

Butchart, Cuthbert Strachan
(1876–)
See List A.

Butchart, John (1854–)
See List A.

Campbell, Benjamin N. (1865–)
Musselburgh Census 1891.
Millhill.

Campbell, Colin
See List A.

Campbell, John (1831–)
Musselburgh Census 1881.

Campbell, William
Glasgow. Glasgow P.O.D. 1899.

Campbell, William
St Andrews Voting Roll 1898–
1902.

Cann & Taylor
See List A.

Cardwell, Claude
Glasgow. *Slaters* 1911.

Chisholm, James
St Andrews. Valuation Roll 1903,
10, 11.

Clephane, John and David
See List A.

Collins, Richard (1852–)
See List A.

Collins, Richard (1874–)
Leith. 1906 Professional at Redcar.

Coltart, Alex
Perth. *Slaters* 1907.

Coltart, Frank (1882–)
See List A.

Cossar, David (1788–1816)
See List A.

Cossar, Simon (1766–1811)
See List A.

Cowan, William
Leith. *Slaters* 1893.

Crowley, James (1860–1937)
See List A.

Cunningham, James
Prestwick. 1881 Census.

Cunningham, W. (1872–1938)
Edinburgh. *Slaters* 1911. P.O.D.
1894, '95, 1914.

Currie, Thomas (1878–)
See List A.

Cuthbert, John
St Andrews. Valuation Roll 1897–
1902. Went to Wellington Golf
Club, New Zealand 1906.

Cuthbertson, William (1838–)
Leith. 1881 Census 'and
ballmaker'.

Dalgleish, Joseph (1860–)
See List A.

Dalrymple, David
St Andrews. Valuation Roll 1895–
1903; 1910/11.

Dargo, J. H.
Edinburgh. Trade entry 1905–15.
Slaters 1911.

Davidson, Charles
Musselburgh. *Slaters* 1896, 1900,
'03, '07, '11, '15.

Davidson, Robert (1801–1875)
See List A.

Davidson, William (1876–)
Gullane. *Slaters* 1891, 1903, '07.

Day, Walter (1837–)
See List A.

Denholm, David (–1820)
See List A.

Dick, William Jr (1868–)
Largo, Fife. Fife Directory 1893/4.
Slaters 1893, '96, 1900, '03.

Dick, David (–1731)
See List A.

Dickson, Alexander (1861–1926)
See List A.

The Dickson Family
See List A.

Dickson, J. & A.
See List A.

· **Doig, R.**
Musselburgh. Foreman in W.
Park Jr.'s 'shop'.

Doleman, Frank
Edinburgh. Trade entries 1895–
1914. There was also a William
Doleman. See history of Doleman's
Golf Illustrated, October 20, 1899.

Dougall, J. D. & Sons
Glasgow. P.O.D. 1899. Also
gunmakers.

Dow, Robert (1832–1909)
See List A.

The Dunn Family
See page 104.

Ellis, Thomas J. B.
Glasgow. P.O.D. 1899.

Fergie, William (1856–1924)
See List A.

Ferguson, Robert (1846–1915)
See List A.

Fernie, William (1858–1924)
See List A.

The Forgan Family
See page 96.

Forrester, George (1847–1930)
See List A.

Foulis, James (1842–)
St Andrews. Valuation Roll 1896,
'98. Census 1881.

Frier, William (1842–)
Edinburgh. Trade entries 1886–91.

Galloway, Thomas
Pittenweem, Fife. *Slaters* 1915.

Gatherum, John (1859–1927)
St Andrews. Valuation Roll 1894–
99.

Gibson, Charles (1864–1937)
See List A.

Given, David
Earlsferry, Fife. Valuation Roll
1901/2.

Goudie & Co
Edinburgh. P.O.D. 1895, 1905,
1914.

Gourlay, James
Glasgow. *Slaters* 1911.

Grant, David
North Berwick. Voters Roll 1890,
92. Brother in law to Ben Sayers.
Obit: *Golf Illustrated* 3rd July 1903.

Gray & Co.
Edinburgh. Started as Billiard,
Bagatelle and Fishing Tackle
Manufacturers 1890, '91, '94.
P.O.D. 1895. Golf Club and
Ballmakers.

Green, William
Monifieth, Dundee. *Slaters* 1911
and 1915.

Greig, Alexander Jr.
See List A.

Grieve, David
St Andrews. Valuation Roll 1896–1902.

Grieve, John
Edinburgh. Trade entry 1894, 95, 1905, 14.

Heggie, John
North Berwick. Voters Roll 1895–1901, 1914.

Henderson, William
Monifieth. *Slaters* 1896.

Herriott & Co
Glasgow. P.O.D. 1899. Also engineers.

Herriott, Robert
St Andrews. Valuation Roll 1901–03, 1910/11.

Hood, Thomas (1843–1909)
See List A.

Hunter, Charles (1837–1921)
See List A.

Hunter, John
Prestwick. 1891 Census (son of Charles Hunter).

Hutchison, James H. (1847–1912)
See List A.

Hutton, James D.
St Andrews. Valuation Roll 1894–1903, 1910.

Ife, A. J. (1870–1927)
See List A.

Jackson, John (1805–1878)
See List A.

Kerr, Robert
Leven. *Slaters* 1893.

King, Thomas
St Andrews. Valuation Roll 1893–98.

Kirk, Robert (1810–1891)
St Andrews. Fife Directory 1862, '66, '91.

Kirk, Robert Jr. (1845–1886)
See List A.

Lang, Bennet (1849–1913)
See List A.

Lloyd, Joseph
See List A.

Lorimer, George (1864–   )
St Andrews Valuation Roll 1897–1903.

Lyall, David
St Andrews Valuation Roll 1899–1903.

MacAndrew, Robert
St Andrews. Valuation Roll 1895–1899.

McDonald, Charles
North Berwick. Voters Roll 1898–1907.

McDonald, Walter (1836–   )
See List A.

The McEwan Family
See page 100.

McGregor, John (1862–   )
See List A.

Mackay, Donald
North Berwick. Voters Roll 1898–1907.

MacLeod, Angus
Leith. Edinburgh & Leith P.O.D. 1886–93.

McNicoll, Duncan
Aberdeen 1907, '11, '15. *Slaters*.

Manderson, Alexander (1813–1891)
See List A.

Martin & Kirkaldy
Edinburgh. A. Kirkaldy (1860–1934). Golf Professional at St Andrews.

Martin, Robert (1855–1917)
St Andrews. Valuation Roll 1894–96. Census 1891. *Nisbet* 1906 – clubmaker to Tom Morris.

Mayne, William
See List A.

Miller & Taylor
Glasgow. *Slaters* 1911.

Miln, Henry (–1755)
See List A.

Mills (aluminium clubs)
See List A.

The Morris Family
See page 114.

Muir, John
Edinburgh. Trade entry 1891, '94, '95.

Munro, Alexander (1796–1847)
See List A.

Neaves, Charles (1871–   )
Leven. *Slaters* 1896. *Nisbet* 1906.

Neil, Robert (1873–   )
Troon. 1891 Census.

Neilson, Robert (1719–1767)
See List A.

Neilson, Robert
Musselburgh. *Slaters* 1903, '07, '11, '15. Clubmaker with W. Park Jr. at Musselburgh.

The Park Family
See page 110.

The Patrick Family
See page 108.

Paxton, Peter (1859–   )
See List A.

Paxton, James B. (1874–   )
See List A.

Pett, James (*c*.1627)
See List A.

Philp, Hugh (1782–1856)
See page 96 (Philp-Forgan family)

Porteous, William M.
Glasgow. *Slaters* 1911.

Purves, Robert
North Berwick. Valuation Roll 1896–1906.

Redpath & Co
Glasgow. *Slaters* 1911.

Rintoul, Thomas
1871–1926. St Andrews.
Valuation Roll 1898–1903, then
1910/11.

Robertson, David
Kinghorn 1915.

Rourke, T.
Musselburgh. Musselburgh
Directory 1903.

St Andrew Golf Co Ltd
Glasgow. *Slaters* 1911.

Sandison, Ludovic (1825–1884)
See List A.

Sayers, Ben (1857–1924)
See List A.

Scott, A. H. (1875–   )
See List A.

Scott, Richard
St Andrews. Valuation 1895–97,
then 1910.

Simmons, Henry G.
North Berwick. Voters Roll 1908–
10.

Simpson, Robert (1862–1923)
See List A.

Simpson, Archie (1866–   )
See List A.

Slazengers Ltd
See List A.

Smart, James (1871–   )
St Andrews. Census 1891.
Valuation Roll 1893–97.

Smith, James & Son (1834–   )
Monifieth/Dundee. *Slaters* 1896 '&
Son' *Slaters* 1900, '03, '07, '11, 15.

Smith, T.
Musselburgh. 1903 Musselburgh
Directory.

Somerville, Andrew (1861–   )
Dunbar. Census 1891. Ardeer Golf
Club, Ayrshire. *Slaters* 1907.

Spalding, A. G. & Bros
See page 133 and List A.

Spinks, Charles
Leith. *Golf* 18.9.1891 records
special machine for turning out
shafts of golf clubs, p.147.
Illustration of his sawmill
'Established 1810'. *Golf* 4.5.1894,
p.148 says he has a golf material
factory at Pirrie St, Leith. He
seems, in fact, to have been a mass
producer of shafts for the trade.

Standard Golf Company, The
See List A.

Stark, William
St Andrews. Valuation Roll 1901–
03, 1910/11. *Slaters* 1900.

Stephen, Alexander
St Andrews. Valuation Roll 1892–
1903, 1910/11.

Stewart, John (1864–1947)
St Andrews. Valuation Roll 1896–
1900. Census 1891.

Strachan, James
Leith. *Slaters* 1893.

Strath, Andrew (1836–1868)
See List A.

Strath, David (1840–1879)
See List A.

Strath, George (   )
See List A.

Tait, Alexander (1865–   )
Musselburgh. 1891 Census.
Musselburgh Directory 1903.

Taylor, J. H. (1871–1963)
See List A.

Thistle Golf Co Ltd
Glasgow. *Slaters* 1911.

Thomson, J. (1865–1939)
St Andrews. Valuation Roll 1892–
1902, then 1910/11.

Tingay, Albert (1869–   )
St Andrews. Mentioned as a
clubmaker of Tom Morris's,
particularly expert on wooden

putters. Club in Spalding Museum.
Recorded also as a good golfer.

Tullock, John
Glasgow. *Slaters* 1911. P.O.D. 1899
and ballmaker.

Vardon, Harry (1870–1937)
See List A.

Waggot, Thomas P.
Musselburgh, Aberlady. *Slaters*
1896, 1907, '11, '15. He had a shop
at Aberlady.

Walker, James
Edinburgh. Trade entry 1885, '86,
'87. *Slaters* 1882, '84.

Walker, John
Earlsferry. Valuation Roll 1911,
1913.

Walker, Thomas (1842–   )
St Andrews. Valuation Roll 1886–
1902.

Waters, John (1876–1948)
St Andrews. Valuation Roll 1900–
01, then 1910/11.

Watson, James W.
Monifieth, Dundee. *Slaters* 1900.

Watt, William (1867–   )
Perth. *Slaters* 1896. North Berwick.
Census 1891. Club in Spalding
Golf Museum.

Watters, Henry
St Andrews. Valuation Roll 1900–
02.

White, Jack (1873–1949)
See List A.

Whitelaw, Peter (1876–   )
Musselburgh. 1891 Census.

Wilson, James (1803–1866)
See List A.

Wilson, Robert Black
St Andrews. Valuation Roll 1895–
1903.

Yeoman, Wm.
St Andrews. Valuation Roll 1894–
98.

The clubmakers in the USA

From the time golf started in America in 1888, the clubmakers took just about ten years to establish their own factories and to begin 'taking coals to Newcastle' by exporting to Britain. This will surprise many people but their astonishing success was only equalled by the enthusiasm with which their nation took up the game and the speed with which golf equipment became big business.

The demise of the craftsmen clubmakers in Scotland has already been discussed. When the boom in golf arrived they were ill-adapted to change to the role of mass producers, and enterprising as the Scots were abroad, at home none was prepared to put any capital into making golf equipment on a big scale. Instead, the clubmakers and golfers emigrated to make their fortunes.

Raw materials had already become a problem. Hickory had been imported from the USA for many years, but now persimmon had come into use for clubheads and this also had to be imported. The Americans had direct access to both, and they undoubtedly selected and matured the wood better. They then added an entirely new dimension to clubmaking – the scientific approach, coupled with mass production methods. They enlisted from Britain the men who could design clubs and make them by new methods with first-class material. Before long they were also making iron clubheads using steel by means of a new method of 'drop forging' – with a huge hammer which forged the head in one piece, and achieved a degree of accuracy in reproduction not previously possible.

By the end of the century the phrase 'machine-made' clubs was being bandied about – but all this meant was that the hard work had been taken out of clubmaking and the rough-hewn heads were still to be finished by hand. A. G. Spalding & Bros. even had to put out an advertisement in America saying that all their woods were hand-made and 'that there was no machine in existence that could possibly make a golf club'.

Throughout the 1890s the leading British clubmakers were doing an increasing export business to the USA and the British Empire and the British home markets were expanding also. The Americans stepped in and mass-produced good clubs for export to the UK, having almost no home market of their own but having first access to the best materials in their own country. Three leading firms made golf clubs, both woods and irons, prior to 1900. These were:

1　Bridgeport Gun & Implement Co., Bridgeport, Conn.
2　Crawford, McGregor and Canby, Dayton, Ohio.
3　A. G. Spalding & Bros., Greenwich, Conn.

It is controversial which of these was first, or best, and they have been listed here in alphabetical order.

1　*Bridgeport Gun & Implement Co.*
Records have shown that this company started clubmaking around 1896/7. At that time Willie Dunn Jr. and his nephew, John Duncan Dunn, were in partnership together at Dobbs Ferry, New York, and

Bridgeport Gun & Implement Co.
Mark on all-in-one club.

Bridgeport Gun & Implement Co.
Cleekmark.

first of all Willie Dunn Jr. became the designer for BGI and in 1898 John Duncan Dunn became their manager. It is probable that the Dunns' business at Dobbs Ferry was then closed down. At any rate, thereafter, the famous Dunn 'all-in-one' club made from a single piece of hickory was being made and sold by BGI (see p. 108 of this chapter). The BGI iron clubheads were made by William Bros. of Brooklyn, N.Y. and were shafted and finished in Bridgeport. The initials BGI were in script.

In wooden clubs they made heads 'in the rough' using a copying lathe and they also used lathes for fining down the hickory shafts and machines for making the groove for the lead and for the horn. Machines were also used for making the hickory pegs used to hold the horn in place. They used a conveyor-belt technique so that the wood came in at one end and the finished club with a grip on appeared at the other. That they were a successful company is borne out by a statement in *Golf Illustrated* of 17th November 1899 which refers to the BGI as doing one of the largest trades in golf clubs and balls in the USA. Despite this apparent success story they closed in 1906–7 for reasons that are not evident. Their iron clubs are rare in the USA now, probably because the firm existed for only a few years. Their 'all-in-one' wooden clubs, which were only a part of their wooden-club production, are extremely rare. See also the cleekmakers' marks in Chapter 6.

2   *Crawford, McGregor and Canby & Co.*
This firm began life in 1829 as a maker of shoe lasts and became a large manufacturer owning its own forests and blockmills. In 1896 there was a depression in the shoe-last business and in that year Robert White, master cleekmaker from St Andrews, came to Dayton with a 'set' of his handforged irons. He met Mr W. H. Crawford, head of the firm, and introduced him to golf. Crawford took to the game with enthusiasm and when later in the same year he broke the shaft of his driver, he decided to try and get it replaced in his own factory instead of suffering the inconvenience of having it sent back to Scotland. He took it to his chief engineer, Mr George Mattern. Mattern was interested, not only in repairing the shaft but in the wood of which the head was constructed and suggested that persimmon, a tough wood from which shoe lasts were made, would be better than the beechwood which was then in use. They concentrated first on making clubheads of persimmon and did not go in for shafts. Because so few Americans played golf at this time their main business was exporting to the British Isles, and heads were shipped all ready for splicing to the shaft. By 1897 they were making shafts also and very shortly after were making complete clubs. In the spring of 1898 they produced socket-head clubs and were advertising that they made clubs 'From tree to tee'. They employed a man from St Andrews to supervise the forging of iron heads and he was in charge for a number of years. They also established a private golf course and allowed their employees to play. In 1896 they exported 28,000 clubheads to the UK and by 1900

were exporting 100,000 complete clubs to the UK. The wooden clubs had the name on them: the iron clubs a mark like that of Condie of St Andrews, i.e. a rose and on some also an arrow similar to Anderson of Anstruther.

A look at the pre-World War I catalogues shows at once how sophisticated they were in presenting their models, with complete measurements for each club including the loft in degrees. From the earliest times they settled on the brand name 'J. MacGregor' and so it has been ever since. It has been suggested that he was John McGregor, clubmaker of St. Andrews, originally employed by Forgans (see ill. p. 98) who went to the USA but returned after a comparatively short stay there. This awaits definite confirmation.

Guaranteed handforged par irons, from the McGregor catalogue. (Left) XC Driving Mashie, (Centre) XM Mid Iron, (Right) Driver.

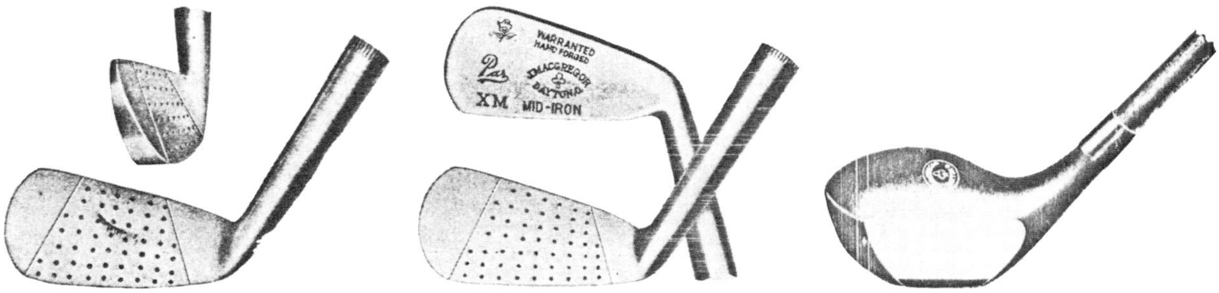

Model	Depth of Blade inches	Length of Blade inches	Loft of Blade inches	Weight of Club ounces	Lie of Club degrees	Length of Club inches
XA Driving Iron, beveled heel	1⅜	3⅛	⅝	14¾	55	40
XB Driving Cleek, short compact blade	1 5/16	3	⅜	14½	54	40
XK Driving Cleek, long narrow blade	1¼	3¼	3/16	14¼	57	39
XC Driving Mashie, medium blade	[illegible]	3	½	14¾	55	39½
XB Mid Iron, straight back, heavy weight	[illegible]	3⅝	¾	15¾	57	39
XM Mid Iron, standard model	[illegible]	3⅛	⅞	14½	56	38½

3 *A. G. Spalding & Brothers*

In 1892 this firm were importing golf clubs from the UK when Mr Julian Curtis, a director, went abroad and brought $500 worth of golf clubs back to the USA. At that time the firm considered this was more clubs than they would sell in a lifetime. Curtis and his brother, together with a Mr Freeman, had a 4-hole course built and started using some of the clubs, much to the amusement of their friends. In 1893 there were enough enthusiasts to form a small Club, destined to become the Greenwich Country Club. By 1896 Spaldings were making golf clubs and one of their early specialties was the Harry Vardon set of clubs being reproductions of those which he designed. In 1900 they paid Vardon to come to the USA and play a series of exhibition matches, a tour which was a great success. The cleekmaker's mark in the earlier irons was an anvil, in the drop-forged irons that came in a little later, a hammer. The authors have learned from American sources that all Spalding irons in America, in addition to the anvil mark, were stamped 'Dysart – Fife'.

That these three firms were an outstanding success in the golf world is due to the fact that, in the first place, they used only the best materials, properly seasoned. The wood exported to the UK was not the best American wood and, on arrival in the UK, was kiln-dried in less than three months and left brittle by the process. However beautifully handmade it might be, the resulting club was often second-class because of the faulty wood. The hickory used in America was specially selected by experts who picked out only the best trees on the farm. The trees were marked and cut down only when the sap was in the ground. The selected trees would then be cut into square laths, roughly the size of a golf shaft, and air-dried for two years before being used. For heads, persimmon was specially selected and seasoned over a long period of time, the moisture being dried out of the blocks by a special drying process which got rid of the resin in the wood and left the wood cells with air in them. In the second place they produced large numbers of rough-shaped clubheads, all the same, being produced from a single master model by the use of a copying lathe. Machines were also used for cutting the back of the head to take the lead, the sole to take the horn, and even the wooden pegs used to hold the horn in place were machine-made. The final touches were done by hand. It is interesting that the copying lathe and other machines used were simply improvements on machines used in England for many years. Thirdly, the American manufacturers were prepared to spend money on sales promotion, the classic example being Messrs A. G. Spalding's contract with Vardon who was engaged to spend three months in the USA every year for three years at £900 per year, playing exhibition matches and promoting golf equipment. He had a great success. As a result of American enthusiasm for the game and similar promotional schemes the Americans, with great rapidity, developed a large home market.

Cann & Taylor were the only British firm to manufacture in the USA at that time, although Slazenger and Willie Park both had businesses selling golf equipment in New York.

Chapter 5
Wooden Clubs

In order to understand something of the sort of people who made clubs and balls in the middle or latter half of the nineteenth century, it is useful to have some knowledge of the various categories of club servants that existed at that time. The arrangements were referred to briefly by Horace Hutchinson in the book *Badminton Golf* published in 1892. He states: 'There are a certain number of clubmakers and smiths who forge iron heads, and others who only make golf balls, who have no pretension to be golfers.'

There were three classes of people who derived a living from golf at any sizeable Golf Club.

1 *The Keeper of the Green*
This title, rather more grandiloquent that that of a mere greenkeeper, was quite justifiable for he was an important man. He received an annual salary from the golf club. This was given him so that he might look after the course, arrange the tees and cope with the organisation of the caddies. He was nearly always allowed a workshop in which he could repair or make clubs and might well employ several men who were apprentices. Gibson at Westward Ho! in 1880 had five or six men at any one time and Willie Fernie at Troon had nineteen or twenty men somewhat later in the century. The clubs were made or repaired entirely by hand and it was not until 1890–1900 that certain mechanical methods came to be employed, notably the use of copying lathes which were machine-driven (see Chapter 4 for details on this). But, to return to the Keeper of the Green; he also had control of several people outside his shop, such as those who could mow the grass, rake the bunkers, etc.

2 *The Professionals*
Under the Keeper of the Green also, but only partly under control, by threat of reporting misconduct to the Secretary, would be one or more professional players. They made a living by playing games with amateurs, for which they were paid. Their rate of pay was usually 7s 6d a day by playing two rounds or 3s 6d a day by caddying for two rounds for, if they were not required to play, they made some money on the side by caddying. They also made a certain amount of money by teaching those with whom they played or for whom they caddied, something of the rudiments of the game. Some were, in fact, engaged as sort of body servants, being paid £1 a week with a free breakfast at the master's house, but having also to black his boots and look after his clubs. They sometimes made a shilling or two on bets. Whisky and golf were their principal interests and generally speaking they were rather feckless, uneducated men with but little sense of responsibility; only a few were suitable for promotion to the responsible and well paid job of Keeper of the Green. They did not make much money and were dependent on the whim of those who asked them to play; there was little or no work to be had in bad weather and therefore little work to be had in the winter, and in consequence of this, many such men had rather sporadic jobs on the side, working as stone-breaker, mason, shoemaker, weaver, slater, etc.

3   The Caddies

The third category comprised the caddies, who might be aged men or young boys or professional players who had not at that moment got a job. They were not particularly well dressed and many of them in the early days had no shoes. They usually wore the cast-off clothing of those for whom they regularly caddied. At many courses they were issued with a club badge or a brass half-band to fit on the arm, which badge or band could be removed for misbehaviour reported to the Keeper of the Green.

The important man of these three groups was the Keeper of the Green who had many duties, a certain amount of salary and was able to make money by repairing and making golf clubs. Many Keepers of the Green were only known locally and had no great fame outside their own club, frequently having no great pretentions to being good golfers.

The days when the professional became a more important man came later, when tournaments and exhibition matches began to be

Sketch of a caddy, c. 1875. Note the marked preponderance of wooden clubs. No shoes or stockings; no golf bag.

played more frequently. Towards the end of the nineteenth century men appeared who, because of prize money and enough tournaments, exhibition matches and challenge matches, could make a living by their prowess with a golf club. So the playing professional became a more important man and the greenkeeper descended in the scale; by the early part of the twentieth century, the professional had a shop and made and repaired golf clubs, and the Keeper of the Green, whose sole job was to look after the greens and bunkers and ensure that the course was in good condition, became a mere 'greenkeeper'. It is interesting that in recent years the greenkeeper has begun to return to a position of considerable importance. This is not in the same sense that he was a Keeper of the Green before, but because the continued and relentless pressure to keep golf courses in good condition throughout the year has meant that the head greenkeeper must be a very knowledgeable and responsible man and in consequence his salary and general terms of office have improved very considerably.

Old Tom Morris was probably the most famous Keeper of the Green that ever was. He was Keeper of the Green at Prestwick for fourteen years, and subsequently returned to St Andrews and was Keeper of the Green there. He was also, as it happened, a great golfer and a considerable clubmaker, but there were many other Keepers of the Green who made no pretensions to being golfers and therefore names sometimes appear on old clubs which have little or no meaning outside the immediate locality.

It has been stated that the Keeper of the Green usually had a workshop and some apprentices, and that there he made and repaired wooden clubs. The latter activity required quite a lot of work, for example, re-gripping clubs, repairing cracked heads and cracked shafts or replacing them, replacing worn horn inserts and replacing leads or parts of leads which were damaged. These activities probably constituted the bulk of his work but, in addition to this, of course, he made new wooden clubs as well. In those far-off times each club was very individual, and if it were severely damaged, it could not readily be replaced by another club with the same feel, so that constant repairs and renovations were required throughout its life in order to avoid such damage that the player might have to acquire a new club. The care of wooden clubs was therefore of great concern to their owner. The most important part of the club was the shaft. The other parts were the grip and the head. The relationship between the three parts was complex and gave to the whole an entirely individual feel which was highly characteristic to the player and which would have enabled him, blindfolded, to identify his own club from any other. If a grip became worn it could be replaced, but the new grip must be of the same thickness as the old and however carefully matched, the club would feel slightly different after a change of grip. The weight of the head was of importance because it was matched to the spring of the shaft and any alteration in the weight of the head would lead, not only to a difference in the weight of the club, but also in its general balance and in the general 'springiness' of the shaft. Nevertheless, it was possible to replace one head with another, provided the second was of the same weight and approximately the same shape, and to achieve a reasonably similar feel to the original club, although the club would never be quite the same. But the shaft could not be changed with any hope of achieving the same feel because of the minute differences of grain and spring in different pieces of wood. In the shaft, of course, of great importance was the site of the whip or spring which would, in drivers, be about 7 inches above the scare or splice. To achieve the right point of whip or spring required, the shaft had to be fined down with sandpaper, by hand, until the feel of the club was right. As this feel depended on the weight of the head and also to a certain extent on its shape, the final sandpapering of the shaft, when a club was being made, took place after the head had been fixed to the shaft.

The marrying of these two components to make a club with a

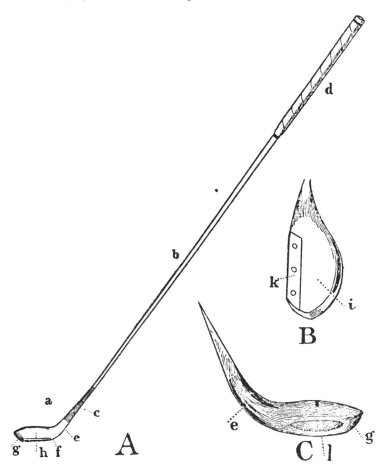

FIG. 1.—A WOODEN CLUB

A, the whole club; *B*, the 'sole'; *C*, back view of the head; *a*, the head; *b*, the shaft; *c*, the 'scare,' or part where head and shaft are fastened and bound together; *d*, the leather grip or handle; *e*, the neck; *f*, the heel; *g*, the toe or nose; *h*, the face; *i*, the sole; *k*, the bone; *l*, the lead.

Parts of a spliced (or 'scared') wooden club (reproduced from *The Game of Golf*, W. Park Jr., 1896).

certain 'right' feel was completely empirical and only to be learned by long experience and right judgement. In this respect, above all, the clubmaker was able to demonstrate his skill in the making of a very highly individual club.

Of course the customer had some say in the matter. If he were a beginner or very inexpert and if he were wise, he took the clubmaker's advice, because the latter with his experience would be able to advise the player, having regard to his height and general muscular build, what sort of club would suit him best. If the customer were an expert golfer, then he and the clubmaker would between them evolve the right club for him. There might be much coming and going and trials of the club, with subsequent small alterations in the shape of the head, the amount of the lead in the back of the head, alterations of depth and loft in the face, fining down of the shaft at certain places and alterations in the thickness of the grip: the final result was a highly individual club suited to the player. Small wonder, therefore, that such clubs needed to be looked after properly and to be kept in a reasonable state of repair, so that they might continue in service a long time. Small wonder also that the clubs had names and not numbers and often, in fact, a nickname coined by its owner.

We have all heard, in later years, of Robert Jones's putter, Calamity Jane, but many years before that names for nearly all the clubs were coined. Willie Park Jr. had a wooden putter 'Old Pawky',[1] Allan Robertson, the feather ball champion of Scotland in the early and middle nineteenth century, had names for all his clubs. One was called 'The Doctor', another 'Sir Robert Peel', while his iron was called 'The Frying Pan' ('Thraw-cruik').[2] Captain Molesworth of Westward Ho!, one of the early members of the Golf Club, in 1864 only carried three clubs – driver, lofting iron and putter, called respectively Faith, Hope and Charity.[3] A famous legal gentleman at a slightly later date called his niblick Faith because, as he was wont to explain, 'Faith can move mountains'.[4]

Care and attention by the owner for his clubs was always necessary but more so with the advent of the gutta ball, which was hard and tended to crack the clubface. These were then repaired with leather or vulcanite and, in time, some clubs were made initially with leather or composition faces. Willie Park Jr. commented: 'Leather faces were originally devised for repairing clubs that had become damaged by wear and tear but they are now frequently put into quite new heads. A leather face put into a new club helps to make it last better.'[5]

The owner of such fragile weapons was not able to practise in the way the modern golfer practises. Not for him three hours and 500 shots on the practice ground. If he did, the shaft would lose its liveliness, the clubface might be damaged and, in fact, the whole club would be ruined. Later in the nineteenth century a good playing professional had two sets of clubs. The really good ones, that he personally liked, were kept for the important occasions and the reserve set for friendly games, exhibitions and generally less

[1] This putter is in the Woking Golf Club Collection.
[2] Robert Browning, *A History of Golf*, 1955, p.148.
[3] Ibid., p.148.
[4] Ibid., p.149
[5] W. Park Jnr., *The Game of Golf*, 1896, p.32.

important use. Among amateurs, particularly those who were rather more expert, it was customary to carry at least a second driver in case the first one broke.

Because of the need to preserve golf clubs, much advice concerning the care of clubs was included in books and articles about golf. Willie Park Jr. gives this advice:

'The keeping of clubs in order is a matter to which a good share of attention has been directed and it is frequently recommended that the shaft and head should be kept slightly oiled. If the clubs are properly cared for and not kept in too damp or dry a place, I do not advise oiling as I find it is apt to cause cracks in the wood. Before a club leaves the maker's hands it receives a coating of oil and varnish and this ought to last for a long time.'[6]

He goes on to say that a touch of oil, if the shafts are a bit dry, will render them less brittle and recommends re-varnishing if this begins to wear off. He continues:

'A really fine club should not be used on a wet day if it can be avoided as not only the head will probably be ruined, but the shaft also. I have seen some splendid shafts with just the right spring in them rendered wobbly and useless through their getting thoroughly soaked by playing in wet weather.'

James Braid:

'This question of the selection of the shaft is really one of enormous importance for it is infinitely easier to get a head to suit you exactly and to be, to all intents and purposes, perfect, than it is to get a perfect shaft. The latter, indeed, is a comparatively rare thing.'[7]

Horace Hutchinson:

'A good club deserves good treatment like a good servant. It is ruination to wooden clubs to use them on a grassy course after rain and a "scratch pack" kept in reserve to save the better sort will be useful in these circumstances.'[8]

Vardon, writing about the care of clubs:

'More often than not, the shaft is never given a thought and yet a perfect shaft that just suits the man who has to play with it is one of the rarest and most difficult things to discover . . . It needs constant care and attention. It should be your invariable practice when you have been out on a wet day, first to see that your shafts are properly dried and then to give them a thorough good oiling with linseed oil, applied with a rag kept especially for the purpose.'

[6]Ibid. pp.47–48.
[7]James Braid, *Advanced Golf,* 1908, p.20.
[8]Horace Hutchinson, *Golf and Golfers,* 1900, p.289.

Vardon then goes on to advise that the shafts should be oiled but that one must be very careful never to get the oil on the face of the clubs as it might open up the grain.[9] This is advice which has been reiterated by a number of other experts.

In similar vein there is advice about not playing on frosty days because to strike the very hard ground might damage both head and shaft.

When one considers that it could be ruination to one's clubs to play on a wet day (and it must be remembered that in the days of the feather ball, the ball became a sodden mass of feathers as well), that it was not advisable to play on a frosty day, that striking the ball in the heel of the club might well fracture the neck in the days of the gutty ball, and that, moreover, the club required constant attention, drying, oiling, etc. and when one then considers the number of wet and frosty days in Scotland in any one year, it is clear that the golf-playing Scot had an enthusiasm bordering on the fanatical for his chosen game. These facts also underline the advantages of East Scotland in the early days of golf, where links-type courses abounded and the climate was noticeably drier than that of West Scotland. The fact that sea-level links afforded golf less susceptible to frost and snow and that even if there were rain, the water would quickly drain through the sandy subsoil, were all good enough reasons why the East of Scotland should have seen more golf than other parts. Added to this it is clear that those who had money and leisure were in a position to pick the better days for playing golf, and as Edinburgh was the fashionable centre of leisured Scots society at that time, it was natural that many of the earliest links were situated within easy reach of the city.

Materials used in the making of wooden clubs

Kincaid, 1687, said that the shafts were made of hazel. He does not mention the composition of the clubheads at this time. Some early clubheads were made of 'thorncuts'. The thorncuts, which were probably used by James McEwan (1747–1800), are said to have been made out of small 'cuts' from hedge thorns.

> 'These thorns were planted horizontally on sloping banks, with the result that the stem of the tree or bush grew at an angle at the root, giving a piece of wood with a natural bend for the neck or the head. The 'cuts' were split with wedges through the centre, the back was roughly shaped and then trimmed with a handsaw, and the turnup of the 'scare' (the prolongation of the neck to be spliced to the shaft) was treated in the same way.
>
> These thornheads, often stamped with a thistle, were neither varnished nor stained, but instead were rubbed over with red keel which emphasized the grain of the wood and gave a beautiful finish. This substance, the composition of which is unknown to us, was used on clubs prior to 1820, when resin varnish came into use.'

[9]Harry Vardon, *The Complete Golfer*, 1905, p.50.

Although McEwan and Philp used the thorncuts, which were a very hard wood, other makers used different woods, the principal woods being apple and pear.[10] The noticeable quality of all these three woods was that they were very hard and in connection with other woods George Cann has some interesting facts to relate.

The quotation goes as follows:

> 'The great difficulty which golf clubmakers have always experienced has been the obtaining of good wood suitable for the purpose of headmaking. Beech, which is more used than any other wood, grows in great abundance both in England and Scotland, but notwithstanding the amount obtainable it is exceedingly difficult to get it really good. A great deal depends on the manner in which the tree has been grown; if in some sheltered spot where plenty of nourishment has been afforded, it will generally be very soft, but, if in some exposed quarter, where growth has been slow and difficult from the force of the prevailing winds and the lack of soil, it will then be hard and durable. Under the latter circumstances no wood can be more suitable for making into golf clubheads, for while it is hard enough to wear well, there is not that stony hardness, which is sometimes found in holly, hornbeam, rockwood, etc.
>
> Apple is also often used but being a more brittle wood than beech it is not easy to foretell what will happen to it. If it stands for the first few rounds it will probably last for years, but with rough usage it is very liable to break in the neck. This is not so plentiful a wood as beech as the trees do not grow very large. The hardness of applewood does not depend so much on where it has been grown as is the case with beech. It is nearly always hard but the sour apple trees are the hardest. There is a great deal of waste with this wood in cutting it up as the trees are so small. It is also very treacherous to work as there are often little flaws in it which cannot be seen at first, one of which may, however, appear in the neck of the club just when it is nearly finished and, of course, labour in that case, has been spent in vain. Thorn, which is also sometimes used, is very like apple in all respects.'[11]

It must be remembered that this account by George Cann was written in about 1890 at a time when the gutty was at its zenith. In the days of the feather ball, which was a relatively soft and resilient ball, a hard and unyielding wood such as thorn or applewood would do very well, but in the later days of the gutty ball which was as hard as a stone, it was necessary to use a wood with a little more give in it, partly to lessen the shock of impact on the player, and partly because the impact of a composite gutty ball on very hard and rather brittle wood, was liable to cause cracks to appear in the wood, and occasionally to cause dissolution of the ball as well. So applewood, thornwood, etc. were used with the feather ball, but gave way to beech, which had suitable qualities and was available in large

[10]Sir G. Campbell, *History of Golf in Britain*, p.75.
[11]J. H. Taylor in *Golf and Golfers*, 1900, p.259.

quantities, when the gutty ball came into being. Beech continued to be the wood for clubheads almost until the turn of the century. In 1896 the USA began exporting persimmon clubheads into the UK and, by the end of the century, were exporting 100,000 clubheads a year. Persimmon wood, which was like applewood, was easily the best wood for clubheads and it rapidly took over from beech.

W. Park Jr., who was a man of inventive turn of mind, was also trying to make wooden heads less frail, and stated (1896):

'Complaints about the frailty of all wooden clubs have been frequently made to me. I endeavour to manufacture a clubhead which, while able to stand more strain than a beechhead, would yet not be inferior in driving power, and for some time past I have been making clubheads of wood compressed and otherwise treated to make it more endurable. In this club the wood forming the head is bent so that the grain runs down the neck and along the head, making it practically unbreakable and, in fact, I guarantee that with ordinary wear and tear such heads are indestructible.'[12]

It would seem that Park, apart from treating the wood, the method of which he does not specify, in using a club with the grain going down the neck and bent into the head, is reverting to a method that had been found nearly one hundred years previously in the use of thorncuts which had the grain similarly arranged. With the advent of the softer rubber-cored ball in 1904, there was less need to avoid damage to the neck and face of the club: plain persimmon heads did very well.

Even so, the changeover to persimmon was not instantaneous and as late as 1911, Jack White, of Sunningdale Golf Club in Surrey, was advertising 'Beautifully grained beech heads, with specially selected split hickory shafts. Recommended by first class players.' (*Golf Monthly*, August 1911.) Persimmon was a hardwood which would stand up to the strain of hitting the gutta percha ball. It remained eminently suited to hit the softer rubber-cored ball. Even so, during the years of the gutta and particularly of the composite gutty, it became the habit to introduce an insert into the face. These inserts were of a bewildering variety (see Chapter 8 on Patents.)

Materials for wooden club shafts

In the time of Kincaid it appears that hazel was the wood used for the wooden club shaft, but in the first half of the nineteenth century ash was the wood in common use for club shafts. It was supplanted by hickory from America.

There are rumours in golfing history that the first hickory to arrive came from Russia, as ballast, in a ship which arrived at Dundee. There seems to be no written record that this, in fact, was the case and it could be that this is one of the interesting, but not entirely factual, tales about early golf and its implements. What seems much more certain is that hickory began to arrive from America in about the 1850s for use as axe-handles, pit props, rake handles, etc.

[12]W. Park Jnr., *The Game of Golf*, 1896, p.32.

Robert Forgan is popularly supposed to have been the first clubmaker to use hickory for club shafts. Curiously, the exact date at which all this occurred is not known but J. B. Farnie in 1857 states unequivocally:

> 'The timber best adapted to driving shafts of all descriptions is red hickory. This wood is peculiarly tough yet at the same time possesses a powerful spring without the drawback of too great flexibility, qualities which give it an infinite superiority over ash, which is generally too supple and not nearly so strong as hickory.'[13]

It would seem, therefore, that hickory shafts must have arrived in the early 1850s. Certainly by 1890, all golf clubs are referred to as having hickory shafts and the ash shaft seems to have disappeared entirely. The hickory came from the Tennessee hickory belt in America and was most peculiarly suited to golf club shafts, being not too heavy a wood and having a very resilient and steely spring with a minimum of torsion and being also, very importantly, impervious to the weather if properly seasoned and treated before use. Willie Park states:

> 'The words, "good shaft" have a world of meaning. Here are some of the requisites. The wood must be light in actual weight. The grain must run straight down the stick; it must be supple and yet not wobbly and have a fine steely spring without being too stiff. Throughout all its length, gently tapering from the leather grip to the scare.'[14]

Hickory was sometimes described as being white or brown or red but apparently they all had the same qualities: there was no doubt that split hickory was better than sawn hickory, that is, hickory split with an axe, along its grain, and not cut with a saw. The hickory must come from the mid-country in Tennessee. Those laths of wood that came from too far down the hill were soft and not springy and known frequently as 'swamp hickory' whereas those that came from the highest parts of the hill were rather too brittle.

An old friend of ours, Jack Gibson, son of the late Charles Gibson, professional at Westward Ho! and himself a clubmaker and professional of many years' standing, had, at one time, a factory in America in the hickory belt in Tennessee where he produced about 100,000 shafts a year and also, incidentally, the spokes for the wheels of Model T Fords. He said that it was possible to tell at a glance whether hickory came from too low or too high in the mountain. It was possible to tell, on slightly closer examination, whether the hickory had grown on a slope facing the sun or facing away from the sun and with care it was also possible to decide whether there had been a hard winter or not, in the year previously, up in the hills. The hickory was brought in by the 'hill-billies' of the local countryside and was cut into laths which were rectangular in cross-section and

[13] *The Golfer's Manual* by 'A Keen Hand', 1857.
[14] W. Park Jnr., *The Game of Golf*, 1896.

about one and a half inches square. They were subsequently fined down and rounded, entirely by hand, with scraper and sandpaper but later in the century, with the use of a lathe. The selection of the shaft to meet the requirements of the weight of the head and also having regard to the use to which the club was to be put, was a matter of difficulty and required considerable experience, and the late Miss Gibson, daughter of Charles Gibson of Westward Ho!, has told us how her father would take as many as twenty or thirty laths of wood, and sandpaper them down or use the lathe, and might well discard twenty shafts at a time before lighting on the right shaft for the club he had in mind.

The best shafts were of 'ring hickory', these being made from laths cut from the centre of the hickory tree where some of the grain had an appearance of a ring around the shaft: such shafts were said to be unbreakable.

Other woods used in shafts

Park points out that 'hickory is the right shaft': ash is quite good but too supple for anything but a light head, greenheart is too heavy for any clubs except for niblicks and for putters. Lemonwood or lancewood makes a good shaft but is somewhat heavy: it is particularly good for iron clubs having a very 'steely' quality and is not liable to warp.[15]

The grip

When there was a grip it was made of leather and in some of the earlier clubs this was, in fact, sheepskin, but later cowhide or horse was used. The grips of the earlier clubs were thick, as has already been mentioned. This was partly so that the club could be gripped in the palm of the hands rather than in the fingers and also to lessen the shock of hitting a rather hard and unresilient gutta golf ball (after 1848). Though grips were thick, this was not universally agreed as being the best idea and J. B. Farnie, in 1857, states quite emphatically that 'the leather grasp on the shaft should not be thick but raised a very little above the wood. Thus a wonderful command is obtained over the club which is in a manner lost when the golfer has to compass an unwieldy bundle of rind more resembling in shape the handle of a cricket bat than that of a slim and graceful play club.'[16] His reference to the rind is that this was the name given to the linen strips that were put on the shaft directly to go under the leather grip so as to make a general thickening. The strips were also sometimes called 'listings'. Some of the earliest clubs had no grips at all, the shaft presumably being sufficiently thick that they could be gripped satisfactorily without a grip being required.

Having discussed the materials of which golf clubs were made, it is logical to continue with a description of how golf clubs were made. The old wooden clubs being entirely of that material, it is obvious that a craftsman who started making these clubs needed to be an expert craftsman in wood. This is borne out by the history of many of the great clubmakers. The earliest McEwan in the middle of the eighteenth century was originally a joiner. Hugh Philp at the beginning of the nineteenth century originally was a 'wright'. At

[15]Ibid.
[16]*The Golfer's Manual* by 'A Keen Hand', 1857.

about the same time as Philp there were also Sandison and Munro in the Aberdeen area, and both these men also made fishing rods. The firm of R. Anderson & Sons in Princes Street, Edinburgh, about 1890, made golf clubs, but the other part of their business was making fishing rods.

These then were the sort of men who began to find an interest in making golf clubs when there were few Golf Clubs, i.e. associations of golfers who played on a links and organised their association such that they had a Keeper of the Green and caddies, etc.

Long before the Golf Clubs came into existence, people were playing golf and because they played golf, other people were making golf clubs for them and these sorts of trades produced men with that capability; if they found that they had a particular bent for it, they made rather more golf clubs and had less time for the other part of their usual activities but, no doubt, because the number of golfers was few and the demand for golf clubs not great at that time, they continued to ply their second trade as well, and it was only with the advent of more golfers and the formation of more Golf Clubs that it became worthwhile having a Keeper of the Green. No doubt this later generation of wooden clubmakers learnt the trade from the Keeper of the Green and possibly had no other occupation, being wooden clubmakers only. In some areas people with resource and a knowledge of wood often did many of their own repairs and even made their own golf clubs. One such person who is recorded is Mr Robert Duthie of Aberdeen. The Rev. T. D. Miller, writing in 1911 of Mr Duthie who was then 80,[17] and was speaking of fifty years before, makes, among others, the following points: that Mr Duthie had for long been a partner of the old firm of shippers and shipbuilders, John Duthie & Sons. Mr Duthie excelled not only in the game but in the handicraft of club- and ballmaking, and where there was no clubmaker at hand, the acquisition was a valuable one. The Rev. Miller goes on to point out that Mr Duthie had much to do with the introduction of gutta percha and the making of the first golf ball mould ever used north of the Tay: it seems that the gutta percha came as a gift from one of the Company Schooners from Batavia in 1857. He also goes on to say that for many years prior to the last decade of the nineteenth century, Aberdeen could not support a clubmaker. 'There were too many amateur experts engaged in the business.' In this, Mr Duthie's memory was at fault, because we have factual evidence that there were at least two clubmakers in Aberdeen at that time – Munro and Sandison (see the list of clubmakers). He mentions that Mr Duthie was responsible for sending his first consignment of hickory to Bob Dow, the Montrose clubmaker, and also helped the St Andrews professionals to obtain not only hickory but, from slaughtered sheep and oxen, leather for grips. No doubt there were many areas, probably Dornoch is typical of them, where golf had been played for many, many years before there was organised golf in the form of Golf Clubs and in consequence many of the local golfers made and repaired their own clubs and were quite independent of any

[17]'Memories of an Octagenarian', *Golf Illustrated*, 1911.

professional maker. It would seem, too, that much the same has happened in the Edinburgh area (see Chapter 4, page 93, Andrew Bailey's letter). How then, was a golf club made in the mid-nineteenth century and possibly for many years before that? Probably as good a description of the making of a wooden club as any is that which is given in Horace Hutchinson's book *Golf and Golfers* in a chapter by John Henry Taylor. John Henry Taylor, of course, never made a golf club, which he freely admits in his autobiography, and there is no doubt that the chapter was, in fact, written by his partner, Cann, who was a very expert clubmaker (see Chapter 5, Appendix 1 for details).

Although the simple scare/splice system seems to have been the accepted method of making a club, a method passed on from master to apprentice probably for over 250 years, in the nineteenth century there were experiments to alter this type of joint: one such was a combination scare and a form of mortice and tenon joint which we have seen in a wooden putter stamped H. Philp/Forgan and which therefore can be accurately dated as between 1852–56. The form of the joint is shown in the accompanying illustration. The joint is ingenious but would require a considerable craftsman to make it: the simple scare was so much simpler that few of these complicated joints were made.

Later in the century mechanisation began to appear. Machines were used to help the clubmaker. Probably Scott of Elie was the first

A putter stamped Philp/Forgan, i.e. made at about the time that Forgan began to take over the firm from Hugh Philp, 1852–56. The first view shows the whipping removed to reveal the joint, which appears from this angle to be a scared or spliced joint but with a further joint running forward at the lower end. The second view is of the head separated from the shaft, displaying the mortice joint. The third view shows the shaft separated from the head; on the right side, at the lower end is a long, 'fine' scare. The tongue of wood (unstained) which fits into the head mortice is well seen.

The same Philp/Forgan putter
restored. Note the long, narrow,
tongue-like mortice joint.

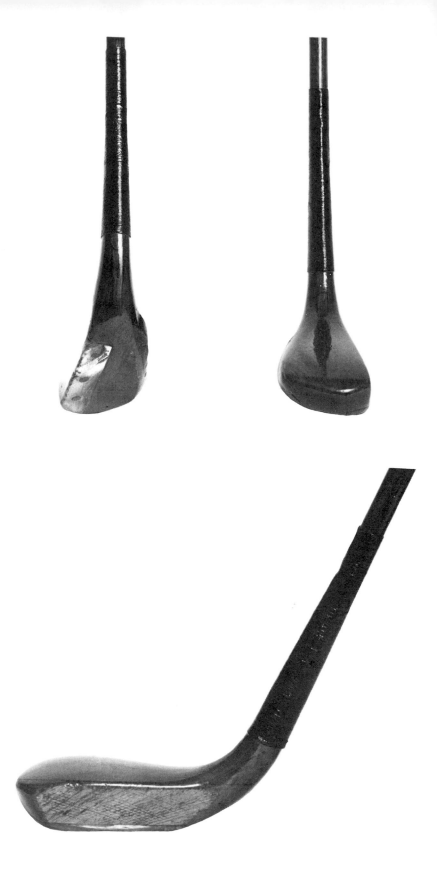

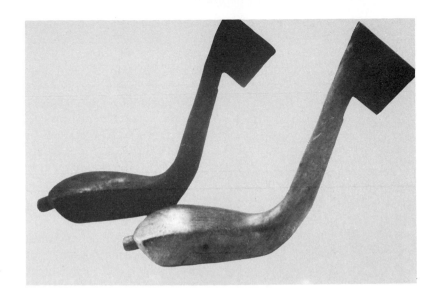

The clubhead in the foreground is the wooden model and that in the rear is the iron copy which enabled the copying lathe to reproduce clubheads in quantity from wooden blocks.

one to include some machinery in his factory, but Forgan certainly did the same thing and by the end of the century mechanisation had been introduced into the making of golf clubs (see Chapter 4). It will be noticed that John Henry Taylor in his article says that he sees nothing wrong in adding mechanisation to the making of golf clubs as long as the finish of the club is done by hand and that the rough shaping is better and more quickly done by machine (see Chapter 5, Appendix 1). The wooden clubs made by the mechanical process were socket-headed clubs; the days of the scared heads were over. Socket-headed clubs appeared in great numbers at the beginning of the century and from this time the scared-head clubs steadily disappeared (see Chapters 4 and 8 for further details). Among the 'old hands' who had played for many years with scared-head clubs, there were sounds of disapproval and even talk of increased torsion at the neck, but these criticisms were soon silenced and the socket-head clubs have remained ever since that time. Nevertheless, the great Walter Hagen won his first American Open with a scared-head club in 1914. He used it in many events and exhibitions and used it again when he won the American Open in 1919; he was still using it when he won the British Open in 1922. He retired the club in the following year because of age, but was so fond of it that he had three copies made.

In an article in *Golf Illustrated* of 1909,[18] there is a discussion on the changes that have taken place in the characteristics of golf clubs in the last twenty or thirty years, and it is pointed out here that the greatest change is in the shape of the wooden clubs, that their heads which now are broad and squat, were at one time long and narrow shapes as made by Forgan, McEwan, Philp and old Tom Morris and other makers of the period. The author states:

'There can be no doubt that the old clubs were more graceful in appearance. As a general rule also the shafts of modern clubs

[18] 'Clubs Old and New', by C. Gardner Smith, *Golf Illustrated*, 10th Sept., 1909. An Aberdonian, a golfer and a writer on golf who was well known in his day.

are thicker and not so tapered and they are in consequence much stiffer than the old playclubs. The suppleness or give in the shafts occurred 3–4 inches above the whipping in the old clubs, but in the modern clubs, if the shaft has any give at all it is much further up and, as a rule, is more evenly distributed throughout the shaft. The old clubs were made for the swinging blow whereas the modern ones are adapted more for hitting and suppleness has therefore given way to steeliness. Another great change which is also pointed out has been the deepening of the faces of all the wooden clubs. The old clubs had narrow faces, those of drivers and putters including the horn seldom exceeded 1 inch in depth and the faces of spoons were almost invariably a little less.

'The rubber-cored ball is much more resilient than the gutty and flattens more on the club face and it therefore requires a deeper faced club. Probably the deep face also is in part due to the fairways of courses.'

The author goes on to point out that in the old days it was the rarest exception to get a ball really 'sitting up', as it usually does nowadays, anywhere on the fairway of the course. Usually it was lying cupped, or if not cupped, very close to the ground. The narrow-faced spoons were very much more efficaceous for getting down to these tight-lying balls than the deeper-faced weapons that superseded them. He also goes on to point out that another notable change is the piercing of the head and the insertion of the shaft through to the sole. The old wooden clubs were always spliced on the shaft and whipped with pitched string.

'Many players find that even with the stiffer shafts now used, the new method is apt to produce torsion of the shaft in swinging and some are going back to the old-fashioned scare and splice.'

The author goes on to bewail the fact that clubs are no longer individual in appearance and that the maker's name may be put on anywhere, whereas with the handmade clubs, the maker's name was always put on at right angles to the face and immediately opposite the striking point. Another matter of which the author disapproves is the colour of the wooden heads. He says that, in the old days, it was comparatively rare to see anything but a light-coloured head. So much so that it was the custom to regard a dark head with suspicion. The idea that the clubmaker had stained it dark might be to cloak some imperfection in the grain or quality of the wood. The usual stain was simply a coat of varnish and the proper colour, after age and use had mellowed it, was the rich amber obtained by old violins. He goes on to say:

'Whether the secret of the varnish has now been lost or not, one never sees it now, but as a matter of fact most clubs are now stained dark, probably the constant chipping of irons in the confinement of the caddy bag is bad for clubs of fair complexion.'

Some notes on the general shape of clubheads through the nineteenth century

In the early part of the nineteenth century, all the clubheads were long, relatively narrow, particularly at the neck, and many were made with a marked hook at the toe.

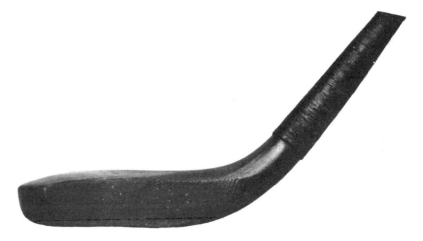

A long-nosed, shallow-faced (1in.) driver by Philp. This club would have been used with a feathery ball. Note also the very 'flat lie' of the club.

Measurements of a driver by Hugh Philp

Length of shaft		45 inches
Weight		400 grams
Angle of head to shaft		120°
Head:	Length	5 inches
	Width	2 inches
	Face depth	1 inch

Sometimes these clubs are described as having concave faces. They were not originally made in that way and most of them are not exactly that shape. For the most part, the toe part of the face is decidedly 'hooky' and the heel part of the face is set about at right angles to the shot; in some old clubs there is apparently a slight concavity from the heel to the centre of the face but this is probably due to use, as the centre of the face tended to be driven back by constant striking of the ball and it is probable that the 'hooky' quality of the toe was less marked when the club was new, than it is as seen today. This obvious hook shape to the faces is particularly noticeable in the Simon Cossar clubs and in the early McEwan and Philp clubs: it is more marked in the early part of the century. Later in the century, faces are virtually straight and the club face, although long, is less long than before; the neck of the club is somewhat thicker than that of the early clubs, which had to strike a feathery golf ball, and were less liable to have such great strain on the neck as to fracture there (as was to happen when the gutta was first made).

Two wooden clubheads. The one on the left has a head that is shorter and wider and has a straight face. The one on the right is longer, narrower and has a curved, 'hooky' face. The right-hand club is from the earlier part of the nineteenth century: the left-hand club from the latter part.

Between 1885–90 there appeared the bulger driver. Park claimed to have invented this in 1884 and to have played in the Open Championships with it in 1885. Much controversy was aroused in the golfing world at about this time, because Mr Henry Lamb, an amateur golfer from Angus, also conceived a bulger driver which was made for him by Simpson of Carnoustie and which of these two gentlemen invented the bulger driver has never been entirely satisfactorily decided. Robert Harris said 'from Bob Simpson's shop emerged the bulger driver and the idea was Henry Lamb's.'[19] This was, of course, vigorously denied by Willie Park Jr. who sent more than one indignant letter to *Golf Illustrated* of about that time, to say that he had thought of the bulger driver before Mr Lamb.[20] Whatever the rights or wrongs of whoever invented it, the bulger driver had a convex face and heralded a new and important shape of clubhead. The bulger had a short, round head and in general was much nearer the shape of a modern driver. The early ones were somewhat clumsy in general appearance but later became more elegantly shaped, while maintaining the same general proportions. The typical dimensions of a bulger driver were:

Length of shaft	42 inches
Weight	400 grams
Angle of head to shaft	125°
Head: Length	4 inches
Width	2.25 inches
Face depth	1.25 inches

Two views of a 'bulger' driver. Compared with earlier clubs, the head is much shorter, the face is deeper and, far from being 'hooky' is slightly convex. This is a spliced or scared club.

[19]Robert Harris, *Sixty Years of Golf*, 1953.
[20]*Golf Illustrated*, Oct. 17th, 1890, p.70. Letter from Willie Park.
[21]H. Hutchinson, *Badminton Golf*.

It is said by Hutchinson[21] that Henry Lamb and R. A. Proctor, who apparently was a mathematician and was able to decide the curve of a baseball in the air, advanced a theory in support of this shape to prove that a ball struck on the heel of such a club would not slice as much as one struck off a straight or concave face and the same also obtained for the toe of the club and the amount of hook. Certainly the bulger driver became a very important club in a short time. As Robert Harris says:

'At once it became the prince of drivers and this club was to be taken by enterprising young clubmakers and professionals from Bob Simpson's shop later to give golf in America its greatest boost. In a great emigration these young men took the Carnoustie swing to the USA and the bulger driver and brassie were taken to supply the fundamental instruments. Certainly the bulger driver, although it had a short head, began to become a more graceful shape and completed the transition from the 'curved on flat' hooky faces of the early part of the century to club faces much shorter and of an exactly opposite curve.'[22]

Those who extolled the virtues of the bulger driver were at some pains to point out that the hook-faced wooden clubs gave rise to inaccurate driving, and, consequently, this shape of face, so elegantly produced by Philp and McEwan from their long years of experience, was immediately condemned. Indeed, one gains an impression from the literature in the 1890s that Cossar, Philp and McEwan had been labouring under a delusion for many years and their whole design of golf clubheads had been entirely wrong and merely made the game difficult. Personally, we have too much respect for the craftsmanship of people such as these to believe that they made clubheads of this shape by mistake and, worse than that, in order to make the game more difficult: they were ingenious and clever craftsmen and it is inconceivable that they should have continued to use this shape of wooden club unless it was of some benefit to the player. Our own view of this problem is that in the early days of the century, with the feather ball, the club was swung in a great circle and with a considerable shoulder turn and the ball was swept away. The clubs were long. The shafts were made of hazel or ash, and, as anyone who has handled one of these clubs will realise immediately, there was a great whip in the club and, in addition to that, the head could twist through several degrees. That is to say, not only were the shafts whippy but there was a very considerable torsion. The long and shallow head was the most suitable shape for getting the feathery ball in the air but at the same time, this shape of head, together with the large quantity of lead which was let into the back of the club, must have caused a considerable torsion in the shaft as the club was swung. It was only too likely that the toe of the club as it approached the fastest part of the swing, i.e. as it was approaching the ball, was 'left behind' and that, due to this, the hooked angle of the face was eliminated at the moment of impact and the club face came square into the ball. Had the face been straight, it is almost certain that the heel would have led into the ball with the toe behind and the ball would have been hit with a slice, or down the right-hand side of the fairway.

Golf Illustrated (1904) appears to agree with this theory. The editor comments on the 'new' socketed-head clubs and compares them (to their disadvantage) with the older scared-head clubs. He says:

[22]R. Harris, *Sixty Years of Golf*.

153

'In other words the head is more apt to twist and its face to be diverted from the proper angle in striking . . . and it is doubtless to compensate for the increased torsion that so many clubs are now made with a large amount of hook on their faces.'[23]

Later in the century, after 1850 and particularly after 1887, when the bulger driver came into being, clubs were shorter. There was a considerable steely spring to hickory and considerably less torsion, not only because the nature of hickory allowed shorter clubs, but also because the head was shorter and more compact: in consequence there was no need to have a hook face: the hands and forearms could be forced into the shot to bring the club back to square to the line of play. This was something which could never have been done with the long supple whippy clubs of an earlier era.

Having discussed what wooden clubs were made of and how they were made, it is now time to consider what sorts of clubs were used at various times during the nineteenth century. One avoids the phrase 'sets of clubs', because clubs were entirely individual and not in sets at all. Our knowledge of this before 1800 is very slight. Unfortunately, Kincaid does not talk about how many clubs he carried or how many clubs should be carried, so from his writing we have no knowledge of what sort of clubs were in use. In the letter of 1735 by Andrew Bailey (see Chapter 4, page 93), the writer seeks clubs from him – these to be nine in all, three play clubs (these would be drivers), 'three scrapers' (one of which was to be a half-scraper or spoon) and three putting clubs, etc. The three putting clubs would certainly have been of wood and would probably have constituted a 'green' putter, a driving putter and perhaps an approach putter. It is difficult to decide what a 'scraper' was. In view of the fact that one of the scrapers was to be a 'half-scraper' or spoon, it seems possible that, although at first sight the term scraper implies an iron club, undoubtedly the term spoon implies a wooden club, and one would suspect that the three scrapers were three sorts of spoons, the shortest of which must be a short spoon and the others what probably later became middle and long spoons. It is possible that the term scraper does not imply, as one might think, an iron weapon for scraping, but a club to get a golfer out of scrapes or difficulties; however, this must be conjecture. *Hoyles Games*, 1826, states:

'There are six sorts of clubs used by good players; namely the common club, used when the ball lies on the ground, the scraper and the half-scraper, when in long grass, the spoon when in a hollow: the heavy iron club when it lies deep among stones or mud; and the light iron ditto when on the surface of shingle or sandy ground.'

The scraper and half-scraper are placed in this account between the driver, made of wood, and the spoon, made of wood, the iron clubs being brought in later: this, again, would suggest that the scraper and the half-scraper were wooden clubs: probably forms of long,

[23]Editorial in *Golf Illustrated*, 1904.
[24]*The Golfer's Manual* by 'A Keen Hand'.

154

middle or short spoon. The term 'spoon when in a hollow' probably refers to the baffing spoon.

That they were all to be used with a feathery golf ball makes it more probable that they were all made of wood.

The next information concerns the clubs that were used in 1857, that is to say some nine or ten years after the introduction of the gutta percha golf ball and is taken from the *Golfer's Manual*.[24] The author describes a complete set of golfing clubs as being divided into four classes – drivers, spoons, irons and putters.

The drivers or play clubs

The drivers or play clubs, he points out, are distinguished by their long tapering flexible shafts and there are two sorts of driver – the play club and the grassed driver. The grassed driver was a driver with a slight loft to it – the term 'grassed' meaning 'loft'. The drivers would, in such a golf bag, be two, with probably a spare driver in case the one in use broke or became damaged.

The spoons

The spoons comprised long spoon, middle spoon, short spoon and baffing spoon. The spoons have got stiffer shafts and more loft on the face than the grassed driver and are, in fact, referred to as being 'well spooned', i.e. well lofted. The fact that they are called long, middle, short and baffing spoon refers mainly to the length of the shaft but it also carries an indication of the degree of loft in the face. The long spoon was nearer to the grassed driver and the baffing spoon had the most loft of all. The difference between the short spoon and the baffing spoon was not great. The clubface in each case would be long and well spooned back and it would almost certainly be shallow. The baffing spoon probably had a stiffer shaft than the short spoon. The short spoon was for getting the ball out of difficult lies and was used in making half strokes to the green when the swing was largely confined to a wrist stroke, the shoulders and the legs being scarcely used and the shot being referred to as 'off the wrist'. A baffing spoon had a special name because the ball was 'baffed' with it and this particular club was used for skying the ball over a hazard onto the putting green when the stroke was too short for any other spoons. In use, the club was made to hit the ground at the same time, or fractionally before, the ball was hit and this made a characteristic noise and was the form of stroke known as 'baffing'; no divot, of course, was taken. Sometimes the baffing spoon was referred to as the 'cutty': one does not know why this name was ever coined but it might be because the ball was 'cut up' into the air with it. There is no doubt that the baffy, in skilled hands, produced a beautiful and reasonably accurate stroke but it must have been difficult to judge the exact strength with which the ball was going to be struck and the distance which it was going to fly, when the player had to consider how much he was going to hit the ground and how much the ball. It would seem, too, that this club was particularly useful in the days of the feathery ball when the nature of the ball was

A 'grassed' driver. That is, a driver with a little loft.

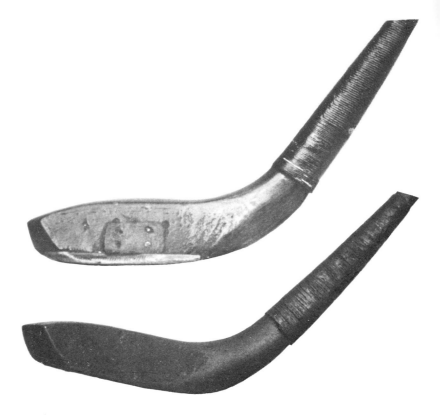

(Left and top right) Two views of a long spoon – well-hooked face, well spooned, i.e. lofted. The central part of the face has been repaired by a leather insert. The damage was probably done by a gutta.

(Bottom right) A baffing spoon. A long-nosed, scared-head club with a shallow face and well spooned or lofted. Used for playing approach shots before the days of iron play. The long face made it difficult to play out of ruts and 'cuppy' lies.

such that it would readily rise into the air; the baffing spoon became much less useful with the relatively inert gutty ball and already in 1857 the author of the *Golfing Manual* points out that the iron club 'is employed by many players for effecting the same stroke, thus superseding the use of this spoon altogether'. By 1890 this club is being referred to as 'one used by golfers in far-off days'.

The wooden niblick
There is another club which would have been in the golfer's bag at this time. This was known as a wooden niblick, and when discussing clubs in the early 1800s and even up to the middle of the century, it is common to refer to a wooden niblick and an iron niblick in the bag. A wooden niblick had a small head and was well spooned back, and the shaft was stiff. The club was short and the idea of it was that the smaller head would fit into a rut or hole in the ground which the longer head of the baffing spoon or short spoon could not deal with. In its time, it was undoubtedly a very useful and much used club but with the advent of the gutty ball and with that ball, the great proliferation of iron clubs of all sorts, the wooden niblick disappeared and such strokes were played with an iron club.

The brassie
In 1890, Hutchinson writes:

'The baffy with which the golfer of old used to approach the hole is now replaced by the lofting iron. But in place of the

A wooden niblick. This club is well spooned or lofted. It has a brass sole and underneath the brass is a horn insert in the leading edge. The length of the clubhead is much the same as for the bulger driver, but this type of club was in use before 1885, when the long-headed wooden clubs were in use. The relatively short clubhead would fit into small cups and ruts better than the baffing spoon. The earlier wooden niblicks did not have a brass sole.

numerous spoons of a nearly bygone age, there has come into general use, a club that is named a "brassie" (equivalent to the present-day No.2 wood). This weapon is shod or soled with brass whereby its wielder is enabled to play off roads and hard lies without injuring the head. Moreover, when this club is made very short in the head, it is then given the name of a wooden niblick: this small head enables it to fit into many a rut where its more elegant brethren could not follow it.'[25]

With regard to the wooden niblick, then, there does seem, by the 1890s, to have been a slight change. The club described by Hutchinson has got about the same loft as the brassie, albeit with a much smaller head, whereas the early wooden niblick was described as very well spooned back. Thus, the early wooden niblick was like a baffing spoon with a very short head and the later wooden niblick was like a brassie with a very short head.

The brassie came into being probably in about 1875 or 1880, a brass sole being screwed onto the bottom of the club to protect it against a hard surface. At first, the club was made in the usual way with a bone leading edge and a brass plate was screwed over the bone. Later the bone came to be discarded and the brass plate was screwed directly onto the sole of the brassie. In 1896 Willie Park Jr. remarked:

'With regard to brassies, I would point out that some makers, considering the brass sole to be sufficient protection to the clubhead, omit the usual bone with which all wooden clubs

[25]H. Hutchinson, *Badminton Golf*.

Two views of a brassie by Harry Vardon. The club probably dates from 1896–1903. The notable features are: (1) a very small head; (2) a very long fine scare, such that the club could be mistaken for a socket-head club; (3) the club has a brass sole but a horn leading edge has also been inserted.

should be protected at the bottom of the face, but players should not accept such clubs. Without the bone the wooden face gets hammered in by repeated strokes and the result is that the brass sole, being left projecting, cuts the ball, not to say the turf of the links. See, therefore, that the brassie has bone in it.'

As the century advanced and the composite gutty ball took hold of golf, iron club play became much easier and more practical and the number and shape of irons increased as also did their quality of making, because of demand. As the iron clubs had taken the place of certain wooden clubs, being more easy to play with, the proportion of iron clubs to wooden clubs increased steadily throughout the years. The 'early' Troon clubs consist of six woods and two irons. The 'early' Blackheath clubs show approximately the same proportion of woods to irons. In the middle of the nineteenth century, it is recommended in the *Golfing Manual* that there should be seven wooden clubs and three iron clubs. Andrew Kirkaldy, talking of about the year 1875, states that

'nearly all the clubs were wooden and a complete set would consist of a driver or play club, a grassed driver, long, middle spoons and baffing spoon, a sandiron "like a battleaxe", wooden niblick, iron niblick and a wooden putter.'[26]

Bernard Darwin says:

'I respectfully submit that in England in the "80's", the average golfer's bag contained a driver or a brassie, a cleek or a driving iron, a lofting iron, a niblick and a putter.'[27]

[26]A. Kirkaldy, *Fifty Years of Golf. My Memories,* 1921, p.159.
[27]Bernard Darwin *et al., Golf in Britain,* p.10.

158

By 1905, the wooden clubs in a set would usually comprise a driver, a brassie and a spoon, roughly equivalent in modern times to a driver, a 2 wood and a 3 wood. The spoon, or 3 wood, was the lineal descendant of the short spoon and, also, perhaps, because of the generally shorter shaped heads of wooden clubs of this time, it could well have been considered to have been a first cousin to a wooden niblick.

Just before the First World War, Charles Gibson at Westward Ho! was asked by the late Hon. Michael Scott (who was an international golfer and subsequently became the oldest man to have won the British Amateur Championship) to make a wooden club as a substitute for a cleek, the idea being that the wooden club should have a shallow face with plenty of loft, as in the cleek; Charles Gibson's son tells us that his father made, in all, some three or four hundred of these clubs which were sold under the title of 'wooden cleek'; this type of club would be familiar to modern golfers as the No.4 wood.

Mention must be made of two types of club which enjoyed a vogue in the early part of the twentieth century.

The Dreadnought driver
The feature of this club, a socket-headed club, was a rather large head and an unusually whippy shaft. The name was derived from the new iron-clad battleships – the Dreadnought class. They were much in vogue in about 1908 and were made by Ben Sayers at North Berwick, Jack White at Sunningdale and Charles Gibson at Westward Ho! No doubt many other professionals made them also, in response to popular demand.

Fishing rod drivers
These socket-headed clubs appeared somewhat earlier, in 1901–2, and were still talked of in 1912 (*Golf Monthly*). The prominent feature was the length of the shaft which was about 3 inches longer than the usual driver and which was therefore very whippy. They were particularly useful to men of small stature and Ben Sayers used them to good effect. Some claimed that he invented them: others that the club was thought up by Charles Gibson of Westward Ho! Certainly, the Hon. Osmond Scott (of Westward Ho!) used one in the Amateur Championship of 1905 and Gibson, after that, had a lot on order.

Putters

Putters are being treated as a special subject because, although in general, there is some standardisation of other clubs, the putter remains a very individual club: indeed, even the method of using the putter remains very individual and there are almost as many methods of putting as there are putters. It is a club which requires a delicate and sure touch in its handling and it is noticeable how many of the great professionals and amateurs of today remove the left hand glove with which they play other shots in order to improve their feel of the putter. There are many different ways of gripping the putter and of swinging the putter and many of the large number of variations are to be seen among the great golfers. Individual preference still rules the day and the difference and shape of the putters used by the great golfers of today clearly indicate that putting is an individual skill, in which one man's meat is another man's poison. Not only is the shape of a putter subject to great variations but so, also, is the material of which it is made and today putters may be made of wood, steel, aluminium, plastic, fibreglass,

A short putt. In the background 'green' and 'fairway' are indistinguishable.

George Glennie, the famous amateur golfer of the early gutta ball period, putting at Blackheath with a putting cleek. Here again the 'fairway' and the 'green' are indistinguishable. (Painting by Heywood Hardie, RA, courtesy of Royal Blackheath Golf Club).

160

etc. An expression of the individuality of the putter is that it still retains its name and nobody has ever attempted to call it by a number. It is, in fact, a very unique golf club and has a closer personal relationship with the player than any other club.

In the early days of golf the putter was made of wood and it served a number of functions. The green was then a roughish patch of grass, not greatly different from a good piece of fairway and even, on occasions, indistinguishable from a poor piece of fairway. The early rules of the game (1744) defined a putting green as ground within 'one club's length of the hole' (Honourable Company of Edinburgh Golfers, Rule I). In 1777, the area was extended to four clubs lengths and, in 1828, to eight clubs lengths. The definitions were particularly necessary in those days because the fairway, the green and the teeing area for the next hole might all be indistinguishable from one another.

It is no accident that in Willie Park Jr.'s book on *The Art of Putting* instruction is given in how to putt out of a poor lie.[1] Up to the early part of the nineteenth century there were three clubs recognised as putters, the driving putter, the approaching putter and the putter.

The driving putter was not really a putter at all. That is, it had nothing to do with the putting green. It was a short club with a stiff shaft and the face had little or no loft on it. It was used in particular for driving the ball very low into the wind and was largely superseded by the cleek, driving iron or driving mashie when the gutta ball came on the scene.

The approaching putter was used for approaching the green from 80–100 yards when there was no hazard or other obstacle in the way. The shape was generally that of the putter used on the putting green but there was a definite loft to the face. The putter used on the green was shaped not unlike a driver or play club but the head was somewhat shorter and the lie of the club was definitely upright, more so than the driving putter and slightly more so than the approaching putter. Putters were somewhat heavier than the other wooden clubs. Of eight drivers and brassies weighed by us, the weight was between 350 and 410 grams each; seven putters weighed about 400 grams. Many putters by Philp and McEwan were so driver-shaped that they even had the hook face and there was a well-rounded back to the putter, so that it was a fairly substantial wood head. This was, to a certain extent, necessary because, if the putter were to be 400 grams, a fairly large quantity of lead must be let into the head, and this was clearly easier to do in a large head than in a relatively short and narrow head where there would be but little rim of wood on the upper and lower surface by the time the weight was achieved. Nevertheless, it could be done if it was seen to be necessary. One advantage of the narrower putter head was that it could be soled on an uneven surface more easily than a wider one. Tom Morris Jr. of St Andrews, who won the Championship Belt outright by winning it three years in a row in 1868, –69 and –70 and was, in his time, the recognised genius on the golf course, used a

Driving putter. The head and neck. There is a substantial scare or splice. The club is of a flatter lie than a 'green' putter.

[1]W. Park Jr., *The Art of Putting*.

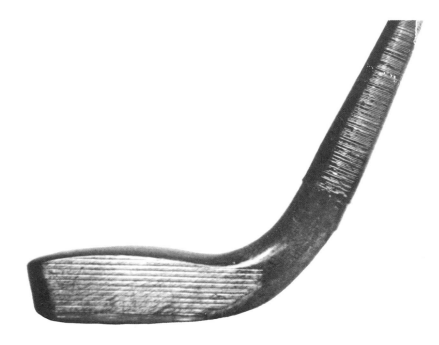

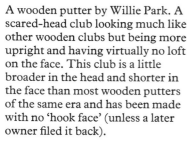

A wooden putter by Willie Park. A scared-head club looking much like other wooden clubs but being more upright and having virtually no loft on the face. This club is a little broader in the head and shorter in the face than most wooden putters of the same era and has been made with no 'hook face' (unless a later owner filed it back).

putter with a relatively narrow head: Tom Morris Sr. of St Andrews, also an Open Champion on four occasions, had noted this and got one of his senior workers in the shop to make quite a large number of narrow-headed putters which were also (like Tom Morris Jr.'s) shallow-faced, that is the face was less than 1 inch in depth. That the Philp putters were hook-faced is mentioned by Bernard Darwin who says that he was given a beautiful Philp putter with which he putted very well 'after I had filed the hook off the nose'.[2]

In 1857 the 'Keen Hand's' *Golfer's Manual* states unequivocally that 'the putter is made of wood'.[3] In a beautiful presentation set of clubs made in 1866 by Forgan, the putter is also made of wood. In 1887, Walter Simpson makes two remarks about putters which clearly indicate his views on them:

(a) 'Then there are putters. A good one ought to have the name "Philp" stamped on it by somebody who must not tell you that he did it himself.' (b) 'There are putting irons which are not irons but putters. People who putt badly are happy with them, although they only put it out of their power ever to putt well.'[4]

Willie Park, Jr. in 1896 says:

'Putting has changed a good deal of recent years. Formerly the only club used was the wooden putter. In more modern times innovations in the shape of putting cleeks and iron putters began to appear and these have now, to a large extent, displaced the older implement. It is difficult to say whether the change is for the better or not.'

[2]Bernard Darwin *et al., Golf in Britain.*
[3]*The Golfer's Manual* by 'A Keen Hand' (J. B. Farnie), 1857.
[4]Walter Simpson, *The Art of Golf,* Edinburgh, 1887, p.23.

He goes on to say that for approach putting from 30–40 yards the wooden putter is unequalled and he thinks it is probably best on perfectly smooth greens but advocates an iron putter if the green is not smooth as the ball will tend to jump off a wooden club face.[5]

Thus it can be seen that there was a general move towards metal putters by the end of the nineteenth century but by no means all golfers agreed on this and, even today, wooden putters are in use. Nevertheless, because fewer wooden putters were required, and as those who were expert at making them died or retired, those who came after lost much of the art of making these beautiful clubs and quite probably, because they were not made well, they fell into disrepute.

It seems that the making of a really fine, beautifully balanced wooden putter required a special skill and also careful, slow and loving craftsmanship which not every clubmaker was prepared to give, especially when the golf 'explosion' came, and it became necessary to produce large numbers of golf clubs quickly. This may well have hastened the disappearance of the really handmade and beautifully balanced putters of earlier times. John Low, a fine amateur international golfer, and also a prominent member of the Royal & Ancient, was a staunch believer in the wooden putter and he was also a particularly fine exponent of the art of putting with it. Horace Hutchinson (1899) mentions John Low, observing:

'He is so good a putter that we cannot for the moment name a better and it is a point especially to be noted that he putts with a wooden putter. This is a weapon that was universal for the short game 20 years ago. One hardly ever sees them today.'[6]

John Low wrote a book *Concerning Golf* in 1903 and Chapter 7 is called 'Concerning Putting'.[7] The first part of the chapter is devoted to the club and much of this chapter is reproduced here because the opinions of one who had such skill with, and love for, wooden putters, must carry weight and also because they make clear the importance of individual craftsmen in making them. He says:

'With the (wooden) putter the ball is struck with exactly the same kind of blow that a cue gives a billiard ball and in the centre of the club. I do not know of any club which is capable of giving as free, true hit to the same degree as the wooden putter.

And then, on another occasion:

'When it is recognised that a putter may cost from 1s 0d to half a sovereign (10s 0d) to produce out of the same material, the fallacy of the saying "The good player can play as well with one club as with another" will partly be understood. The truth is that good clubs cannot be made quickly or by unskilled work-men, nor are the clubs worth buying unless they are well and

[5]W. Park Jr., *The Game of Golf*, 1896.
[6]H. G. Hutchinson, *The Book of Golf & Golfers*, 1899, p.154.
[7]John Low, *Concerning Golf*, 1903, p.116.

carefully fashioned. George Lorimer, one of the best of club-makers, has said that he liked to have a week in which to make a putter. His habit is to take up the head in the morning and look at the work of the day before with a fresh eye: after half an hour's touching up he will put his work down again so, working at intervals, at last turn out a beautiful and cunningly formed thing.'

John Low goes on, later, to explain the importance of getting a putter made properly:

'But if you wish a good putter of wood, you will hardly expect to find one in a clubmaker's ready-made stock, far less in a toy-shop or a tobacconist's window. The putter must be sought for with care and not hastily for she is to be the friend, be it hoped, of many years. First, then, find out a workman of repute as a maker of putters – and in these days of "reach me down" clubs, there are few such artists, – and having found him proceed warily. It will never do to go and order him to make one, you would probably receive only the work of an apprentice. Wait your time and you will find the great man about his shop or on his doorstep at the dinner hour and may remark to him that the day is fine. This will be a safe opening, even though rain be falling in torrents, for it will give him the idea that you are a simple fellow and so throw him off his guard. If a half-empty pipe lies beside him, offer him a cigar and mention that you are afraid that it is not as good as you would have wished, being the last of the box, at the same time giving him to understand that another box is expected that evening. The cigar having been accepted and lighted, you may in course of conversation allude to a very fine putter made by a rival clubmaker which, you will tell your friend, is being much talked about and copied.'

John Low continues in this rather lighthearted vein but it is clear that his more serious indication is that good makers of putters were difficult to find, were not necessarily men who made other clubs well and that it was very important that you should have, after due discussion about weight and lie and size and such like, a club that really felt individual to your needs and in which you had confidence. He later talks about the shape of putters:

'There is probably no club which has received so little attention in recent years and been so uniformly made badly as the putter of wood. Until Mr Mills introduced his putters cast from good wood models (the Mills Aluminium putter – see Chapter 4), the idea for a proper shape for a clubhead seemed to have been almost lost. A couple of years ago I do not suppose that there were more than a dozen putters in England which could, by any stretch of imagination, have been called fit to play with. At St Andrews, owing probably to the fact that the putter is the only club permitted to appear on the "Ladies Green", the art of putter making was to some extent kept up.'

John Low then shows his considerable interest in makers of putters:

'Three very fine putters were made in Tom's (Old Tom Morris of St Andrews) shop. One for Mr James Cunningham, one for Mr Peter Anderson and the third for Hugh Kirkcaldy. They were made, if I mistake not, by Tingay, who was at that time apprenticed to the grand old man and were copied from an old putter, but whether it was young Tommy's (Tom Morris Jr.) or one belonging to Mr Cunningham, I cannot at the moment remember. The feature of these putters is the narrow long head and the thin straight face.'

He adds later:

'These two features, the thin (shallow) face and the narrow heads seem to me essential to a good putter and are seldom found in the ordinary wooden club. The ordinary wooden putter is a dumpy headed, clumsy fellow, with a broad head, a thick neck and a deep face. Even the famous Philp putters were by no means fair of countenance and were, moreover, in their original shape – that is before the face was much filed – very hooked in the nose.'

He proceeds to describe in considerable detail, giving measurements, what he considers to be the proper shape, size and weight of a wooden putter. It is clear, in fact, that he feels very strongly about wooden putters with which he was a considerable expert and it may well be that the introduction of mass methods of production and the lack of individual attention to such a delicate club was what sounded the death knell of the wooden putter, although there are those today who use wooden putters and consider them good.

Later in the chapter he describes the importance of the bend in the shaft of a wooden putter (most wooden putters were made with a curve in the shaft). He points out that the bend in the shaft should be at the foot of the leather grip when the grip is of ordinary length, say 12 inches. He continues:

'In other words, if the direction of the leather-covered grip of a putter be produced as a line, it should end in the hitting point of the clubhead and not in the heel or toe. This matter of the bend in the shaft is so important that I may say that I have never seen a putter of wood or aluminium without this bend which balanced properly in the hand.'

Having examined some twenty-five to thirty old wooden putters, if what John Low says about the bend in the shaft is correct, then very few of them are properly made. The faults are usually that the bend in the shaft is either in the wrong place or insufficient.

He goes on towards the end of the chapter even to describe the lead that should be put into the back of the wooden putter, saying that the lead should be soft 'for a hard lead would not unite itself with·wood in a satisfactory manner to give the right feel'. Finally he has something to say about the shaft of putters which would seem to be of considerable importance:

'It is a fact, perhaps not always recognised, that the shaft and the head of a putter stand in quite a different relationship to each other from the shaft and the head of other wooden clubs. The putter shaft is much more part of the head for it is necessary that the player's hands be in touch not with the head only but with the ball. From the fingers, through the shaft, past the whipping to the face of the club to the very ball itself, the sense of touch must go if fine and delicate work is to be accomplished. It is obvious, therefore, that the shaft and the grip must be in perfect harmony with the head of the club for they are the medium which communicate from the fingers to the head the message to the ball.'

It would seem likely, in view of these remarks about the shaft, that one had to look after the wooden putter very well, to protect it from the weather and to be particularly careful not to break the shaft as with this sort of club, in particular, a replacement of the shaft would completely destroy the balance; it is also clear that, if the sense of feel from the fingers should be transmitted as directly as possible to the ball, the scared or spliced method of fixing the head to the shaft by which some 4 inches or 5 inches of the shaft were in contact with the wood of the head, the two being bound firmly together, was better than the socket-headed type of club in which the shaft was let into the head of the putter.

The mention that he makes of Mr Mills making aluminium putters from good wooden models is of some interest and importance because it is quite clear that John Low, who felt himself to be very expert on wooden putters, was quite able to accept the aluminium putters. These putters had the great advantage, when properly made and balanced and copied from a good wooden model, that they were not as subject to damage as the wooden-headed putter. Some of the aluminium-headed putters of an earlier time that we have seen are beautifully shaped and in all respects like their wooden forbears. So much then for wooden putters and a brief mention of the value of the aluminium putter. The other sort of putter to be discussed is the iron putter.

Putters made of iron were quite early to appear but gained little ground until well into the gutta era. The earliest were the putting cleeks, shallow-faced, long-headed and with rather less loft than the ordinary cleek; perhaps on occasions more upright in lie. The shaft was stiff and shorter than the usual cleek length. The particular virtue of the putting cleek was that the lofted face enabled the golfer

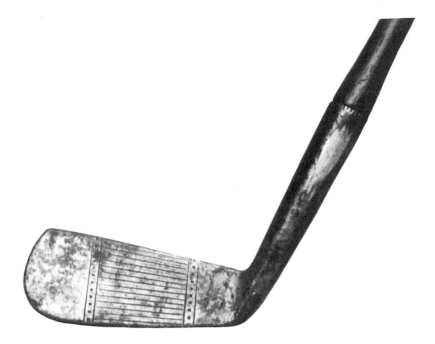

Two views of a putting cleek, a club
with a rather long shallow face,
with less loft than a cleek but more
loft than an ordinary putter.

to hit the ball smoothly out of a doubtful lie; also it allowed the ball
to be hit more firmly than with the wooden putter because the little
bit of backspin imparted by the loft caused the ball to pull up
quickly: short putts could be tapped quite smartly without going too
far past the hole. Other advantages were that the narrow blade
would sole easily on an uneven lie where the wider wooden putter
might have difficulty. Some players also found it easier to line up the
club face when a narrow blade was used. Lastly, but by no means
least, the metal putter was less liable to be damaged or affected by
wet weather.

Following the putting cleeks came the iron putters which were, in
fact, often made of gun metal. They were usually shorter and deeper
in the face than putting cleeks but still had an appreciable loft
compared with the modern putter. Towards the end of the
nineteenth century came an important invention by Willie Park Jr. –
the wry-necked putter. In his book *The Game of Golf*[8] he mentions
that he discovered, somewhat by accident, that when the shaft of one
of his putters had become warped so that the shaft was in front of
the head of the putter when the ball was addressed, he had found
that he could putt rather better with it. Others have said that the
putter arrived by accident because Willie Park used to drive a
dogcart to get out to the farthest holes at Musselburgh and he
usually took his putter with him so that he could have a few putts
while he was there, and that on one occasion the putter fell off the
cart and the wheel went over it and bent the metal at the neck. This
story has been repeated many times and it makes an attractive tale
but we cannot verify the truth of it. Of course, the iron putter heads
were made by cleekmakers. They frequently had the cleekmaker's
mark on the back, as with any iron club; they were made by

[8]W. Park Jr., *The Game of Golf*,
1896.

167

An 'original' Willie Park, Jr. wry-necked putter. Made by him for his daughter, herself an international lady golfer, who used this putter throughout her competitive golfing years.

blacksmiths or by those blacksmiths who had turned entirely to cleekmaking. Willie Park Jr., himself, made many of his own putters.

There were many different shapes of putter and this club, in particular, seemed to inspire weird and wonderful ideas. Most of them appear in the Patents chapter but perhaps the 'Schenectady' centre-shafted putter deserves special mention. It was the first centre-shafted putter and was brought to Britain from America by Walter J. Travis. Travis was a slightly 'tetchy' man and not, as regards the long game, a particularly impressive golfer but, when he arrived at the green, he became superlatively good and it was his putting which won him the British Amateur Championship in 1904. After his win, centre-shafted putters were barred by the Royal & Ancient and this was the cause of some ill-feeling in America. The ban on centre-shafted putters was removed by the Royal & Ancient half a century later.

Chapter 6

The Cleekmakers

By tradition the iron clubmakers are called cleekmakers. In the early days of golf, i.e. when the feathery ball existed, the great preponderance of clubs were wooden but iron clubs did exist and one of the oldest known collections of clubs, at Royal Troon Golf Club, South West Scotland, has two iron clubs and six wooden clubs. The clubs at Royal Blackheath Golf Club show similar proportions. Whereas the makers of wooden clubs were essentially people who were used to working in wood, there were no people at that time associated with golf who were experts in metalwork and it was left to the blacksmiths to make the earlier iron clubs, presumably under some instruction from the wooden clubmakers as to what sort of clubs they required. The clubhead only was made by the blacksmith; the rest of the club was put together by the wooden clubmakers who shafted it and put on the grip.

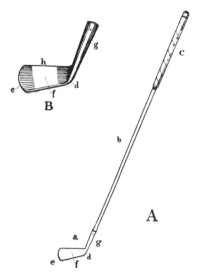

The parts of an iron club (reproduced from *The Game of Golf*, W. Park Jr., 1896).

The 'ancient' clubs of Royal Troon Golf Club.
This illustrates the 'cut-off nose' appearance of the early iron clubs. It also shows the proportion of woods to irons in the early sets of clubs, i.e. before 1800; the very 'flat lie' wooden clubs with shallow faces; and the fact that five of the eight clubs have no grips.

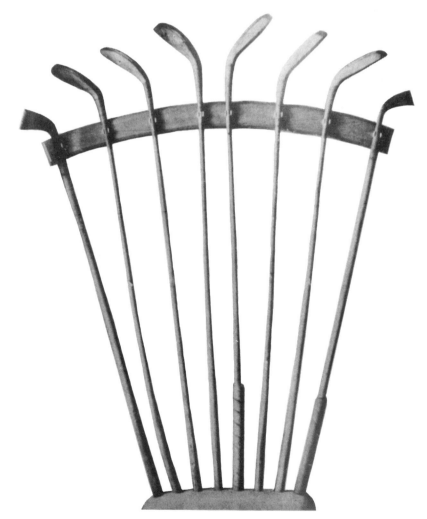

In the early days the blacksmiths made very crude clubs and some, perhaps, had no great interest in the matter, but slowly, with the beginning of the nineteenth century, and especially after the gutta appeared in 1848, iron clubs began to be made by blacksmiths who found it paid to go over entirely to the making of these articles. The iron club, if it 'topped' a feathery ball, was liable very easily to burst it and it is probably because of this sort of accident that there was no great growth of iron play until the advent of the gutta golf ball in 1848. The pre-1800 iron clubs were notably crude and heavy and they were almost certainly used merely as last ditch resorts when the ball lay in such places that either a wooden club was incapable of getting it out or that the head of the wooden club might smash if a shot were attempted; a specific difficulty was that the long wooden clubhead could not fit into a cartrut or small hole.

Iron clubs, probably before 1830. The clubhead is crudely formed. The faces are concave from upper to lower edge and from heel to toe. The hose is long and massive: the nicking or knurling at the top of the hose is deep and, on the left, long. The hammer marks on the faces can be seen, especially on the right. These marks could easily be seen with the naked eye and very easily felt also. There are no face markings and no cleekmaker's 'mark'.

The making of iron clubs

Early iron heads were made by blacksmiths. Often this was only a small part of the blacksmith's trade. He did not make many clubs because, in the time of the feathery ball, few irons were needed. He worked with perhaps one assistant, and the operation was a purely hand operation. He had only one special tool, a mandril, which was a metal instrument: it consisted of a straight bar with a handle at one end; at the other end the bar, which was circular in cross-section with a diameter of about $\frac{1}{2}$ inch, tapered to a tip over a distance of 3–4 inches. The other implements were the usual blacksmith's armamentarium of anvil, various hammers and tongs.

The head was fashioned from a piece of iron 6–7 inches long, about 2 inches wide and $\frac{1}{8}$ inch thick. After the heat had rendered the iron malleable the first step was to hammer one end around the mandril, thus making the tapered socket into which the wood shaft would subsequently be fitted. The forming of the socket around the mandril caused the rest of the piece of iron to double in thickness and at this stage the socket was in line with the rest of the bar.

The next step was to form the angle of the head to the socket, thus giving the clubhead the appropriate 'lie'. This was done partly by hammering the iron, when malleable, over the cone end of the anvil or by putting the end of the part which was to form the face into the 'hardie'; this latter was a square hole at the end of the anvil, which was normally used for holding various extra pieces of equipment. By the use of tongs, or with the aid of the mandril in the socket, the face could be bent to the necessary angle with the socket. After this the face could be turned at a suitable angle to the socket, while maintaining the angle of the lie, to give the necessary loft. The face of the club could also be shaped to give the necessary depth and shape. After the shaping was completed a hole would be punched in the socket, on each side, at right angles to the line of the club face. This hole was for a rivet which the clubmaker would use subsequently, to fix the wood shaft into the socket. The top end of the socket would be 'nicked' or 'knurled' all the way round to help grip the wood shaft when it was driven in. This nicking in early irons was larger and cruder than in later irons.

After this process was complete the iron head would be filed to get all the rough edges off. If the face was to have a pattern, this was usually done by punching the face with a pointed instrument to give a pattern of dots or holes. Many irons of this era had plain faces. Sometimes the back of the iron was marked with a cleekmaker's mark and stamped with the name of the clubmaker who would shaft it, but this was unusual.

The cleekmakers were very expert and it was accepted among the better ones that the line of fusion of the metal when the hose was hammered around the mandril should be invisible: if this were not so the clubhead was regarded as defective and discarded. Such defective irons were often bought very cheaply by those who could afford it; the owner would then shaft it himself.

The blacksmith then passed the head on to the clubmaker who

A rut-iron head with socket hole taken right through to the sole. The shaft end would have been shaped so that the wood traversed the whole length of the socket and protruded at the base, where it was cut off flush. In this case, age and use have caused the lower segment to disappear. There is no cleek-maker's mark.

would select a suitable shaft, taper the end, insert the tapered end into the socket and retain it there by knocking an iron rivet through the two holes provided by the cleekmaker. It was of some importance to ensure that the tapered end of the shaft was really well 'fitted into the socket as this had an effect on the feel of the club and its driving power. In some clubs of this era, the tapered socket was carried down to the sole of the club, so that the shaft could be driven down until it came out at the sole: the excess was then cut off, flush with the sole; this type of iron head made it easier for the clubmaker to get a really well-fitting shaft. When the clubmaker had roughly shaped a shaft from a lath of wood, he tapered the end and fitted it into the socket, securing it with the rivet. He was careful to set the grain of the shaft in the line of the shot which the club would make, i.e., at right angles to the head. It was only after this that he set about shaping the shaft with sandpaper, by hand, so that he got the right degree of stiffness and site of maximum whip, at the right distance above the head. These factors were all important, if the club was to be properly balanced. He had to consider what type of iron he was shafting; the weight of the head and the 'springiness' of the wood shaft. He also had to bear in mind what length of shaft was right and what the whole club would feel like when the thick grip had been put on. All this was completely empirical and its successful accomplishment was due to experience, a sound apprenticeship and a certain 'flair'. He would, of course, often know his customer and his preferences and also take into account the physical build of the man. No doubt all this was achieved by innumerable 'waggles' of the club and, when it was finished and sold to the customer, there would be possible adjustments to the shaft and grips from time to time. It was necessary for lofting irons and rutters, or track irons, that shafts be stiff and strong.

Before hickory appeared on the scene, in about the middle of the nineteenth century, ash was the common wood for shafts. This wood was adequate for the wooden clubs but was rather resilient and whippy for use with iron clubs. Various other woods were tried. Greenheart was tried and had some desirable qualities, i.e. it was stiff and had a good steely spring to it, but it was heavy and brittle. It was quite well suited to putter shafts and continued to be used for this purpose by some putter makers until the end of the century. Lemonwood (or lancewood) shafts also had these qualities of stiffness and, in particular, were said to be resistant to warping but were rather heavy. Hickory, especially 'red' hickory, was light, had a steely spring and was, when properly varnished, weatherproof or, at least, much less affected by the wet than any other wood. It became the wood for all shafts and, except for some putters, all other woods ceased to be used.

When the gutta ball was introduced in 1848, the use of iron clubs increased very rapidly and so did the number of golfers. The consequence of this was a marked increase in the number of irons produced and a considerable increase in the varieties of irons produced. Not least among the iron clubs was the virtual abandonment of the wooden putter for the various forms of iron putters, in the latter part of the century.

To cope with the big demand some of the blacksmith/cleekmakers became cleekmakers only. They took on extra men and enlarged their workshops. Apprentices now learned the art of making iron clubs and became specialist cleekmakers. Grinding wheels, emery wheels and various forms of polishers, driven by steam power, appeared.

There was a special type of iron developed for making clubheads —'Waverley' iron. Cleekmakers began to shaft their own irons.

We are indebted to Mr George Gibson, late Secretary of the PGCA and son of the late William Gibson of Kinghorn, Fife, who was a large-scale maker of iron clubs, for a description of the general arrangement of his father's factory in 1907.[1] He writes:

'I can well remember my father's cleekworks in about 1907 when there were 16 forgers, eight either side of the smithy, each with his own fire and bellows. The finishing shop (grinders, finishers and polishers) and the big engine room were beyond that. Two big hammer men were in the centre of the smithy at the call of the forgers when beating out the heated bar in readiness for making the hosel. The forger and the hammerman struck alternate blows to flatten approximately $3\frac{1}{2}$ inches of the iron bar. The hammerman was called upon when cutting off the required length of the bar for the blade. The forger had templates for lofts and lies for each iron.

'After completing the welding of the hosel, using a mandril he bent the heel around the cone end of the anvil to the required lie. A forger always made the complete head and usually made one type, cleek, mid-iron, mashie, etc., but could make any club.

'A bucket of water stood by the anvil and, after every operation, the head was dipped into the water before being put into the fire for re-heating. During these operations, flakes would form on the iron and the forger used a heavy rasp now and again to remove them.

'The men worked from 6 to 9 a.m., 10 a.m. to 1 p.m. and 2 p.m. to 5 p.m. from Monday to Friday and on Saturday from 6 a.m. to 9 a.m. but from 10 a.m. to noon they cleaned out their fires and relaid them in readiness for the following Monday morning. During this latter period there were usually feats of strength such as lifting an anvil or taking a bar of iron between the forefinger and middle finger and raising it to the horizontal – no mean feat!

'The iron used for making heads was called Waverley Iron, source unknown to me. The iron came in bars, forty inches long, $1\frac{1}{2}$ inches wide and $\frac{3}{8}$ inch thick.

'The iron head then went through to the finishing shop where there were grinding wheels, emery wheels and a "Dolly", the latter was a wheel covered in linen on which was applied a black greasy substance: it was a polishing buff.'

[1]Personal communication from Mr George Gibson.

The forming of the socket around the mandril continued to be the common method until 1914 and even after that.

The 'nicking' or 'knurling' at the top of the hosel was done by hand also and was done in order that the shaft could be better gripped by the socket.

The trade mark, professional's name, face markings, etc., were put on the stamper when the head was cold and after it came from the emery wheel. To do this the head was laid on a lead base and clamped in position.

'A stamp for punched faces had a series of points and for line faces, just one line. Hundreds of name stamps were held by each maker. A stamper was a very skilled worker and worked unbelievably fast.

'Around 1910, when musselbacked (round back) and concentrated back irons were introduced, moulds were used for shaping the backs.

Shafting irons

'A clubmaker was usually given twelve irons at a time for shafting. He took the heads and shafts to a permanent lathe worker, who pointed the shafts to a near fit, so minimizing the work of the clubmaker. The shaft was then planed, scraped and sandpapered by the clubmaker; after this the shafts were rubbed with pitch and linseed oil to bring out the grain and preserve them against the weather: the excess oil was burned off by passing the shaft quickly through a gas jet. After that the shaft was varnished. Basil grips were in common use at this time and were built up into thick grips by "listings" – strips of cloth wound round the shaft over which was put the grip.'

The process described was a development of the simple method of the early blacksmith, in order to make more clubs. It involved more workmen; specialisation; the use of machine-driven lathes, grinders, polishers, etc., and the introduction of a clubmaker to do the shafting. Nevertheless, the process was still basically a craftsman operation and remained so until World War I, and even after, in most British cleekmaking firms.

Some cleekmakers had dispensed with the hammermen and used a steam-driven hammer even before World War I.

In about 1906 Spaldings, of America, started a factory in Fetter Lane, London, They introduced a method of making iron heads known as drop-forging, which they had developed in the United States.

An American magazine in 1900 comments:

'Improvements in clubmaking have been remarkable in recent years. Hand-made wooden clubs are still considered superior to machine-made ones but a big advance has been made in the manufacture of iron clubs. Irons are now drop-forged; formerly makers were obliged to form the sockets by welding the material and used iron because it was easier to weld and work than steel. Steel heads are less likely to injury by contact with a stone . . . in hand-forging poor material could be used but the nature of the drop-forging process forbids anything but good material. An advantage of the drop-forged club heads is that they are all alike. No two hand-made clubs are alike, thus a player who breaks a hand-made club can never exactly replace it. The shanks of drop-forged clubs are practically unbreakable as the neck is forged solid and then bored. In hand-made clubs the neck is made flat, then bent over a mandril and welded. If the welding is imperfect, the shank will break off where the neck joins the heel. The surfaces of drop-forged clubs are uniformly good, while the holes in the neck are bored to a uniform taper.'[2]

The system of drop-forging consisted in pouring molten steel into metal moulds. Once the mould had been made, large numbers of heads could be turned out rapidly, all that remained was to bore out the socket and polish the head on an emery wheel, etc. The system was clearly well-suited to making the matched set of irons. Some moulds used in drop-forging may be seen in the Spalding Museum, Dundee, where many of the work tools of Forgan's old shops are on exhibition.

The various identifying marks on iron clubs tend to be lost over the years because the irons had to be cleaned regularly with fine emery paper to clean off rust. Efforts were made to prevent rust. An iron in the Woking Golf Club Collection is a non-rusting iron marked 'Hunt non-rustable'. It appears to have been 'tinned'. Horace Hutchinson mentions 'tinning'[3] – this is the process of dipping the iron head in melted tin, having previously treated the iron with salts of soda to form a flux with the oxide of iron. Hutchinson points out that the tinning prevents rusting and therefore the need for cleaning and also that the face is not slippery, as is the case with nickel-coated irons which, he says, have a slippery surface which seems to get little grip on the ball – even in 1900 nickel-coating to prevent rust was an established process.

Iron clubs: track irons or rut irons

The measurements of a typical track iron are:

Length of shaft	33 inches
Length of face	$2\frac{1}{2}$ inches
Depth of face	$2\frac{1}{2}$ inches
Length of hose	$4\frac{3}{4}$ inches
Weight 410 grams	

Because of the need to fit the iron clubhead into small holes and cartruts, some early irons were heavy, upright in lie, well set back, with a very small head and a long thick hose. The head, in fact, was but little larger than a golf ball; because they could be used for getting balls out of small cups and cartruts, they are sometimes

[2]*Chicago Inter-Ocean Magazine,* May 1900.
[3]*The Book of Golf and Golfers,* 1899, p.290.

Example of a 'tinned' mashie. A part of the back of the head has been cleaned of tin to show the unrusted metal beneath.

known as 'rutters', track irons or rutting irons. Although the earliest irons to appear in the armamentarium of people who played golf were the short, heavy small-headed rutters, other clubs certainly existed, still mainly for the purpose of getting out of such lies as were almost impossible with a wooden club, but of a different shape. They were given a general name of 'Iron'. Their principal characteristics were that they were heavy and had a very large hose, the 'knurling' on which was proportionately large. Both the back and front of the iron were plain. The face was often concave and had a 'hooked' appearance. Some of the very early irons had no 'toe' to the club face, the face ending in a straight vertical line and having a generally 'cut-off' appearance. Somewhat later irons of this pre-1820 period retained the general shape of their earlier forebears but had a rounded toe. Few players used them for deliberate shots in preference to wooden clubs. It is said by more than one authority that the first man to start using iron clubs for approach shots to the green was Allan Robertson (1815–1859) who has been given the title 'Feather Ball Champion of Scotland', quite unofficially. He did not apparently start using these clubs until the advent of the gutta percha golf ball. Whether or not Allan Robertson started to play with iron clubs, young Tom Morris (1851–1875), a great golfer who won the Championship outright by winning three times in succession, made the use of iron clubs for ordinary approach shots popular and had a great deal to do with the development of iron clubs in consequence.[4] It is said that he started using the rutter for playing approach shots to the green when faced with the need to carry a bunker. If this is so, he must indeed have been an accurate golfer for the clubhead is about the same size as a golf ball and without the most accurate striking it must have been all too easy either to socket the shot or to hit it off the very outside of the toe. It was customary in a bunker not to attempt to hit the ball direct but to hit the sand behind it.[5] That is to say that the 'explosion' shot is one of the early golf shots.

The 'rutter' or rut-iron or track-iron – one of the early golf clubs. This club is unusual in having a short hose. It has a small head (to fit into ruts and cart tracks) and is heavy. The dents in the head show that this club has been put to stern use.

[4]Robert Browning, *A History of Golf,* p.145.
[5]W. Park Jr., *The Game of Golf,* 1896.

Once the iron club had come to be found of use other than merely as a last-ditch resort and with the advent of the gutta golf ball, its development was very rapid indeed. The gutta ball was hard and sprang off an iron face well. It also flattened slightly on the face and needed, therefore, a deeper face with which to hit the ball and both the wooden clubs and the iron clubs after 1850 began to have deeper faces. One of the earlier developments to occur after this preliminary period was that the head of the niblick became somewhat larger and this tendency ran on unchecked until the middle and late 1920s when the most giant-sized niblicks were produced. Of the other clubs to appear, the first, after the rutter and the iron, were the lofting iron and the cleek.

Lofting irons

Lofting irons have a definite loft or spooned face. They are solid, heavy irons with long faces. The face is quite deep and the upper and lower edges of the face are not parallel, the toe of the club being wider than the heel. The earlier lofting irons often had a concave face from heel to toe and also were concave from upper to lower edge, but in later ones these two curves are minimal. The faces are plain but, of course, some may have had a patterned face which was rubbed off over many years of cleaning with fine emery paper. The blade is thicker at the bottom than the top. The hose was long and heavy and the knurling also. The shaft of the lofting iron was strong, with little or no whip. It could be used to get the ball out of difficult lies or out of sand and was also used for deliberate shots to the green, taking the place of the baffing spoon, an innovation which made for increased accuracy of approach shots but introduced the practice of taking divots out of perfectly good fairways.

The measurements of a typical lofting iron head are:

Length of shaft	39 inches
Length of hose	$3\frac{3}{4}$ inches
Length of face	$4\frac{3}{4}$ inches
Depth of face	$1\frac{3}{4}$ inches
Weight 350 grams	

The lofting iron, an early iron club. It was longer in both face and hose than the later mashie. A slight hook exists in the face. The size of the hose and of the shaft proclaim this club as an altogether larger and heavier club than the mashie. The face is deeper than a cleek and the toe part of the face wider than the heel.

The cleek

The word 'cleek' is a Scots word meaning a hook. The cleek was to the iron clubs what the driver or play club was to the wooden clubs. It was the iron club which hit the ball a long way. The cleek came on the scene after the lofter and became a much used and famous club. For the most part cleeks were long and shallow in the face and were not such a heavy and solid club as the lofter. They also did not have as much loft and the upper and lower edges of the face were nearly parallel, that is, the toe and heel of the club were nearly of the same depth. The shaft, while stiffer than that of a wooden club definitely had some play or whip in it. The hose was neither as long nor as heavy as the hose of a lofting iron. It was altogether a lighter and more delicate weapon than the lofting iron and was used for long shots through the green out of doubtful or hanging lies. It was not used for punching the ball or jerking the ball out of cuppy lies.

The measurements of a typical cleek are:

Length of shaft	40 inches
Length of hose	3 inches
Length of face	$4\frac{1}{4}$ inches
Depth of face	$1\frac{1}{4}$ inches
Weight 300 grams	

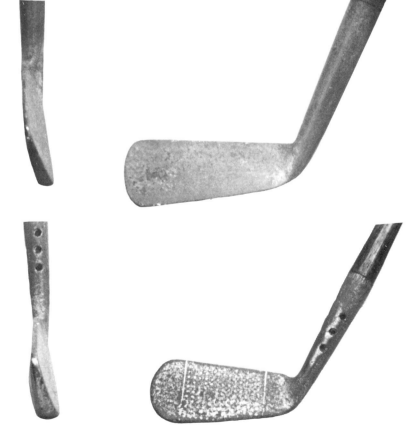

An early cleek. Note that the face is long and the upper and lower edges almost parallel. The hose is much more substantial than the later cleek and, in fact, the whole club-head is much more solid and robust than the 'Maxwell' club.

'Maxwell' cleek. This type of club was characterised by holes drilled in the hose to lighten it. This cleek was probably made between 1905 and 1912. It is somewhat shorter in the face and finer in construction than earlier cleeks. Most of the 'Maxwell' type clubs were made by Gibson of Kinghorn, Fife.

178

As the cleek was the long iron, efforts were constantly being made to enable it to hit the ball further. The best way to achieve this was to concentrate the weight in the head rather than the hose and, even more, in the centre of the head and fairly high up in order to hit the ball low. To achieve this, various methods were employed. Firstly the hose was made lighter, being both thinner and shorter, thus allowing a club of the same overall weight but the weight being more in the head. To this was added a shortening of the head and also a build up of metal in the centre of the head, rather high on the back. In consequence, some of the later cleeks are smaller in the hose, shorter in the face and some have a back which is built up with extra metal. The extra metal at the centre of the back of the club was achieved in a number of ways toward the end of the nineteenth century, involving the diamond-backed club, round-back clubs and mussel-back clubs.

These three clubs, the small-headed (track or rut) iron, the lofting iron and the cleek, were what may be termed the primary iron clubs: all the irons which subsequently developed were hybrids of these three primary clubs.

The mashie

An important and early hybrid, developed from the lofting iron, was the mashie, the direct forerunner of today's No.5 iron. It appeared and became rapidly popular between 1886 and 1890. Bernard Darwin (an international amateur golfer who became a noted writer and authority on golf) says that he learned to play golf with a lofting iron. He writes:[6]

'I was playing golf before the mashie age, not long, but definitely before it. I, at least, dimly recall its arrival just as I do that of the bulger: I am pretty sure that there was no such hybrid as the mashie in 1885 and by 1890 it had become essential ...'

He goes on to say that, for him, the lofting iron was a better club.

The mashie. First appeared about 1885 and rapidly achieved success as a club for pitching the ball on to the green. It was a development of the lofting iron, being shorter in the face than the lofting iron, somewhat more lofted and with upper and lower edges almost parallel.

[6]Bernard Darwin *et al., History of Golf in Britain*, p.9.

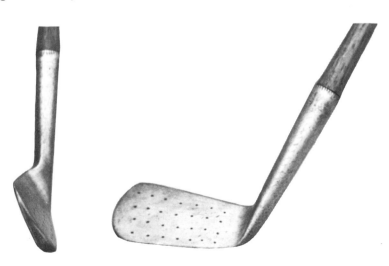

By 1890 J. H. Taylor from Westward Ho! was an up and coming professional and by 1894 had won his first Open Championship. He was a virtuoso with the mashie and his rise to fame, using it, set the seal on the mashie. What sort of club was this important development of the lofter? The mashie was markedly shorter in the face than the lofting iron: was not so heavy, had a shorter hose and was rather more lofted. It had a deeper face and the upper and lower edges were nearly parallel, i.e. toe and heel were about the same depth. It had a really stiff shaft. It was used for playing approach shots to the green and it was possible to get definite backspin.

The measurements of a typical mashie are:

Length of shaft	$37\frac{1}{2}$ inches
Length of hose	$3\frac{1}{2}$ inches
Length of face	$3\frac{1}{4}$ inches
Depth of face	$1\frac{1}{2}$ inches
Weight 325 grams	

Taylor made accurate approach shots look easy and, as a result, it became the answer to the general prayer and everyone attempted to emulate him. The word 'socket' or 'shank' became golf terms frequently in use.

Clubs derived from mashies

1   *The mashie iron or driving mashie.* This club had less loft than a cleek and retained the short mashie length of head and the mashie depth of face. It was used off the tee at 'long' short holes and also for long iron shots through the green. It did not fulfil the early promises made for it and did not, therefore, survive long as a club.

Face of a 'mashie iron'. The short deep mashie-shaped face can be seen: there is a minimum loft and the sole is slightly rounded. This was a straight-faced iron, usually used off a tee. The face marking was quite common.

The measurements of a typical driving mashie are:

Length of shaft	39 inches
Length of hose	4 inches
Length of face	$3\frac{1}{2}$ inches
Depth of face	$1\frac{3}{4}$ inches
Weight 300 grams	

The sole was usually slightly rounded.

2   *The mashie niblick*. A club more lofted than the mashie and also slightly deeper in the face. It was slightly longer in the face due to the rounded toe and with the upper edge and the lower edge of the club face rounded also.

The measurements of a typical mashie niblick are:

Length of shaft	35 inches
Length of hose	4 inches
Length of face	$3\frac{1}{2}$ inches
Depth of face	2 inches
Weight 320 grams	

With the advent of this club the term 'socket' and 'shank' became household words. The mashie niblick was the forerunner of the No.7 iron.

A mashie niblick, face view. The rounded toe and the rounded upper and lower borders are readily seen.

3   *The spade mashie*. This club retained the general mashie shape but was slightly more lofted than the mashie and had a deeper face. It was of particular use in hitting the ball out of lush grassy lies where it was all too easy to pass the club under the ball. An emasculated version of it exists today as a No. 6 iron, being, by now, indistinguishable from the No.5 iron except that it has slightly more loft (see illustration on page 184).

The measurements of a typical spade mashie are:

Length of shaft	36 inches
Length of hose	$4\frac{1}{4}$ inches
Length of face	$3\frac{1}{2}$ inches
Depth of face	$2\frac{1}{4}$ inches
Weight 310 grams	

Hybrids from the cleek

Apart from variations in the shape of cleekheads already mentioned, cleeks were used for other purposes.

1 *The putting cleek.* See Chapter 5 on putters.
2 *The approaching cleek.* A cleek with more loft than the usual run of cleeks and with a rather shallower face. The shaft was somewhat shorter than for the full cleek. Two variations on this theme appeared in the early 1900s.

(a) *The jigger.* A very shallow-faced and well-lofted cleek with a flat back, and

(b) *The sammy.* Precisely the same but having a rounded back.

Both these clubs had a rather shorter face than most cleeks but the principal feature was the shallow face – only about 1 inch deep.

Typical measurements of a jigger were:

Length of shaft	37 inches
Length of hose	3 inches
Length of face	$3\frac{3}{4}$ inches
Depth of face	1 inch
Weight 400 grams	

The jigger. A form of approaching iron, with a face like that of a shallow cleek and with rather more loft than a cleek.

Fairlie irons

It is important to mention specific types of club which were of unusual design and which were in common use at the beginning of the twentieth century.

In about 1892, Frank Fairlie, an amateur, designed some clubs which had no socket and which, equally importantly, had the lower edge of the face in advance of the hose. This shape had two effects: it eliminated socketing and it allowed the ball to be nipped out of bad lies more easily. These clubs were a great boon to those prone to socket and it is difficult to understand why they have gone completely out of use: the fashion of socketing is still ever present in golf and there are those whose game has been ruined by a particular frailty in this respect.

The 'Fairlie' niblick. The characteristic of this club is that it had no socket and the leading edge of the face was in front of the hose. As a result 'socketing' could not occur and the ball could be 'nipped' out of a cuppy lie more easily.

F. G. Smith's model irons

A few years later F. G. Smith's model irons appeared. These were something of an improvement on the Fairlie irons, being also socketless but having a wry neck in addition. They were made by Gibson of Kinghorn, Fife.

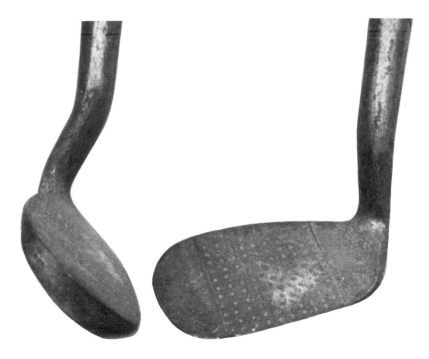

Smith's model niblick. An improvement on Fairlie's club, in that while there is virtually no socket and the lower edge of the face is in front of the hose, the club is better balanced, due to the wry neck.

Maxwell irons

Spade or deep-faced mashie. A 'Maxwell' club by Gibson of Kinghorn.

Irons with perforated faces

These irons attempted to place an even greater proportion of weight in the head of the iron by drilling holes in the hose to make it lighter. They were patented and were made mainly by Gibson of Kinghorn, Fife. They were finely balanced clubs and achieved considerable popularity, especially in the more lofted irons. The additional weight that was thus allowed was placed in the sole of the club which had a flange along the whole lower edge. They also incorporated the 'Genii Iron' principle, which Gibson of Kinghorn had produced in other irons. This was the wry-neck iron, invented by Logan, who worked for Gibsons: the effect of this bend was to minimise the socket part of the iron, without completely eliminating it, as in the Fairlie clubs. The disadvantage of the holes in the hose was that water got into the shaft through them and rotted the wood. These clubs often made a whistling noise in the downswing, owing to the holes in the socket.

Irons with perforated faces have existed from early times but most of them stem from the late nineteenth century or early twentieth century

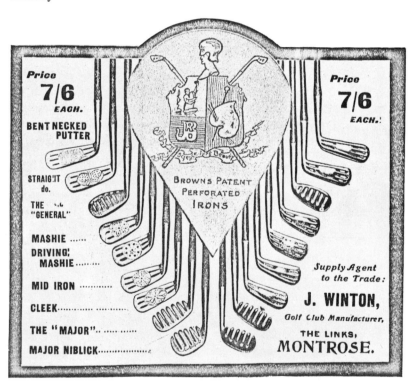

Examples of irons with perforated faces. Advertised in 1906.

'Water' mashies

Mashies with various slots cut in the face, possibly to decrease resistance to sand or water or even air.

Although many of the early irons had plain faces, or, at least, appear today to have plain faces, later irons have a pattern on the face, to enable the player to get backspin on the ball.

184

The earlier irons had faces in which the marking was done by hand; perhaps because of this, many show quite original and pleasing designs.

In the middle of the nineteenth century the typical clubs with which golf was played were:

Wooden clubs: Driver, Grassed Driver, Long Spoon, Short or Baffing Spoon, Wooden Putter

Iron clubs: Cleek, Iron, Lofting Iron, Rut Iron

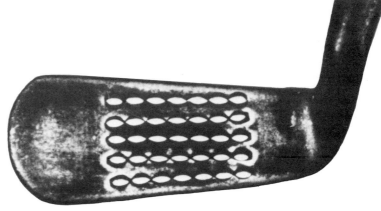

Above: water mashie.
Top right: face of a wry-necked putter by Condie of St Andrews to show unusual face markings.
Centre right: face of a child's mashie to show diagonal lines and hole-punched face.
Bottom right: face of a mashie with a circular punched-hole face.

By 1896 the typical clubs were:
  Wooden clubs: 'Bulger 'Driver, Brassie, Spoon, Brassie Niblick
  Iron clubs: Cleek, Lofting Iron, Mashie, Iron-niblick, Putter

A presentation set of clubs made by
Forgans in 1865–6. Nine clubs in
all.
Woods Driver
         Grassed driver
         Long spoon
         Short spoon
         Putter
Irons Cleek
         Iron 'general'
         Lofting iron
         Rut iron

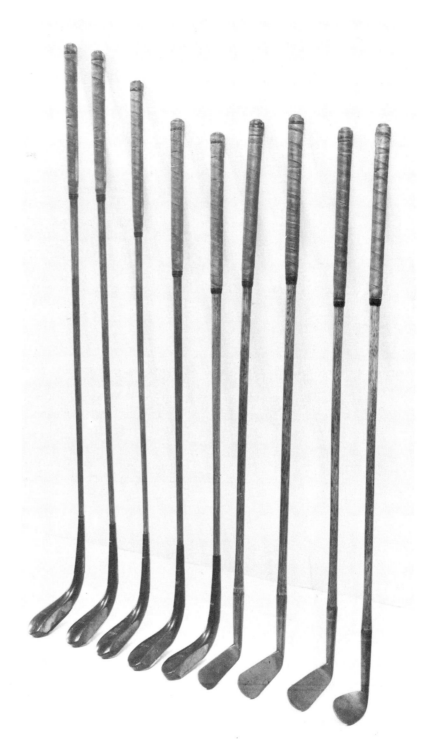

The story of the cleek-maker's marks

Cleekmakers, like potters, had their own marks. It is commonly supposed that the name of the professional and his Golf Club stamped on the back of an iron club implies that he made it. This is not so.

After the metal head had been rough filed, smoothed with the emery and finally polished, usually the blacksmith's mark would be placed on the back of the club but it was not common for his name to appear. The name on the back of the club was that of the wooden clubmaker who had shafted it and put on the grip and it was also of course an indication of where the iron club had been sold. In those days there was no such thing as a Trades Description Act, and very commonly the blacksmith did not put his mark on the club which was then sold by the wooden clubmaker as his own club. Although at first sight this may appear to be somewhat unfair to the blacksmith, it must be remembered that the entire balance and value of the club depended, not only on the shape of the head, but on the fact that it should be shafted properly with the right shaft and have the right grip. Whatever the rights and wrongs of this, it seems that the blacksmiths were content to be unknown in many cases and allowed those who put in the shaft to take all the credit for the club. This makes the identification of old iron clubs both interesting and difficult, for if the blacksmith did not put his mark upon the club at all, then it is not possible to say with certainty who made it. Certainly it was not made by the man whose name and Golf Club are stamped on the back. He was only the man who bought perhaps fifteen or twenty heads from the blacksmith and shafted them in his shop. The blacksmith had the necessary stamp so that he could put the professional's name on it. Thus an iron club may have stamped on the back of it 'James Smith, Potato Pit Park Golf Club', but it must be realised that this means, in the latter part of the nineteenth century, that he shafted the club and had his name put on the back of it, but in the early 1900s it probably means that he had no hand in making the club at all and that the manufacturer not only shaped the iron head but shafted the club and put on the grip.

A selection of cleek marks

1 John Gray, Prestwick
2 Anderson of Anstruther, Fife (early)
3 R. Wilson, St Andrews
4 Hewitt, Carnoustie
5 Carrick, Musselburgh
6 A. J. Ife, The Hague
7 Spalding, Britain and USA
8 C. Brand, Carnoustie
9 Cochrane, Edinburgh; 'false' cleek mark
10 Spence and Gourlay, St Andrews
11 Robert White, St Andrews
12 Cochrane, Carnoustie
13 J. and W. Craigie, Carnoustie
14 Condie, St Andrews
15 Stewart, St Andrews
16 Stewart, St Andrews (Ladies club)
17 Johnson, London
18 Gibson, Kinghorn, Fife
19 Gourlay, Carnoustie
20 Gourlay, Carnoustie
21 Anderson of Anstruther (late)
22 Bishop & Hendry, Leith
23 Gibson, Westward Ho!; 'false' cleek mark
24 Scott of Elie; 'false' cleek mark
25 Nicoll of Leven
26 T. Harrower, Carnoustie

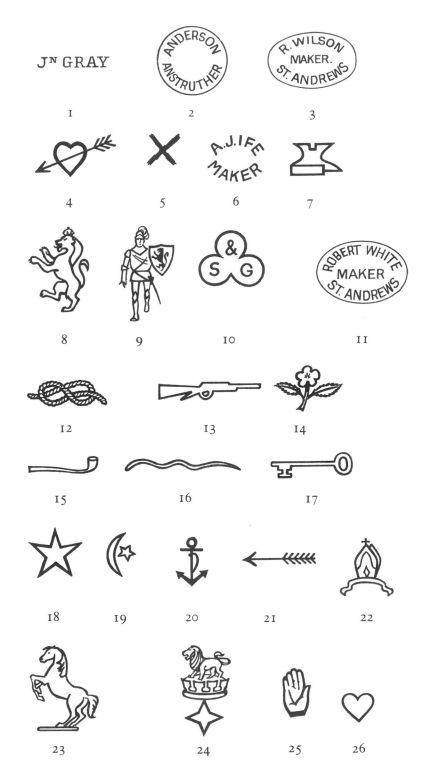

List of cleekmakers

Anderson & Son, Anstruther

James Anderson (1845–1895). A master blacksmith and cleekmaker. Listed in *Slaters* 1893, 96, 1907, 11 and 15.

Anderson, Alexander (1879–1952)

Son of James. The Census of 1891 records James Anderson at 46 residing at 127, St Andrews Road, Anstruther. *Golf* states that James Anderson began as a smith and a farrier in 1862 and shortly after began to make irons. He is said to have made up to 500 irons per year. All the forging of the clubs was done by hand and in 1892 he had 14 forges at work in his shop. At this time the polishing and finishing was done by machine. In 1892 his works used '16 tons of the finest steel' and he was making 40,000 iron heads per year. He also made the iron clubheads for A. H. Scott of Elie and made Forrester of Elie's centre-balanced cleeks and I. Carruther's cleeks. His irons were made to a high standard and a large number of them exist. His mark was an arrow but in some of his earlier irons the name is impressed on the back of the club.

Ayres, F. H.

111 Aldersgate Street, London EC (Est. 1810). Sports equipment manufacturers. An advertisement in *Golf Illustrated* (June 1911) among golf bags and balls, states that they make the well known Maltese Cross Brand of Irons 'warranted hand-forged in our own workshops'.

Bishop & Hendry, Leith

Later Hendry & Bishop of Musselburgh. They were harness makers pre-1902 and made some iron heads for W. Park Jr of Musselburgh – notably some of his wry-necked putters. Their mark was a Bishop's mitre. They made good irons and their 'Cardinal' irons were well known.

Brand, Charles (1849–1922)

Ferrier Street, Carnoustie. Listed in *Slaters* 1900, 03, 07, 11 and 15 and in the Fife Directory 1890 and 1892. He was Keeper at the Caledonian Club House.

Carrick

A family from Musselburgh. The father, Alex Carrick, was a blacksmith, married on 8 July 1785. He had two sons and a daughter, Francis 1787–1855 and Archibald 1789–1817, and Margaret. The sons formed F. & A. Carrick, Edged Tool Makers, at Musselburgh in 1840. The firm continued in business after they died, being carried on by Alex Carrick (1820–1901), son of Francis, and Archibald Carrick, son of Archibald Snr., born 1830. The firm of F. & A. Carrick ceased to exist in 1904. As a small sideline to their business they made iron clubs and were one of the pioneer cleekmakers in Scotland. They certainly made some fine well balanced cleeks. Their mark was a rough cross and some of the irons also had F. & A. Carrick, Musselburgh, impressed on the iron.

Condie, Robert (1863–1923)
St Andrews
A cleekmaker of some renown in his time. He appears to be one of the 'second generation' of cleekmakers, that is, as far as trade directories are concerned he was a golf cleekmaker only and was never listed as a blacksmith. Listed as golf cleekmaker in *Slaters* 1896, 1900, 03, 07, 11 and 15. Listed as 'Clubmaker' in St Andrews Valuation Roll 1892. His mark was a rose. He made many iron heads and, in his day, was regarded as one of the great craftsmen.

Craigie, John (1854–1928)
Montrose
Craigie, William (1859–1936)
These two formed J. & W. Craigie, listed in *Slaters* 1895 both as clubmakers and also as joiners and builders. In 1900, 03, 07 and 11, they are listed in *Slaters* as cleekmakers. They were a small firm compared with Winton & Co. and therefore there are relatively few clubs of theirs. When William Craigie died, the foreman and some other worker friends took over Winton & Co. (which had ceased in the same year) and continued to make clubs until World War II. Their cleekmaker's mark was a gun.

Gibson, William (1868–1921)
Kinghorn, Fifeshire. Blacksmith. He started doing wrought iron work at Kirkcaldy, Fife, and learnt how to make iron clubs from Anderson at Anstruther. He set up on his own at Edinburgh in 1890. In 1902 he employed 22 men and in 1908 started making wooden clubs as well. He was said to be the largest manufacturer of golf clubs in the world, at that time. He supplied many of the leading professionals of the day. His best known lines were James Braid irons, Maxwell irons, Genii irons, F. G. Smith non-socket irons and Montmorency push-irons. His mark was a star.

Gourlay, James
Carnoustie
Listed in Dundee Directory as a blacksmith 1905, 1906 as a cleekmaker. We think this refers to the son.
There were two James Gourlays, senior and junior, according to Robert Simpson of Carnoustie,

whose family have been professionals and clubmakers in Carnoustie for about 100 years. In a personal letter he says that James Gourlay, senior, was before his time: he started making iron heads in Carnoustie and worked from premises where they also shod horses. When he died his son carried on the business but left for Canada and from there to Chicago where he started up a clubmaking business. When James Gourlay left for Canada the business was carried on by his sister and an uncle. Simpson says that the Gourlays were a small business who handforged the iron heads and Simpson does not think he ever employed more than six men. Whether the two Gourlay cleekmarks were for father and son respectively, we do not know. The Gourlay irons are well made and finished.
The cleek marks were a crescent moon and star, and an anchor, respectively.

Gray, John (1824–1904)
Prestwick
A blacksmith and a keen golfer, being one of the original members of the Prestwick St Nicholas Club. He became the only cleekmaker in the West of Scotland. He was apprenticed to the trade of smith in Glasgow. In 1851 he began forging iron heads and made this business very successful, supplying most of the iron heads for the West of Scotland. He was a Freeman of the Burgh of Prestwick and Captain of the St Nicholas Club at Prestwick

1852–3. All his clubs were handforged and to a very high standard. He impressed his name only on the back of his clubs either JOHN Gray, JN Gray or J. Gray.

Hewitt, Walter Reynolds
(1862–1940)
Carnoustie
A cleekmaker who handforged all his clubs. He was locally known as 'Sandy'. He had a brother who helped him at one time but went to America as a professional golfer, returning later in life to Carnoustie and dying there. Hewitt appears to have been more or less single-handed. His production of clubs was therefore not high in quantity but was high in quality. He is in the Forfarshire Valuation Roll, 1905, 10 and 14 and in *Slaters* 1900, 03, 07, 11 and 15, listed as blacksmith and cleekmaker. His mark was a heart with an arrow through it.

Ife, A. J. (b. Hayling Island 1870) –
see also clubmakers' chapter on page 122.
Professional at The Hague 1904 and remained until he died in 1927. He made iron clubs as well as wooden clubs. Some fine irons of his are at Rye Golf Club and are stamped: A. J. Ife, Maker.

Frank A. Johnson Ltd
29 Paternoster Row, London EC. Started in golf equipment in 1901 and finally set up a small factory engaging, early in 1911, Hugh Logan, the designer of Genii irons for Gibson of Kinghorn, to manage the factory. Unfortunately by December of that year, Johnson's had gone bankrupt. There must have been a small output. They advertised in *Golf Illustrated* (18.2.1910 p.188) 'The KEY is the trade mark on the finest iron heads.' The key mark must therefore be rare – an iron with this mark has been seen.

MacArthur, Daniel (1810–86)
St Andrews
His name occurs in several early books on golf. He is listed in the 1881 Census as Master Smith and Ironmonger, resident at 69 Market Street, St Andrews. We have seen no clubs of his and do not know of his 'mark'. He is included because of references to him as a pioneer cleekmaker of skill.

Nicholson, T. (1864–1900)
Pittenweem
Listed *Slaters* as blacksmith. 1891, 93, 96, 1900. Awarded a gold medal at the Edinburgh International Exhibition 1891 for 'a case with golf cleeks'. Examples known marked with his name and the gold medal award.

Nicoll, George (1861–1945)
Leven
A cleekmaker who originally was a blacksmith. He also made bicycles and owned a cycle shop. He founded the cleekmaking business in 1881 but remained principally a blacksmith, making some golf clubs until World War I, when the firm became involved in iron clubmaking entirely. In 1882 he employed 12 men.

Nicoll, Robert (1884–1946)
He was really responsible for the subsequent development of the firm. He was the son of George and joined him in the family business. They made well-balanced irons and were master craftsmen. They made clubs for F. G. Tait, a famous amateur, and Arnaud Massey, a famous French professional who won the British Open Championship at Hoylake in 1907. The firm of Nicoll survived the age of mechanisation. In 1925 they took to making wooden clubs and the firm is now known worldwide.
Nicoll's cleekmark is the 'hand of friendship'.

Park, William, senior
See Chapter 4.
A clubmaker and professional golfer of renown. He also made iron clubs, examples of which we have seen. He was the first Open Champion in 1860 and subsequently won it 1863, 1866, 1875. A renowned putter.
A maker with the expertise to fashion both wood and iron heads is unusual. Park senior was a master craftsman in both. His son, Willie Park junior, joined him in the business in the 1880s, forming W. Park & Son, Musselburgh. His iron clubs were stamped 'W. Park, Musselburgh'.

Park, William, junior
See Chapter 4.
Joined his father in the business. He too made iron and wooden clubs. His daughter has told us that he used no cleekmaker's mark on the iron clubhead but put a 'P' on the shaft.

anvil mark on the earlier irons was quite detailed but later became much simplified. In 1911 they were advertising 'Spalding Model "V"' golf clubs. These were both woods and irons and had a special Spalding mark (see illustration) which was not an anvil mark. The trade mark was the same for both woods and irons. In the same advertisement they point out that they make twelve other models of wooden clubs and twenty other models of hand-forged irons.

Spence and Gourlay
St Andrews
Spence, James Hampton (1870–1929) and Gourlay, George Longmuir (1880–   ).
According to Robertson in *St Andrews Home of Golf*, these two men occupied the old lifeboat station at St Andrews from *c*.1895. In 1920 they became incorporated in Forgans business. Prior to this their mark was a shamrock or, for those who prefer, a 'club' – as in a pack of cards, with letters S & G.

Spalding, A. G. (1852–   )
Rockford, Illinois, USA
They were founded in 1878. Their first factory was in Fetter Lane, London, and they subsequently moved to larger premises at Putney, London. They were the first to introduce drop-forging into England and these clubs were stamped 'Hammer Brand', the earlier clubs being marked 'Warranted hand forged'. They made woods and irons and their mark on irons was an anvil. The

T. Stewart, senior
Carnoustie
T. Stewart, junior
(1861–1931)
St Andrews
Tom Stewart senior was a blacksmith who made iron clubs at Carnoustie – notably for George Morris, then professional at Carnoustie and brother of 'Old Tom' Morris of St Andrews. His mark was a pipe. He made fine clubs.
His son, Tom Stewart junior,

was apprenticed to his father and for some years worked as a blacksmith at Carnoustie winning prizes for horseshoes at many agricultural shows. In 1890 he joined Robert White as a cleek-maker at St Andrews. In 1893 he became a master cleekmaker and took over the firm a little later when Robert White went to America. He was a prolific cleekmaker and made clubs of a quality which were a credit both to his father and his teacher of later date, Robert White. The earlier clubs by him have a simple pipe on the back: later clubs have, in addition, 'T. S. St Andrews. Trade Mark'. After the early 1900s, he used polishing wheels of various sorts, driven by a steam engine. He probably also used a steam-driven hammer to produce the number of clubs required.
In 1901 he employed eight men and made as well as iron clubheads, tins for holes (said to be his invention), flags, holecutters, ball-presses and ball-moulds. (*Golf Illustrated* 12.7.1901, p.37). He appears on the Valuation Rolls of St Andrews as cleekmaker 1897, 98, 99, 1900, 01, 02. Also in Barton's *Scottish Trades Diary* as Golf Cleek and Ironmaker 1903. *Slaters* 1903, 07, 11, 15. Stewart's ladies clubs usually have a snake on them. When Stewart died his sons carried on the business until the Second World War.

White, Robert (b.1857 in England) St Andrews
Originally a blacksmith, turned to cleekmaking. He appears in the 1881 Census aged 24, also in the *Fife Trade Directory* 1893–4. He worked at Cathedral Pends and was the last man to use water from the Mediaeval Mill Leat there before it was filled in (see Robertson, *St Andrews Home of Golf* – J. & G. Innes 1967). A considerable pioneer cleekmaker and made, in particular, fine cleeks and lofting irons. Thomas Stewart was apprenticed to him from 1890–3. He emigrated to America in about 1894 and was involved in

the setting up of Crawford, McGregor & Canby in the manufacture of golf clubs. (see Chapter 4). He impressed his name on the back of his irons.

Wilson, Robert (1845–1906)
St Andrews
Death certificate lists him as a blacksmith of 144, North St., St Andrews and son of Alex. Wilson, also a blacksmith.
Said by Robertson, *St Andrews Home of Golf* (J. & G. Innes 1967), p.56, to be one of the pioneer blacksmiths-turned-cleekmakers and to have made very fine irons particularly cleeks. He is mentioned also by Sir Guy Campbell in *History of Golf in Great Britain* as an early and highly-skilled craftsman. Despite this, the only certain reference to him is 'R. Wilson of St Andrews' listed as a cleekmaker in *Slaters* 1900. He had a mark, a bent nail on the back of the heel of the club or

on the hose, described as small but readily identifiable. He also impressed his name on the back of some of his clubs.

Winton, James (1835–1909)
Montrose
1861 Census records James Winton aged 26 as a journeyman miller born in Kincardineshire.
Slaters lists him as a cleekmaker 1896. W. M. Winton & Co. are listed as cleekmakers 1900, 03, 07, 11, and 15.

Winton, Robert (1862–1926)
Montrose (son of James)
The firm ceased to exist in 1936. The cleekmakers' sign of Winton & Co. was a diamond. The sign is often accompanied by a number. They seem to have made good clubs and also made large numbers, for there are many clubs to be found with a diamond on them. At one stage they had a second factory at East Acton, London.
His elder son ran the business for a few years after his father's death and then sold it to his brother William.

W. M. Winton & Co., Ltd.
William M. Winton (son of James) c.1884 went to Australia and worked in the hardwood forests of Queensland. In 1897 he returned to England and became a golf professional at East Finchley – later on at Acton. In 1910 after 10 years at Acton, he left and started his own factory with a Mr A. C. Clayson, making woods and irons at Hemp Row, Walworth, London. He was

so successful that he took over his brother's business at Montrose (See *Golf Monthly* Feb.1914). The firm eventually closed down in 1936.

Some 'false' cleekmarks
Occasionally a clubmaker would order iron heads from a cleekmaker and would have not only his name stamped on the back, but a special mark of his own. Often the cleekmaker would leave his own mark off: in such cases it is easy to assume, falsely, that the mark is the cleekmaker's mark. We know of two but there may be more.

1. **Charles Gibson** of Westward Ho! in his earlier days had a prancing horse stamped on all the irons he ordered: most of these irons came from Gibson of Kinghorn; some from Anderson of Anstruther.

2. **A. H. Scott of Elie.** Had a crown and star stamped on his iron clubs after he got Royal Patronage. The iron heads were made by Anderson of Anstruther. See page 188.

Prince of Wales Feathers stamped
on a Forgan iron made between
1863 and 1901 when he was By
Appointment to HRH The Prince
of Wales. A 'false' cleekmark as
Forgan's did not make the iron
head.

Crown on a Forgan's iron made
after 1901, when the Prince of
Wales became King Edward VII.
A 'false' cleekmark also.

A list of cleekmakers, not included in the lists of major cleekmakers, whose names have appeared in the course of
research. Some are cleekmakers in their own right but we think it likely that many were employed by the master
cleekmakers as skilled workers and would therefore not have their own 'mark'.

Brodie, Robert	1837–1907	Anstruther.
		Occupation on Death Certificate – Blacksmith.
Brodie, Robert (son)	1858–1943	Anstruther.
		Occupation on Death Certificate – Golf cleek manufacturer (retired).
Brodie, Robert (grandson)	1880–1963	Anstruther.
Brodie, Robert & Sons	—	Golf cleekmakers. Listed in *Slaters* 1911, 1915.
Brown, David	—	St Andrews. Valuation Roll 1910–11. Cleekmaker.
Brown, John	—	St Andrews. Valuation Roll 1899, 1900. Cleekmaker.
Carstairs, William	—	St Andrews. Valuation Roll 1910, 1911. Cleekmaker.
Harrower, T. H.	—	Carnoustie. Advert 1912. Heartmark.
Himmerman, John	—	St Andrews. Valuation Roll 1910, 1911. Cleekmaker.
Macrae, Andrew	—	St Andrews. Valuation Roll 1910, 1911.
Melville, John	1879–1948	St Andrews. Valuation Roll 1900, 01, 02, 03, 10, 11. Cleekmaker.
Parker, William	—	Carnoustie. Forfarshire Valuation Roll 1907. *Slaters* 1907. Cleekmaker.
Peebles, Thomas	1839–1920	Pittenweem. *Slaters* 1893, 1896, 1900, 1903. Golf cleekmaker.
Ronaldson, James	—	Carnoustie. Forfarshire Valuation Roll 1905. Golf cleekmaker.
Tait, Alexander	1866–	Musselburgh. Golf cleekmaker. *Musselburgh Directory* 1903.
Tait, David	—	St Andrews. Valuation Roll 1897, 99, 1900. Cleekmaker.
Walker, David	—	St Andrews. Valuation Roll 1910–11. Cleekmaker.
Watters, David	—	St Andrews. Valuation Roll 1893, 1895, 1900, 02, 03. Cleekmaker.
Watters, John, junior	—	St Andrews. Valuation Roll 1902, 03. Cleekmaker.
Whelan, William	—	St Andrews. Valuation Roll 1903. Cleekmaker.
Wilkie, James	—	St Andrews. Valuation Roll 1903. Cleekmaker.
Wilson, William	—	St Andrews. *Slaters* 1889, 1893, 1896, 1903. Smith and cleekmaker.

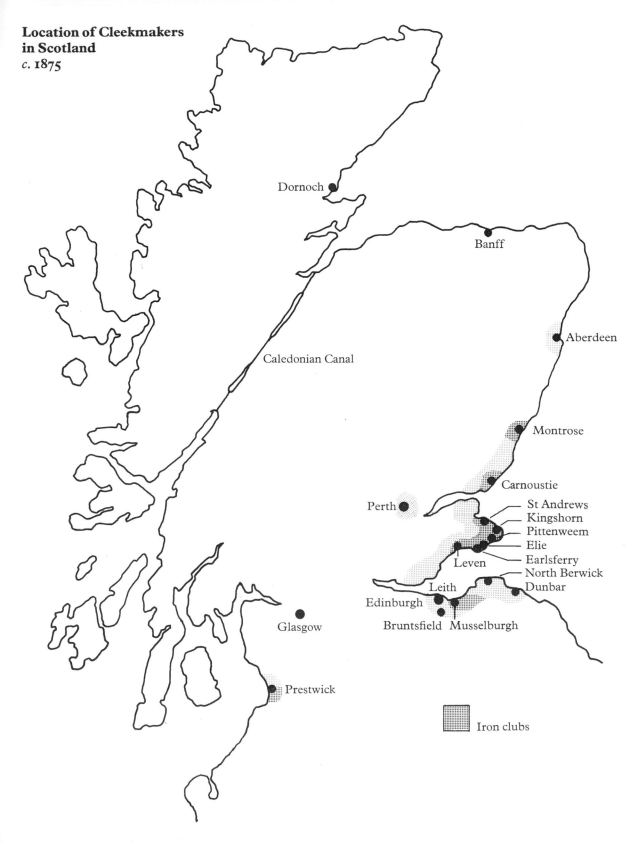

**Location of Cleekmakers
in Scotland**
c. **1875**

Dornoch

Banff

Aberdeen

Caledonian Canal

Montrose

Carnoustie

Perth

St Andrews
Kingshorn
Pittenweem
Elie
Earlsferry
Leven
North Berwick
Dunbar

Leith

Edinburgh

Glasgow

Bruntsfield   Musselburgh

Prestwick

Iron clubs

James Patrick

Chapter 7
Styles and Methods of Play

We have now considered the ancient origins of golf and later, on a more local basis, on what sort of ground golf came to be played and it may be of interest to consider and theorise in very general terms on the changes that took place in the style of play and the methods of play and relate them to the implements and the changes in golfing conditions generally. Apart from one glorious exception, most of the books written about golf and how to play it were written after 1850. The exception is a charming narrative written in 1687 in the form of a diary by Thomas Kincaid, a young Edinburgh golfer and man-about-town. Because it is the only documentary evidence, because it is charmingly written and very detailed, it is quoted in full in the Appendix on page 323.

The musings of Thomas Kincaid – 1687

Kincaid, a cheerful man-about-town and clearly a golf addict wrote, starting in January 1687, about the golf swing as he (and presumably other and better golfers than himself) felt it should be. This is by far the earliest treatise in existence on how to play golf and includes other interesting and contemporary information.

He advises that one should stand as in fencing, i.e. the left foot a little in advance of the right: he is also concerned that the knees should be slightly bent but that the legs, back and arms should be held rigid throughout the stroke. The ball must be straight in front and a little toward the left foot. The weight must be inclined to the right. The body must be bent slightly forward from the small of the back and all the power in the stroke is to be derived from the turn of the body. The body must be kept in the same posture throughout the stroke, neither straightening up nor bending down. The arms are not to move much but to be held rigid and the grip of the club must be very firm. The 'turning about' is what is stressed and the power of the swing is from this. The learner is also advised that the back swing and forward swing are all performed as one rhythmic motion with no stopping. One is advised to hit the ball clean and not strike the ground. Kincaid further reiterates 'You must hit the ball exactly' and goes into some detail about the actual position of feet, body, distribution of weight, etc., which will help to achieve this, including the importance of not 'pressing'.

Apart from the swing, he mentions a number of other facts:

1   The shaft of the club is to be made of hazel.

2   The head must be at a very obtuse angle to the shaft.

3   The shaft should bend as much at the handle as it does at the whipping, i.e. the shaft is very long and whippy.

Altogether this is a remarkably good account of how to hit a golf ball in 1687 and conjures up a picture of a very long, full, flat swing made with a long club with a very whippy shaft. The power of the stroke was generated by centrifugal force – a slow acceleration with rigid arms from a big shoulder turn. In some ways it was not unlike

Opposite: Portrait of 'Old' Tom Morris, St Andrews, by James Patrick.

A sketch of William St Clair of Roslin after the portrait by Sir George Chalmers.
The stance adopted by the feather ball golfers. Right foot drawn well back. Note the whole hands firmly on a thick grip.

the method used in hammer throwing. The sharp acceleration by means of the 'late hit' with the hands and forearms, which is a feature of golf with steel shafts (and, to a lesser extent, with hickory shafts) was impossible.

It will be noted that Kincaid says – in the twelfth note – that the shaft of the club must be of hazel, that the head must make a very obtuse angle with the shaft and that it must bend as much at the handle as it does at the whipping, being very supple and both long and great. At this time, of course, hickory had not come into use and although between the time of Kincaid and the introduction of hickory, shafts were commonly made of ash, it would seem that at this time they were made of hazel. Hazel is a supple wood and has a considerable 'whip' in it. If a shaft of hazel were long, as Kincaid recommends, it would certainly need to be great, i.e. great in diameter, otherwise it would be too whippy and too difficult to use, and it is probably the thickness of the shaft which gives some of the early golf clubs an appearance of clumsiness which they do not deserve.

The 'ancient clubs' at Troon and Blackheath Golf Clubs have well-shaped wooden heads but very thick shafts. This is probably not because they were clumsily made but because the ash shaft needed to be thick if it were very long as it would otherwise be too difficult to swing. He goes on in the thirteenth paragraph to talk about the size of the ball but he also points out that the casing must be of thick, hard leather, so that it is clear that the leather casing with the feathers pressed into it was in use in 1687. It is also noticeable that in the eleventh paragraph he mentions that 'you should tee your ball at first pretty high from the ground'; it is clear from this that from a very early time the ball was teed upon a sand tee. Many of the basic or fundamental points that he makes about hitting a golf ball could well be studied by golfers of today with advantage. There are one or two points that he makes about the method of hitting the ball which show clearly how a golf swing was executed and that this execution differs in many respects from the golf swing of today.

The fact that the head made a very obtuse angle with the shaft means, of course, that the club was of a very flat lie and as it is described also as being long, this must have meant that the player stood at a considerable distance from the ball. We note from Kincaid that 'he should put his left foot somewhat forward' and we further note in Kincaid's article that 'the strength of the stroke is from the swing of the body in turning about'. He also points out, the greater the swing, the greater the stroke.

When one considers the length of the shaft, the whippiness of the hazel and the description of the turning about of the body, it is surely clear that this swing was very much a swing or sweep and that there was no attempt whatever to use the hands to speed up the clubhead. The swing must be long, rounded and smooth so that the ball was swept away off the tee to gain maximum distance. This method of hitting the ball was due, in large measure, to the nature of the club which was, of course, in turn, due to the materials of which it was made. The ball was probably quite lively and resilient when hit, at least when it was new and had not been exposed to wet weather; it is not hard to imagine that a ball with a leather cover, stuffed full of chicken feathers so that it was very tight and firm, would readily fly through the air and, of course, the seams where the leather parts were sewn together would act as good 'markings' which would help the ball in its flight. It is probably no coincidence that Messieux, a Frenchman, in 1836 at St Andrews hit the longest drive with a feathery golf ball and that this was definitely a longer drive than was ever hit with a gutty.

The feathery ball and the long club being in use before the days of photography there is, alas, no picture on record of a feathery ball being struck by a golfer but there is a picture in Sir Walter Simpson's *Art of Golf* which depicts Tom Morris swinging a golf club. The book is written in 1892 which was, of course, well into the era of the gutta percha golf ball, but Tom Morris, in his younger day, helped Allan Robertson to make feathery golf balls. It is likely, therefore, that some features of the swing that he used in order to hit a feathery ball stayed with him and that a picture of his swing may reasonably be expected to give some clue as to the type of swing used

Picture of Tom Morris showing the swing used for a feather ball. Half way on the down swing. Note the flat plane in which the clubhead is swinging and the distance the ball is from the player. The stance is nearly square (but the ball being hit is a gutty, on this occasion).

with a feathery ball. The thick shafts of the ash clubs were so easy to grip that they often did not have a leather grip at all and the ancient clubs at Royal Troon are an example of this. There are, in all, eight clubs and only two have got grips, and those without grips show no evidence of ever having had a grip. A club by Sandison of Aberdeen also has a thick shaft and no grip, and although it appears clumsy, the head is very finely shaped.

With the passage of the years the materials which went into the making of a golf club changed. The shaft was frequently made of ash which had a rather more steely spring to it than hazel and the heads of the clubs were usually made of beech, but the two greatest changes that took place after 1850 were due to the advent of the gutta percha golf ball and the use of hickory for shafts. Feathery balls were very expensive and in their day golf was a rich man's game. The gutta percha golf ball made the game much cheaper and the gutta percha ball was easy and quick to make and could be produced in large numbers. It had very different characteristics from the feathery ball, notably the fact that it was hard and not at all lively. It could resist being mishit with an iron club much better than the feathery golf ball and the improvement in the shafts meant that there was rather more hand action in the swing than there had been in the days of the feathery ball. The hard ball was hit harder and this caused considerable trauma, both to the hands of the golfer and to the clubhead. If a clubhead were applied to such a ball which was to be hit hard, it would probably crack, and it usually cracked at the neck. The better hickory shaft did not need to be as thick as the ash shaft and for this reason and because there was a considerable shock to the player's hands when the gutta percha ball was hit hard, thick grips became the fashion. To lessen the shock still further and to protect the wooden clubheads from breaking, faces of various compositions were inserted, such as leather, vulcanite, bone, ivory and brass. The iron club became more popular and came to be used for deliberate shots rather than being used as a last-ditch saver as in the previous years and the number and complexity of iron clubs increased.

The swing altered as did the stance, not immediately but gradually. The clubs used were somewhat shorter and more upright and had deeper faces and the ball was hit fairly hard with the hands and the forearms. It was difficult to get the gutta percha ball airborne and the old flat swing with the left foot forward began to disappear to be succeeded by a swing in which the player stood square or even with the right foot slightly forward and with a steeper or more upright backswing in order to make the unresponsive gutta airborne.

Many leading amateurs and professionals adopted a more upright swing than before. In the early 1850s the hickory shaft appeared and this had a definite and steely spring to it so that the shaft could be made quite thin and the clubhead could be forced into the shot, using the hands and the forearms. Around 1897, persimmon began to be used for clubheads and this enabled more force to be applied to the shot so that towards the end of the gutty era, the swing continued to change and to become more upright, more forceful and, in general, more like the modern golf swing.

With the advent of the Haskell ball, 1902–1904, things changed yet again. The Haskell ball was much livelier off the clubface than the gutta percha ball. So lively and resilient, in fact, that it flattened considerably on the clubface when hit and tended to climb the clubface slightly, particularly with the irons. In consequence, the problem that faced the golfer was different entirely to the one that he had faced with the gutty. He now had to consider how to keep the lively ball down and prevent it climbing too high and he also had to have a club which would allow for the climb-up on the face by the resilient Haskell ball. Thus, clubfaces generally became deeper. As an example of the change, club faces of wooden clubs at this time were probably $1\frac{1}{4}$ inches to $1\frac{1}{2}$ inches deep. Allan Robertson who played with a feathery golf ball and who was the first man to hole St Andrews in 79, did so with the clubs in which the face of the wooden clubs was $\frac{15}{16}$ inch deep.

The two great schools of golf in Scotland, in the days of the gutta, were St Andrews and Carnoustie. Later, the English golfers came into the reckoning and there is described from time to time in the books on golf at that time, three different swings – the St Andrews swing, the Carnoustie swing and the English swing. The English swing was really a swing that was developed to meet the circumstances of the improvement in clubs and in the golf ball. When the English took to golf in large numbers, there was a tendency for the right foot to come forward, as mentioned, for the swing to be more upright and the clubfaces to be deeper and the swing, in general, to be slightly shorter than it had been previously. This was because of the improved hickory shaft, the persimmon heads and the continued improvements in the gutta percha ball, and it is only too likely that many golfers in Scotland had adopted the same system: it is doubtful if, in fact, this should really be called an English swing.

The difference between the St Andrews swing and the Carnoustie swing was somewhat difficult to describe. Robert Harris, in *Sixty Years of Golf*, talks of the old days at Carnoustie where he was brought up:

> 'These old time players had the perfect body turn, the chin pointed to the ball at the top of the back swing. All of them turned their wrists and took the club back with the hands moving low around the back of the neck. If the hickory shaft was sufficiently supple it seemed that the clubhead must inevitably hit the left knee but with a down swing of unhurried pace and a smooth follow through, they swept or "carted" the ball away with a gentle rising flight to flutter and descend, pancake fashion, on the selected spot. There was no hard hitting or forcing. The "dunch" and "dig" and the taking of turf was still many years away.'

From the description of this swing and the fact that he was talking

The 'palm' grip.

about the old-time players, he seems to be describing the sort of swing that is a development of the swing which Kincaid describes. Subsequently, in the same book, he talks about the swing of F. G. Tait, who was a St Andrews golfer:

> 'From the top of the swing the stroke followed through to the end in the real St Andrews follow through with the strong un-hurried turn of the shoulders until the hands came again to the back of the neck, the club lying horizontally with the wrist turned and the toe of the club pointing to the ground.'

The swing that he describes as a St Andrews swing sounds very like the swing that he describes as a Carnoustie swing but there is no doubt if Robert Harris had seen an expert golfer from either St Andrews or Carnoustie, he could have said immediately from which locality he derived his swing.

The grip

Kincaid points out that 'there must be little movement of the arms and forearms in the swing but that the grip of your hand must be very fast' and, in the days in which he was describing such a swing and method, the club was gripped in the palm of the hands and not in the fingers. Indeed, this was so through much of the gutty era and it was not until an improvement in the shaft and the head and the subsequent improvement in the form of the Haskell ball came about, that the club was held more in the fingers, although there was a move towards it before this. The Vardon grip with the overlapping of the finger, as described by him, was essentially a finger grip and this grip, in fact, was not invented by Vardon. It had been used by J. E. Laidley of North Berwick at least fifteen to twenty years before Vardon appeared on the scene.

The swing

It is instructive to examine the nature of the swing for the gutty ball in 1900, when Horace Hutchinson produced his book *Golf and Golfers* in which there were a number of, admittedly, posed photographs. The swings had many features and all differ, perhaps, slightly from one another, but there seem to be three or four points which are common to all. Firstly, the uninhibited raising of the left heel from the ground so that there was, in fact, no tension down the inside of the left leg such as we find in modern golf. A second point in the Scots swing of this time is the considerable turn of the shoulders which no doubt was made easier of achievement by the raising of the left heel. Although Robert Harris describes the chin as pointing at the ball, an examination of the photographs will show that, in fact, the chin was frequently pointing towards the right foot and, indeed, in some of the pictures of these golfers, it is hard to believe that they had the ball in sight at the top of the back swing at all. A further feature of the St Andrews or Scottish swing of its day would appear to have been the marked raising of the right elbow at the top of the back swing and this, no doubt, was what gave the swing its long, free, smooth, slashing appearance. Edward Blackwell

The full swing that swept (rather than hit) the ball away. Even with the ball opposite the right foot the player can only just see the ball: if the ball were opposite the left foot it would not be visible. Clubhead pointing very much to right of target. A St Andrews golfer of the 'Old School'.

Horace Hutchinson, an Amateur Champion. Big shoulder turn, high right elbow, the club close to the back of the neck. High lift of left heel with sole of shoe facing hole.

provides a good example of such a position at the top of a back swing; of his back swing Horace Hutchinson remarks:

> 'This high raising of the right elbow was a feature of the style of an older school.'

In an interesting contrast to the top of this back swing is the picture of Archie Simpson at the top of the drive; Horace Hutchinson comments:

> 'This is the way Simpson really does swing. That is the length or shortness of his upward swing. Simpson does go no further back than this and there must be some other explanation of the impression of length that his whole swing gives.'

The top of the back swing position, as far as the club is concerned and the shoulders, is more nearly like the modern golf swing than any of the others illustrated. It will also be noticed in nearly all these illustrations that, as described by Robert Harris, the shaft of the club is very close to the back of the neck at the top of the back swing. Lastly, Mr Harold Hilton illustrates the looseness of the grip on the club at the top of the swing.

It was quite customary, at the beginning of the down swing, to let the club drop from between halfway up the thumb and index finger of the right hand into the 'V' (see picture on page 205) between the

Above: A swing akin to the modern swing. Moderate left heel lift: sole of left shoe *not* facing the hole. Club well clear of the neck but still pointing to right of the hole. Stance slightly open. An excellent example of the so-called 'English Swing' by John Ball, eight times British Amateur Champion, winner of the Open Championship.

Right: Edward Blackwell, a noted long driver. Observe the free 'lift' of the right elbow, also the very full shoulder turn.

Far right: Hugh Kirkaldy. A huge shoulder turn and a free lift of the left heel. An exceptionally long driver.

hand and thumb, and the general impression of such a grip is of a rather loose and uncontrolled hand action. As an illustration of the so-called English swing it would be difficult to improve on the position of Mr John Ball at the top of the back swing.

This picture shows a number of features which indicate Mr Ball's swing was somewhere between the old-time long St Andrews swing and the modern swing, that is to say, the left heel is raised but not as much as before, nor is the foot allowed to turn. The right elbow is much closer to the side. The shoulder turn is not as great. The club, although somewhat nearer the neck than in the modern swing, is held well clear of the neck. There is no doubt that this back swing position would do very well for a modern golfer with the possible exceptions that the right hand grip is a little high and that the elbow is somewhat higher than is fashionable in the present day. Perhaps the first move towards more controlled swing was in the matter of the right elbow. In the top of the back swing position of Vardon, it is noticeable that although no tension is built up in the left leg as the heel is allowed to come up well clear of the ground and the sole is pointing towards the photographer, the right elbow is fairly well tucked into the side, the swing is upright, the club is well clear of the neck and is pointing at the hole. Indeed, it seems from many of the illustrations that the professionals, as opposed to the amateurs, were beginning to bring the right elbow closer in. As the hickory shafts, persimmon heads and improved gutties all made it easier to hit the ball a good distance, control came to be a more important factor and the swing began to become less full and less free, so that greater accuracy and consistency could be achieved. Mr Hutchinson, in his book, goes on to point out that probably the most typical of the old-time St Andrews swing was that of Hugh Kirkaldy.

It can be seen from this swing, and there is no reason to believe that Mr Hutchinson is not perfectly correct in his statement, that the club is near the back of the neck, the shoulder turn is huge and one really wonders whether the player can see the ball at the top of the

Above: H. Hilton at the top of the swing for the half brassey approach. This picture shows the looseness of the grip. The club has dropped into the V between right index finger and thumb.

Right: Archie Simpson, at the top of the drive. The swing, compact and well balanced, was regarded, in 1890, as remarkably short.

Far right: The great Harry Vardon. Six times Open Champion and once Open Champion of America. The left heel is well 'up' and the sole of the left shoe is pointing at the hole. The right elbow held well in, the club pointing directly at the target and held well clear of the neck. The whole swing is in an upright plane. Vardon was renowned both for the length and accuracy of his wooden club shots.

back swing. In fact, this player could not. His brother says of him:

'Hugh turned his head clean round during the backward swing and followed the club with his eyes till he saw the head come down again and strike the ball.'

The left heel is well off the ground; the sole of the boot is pointing almost towards the hole: the only way in which this swing differs from others described is that the right elbow is fairly well into the side.

Horace Hutchinson has this to say:

'The long dashing swing of the St Andrews school has always been looked upon as the orthodox swing to copy. I remember in my younger days always being told to take the club well round the neck in the backward swing. It was pointed out to me that it necessarily gave more freedom and power to the player. While admitting that natural conclusion, I found out that this extra freedom and power was earned at the expense of accuracy, and even in those days I had learnt the lesson that accuracy is the main essential towards achieving successful results. The longer I play, the more is the wisdom of this theory forced upon me.'

Putting styles

Styles were then, as now, very varied and individual. Some generalities may be permitted.

The putting stroke
Willie Park, Jr., a famous putter, advised that the hands should not move forward or backward in the stroke. The putt was hit by a hinge action of the left wrist with left elbow pointing toward the hole and the left arm and forearm not moving. Many leading amateurs and professionals followed this precept.

Stance
There was a tendency to play the ball rather off the right foot, the stance was open and the right forearm near to the right thigh, if not actually resting on it. The weight was more toward the right foot than the left.

Grip
The grip was as for other shots.

James Braid has his weight nearer the right foot. The stance is 'open'. The hands have moved very little in relation to the left knee – an example of hitting the putt with a hinge action of the left wrist.

Above: J. H. Taylor putting.
Weight, slightly to left, open stance.
Left elbow pointing toward the
hole. Right forearm close to the
right thigh.

Centre: Willie Park putting. The
weight evenly distributed: stance
open. The left elbow not markedly
forward and the ball nearer the
right foot than the left.

Top right: This putting stance was
a common one. Weight central (or
just to the right). Left foot well
back. Two handed grip. This
golfer (John Low) was an
international golfer with a well-
deserved reputation as a great
putter with the wooden putter.

W. J. Travis and the original
Schenectady Putter 1904. A
square stance. One gets an
impression of great concentration
despite the smoke screen.

Ladies

In the illustration of the ladies in 1873 (see Chapter 2, page 31) it can be seen that no great swing could be expected from a lady, partly because of her style of dress and partly because of social decorum. Even the lady who brings the club almost to shoulder height is relegated to the background of the picture – only those demonstrating the genteel art of the short putt are permitted in the foreground.

Later, when the dress fashion and slight relaxation of the social code allowed it, ladies' styles and methods of play resembled those of the men but were less muscular in appearance. The difference in swing toward the end of the nineteenth century and especially after the English Ladies' Championship started in 1893 was not as marked as the difference in, say, 1916. The men's swing in 1880–95 was still mainly a sweep in which a long swing, big shoulder turn and absence of rapid, powerful forearm action were features. The ladies could reproduce this well and despite a costume which was not particularly helpful they were more supple than men and could produce an even greater turn of the body and length of back swing.

This suppleness and length of swing are beautifully shown in the pictures of Lady Margaret Scott on this page. This lady won the first three English Ladies' Championships in succession with some ease. That she did not win yet more is due to the fact that she married after the third win and never competed again. She learned her golf on a private course in the grounds of her father's estate and spent much time playing with her three brothers. The latter were all international amateur golfers who, between them, won a number of national championships including the British Amateur Championship.

Lady Margaret Scott: Despite a long skirt, well nipped-in waist, leg o' mutton sleeves and a saucy boater hat, this lady has achieved a back swing so long that she can barely see the ball. The swing is excellent being well balanced and powerful (note the firm 'palm' grip and slightly separated hands). She won the first three Ladies' Championships with ease: she then married and never competed again.

The swing demonstrates a remarkable suppleness, especially when one considers the hampering effect of the costume. With this suppleness goes strength, the two-handed palm grip, with the hands slightly separated, indicating this. No doubt she had to learn to hit

This swing is like the men's swing of the 1890–1900 era. The sole of the left boot is pointing at the hole.

the ball some distance in order to compete with her brothers.

The second illustration of ladies' style again underlines that the ladies used styles and methods similar to men. This top of the back swing position shows the high lift of the right elbow which was a characteristic of the old Scottish swing. The sole of the left boot points towards the hole and there is a big shoulder turn. On the other hand, the club is well clear of the neck and the club is pointing at the hole, neither of which were characteristic of the 'old' Scottish swing.

Some nine years later, Miss Grant Suttie (page 289) shows an excellent swing, more nearly in keeping with a swing of today. The stance position is good, well balanced, left shoulder is slightly 'up' and the right hand perhaps a little under the club for modern tastes and a somewhat 'palm' grip. The top of the swing position would have suggested to her contemporaries a somewhat short back swing but its length would have been quite adequate by today's standards. The turn of the left foot is more on to the inner edge of the foot and there is a good shoulder turn. The clubface is 'half shut' or square. The follow-through is a little short but shows an admirable balance.

Two years later, in 1910, Miss Cecil Leitch, a famous English Ladies' Champion, shows the run-up approach (page 289). An excellent position and method and the whole shot is played in a thoroughly 'masculine' manner by a lady with powerful hands and forearms.

Chapter 8
The Patents

Anyone with a new idea can in theory obtain protection from someone else intent on copying it, by taking out a patent. In practice it means that if someone does infringe the idea, it is possible to take proceedings against the infringer if they refuse either to desist or to pay a royalty for the use of the idea. It is always necessary for a patentee to protect his own position by taking action against an infringer, as can be seen in the most famous golf patent case of all time – Haskell *v*. Hutchison & Main (see Chapter 3). Legal action of this kind can be an expensive business and in this case the plaintiff was not successful, even though the case was taken to the House of Lords.

Nevertheless, for reasons which today are difficult to appreciate, from the year 1890 onwards hundreds of patents were taken out relating to golf and it is worth examining the table on page 268, which shows the number taken out each year up until 1914. Before 1890 there were only fourteen patents which had anything to do with golf. After that date there was an enormous increase in the number taken out, with the Americans joining in – only ten years or so after the game had been introduced to their country. The table breaks down the patents into various categories and a selection has been made from each category drawing attention to those which made a real contribution to the development of the game. Also included are examples of the more bizarre patents – and there were many – some of which the golf theorists of today may appreciate. Money, effort and thought all went into golf, but few made their fortunes.

It must be emphasised again that there were no regulations as to the size or weight of golf balls during that period and no regulations whatever relating to clubs until 1908. In spite of a powerful movement to standardise the golf ball and to ban the introduction of the rubber-cored ball, standardisation was not brought about until 1922. In the case of golf clubs, by 1908 the Rules of Golf

The Schenectady putter (banned in the UK) in use at the American Open Championship at Wheaton, Chicago, 1912 (see US Patent No.723,534 of 1903)

Committee of the Royal & Ancient had ruled that it would not sanction any substantial departure from the traditional and accepted form and make of golf clubs which, in its opinion, consisted of a plain shaft and a head which did not contain any mechanical device such as springs. By 1909 the croquet-mallet principle had been barred as a result of this ruling and the ban extended to the popular Schenectady centre-shafted putter (with which Walter Travis of the USA had won the British Amateur Championship in 1904). Wry-necked clubs, also in widespread use in the USA and the UK, were to be barred too. A major break between the USGA of America and the Royal & Ancient was narrowly avoided though the Americans continued to use the Schenectady.

From then onwards it became necessary to seek the approval of the Rules of Golf Committee of the R. & A. for any idea which did not clearly fall within the general requirement for a golf club. In 1910 further clarification was announced:

'1. The head of a Golf Club shall be so constructed that the length of the head from the back of the heel to the toe shall be greater than the breadth from the face to the back of the head.
2. The shaft must terminate at the heel of the head or in a socket shank or scare which terminates at the heel.
3. The neck, socket, or hose shall not be bent in such a way that the lower end of the shaft would, if produced, meet the head, or the ground, at a point further from the player than the heel of the Club, when the Club is soled in position for play.'

By then the golf magazines such as *Golf Illustrated*, *Golf Monthly* and *Golf* regularly announced the registration of new Patents and Registered Designs.[1] They sometimes added a comment to the effect that a particular design was unlikely to fall within the new Royal & Ancient rulings and would be illegal.

Prior to World War I steel shafts were not approved by the Royal & Ancient nor by the Americans. The regulations relating to club-face markings were not introduced until after World War I either. The Americans, however, approved steel shafts in 1924, although the British did not follow suit until 1929. It is amusing to note that in the Amateur Championship of 1924, Sir Harold Gillies used a 9-inch tee and a large-headed driver. The Royal & Ancient made an appeal to the spirit of the game adding:

'it is much to be deplored that players, instead of trying to master the use of clubs, should endeavour to overcome the difficulties of the game by using implements which have never been associated with it.'

[1]This Register enables a shape to be protected (the number allotted includes a code for dating) and does not cover the material from which it was made.

Twenty-five years earlier there had been a similar reaction to the arrival of the rubber-cored ball, but that development gave so much delight to the general run of golfers that they were not to be denied.

Historically, the boom in patents at the turn of the century coincides with the growth of the game and formation of new Golf Clubs everywhere. Doomed as many of the early ideas were by the ultimate introduction of standards, many of them convey a message of hope for the inadequate golfer – the under-dog. The scratch golfer of the day needed no help but the thousands of beginners of those days did, and that is what it was all about. The Royal & Ancient membership consisted of the best golfers in the land and together with the USGA felt that the players and not the inventors should guide the development of the game. It was an American Vice-President of the USGA who, just after World War I, said 'A player should not be able to buy his shot in a shop'. The student of golfing history may well point out that it has been the golf ball and its imposed limitations which have controlled the game: and it is fun to ponder whether, if all the way-out ideas for clubs had been freely acceptable, it would have affected the game in any way or established any new idea which could be bought in the pro's shop and which could improve permanently the indifferent golfer's game.

British patents relating to sports are grouped together and are relatively easy to extract. Some are equally applicable to golf and games other than golf, such as grips which can be used for golf clubs or tennis racquets. Early American patents proved slightly more difficult to unearth and are set out in full by comparison with the abridged version of the patents available in the UK Patent Office. The nomenclature of golf also differs – golf 'sticks' and 'handles' being referred to in the USA. As would be expected, quite a number were registered in each country.

Some American golf writers have assumed that the chief improvements in the game sprang from American ideas developed after the game had reached that country. H. B. Martin in *Fifty Years of American Golf*, for instance, devotes a chapter to 'American Inventive Genius'. It is important to set the record straight and to assess accurately the great contribution to the game made by each country. A look through the British patent records shows the wealth of ideas, many before their time, which never really saw the light of day. The British were responsible for a core-wound ball in the 1870s, made by Capt. Stewart, RN, of St Andrews, all sorts of caddy bags, including a wheeled trolley, steel shafts in 1894, twenty-six patents for various kinds of tees, and so on. The Americans, with a larger potential market spread over enormous distances, thought in terms of mass production and promotion of what they had made. Vardon's tour in 1900, sponsored by Spaldings, was historic and promoted not only golf but their products. If Gammeter had not mechanised the production of the Haskell ball, it would have gone the way of earlier British efforts. If one single invention revolutionised golf it was Gammeter's. Neither did it take the Americans long to produce their own clubs and at the same time finally eliminate the craftsman clubmaker. The Americans from the beginning treated the production of golf equipment as a business and made a considerable success of it.

The various groups of patents are now considered, starting with those which have had the greatest influence on the game – those relating to the golf ball.

Golf ball patents

Although more patents were taken out for the golf ball than for any other implement, the figures are somewhat distorted by the story of Eleazer Kempshall. He had made a fortune in America out of manufacturing celluloid eyelets for boots and shoes and also making collars. He became a golf addict and was determined to introduce the use of celluloid into golf balls and even golf clubs, and he spent a small fortune trying to do so. His story is related by J. S. Martin who describes how eventually in 1910 his Scottish associate – the St Mungo Golf Ball Company – took over his American golf ball factory in New Jersey. He took out in various names over thirty-three British patents and seventy American, a total of 103 for the golf ball alone, nearly one third of the total of golf ball patents.

The inventions can be divided into the following categories:

1   *Material and its treatment*. Development of solvents, vulcanisation, etc., which produced compositions using both gutta percha and rubber, but numerous other materials including celluloid were tried out.

2   *The core*. Many ideas for different types of core on which to wind the elastic thread for the rubber-cored ball were tried. The liquid centre or core eventually provided a significant advance in golf ball performance.

3   *The mechanical winding* of the core with elastic rubber tape or thread was varied in many ways but the principle having once been accepted, it remained established.

4   *The cover* of the ball and the method of making it withstand a hack with the club, attracted many ideas.

5   *The marking* of the cover from the earliest days of hand-hammering the gutty became one of the most important factors in achieving the success of a particular ball. We see this again in the application of a bramble cover to the original Haskell, before which the ball had not been performing well.

6   *Paint*. The early pure gutta would not take paint and it was many years before a satisfactory type of paint was developed, or the alternative of a white material for the cover was tried out.

7   *The machinery* of golf ball manufacture. The outstanding patent of the golf ball winding machine was by Gammeter, but other developments followed. These included the re-covering of used balls, which became a regular practice before World War I.

1876

No. 3428 Stewart, D. The first composition ball – use of a solvent for gutta percha, then mixture of ground cork and metal filings. Use of sphered mould. Provision for remoulding, and 'hammered' in usual manner. (See page 59.)

1877

No. 4838 Currie, W. Use of india rubber, blended with ground cork etc., and pressed into moulds and vulcanised. The moulds were lined with canvas to effect a marking. This was the patent for the famous 'ECLIPSE' ball. (See pages 59, 60.)

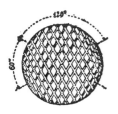

1890

No. 16,862 Park, W. The diamond mesh.

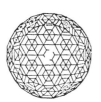

1896

No. 11,761 Park, W. A ball which had flat facings, designed to slow it up on the greens. It was called the 'ROYAL'.

1892

No. 4774 Davidson, A. The rifle mesh, designed so that the ball should travel 'as a projectile from a rifled gun'. There is no evidence that such a ball was produced by Davidson. See also Henry A. patent of 1898.

1895

No. 10,521 Melville, G. Mesh – crossing ridges (a) leaving depressions (b). The Melville ball was on the market.

1895

No. 18,233 Goddard, T. W. A gutta percha ball with metal discs or balls embedded in it, as illustrated.

1896

No. 2235 Lewis, G. A floating golf ball and a net for recovering balls from ponds.

1897

No. 24,667 Fernie, P. G., McHardy, J. & Froy, D. S. Ball provided with isolated indentations.

1898

No. 4360 Henry, A. States quite shortly 'Golf balls are moulded with a series of curvilinear and angular grooves'. In spite of Davidson's 1892 patent, 'Henry's Rifled Ball' was made and put on the market. (See page 77.)

1898

No. 17,554 Boult, A. J. (Work, B. G. & Haskell, C.) Aug. 15 *The Haskell Patent.* This is the abridged specification for the Patent – see USA section.

1900

No. 4165 Boult, A. J. (Haskell Golf Ball Co.) March 5. This is the abridged British patent for the Gammeter golf ball winding machine.

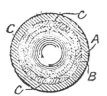

1901

No. 8069 Saunders, A. T. A ball with a compressed air centre effected by means of a hypodermic needle. A ball called the 'PNEUMATIC' was put on the market by Geipel & Lange Ltd. (See pages 74, 75.)

1901

No. 17,413 Gray, R. K. A maker's name-tab to be attached to the ball and readily removed before use. This patent was used by the Silvertown Company for its 'SILVERTOWN SNIPPET' in order to protect its products from inferior balls with imitation marks.

1902

No. 6343 Short, W. M. A cavity in the ball receives a number of small balls which move freely about. See also No. 16,338 of 1903 by Short, W. M.

1902

In this year E. Kempshall filed no less than twenty-nine patents.

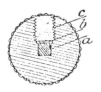

1902

No. 28,750 Southon, W. H. and Southon, H. Mercury is placed into the centre of a ball. In 1904 No. 6172 had the same idea but using the core-wound ball. 'Balls made on this principle have a long and true flight and may readily fall into the putting holes . . .'.

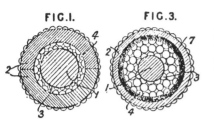

FIG.1. FIG.3.

1903

No. 3230 Roger, J. H. Metal pellets or balls are inserted in the ball 'to give it greater resilience', in two alternative forms – Figs. 1 and 3. Note that a brambled exterior is used.

1903

No. 4591 Greenberg, M. A. and Cowen, I. 'A golf ball is formed by winding a band of pure rubber under tension around a small globular air chamber of glass, etc. This is enclosed in a shell of gutta percha and moulded.' This is given as an example of the many variations of the winding principle under tension that now appeared.

1903

No. 11,785 McDaid, M. A machine for hand-winding rubber thread on golf balls.

1906

No. 9299 McDaid, M. A later machine-winding patent.

1907

No. 852 McDaid, M. Ball moulded under pressure. McDaid was an inventive man who made golf balls under his own name (see Chapter 3 and Scottish Golf Ball Manufacturing Co.).

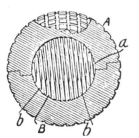
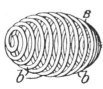

1903

No. 16,128 Thompson, W. P. A ball with a spring core.

1903

No. 16,338 Short, W. M. An inner core of boxwood which is provided with a ball race containing a number of steel balls.

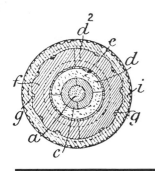

1903

No. 16,800 Gregson, C. A. F. Glass or lead in the centre is enclosed in casings of aluminium.

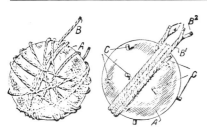

1904

Nos. 1712 and 4960 Appleyard, R. Winding twisted rubber thread over a core. Dr Appleyard was a leading expert on gutta percha.

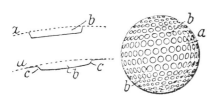

1905

No. 18,668 Taylor, W. To improve the flight of a golf ball, the surface of a covered or solid ball is formed with a number of shallow isolated cavities (see page 67). This was an outstandingly important patent – the dimple has triumphed over all other forms of marking.

1905

No. 20,905 Mingay, F. H. A water, glycerine or treacle-filled bag as a filling for the core of a ball, i.e. a liquid centre. (See page 68.)

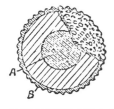

1906

No. 10,463 Hartley, E. and Hartley, J. W. A liquid-filled core of gelatine-wound elastic bands and gutta percha cover.

*c.***1906–08**

At this time there are a number of patents relating to different forms of liquid centres

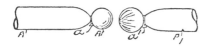

1906

No. 19,981 Miller, H. and Taylor, W. Method of forming a pneumatic core for a ball.

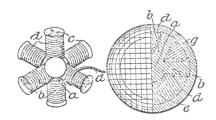

1906
No. 28,085 Thurlow, E. W. A gutta percha cover as illustrated is wound with tensioned vulcanised thread.

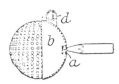

1907
No. 7574 Jones, E. A stencilling device for marking your ball which may be attached to a golf bag.

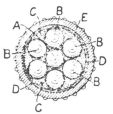

1909
No. 7878 Child, J. & Attwood, B. S. Used a spherical spring as the core.

1910
No. 364 Dimmock, A. F. A series of rubber-wound balls inside a central rubber-wound ball.

1911
No. 5581 Dunlop Rubber Co. & Worth, J. V. The first appearance of Dunlop Rubber Co.

1911
No. 20,778 Johnston, A. & North British Rubber Co. A new mesh design.

1912
No. 3012 Reid, T. & Paull, W. H. A novel marking. Did this ever appear?

1912

No. 16,488 Langstaff, W. 'The core of a golf or other ball consists of a bull's penis first prepared by skinning or drying.'

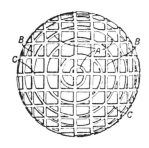

1912

No. 22,179 Hill, W. T. & Milne, R. Unusual marking.

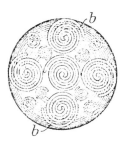

1913

No. 6016 Martin, P. A. & Stanley, J. Different marking. They had a number of patents.

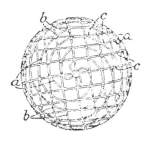

1914

No. 645 Swanborough, F. T. & Avon India Rubber Co. Marking similar to 3012 (1912) and 22,179 (1912) above.

1914

No. 17,159 Fairbrother, H. on behalf of Gammeter, J. R. A new method of producing the cover, using gum as a filling. It is interesting to find Gammeter of the Goodrich Co., USA, appearing again.

The first golf ball patent of all in the USA is No.622,834, applied for on 9th August 1898 by G. Work and Coburn Haskell and granted on 11th April 1899. A short description was as follows:

> 'A golf ball co. manufacturing a core composed wholly or in part of rubber thread under high tension and a Gutta Percha enclosing shell for the core of such thickness as to give it the required rigidity substantially as described.'

> 'A golf ball comprising a central core section of relatively non-elastic material, rubber thread wound thereon under tension and an enclosing shell of Gutta Percha of such thickness to give it the required rigidity, substantially as described.'

This was followed almost immediately by a British Patent (1898) Registration No. 17,554 of 15th August using the name of Boult, A. J. as applicant.

No mention was made at the time of the possibility of machine-winding because development was not complete.

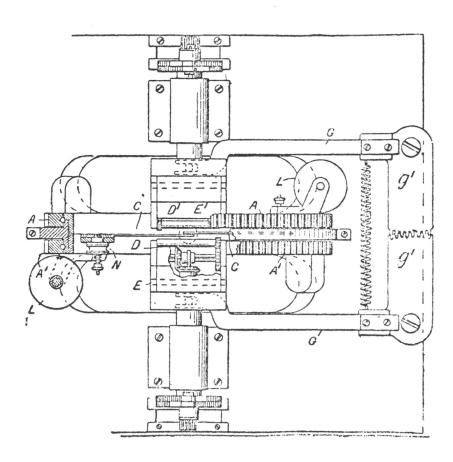

British drawing of Gammeter patent.

1900 J. R. Gammeter then registered his patents Nos. 696,365/6 for his machine without which the Haskell ball would have gone the way of early British hand-wound balls. Gammeter assigned his patent to the Goodrich Rubber Co. and it was registered in the UK, No. 4165 by Boult, A. J. on behalf of the Haskell Golf Ball Co.

The illustrations show the machine measuring approximately three feet long and three feet high as shown from different angles in the US and British patents. It is not intended to describe how it worked, but it was a marvel of ingenuity.

The Haskell patent stimulated even more activity in the USA in 1902 and 1903, than in the UK, with Kempshall the predominant inventor. The main objective was to find some way of doing without the elastic thread-winding process. The common aim was to find a substitute for gutta percha and return to an uncomplicated 'all in one piece ball' (J. S. Martin – Chapter 9 *The Foes of Folderol* which reviews the most interesting of the patents). Nine UK patentees took out US patents during this period.

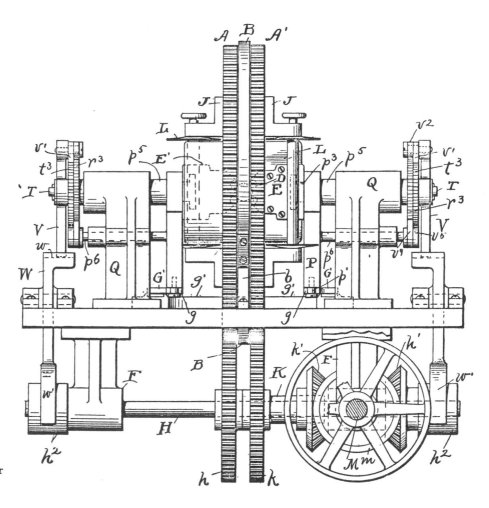

US drawing of Gammeter patent.

Below is an extract from *Golf Illustrated* 20.6.1902, announcing the launching of the 'Kempshall Flyer' in Britain:

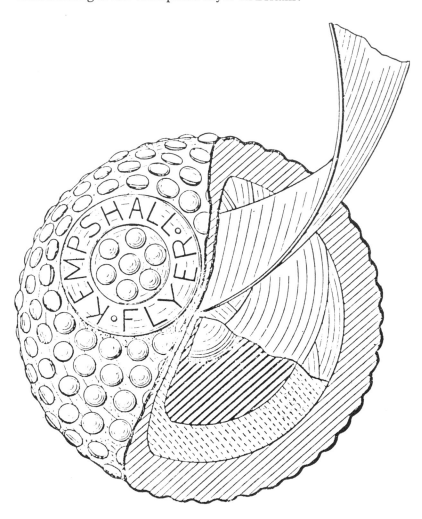

The 'Kempshall Flyer'
'The inventor is Mr E. Kempshall, of Boston and New York, a wealthy manufacturer, who is also a keen golfer. To show the complete way that Mr Kempshall has gone into the matter, it may be mentioned that in the past year or two he has taken out over one hundred patents, in the United States, relating to the structure and manufacture of golf balls. Mr Kempshall's object has been the production of a ball that will fly better than gutta-percha, and yet will be sufficiently dead for approaching and putting.'

Design of clubheads of all kinds and the use of different materials

As early as 1876 there was a patent for a vulcanite or ebonite plastic head in lieu of wood – others were to follow. Even down to the present day no satisfactory substitute has been found for wood or laminates. The 'Mills' range of aluminium-headed clubs were popular for a long time but the Standard Golf Company of Sunderland who made them did not re-establish their business after World War I, although there were other makers who did not achieve the world-wide reputation of Mills.

The most important of the early wooden-head developments was that of the 'Bulger' driver referred to in Chapter 5 which was not patented. (Later on it became appropriate to use the Design Register instead of the Patent.)

A hammer-headed driver and brassie combined appeared in 1892 and this principle was extended to a hammer-headed set of clubs called 'Crossheads', promoted by a Mr L. Everage of Bournemouth, who wrote a booklet entitled *Golf on a new principle*. J. H. Taylor, recent Open Champion, was then at Royal Winchester and, using a set, went round in 78. He used his own putter, however, and putted badly at that – so the clubs did actually perform satisfactorily.

The 'all in one piece' wooden clubs – drivers – were used and success was claimed for them, but with the great mass demand for clubs they must have been difficult to make in quantity. Putters were made of every kind of material and with every kind of device to assist in aiming.

Among the earlier ideas for irons was Low's in 1896 for a matched set of irons. Few of the other designs for irons have any relevance to modern designed clubs.

UK PATENTS

1876
No. 2683 Johnston, T. Heads of clubs formed of vulcanite or ebonite combined with mineral powder moulded to shape.

1890
No. 14,228 Starke, R. The handles of umbrellas, parasols are formed so as to resemble the head of an ordinary golf club and the umbrella used as such.

1891
Nos. 5731 and 5741 Currie, W. Vulcanite composition heads.

1891
No. 5133 Thomson, W. Design of iron with the rear of the blade convex.

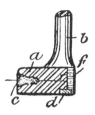

1891
No. 12,207 Morison, A. Head and shaft made of one piece of wood known as the 'all in one piece club' but the club has a driving block of wood (f) with its grain presented endwise to the ball.

1891
No. 21,871 Thomson, W. Metal for the face of wooden club which is toughened by forming diamonds, squares or the like on it.

1891
No. 22,574 Dunn, W. Convex soles for wood and iron clubs.

1892
No. 14,897 Hutchinson, H. G. The toe or nose of wooden club is cut off square with the face. Horace Hutchinson was the well-known player and writer on golf.

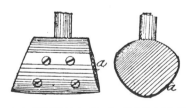

1892
No. 16,148 Dalrymple, Sir W. H. The hammer-head club as a combined driver and brassie.

1893
No. 3822 Ross, W. Iron club with a cavity in the face covered with a thin plate of steel or other suitable springing substance.

1893

No. 8954 Johnson, W. C. Round or oval wooden heads – machine-made with metal socket for shaft.

1894

No. 1959 Gillett, S. W. (Hodgman, W. E.) Another design for an 'all in one piece' club.

1894

No. 9522 Blathwayt, C. R. The right- or left-handed wooden club.

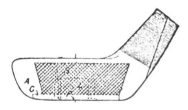

1894

No. 12,019 Jacobs, C. J. Specification for a completely moulded clubhead made of gutta percha, vulcanite, ebonite, etc. This club was commercially produced (see Army & Navy Stores advertisement on page 118).

1894

No. 20,914 Park, W. Wry-necked design for iron clubs.

1894

No. 21,424 Park, W. Compressing and bending hickory, etc. to shape for a wood clubhead.

1894

No. 23,391 Playfair, C. This relates to improvements in aluminium heads, indicating that aluminium was already being used for clubheads.

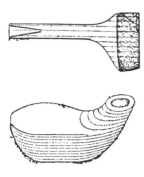

1895
No. 7573 and 11,250 Robertson, D. G. Heads of clubs made of laminated leather.

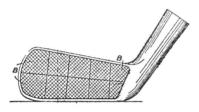

1895
No. 13,545 Mills, W. Development of clubs with an aluminium framework filled in by wood. Clearly a fresh stage in the development of the range of the well-known Mills aluminium clubs. (See Standard Golf Company, page 125.)

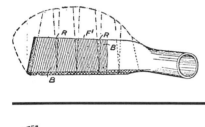

1896
No. 4810 Hunter, R. Metal putter so that the socket terminates and leaves the whole face clear and playable.

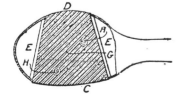

1896
No. 9873 McLachlan, C. D. & Grant, P. S. Hollow metal head with block of wood inserted to provide striking face.

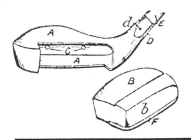

1896

No. 10,211 Young, G. Similar idea to the preceding patent.

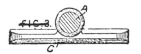

1896

No. 14,812 Munro, J. I. The croquet putter – later banned.

1896

No. 16,560 Lowe, G. Idea for the matched set of irons each 3 inches by $1\frac{3}{8}$ by $\frac{5}{8}$ across the sole; the clubs being named as ordinary irons, lofting irons or mashies and the face being flat all through similar to the 'Fairlie Club'.

1897

No. 12,265 Ward, T. W. Head of a golf club is formed of horn, such as buffalo horn which has been heated so that the pointed end can be twisted or turned to fit the stick!

1898

No. 2930 Brown, J. H. The club is made with its putting face at right angles to that of the ordinary wooden club, the player placing himself behind the back – presumably croquet style. This club could also be used as an ordinary club, in which case a face is also formed on the side of the head.

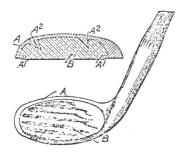

1898

No. 11,350 Ayrton, W. Hollow metallic head for iron clubs, filled in with rubber as a striking face. This type of club was certainly marketed and examples may be seen in museums.

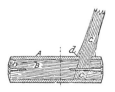

1898

No. 14,169 Cowper-Coles, R. L. & Peake, R. S. C. Convex-faced putter, D-shaped, the convex portion forming the striking face.

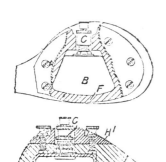

1898
No. 24,274 Jerrard, J. C. This is a double patent. Heads of golf clubs are provided with a pneumatic cushion, covered by a metal or leather face and with an inflating valve. A golf ball with a pneumatic chamber is also described.

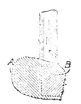

1899
No. 8789 Barrow, P. H. A. Hippopotamus, rhinoceros, walrus or elephant hide to be recessed in the striking face of a wooden club.

1900
No. 4573 Simpson, A. Tapered rectangular socket for irons.

1900
No. 7550 Beldam, G. W. and Winton, W. M. Iron clubs designed with the weight in the top part of head, so that the ball is struck above its centre. This is a strange idea – the advantage is not stated. See also USA Patent No. 655,099 of 1900.

1900
No. 10,051 Boult, A. J. An iron putter has a horizontal rod attached to its back to assist in aiming. The rod could be removed.

1900
No. 12,026 Robertson, W. What appears to be a similar idea to the previous patent. The rod could be folded into a recess in the head.

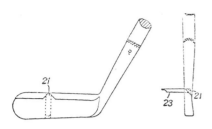

1901

No. 2840 Robertson, W. Further modifications to No. 12,026 of 1900.

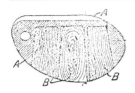

1901

No. 7279 Mills, W. Aluminium clubs with recess for wood blocks in the back of aluminium head. This design was used in Mills heads of the period. (See Standard Golf Company, page 125.)

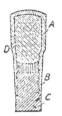

1901

No. 11,118 Wilson, J. Putters have weight put at the top of the handle.

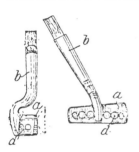

1901

No.12,743 Garlick, W. and Jackson, A. J. Socket for irons placed in the middle of the clubhead.

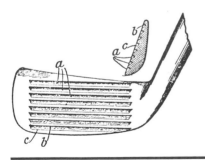

1902

No. 19,988 Burr, E. Rib-faced irons; the overdevelopment of this idea ultimately resulted in strict regulation of the depth and width of the grooves.

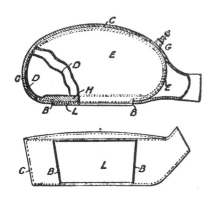

1902
No. 19,675 Taylor, W. Another pneumatic cushion for a clubhead face.

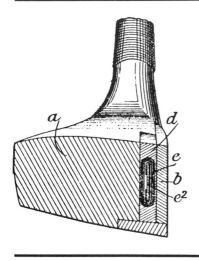

1902
No. 19,242 Byrne, E. J. An elastic pad with a striking face of hard material for the clubface.

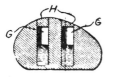

1902
No. 1002 Febiger, H. B. Clubhead with slots containing quicksilver, shot, etc. so as to allow of motion.

1902
No. 11,463 Black, T. H. B. Rollers on the bottom of the club 'to prevent the stroke of the club being spoiled by striking the ground'.

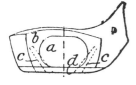

1903
No. 172 Heeren, O. Striking face of glass, quartz or flint.

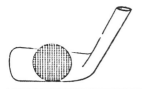

1903
No. 19,725 Simpson, R. Circular face-marking of iron to mark the part which should strike the ball.

1903

No. 20,343 Brown, J. R. Perforations of iron club including, according to the patent, open slots resembling a comb or rake. See also Roger, J. H. 1904 below. Cleeks to this design were made by Winton of Montrose (see page 184).

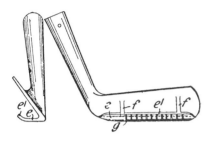

1903

No. 24,834 Brewster, F. W. An extended sole for iron clubs.

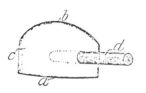

1904

No. 5080 Dunn, W. (Applied for in 1901). A plastic clubhead to be made of pyralin, xylonite , etc.

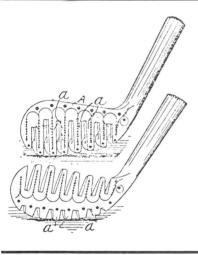

1904

No. 10,736 Roger, J. H. A further development of the principle set out in Brown, J. R. 1903 above; for some reason there is a cross-reference to it in this patent which also says that the club is specially adapted for use in sand bunkers, long grass, etc. Today they are often referred to as 'water mashies' but it appears that they were intended as niblicks.

1904

No. 14,313 Carruthers, J. Back to the pre-1890 principles – a severe concave-faced putter. Its advantages were not stated.

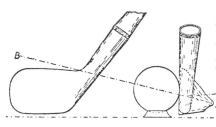

1905

No. 5121 Myles, D. A metal-headed club of the same weight as wood – shortened head – and intended for use with rubber-cored or pneumatic balls.

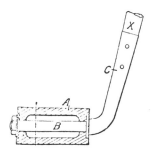

1905

No. 8897 Lloyd, M. G. The revolving 'fluted' roller for the head of a golf club. An advertisement from *Golf Illustrated* 13.12.07 gives a full account of the amazing qualities of this type of club invented in that case by Sir R. Payne Gallwey – no patent being claimed.

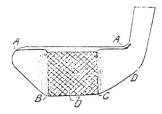

1905

No. 385 Skinner, C. Boat-shaped designs for iron in order to diminish the friction between the ground and the sole of the club. The striking face projects from the face of the club.

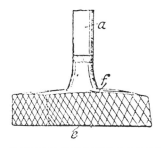

1906

No. 8336 Samuel, Sir E. L. A croquet putter with four faces, two of them lofted.

1906

No. 10,441 Beale, H. Resilient striking faces consisting of steel wires wound round the faces of clubs.

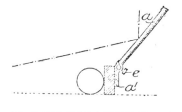

1906

No. 16,834 Maude, A. M. A hinged mirror is fitted at point 'a' to a putter to gauge the direction of travel of the ball.

1906

No. 23,691 Short, W. M. Readily interchangeable faces of wood, horn, bone, metal, etc. See advertisement for Gravitator Golf Ball Company, in *Golf Illustrated* of 6.3.08.

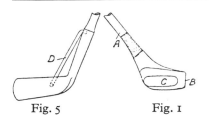

Fig. 5   Fig. 1

1908

No. 3118 Barbour, W. (also Patent No. 19,688 of 1907) Strengthening power behind point of impact by (Fig. 1 Wooden club) – wider socket, cut off toe of club, drop the weight (c) nearer the heel; (Fig. 5 Irons), use of stay.

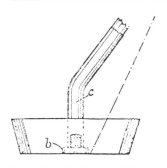

1908

No. 4784 Dagnall, G. F. A channel is formed inside the socket and head of the club with a well behind the club face. A quantity of mercury or small pellets is put into this and rushes into the well on the down swing of the club.

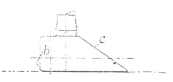

1908

No. 14,199 Southerst, J. & Metcalf, F. T. Glass-headed putter.

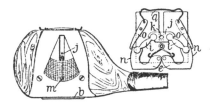

1908

No. 22,400 Evans, R. C. The putter with an alternative end for negotiating stymies (35° loft).

1909

No. 18,616 Collins, S. O. H. & Pearce, H. V. A device contained in the clubhead for recording if you have hit the ball in the middle of club or not. (A further development is No. 28,688 of 1911)

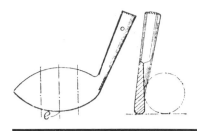

1912
No. 7365 Cannon, W. K. Design for an iron club.

1913
No. 4301 Taylor, J. Protuberances for the iron clubface – subsequently illegal.

1913
No. 9884 Park, W. Step-faced irons with the object of imparting back spin.

1913
No. 20,698 Rose, L. Iron club design – flat extended sole.

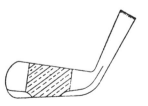

1913
No. 11,264 Simpson, R. Iron club design – sole and heel rounded away so that it cannot cut turf.

1913
No. 15,892 Cooper, M. J. A walking-stick golf club.

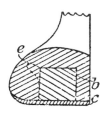

1913

No. 22,206 Auchterlonie, D. & Auchterlonie, W. Putting the weight into the middle of the clubhead.

1914

No. 5340 Taylor, T. Iron club design.

1895

No. 513,733 Gustav, A. Ruemmler, Yonkers, N.Y. A composite laminated head on an extension of the handle.

1896

No. 566,101 Henry R. Sweny, Albany, N.Y. Shank and head turned out of a single piece of wood with the grain lying in a straight line from nose to shank. See also No. 632,885 of 1899.

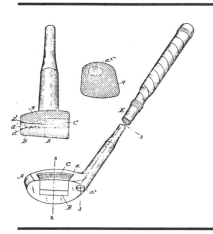

1896

No. 564,655 Edward Slade, Newton, Mass. A golf club having a recess for a block of elastic substance.

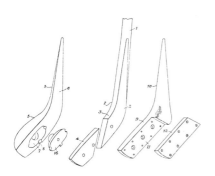

1896
No. 556,042 Warren R. Briggs, Bridgeport, Conn. The head of a driver was made in three sections one of which was integral with the shaft, the others ultimately being spliced to it. In 556,043 filed at the same time he combined the head and shaft into one piece of straight framed wood, with a forked neck to which the shaft could be fitted.

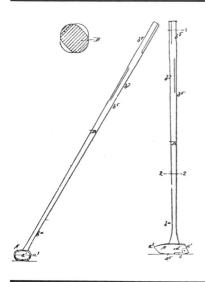

1897
No. 581,331 Francis W. Brewster, London, England; also
1908
No. 894,809
Boat-like, shaped wood clubs (UK patent 9514 of 1897) – the USA patent is visually better.

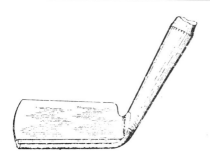

1899
No. 626,347 Walter L. Smith, Elmira, N.Y. Design for an iron club with a longitudinal shoulder along the bottom of the club.

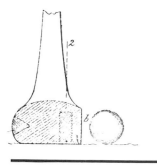

1899
No. 632,885 Harry R. Sweny, Albany, N.Y. (see 566,101 of 1896). This further development contained the design for the striking face and putting weight behind it.

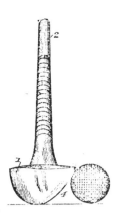

1900

No. 656,099 William Dunn, New York. A design for striking the ball above the centre when the club is held in normal playing position. See also UK Patent 7550 of 1900.

1903

No. 745,044 William Dunn assigned to the Arlington Co., New Jersey. A design for a pyralic compound clubhead, with the shaft set in the middle of the head.

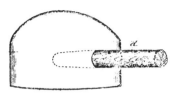

1900

No. 645,942 James Cran, Chicopee Falls, Mass. assigned to A. G. Spalding & Bros., Jersey City. An iron club with an adjustable weight in the rear.

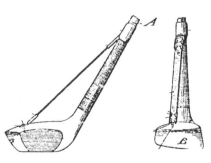

1901

No. 687,539/40 Isaac E. Palmer, Middletown, Conn. A brace connecting the shaft and the head.

1901

No. 677, 811 George W. Mattern, Dayton, Ohio assigned to Crawford, McGregor & Canby Co., same place. A side splice for attaching the head. See also pages 132, 133.

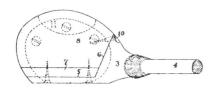

1903

No. 727,819 George W. Mattern, Dayton, Ohio, assigned as above, with a further development of the same idea with elasticity behind the striking face.

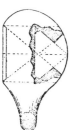

1902

No. 695,579 Charles R. Parmele, New York. A chamber attachment to the shaft having 'a springy metal rod'.

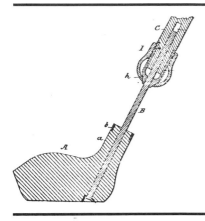

1903

No. 739,458 Walter J. Travis, Garden City, N.Y. (UK Patent No. 10,567 of 1904). Distribution of weight in a wooden clubhead. (Walter J. Travis was the first American to win the British Amateur Championship, in 1904.)

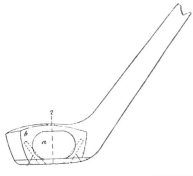
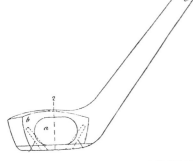

1903

No. 734,065 Oscar Heeren, Biarritz, France. A glass striking face.

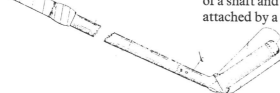

1903

No. 727,086 Clarence M. Burnham, Chicago, Ill. The combination of a shaft and a tubular handle to which the blade of an iron club is attached by a ratchet device.

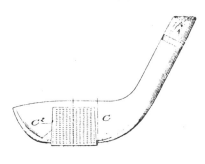

1903
No. 732,136 Frederick W. Taylor, Philadelphia, Pa. A club, presumably an iron although the drawing appears to be a wood, with a flat face at an angle of 55° and a projected striking face having sharp pointed teeth.

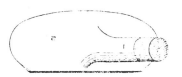

1903
No. 723,534 Arthur F. Knight, Schenectady, N.Y. The 'Schenectady putter' a great success though banned in the UK after 1909. (See illustration on page 210.)

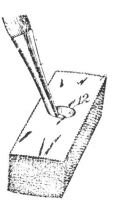

1903
No. 723, 258 Frank B. Felton, Bridgeport, Conn. A metal head and a gutta percha striking face.

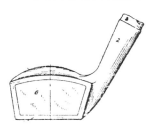

1904
No.749,174 William W. Davis, East Orange, N.J. A putter having four striking faces and the shaft with an adjustable joint, by means of a ball in a chamber and a screw to clamp it in the position required. Also registered as UK Patent 4895 of 1904.

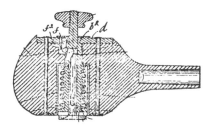

1904
No. 769,939 Charles E. Clark, Lynn, Mass. A spring-load 'back accelerating' device in the clubhead.
Further Patent No. 777,400.

1905
No. 807,736 James Foulis and David Foulis, Wheaton, Ill. A concave design for irons. (See page 65 – Golf ball – J. Foulis's part in re-covering the Haskell ball.)

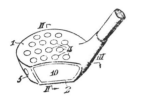

1906
No. 838,284 Charles T. Thompson, Philadelphia, Pa. and Frank P. Mitchell, Laurel Springs, N.J. A metal head with apertures for inserting a resilient substance.

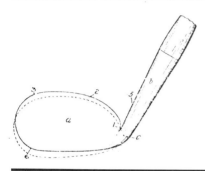

1906
No. 835,735 William Robertson, Oakmont, Pa. A design for what appears to be a broad-faced niblick. Note the shallow connection at the baseline of the head.

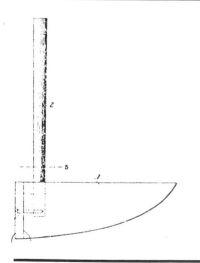

1906
No. 823,082 Frederick H. Robertson, Wichita, Kans. Design for a golf stick – the handle being adjacent to the striking face.

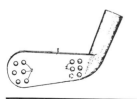

1907
No. 873,423 James Govan, Abington, Pa. Design for irons.

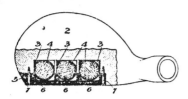

1909

No. 925,389 Charles W. Royce, Montclair, N.J. assigned to Kempshall Man. Co. A face plate compressed against a number of balls.

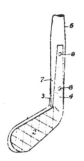

1912

No. 1,026,181 Charles H. Seely, Noroton, Conn. A method of fixing iron heads to the shaft by means of two tangs.

1914

No. 1,096,359 John H. Dwight, Des Moines, Iowa. Design for a driver.

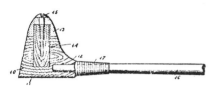

1914

No. 1,089,881 Thomas Taylor, Jr., Hubbard Woods, Ill. See also UK Patent 5340 of 1914. Design for irons.

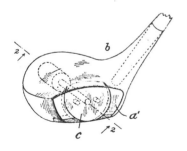

1914

No. 1,091,231 James Millar, Chicopee, Mass. assigned to Spalding & Bros. Design of face plate and weight disposal.

Shafts and the fixing to clubheads

In the chapter dealing with the making of golf clubs, the traditional method of joining the clubhead to the shaft by means of splicing is explained. It was called the 'scared head' technique. With the long wooden heads and the necessity for playing the ball wherever it lay, considerable strain was placed on the spliced joint. With the change in design to much shorter heads around the 1890s it is not surprising that there were many ideas for improving the method of making the joint (see Part I below). As early as 1891 R. Anderson of Edinburgh had patented his idea of placing the shaft directly into the head, and we have a documented club purchased in Edinburgh in 1892 with 'Anderson & Sons Patent' stamped on it. Whether he ever collected any royalties from his development is not known but this method is still used today.

This patent did not prevent a host of other ideas from being propounded nor did it supplant the scared-head principle with a tongue and groove to strengthen it as used for many years. The placing of a shaft direct into the socket of iron clubs was used from time immemorial – but improvements were attempted.

As far as shafts were concerned, nobody claimed any originality for the introduction of hickory shafts. Attempts were made to strengthen the wooden shafts with metal because many shafts were broken in play. Steel shafts have been dealt with in a separate section (Part II below).

Part III relates to adjustable clubs which were designed to play all shots from a single shaft.

Part I Wooden shafts

1890
No. 16,953 Bussey, W. E. & Pinder, J. S. Deals with fixing shafts to iron clubs and a tapered slot for wood clubs.

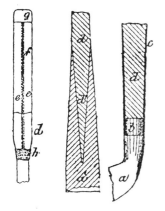

Anderson, R. has the following three patents.

1891
No. 3794 The shaft passes through the neck of the club and is wedged at the bottom. Clubs of this design were stamped Anderson & Sons Patent Edinburgh.

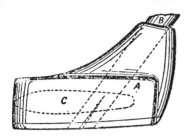

1892

No. 6385 The design for a club with a shortened head and neck with the shaft going right through the centre of the head.

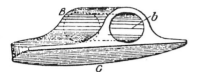

1892

No. 10,187 A design for a centre-shafted iron club.

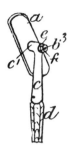

1891

No. 7243 Twist, G. F. An idea for adjusting the angle to the head of the club.

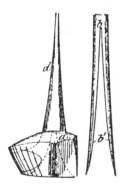

1892

No. 12,093 Gourlay, T. A wedge-shaped shank fitted into a V-shape opening and bound.

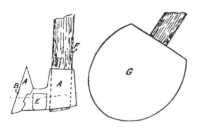

1892

No. 17,929 Grant, G. Shaft is fitted opposite point of impact and the first mention is made of either a hollow or solid metal shaft as an alternative to wood. The drawing shows a special shape for the face of mashies.

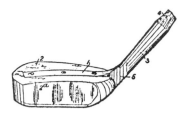

1893

No. 820 Hodgkin, J. A metal frame with fork-like parts which are screwed into the wooden head and a socket into which the shaft is screwed (see also US patent).

1895

No. 21,403 Scott, A. H. A rectangular tapered end to the shaft fitting into a recess in the neck of the club. Note: A. H. Scott, the clubmaker of Elie (see Chapter 4).

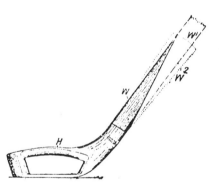

1896

No. 4933 Hamilton, J. F. C. & Jacobs, C. J. A tongue and groove idea using the scared-head method but in this case with particular reference to gutta percha clubheads. See also Patent 12,019 of 1894.

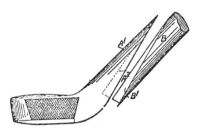

1896

No. 1078 Mills, W. The patent describes the scared-head method of attachment to the shaft of the early Mills aluminium club. (See The Standard Golf Company, page 125.)

1896

No. 7150 Hillman, W. Another method of attaching gutta percha heads for drivers and brassies to the shaft.

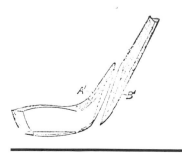

1898

No. 22,763 Butchart, C. S. Scared-head principle with a short-neck clubhead and V-shaped corresponding grooves for the neck and the shaft. Charles Butchart from Carnoustie emigrated to the USA and made W. Hagan's wooden clubs. The latter used Butchart scared-head clubs until after World War I.

1906

No. 25,867 Dickie, J. L. A shaft built up of split cane sectors around a metal steel rod, after the manner of cane fishing rods.

1911

No. 26,976 Gray, L. C. E. The handles for golf clubs are inclined to the shaft.

1911

No. 24,144 Fox, H. W. Greater diameter of shaft near middle of its length. This is a most unusual idea – no club incorporating this principle has yet been seen.

1913

No. 10,910 Seely, C. H. The shaft of iron clubs is rivetted between two resilient steel 'tangs'.

US PATENTS

The US patents number five, of which three are by UK citizens (two of whom did not register a similar patent in the UK).

1901

No. 682,960 Frank L. Slazenger, New York. Screw shaft.

1902

No. 697,179 Frank L. Slazenger, New York, registered a shaft with a separate reinforcing shaft attached. (See Chapter 4, Slazengers Ltd). In 1901 A. E. L. Slazenger (No. 1675) registered Frank L. Slazenger's patent in the UK.

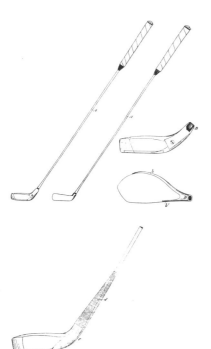

1894
No. 8603 Horsburgh, T. A specification for steel shafts (solid steel rod) and the method of fixing shafts to wood and iron clubs.
This patent was taken out by a thirty-eight year old blacksmith from Balerno (nr. Edinburgh) who played at one time from a handicap of Plus 4 on the nearby Baberton Links at Juniper Green. The shafts were of solid steel rod, thin and resilient, and the ones on exhibition in the Baberton Club House still handle extremely well. The method of fixing the clubheads is shown in the accompanying illustration and a further idea that Horsbrugh had was to have a single shaft and alternative different clubheads. Speaking in 1952, a senior member of the Club, Mr James Graham, said that he frequently played with Mr Horsburgh and borrowed his steel-shafted clubs which he found to be powerful and superior in every way to his own hickory set. Horsburgh could not persuade the club professionals to use the steel shafts in preference to hickory and although he sold the patent to an American it is doubtful if he ever made anything out of it. Nevertheless he deserves his niche in golfing history for an idea that was before its time. He made money from his invention of a horseshoe which did not require nails and died in 1936, leaving the substantial sum of £14,000, but without any benefit from his cherished dream of steel shafts which he lived to see come true.

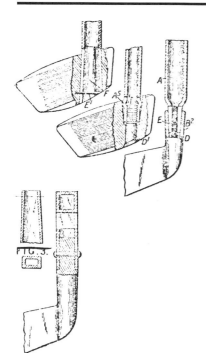

1912
No. 30,050 Scott, E. H. W.; also (below)

1913
No. 26,280 Scott, E. H. W. These specifications relate to shafts of tubular design and the method of fixing them to clubheads. Scott was a clerk in the Stock Exchange living at Beckenham, but nothing more is known as to how far his developments proceeded.

1913

No. 3288 Saunders, S. A. & Accles & Pollock. The shaft consists of a solid drawn tapered steel tube and the method of fixing both iron and wood heads is set out.

Saunders was an engineer with a passion for golf and also fishing and he later developed a tubular steel fishing rod. In conjunction with Accles & Pollock Ltd., Mr Saunders set about producing a number of finished clubs in time for distribution as Christmas boxes to golfing friends for Christmas 1914. An application for a patent in the USA was postponed and the advent of the War also postponed the commercial production of these steel-shafted clubs. After World War I was over, Accles & Pollock Ltd. joined forces ultimately with the American Fork & Hoe Manufacturing Co. which ultimately became the True Temper Corporation.

In 1913 when this patent was taken out, any steel-shafted club would have been banned in both the UK and the USA. There were two reasons for revoking the ban – shortage of hickory and the performance of hickory in certain climates which warped the shafts. In 1924 the USA permitted steel shafts, followed by the UK in 1929, and it is now known that the USA did so with the greatest reluctance. In pressing for the legalisation of steel shafts, claims were made that it would result in the ball being hit still further. This was exactly what the USGA feared and would involve great expense to Golf Clubs in once more having to lengthen their courses. What finally decided them was the depletion of the hickory forests which were being decimated by ever increasing demands for that product. The UK was to follow in 1929 as a result of a request from the New Zealand Golf Association.

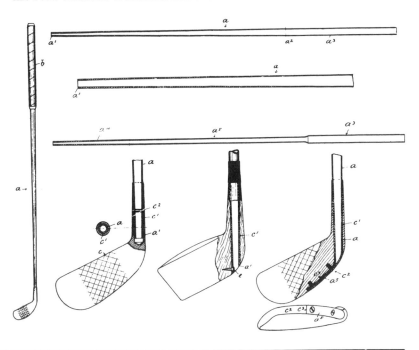

1914

No. 9625 Meguyer W.H. A golf club shaft of steel tube is formed with longitudinal, oblique or spiral slits in order to impart torsinal resilience to the shaft.

Cleeks with steel shafts having slits in them were certainly made, almost certainly after World War I, but little is known about who made them.

1910

No. 486,083 A. F. Knight of Schenectady N.Y. Steel shafts of tubular construction, cylindrical or stepped. He also took out 976,267 in the same year for a torsionless tapering shaft made of steel tubing.

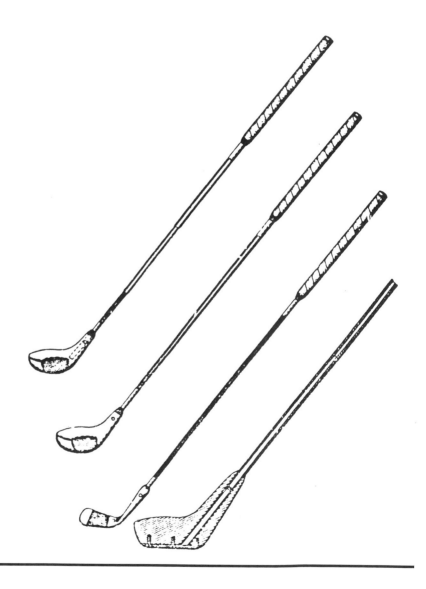

It is doubtful if playing with one club and adjusting the angle of the head as required for each shot was ever intended to be anything but a means of strolling round the course with the minimum of encumbrance. There is no doubt that it was popular and the Urquhart family were outstanding in the development of this club which was a cleek or iron. Other inventors thought of interchangeable heads, which enable woods to be used, but this had the disadvantage that players had to carry clubheads if a full range of clubs were to be used. Today they are a curio of the past.

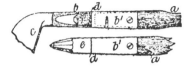

1890
No. 17,211 Stuart, A. D. A single shaft to which different kinds of heads – listed as cleek, driving and lofting mashie, niblick and putter, may be temporarily attached. When not in use the shaft could be provided with a threaded ferrule – presumably for use as a walking stick.

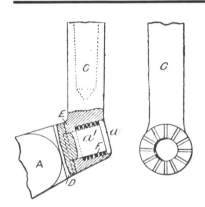

The Urquhart family were active in developing an iron club with an adjustable head and established a company, Urquhart Patents Ltd. at 5 St Andrews Square, Edinburgh which appeared in the Edinburgh Post Office Directory of 1905 but did not appear again prior to World War I. They also took out other patents relating to golf.

1892
No. 8176 Urquhart, R. L.

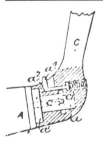

1893
No. 9419 Urquhart, D. I. & R. L.

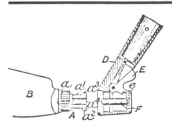

1895
No. 20,642. Urquhart, D. I. & R. L.

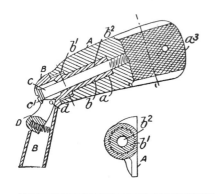

1902

No. 22,590 Urquhart, R. L. & E. M. Improvements to the previous three patents.

1904

No. 776,368 (US) Robert L. Urquhart and Edith M. Urquhart of Dunbar, Scotland. A design which must have incorporated all previous improvements.

Examples of Urquhart clubs may be seen in museums and private collections.

1892

No. 8864 Bussey, W. E. & Pinder, J. S. An interchangeable head, capable of being set at any angle.

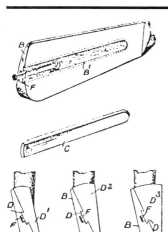

1894

No. 24,771 MacMunn, E. A. S. Insertion of facing blocks to serve as lofting iron.

1895

No. 374 Fawsitt, H. An adjustable head.

1901

No. 23,578 Buchan, C. An adjustable head.

1903

No. 9433 Law, J. & J. S. Interchangeable and adjustable.

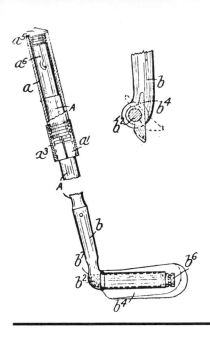

1903

No. 14,891 Burnam, C. M. A different method of attaching the blade to the clubhead.

1903

No. 10,867 Robertson, A. M. Exactly similar idea to Stuart, A. D. No. 17,211 of 1890.

1909

No. 15,713 Ashton, G. T. Adjustable head.

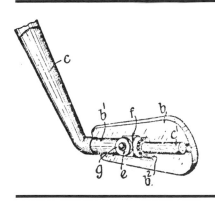

1913

No. 28,312 Pittar, G. F. Adjustable head.

1914

No. 23,839 Nicklin, J. Adjustable head.

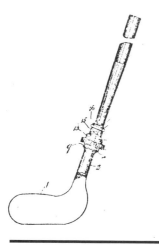

1905
No. 782,955 Albert L. Emens, Lafayette, Ind. Interchangeable clubheads.

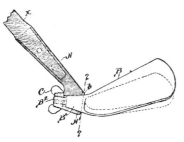

1913
No. 1,058,463 Alexander Pringle, Everett, Mass. Adjustable club.

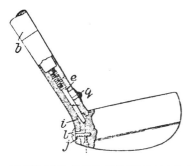

1914
No. 1,083,434 Curry, C. N. of Chicago, Ill. An adjustable club. Also patented in UK Patent No. 9309 of 1914.

The grip

Prior to the introduction of the Haskell core-wound ball, club handles had thick grips because the thickness helped protect the hands from the jarring effect of mis-hitting the hard gutta and gutty balls of the time. Few of today's golfers will have ever seen one. The club-handle was first given several windings of coarse woollen material and was then covered with either soft leather or a smooth finished hide. Starting in 1890 every conceivable idea was explored to enable the club to be held more satisfactorily. Some fifty UK patents and seven American patents were taken out. Many of them dealt with different kinds of material that might be used, and manufacturers were clearly given plenty of new ideas to offer to their customers – the clubmakers.

Here are some of the more interesting developments:

1890
No. 16,953 Bussey, W. E. & Pinder, J. S. This deals also with fixing of shafts – covers leather handles with rubber having a roughened surface or with fish skin.

1890
No. 423 Black, T. H. B. The handle of golf clubs to be made of an oval or similar shape in order to prevent them from turning when in use.

1890
No. 10,701 Currie, W. A vulcanised or unvulcanised tube of ground cork mixed with rubber and celluloid.

1894
No. 24,473 Ben Sayers (see under 'Clubmakers') attached a strip of rubber cloth or leather to the handle of the club so as to form a loop into which the left hand passed to grip the club. 'By this means the club cannot turn in the hand when making a stroke'.

1896
No. 20,738 Gauch Cavanagh, M. R. A tubular grip of rubber mixed with sawdust – 4 to 1 – was prepared so that a person could impress his grip on it before the material set.

1900
No. 11,164 Mollison, W. M. Produced a perforated leather grip and this was undoubtedly widely used.

1904

No. 9816 Sprague, W. H. A cast is taken of the grip of a correct player and you bought the grip of a player who held the club correctly.

1906

No. 27,889 Butchart, W. P. – the oval grip. This idea would indicate that Black in 1890 got no follow-through to his patent (No. 423).

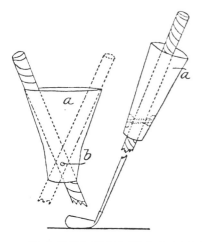

1906

No. 29,058 Cockerton, V. R. This extraordinary patent is quoted in full 'A hand grip for golf clubs – consists of a barrel or collar, in length about the width of the hand, which is pivotted to the shaft of the club. The barrel is open at both ends and is of such shape as to permit the free oscillation of the club inside it.'

1907

No. 6085 Pilcher, N. produced yet another variation of the 1904 patent. *Note:* These became known as the 'anatomical grips' and were taken up by professionals and offered to players.

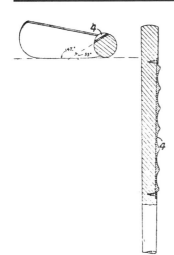

1908

No. 9946 Provan, J. W. A portion of a golf club shaft is provided with finger grooves.

1908

No. 28,465 Thwaite, C. F. A. The top of the golf club handle is thickened for a distance of about $3\frac{1}{2}$ inches. The object of this exercise is not stated.

1908

No. 20,882 Smith, H. H. Riley. The handle is diamond-shaped.

1910

No. 27,613 British Insulated & Helsby Cables & Cole, F. A. This is the first braided rubber grip recorded in the UK.

1911

No. 1792 Cawsey, H. A longitudinal ridge – with a rubber grip, was provided on the side remote from the clubhead.
This idea is used today.

US PATENTS

1899

No. 631,648 Rhodes, G. Lockwood, Boston, Mass. Registers a tubular elastic grip.

1903

No. 742,004 William C. Carnegie, Cumberland Island, Ga. A club provided with elastic material directly attached to the handle and able to be engaged to the wrist of the user. *Note:* This was a similar idea to that of Ben Sayers in his patent of 1894.

1902

No. 712,383 Benjamin A. Joule of Manchester UK registered a rubber handle bound by a spiral cord.

1912
No. 1,017,565 Allan E. Lard, Washington, D.C. A grip comprising a tubular sleeve and a rubber member wound spirally round it.

The golf bag or club carrier

It was not until golf began to catch on in the 1890s that the problem of carrying the clubs without employing a caddy required an efficient alternative method of doing so. Early photographs of golf matches all show caddies carrying the clubs loose under their arms or held loosely by a simple strap hung round the neck.

Various claims have been examined as to who first made or used a golf bag but none are adequately substantiated. A form of bag or contraption for carrying clubs was certainly used in the 1880s, but the mania for patents had not yet caught on and no patent prior to 1890 was taken out.

Reproduced by permission of *Punch*.

MR. PUNCH'S PATENT CADDIE CAR

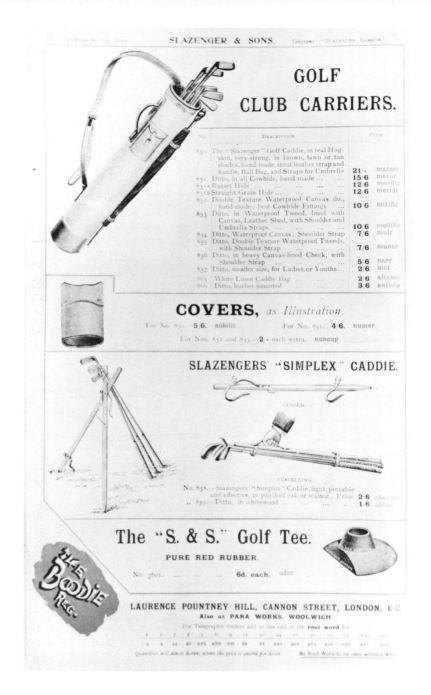

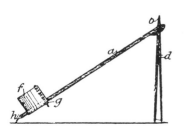

1890
No. 10,390 Anderson, G. C. produced a device for holding the clubs and a tripod to hold it up.

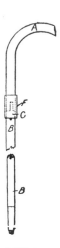

1891
No. 17,918 Buchanan, J. 'To obviate the necessity of having an attendant to carry golf clubs' turns a walking stick or umbrella into a stand by sticking it into the ground and one can only presume resting the loose clubs against the equivalent of the handle.

1892
No. 3584 Baird, J. W. & Eckford, A. The first illustration of the subsequent conventional-type golf bag or club carrier together with a rest, in the form of a spike to be stuck into the ground, thus keeping the bag upright.

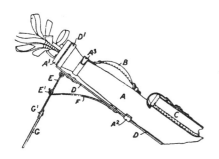

1892
No. 5739 Payne, L. W. describes the golf bag, bound with leather with a pouch for golf balls and a tripod attachment (which is detachable).

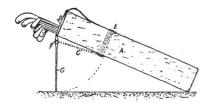

1892
No. 10,175 Chisholm, H. J. Golf club case and stand.

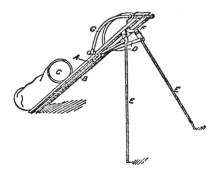

1893

No. 3480 Osmond, J. Golf club case and stand.

Thereafter up to the turn of the century appeared some twenty further patents all concerned with the advantages either of standing the bag plus clubs upright or supporting them by some form of tripod ingeniously contrived to open up automatically as the bag was laid to rest.

1894

No. 25,023 Fisher, J. The drawing attached to this patent is interesting because it shows the golf bag standing upright with the handles of the clubs showing – the heads being at the bottom of the bag. At that time many players were in the habit of carrying their clubs heads downward in this fashion. (See page 296.)

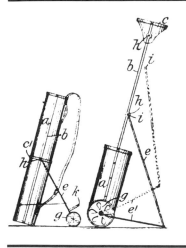

1897

No. 25,415 Boehmer, E. E. B. It would also appear that to Mr Boehmer must go the credit for thinking up the idea of the golf trolley which was not to come into widespread use for another fifty years. He states his case quite clearly: 'Golf – relates to combined dumb caddies and carriages . . . whereby the dumb caddies may be pulled or pushed over the ground on wheels instead of being carried.'

1914

No. 11,992 Pilkington, L. E. had devised a bag which had a compartment for carrying boots, etc., together with a division at the mouth of the bag for separating woods from irons.

The tees

The sand tee was in use from earliest times – and within living memory. Sand boxes are still sitting by tees – empty – and some have water containers attached, because dry sand made an inadequate tee. Prior to the introduction of a box of sand at each tee, caddies carried a little bag with damp sand in it. Between 1889 and 1914 no less than twenty-six UK patents were registered with ideas for teeing up the ball more efficiently.

1889
No. 4901 Alexander, H. G. produced an idea for moulding sand tees.

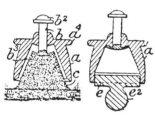

1889
No. 12,941 Bloxsom, W. G. & Douglas, A. S. patented the first rubber tee.

1895
No. 3735 Dalziel, D. A metal frame to be let into the ground on every tee – an adjustment for height. A rubber tee disappeared into a recess, on the ball being struck. The idea was to avoid damage to the face of the driver.

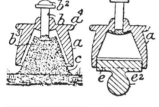

1895
No. 9403 Corlett, S. N. & Hulbert, J. E. Sand mould for tees.

No less than fifteen of the patents in this section related to variations on the theme of tee moulds for the sand.

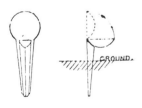

1896
No. 253 Kirkwood, W. We can see the germ of the idea for the modern plastic tee – but in stamped steel.

1896
No. 4409 Hadden, W. I. In the same year another practical idea was produced in rubber.

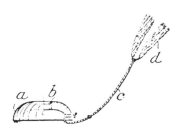

1905
No. 826 Taylor, E. H. Rubber tee and tassel.

1905
No. 4752 Williams, G. J. introduced the idea of cardboard or pasteboard tees which were obviously disposable.

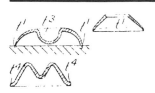

1908
No. 8217 Hartley, C. J. produced the idea of the round rubber tee so that two tees of different level could swivel about the same weight. Tees of this design were undoubtedly popular for many years.

1910
No. 11,967 Hill ,W. A. has a simple thin cardboard collar which fastened into a tee and produced the idea of printing advertising matter on the strips.

Ball pick-ups

To those who make use of the modern plastic tube pick-up for balls, it is interesting to find that the idea of a 'pick-up' was first patented in 1890.

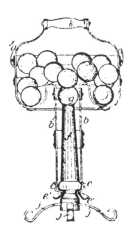

1890
No. 9595 Latham, E. Ball pick-up.

1899
No. 21,000 Bogle, C. D. had an attachment for a golf club which could pick up a ball with the help of four metal arms.

Golf ball cleaners

The painting of a golf ball white in order to assist in finding it has a history of its own, but as courses grew in number, the problem of mud and dirt adhering to the ball became apparent and the golf ball cleaner became a necessary attachment to the golf bag.

1892
No. 12,150 Hulbert, C. E. L. produced a sponge holder, although the specification does not say whether it was to be attached to the golf bag.

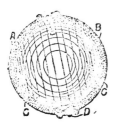

1894
No. 6260 Epstein, L. produced a twin shell cleaner for use in the Club House.

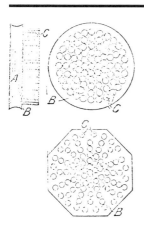

1901
No. 22,725 Wanklyn, H. A. obtained a patent for using straight-forward brushes.

1905
No. 8536 Patchett, J. D. It was not until 1905 that a quite modern-looking design of a rubber sponge-holder for attachment to a 'caddy bag' was produced. It included a small scratcher for removing dirt.

Articles for the golf course

The following patents all contributed to the development of the golf course, and with them a range of grass cutters, mowing machines and the techniques of grass culture.

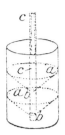

1897
No. 12,165 Cole, A. Design for a golf hole.

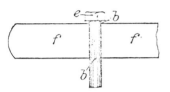

1897
No. 30,300 Cole, A. Design for flagstaffs and flags.

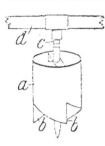

1897
No. 27,159 Cole, A. Hollow auger for cutting out golf holes.

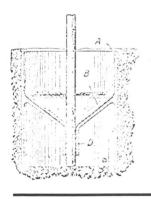

1899
No. 13,482 Turner, E. A. Another design for a golf hole.

1904
No. 29,637 Urquhart, R. L. & E. M. A stand containing tee box, seat, direction post and weather vane for each tee.

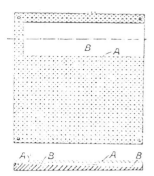

1905
No. 44 King, W. F. A corrugated rubber tee mat for winter use.

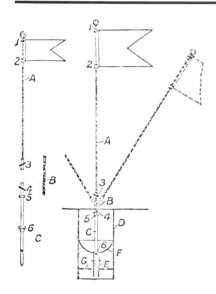

1905
No. 8695 Lander, F. C. A flag-post that will yield should cattle rub against it.

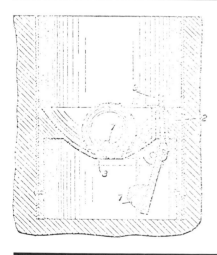

1907
No. 19,031 Dey, A. & J. A device for ejecting the ball from the hole, the mechanism being activated by the 'butt' of a club. Perhaps some such device could now help protect the area adjacent to the hole from the ravages of golfers' spiked shoes when retrieving the ball after holing out.

Golf parlour games

Included under Miscellaneous in the Table on pages 268, 269 are a number of golf parlour games, some of them extending to mini-golf on the carpet and many of them extremely ingenious.

Reproduced by
permission of *Punch*.

" Keep your head still " is the first rule in golf, and Binks
means to do so.

Teaching and practising golf

When golf became popular and new courses were opening up everywhere with small but enthusiastic membership, everyone had to learn how to play. The demand for the professionals skilled in teaching the game was a priority as far as a new Club was concerned.

The following devices, some relating to practice, were mainly designed to help the beginner:

1891
No. 18,814 Jenner, F. Introduction of captive ball for practice.

1902

No. 7726 Clifford, S. Apparatus for teaching the golfing swing – a form of bell had to be made to ring at the start and finish of the swing.

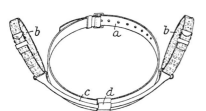

1905

No. 14,452 Ball, F. J. A practice ball with shortened flight.

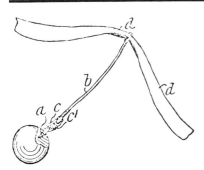

1907

No. 20,463 Longhurst, J. G. The belt is fastened round the waist and the two loops are fastened round the arms just above the elbows. They are thus kept at the correct distance apart during the stroke.

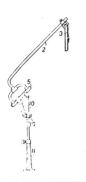

1910

No. 27,103 Logan, H. An apparatus for teaching the correct swing at golf. The apparatus may be attached to a wall bracket and straps are attached to the shoulders of the player.

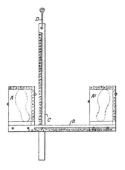

1911

No. 16,930 Brown, R. J. & Barrett, P. F. A device for teaching and registering the correct stance.

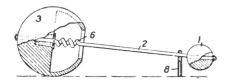

1912
No. 17,420 Heggie, W. A captive ball appliance. The ball swings round an anchor.

1912
No. 17,630 Quill, B. C. A device for indicating the movement of the head while making a stroke. A string is attached to the player's cap and the other end to a weight in a tube. The weight is drawn up the tube if the head is moved.

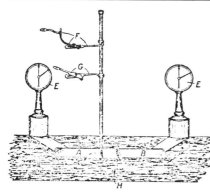

1913
No. 4542 Avery, W. & T. & McGrath, J. M. A remarkable device for measuring weight transference by measuring the weight on each leg whilst making a stroke. Swivelling arms are adjusted against hip and neck and it is suggested that a *cinematograph* or camera is arranged to record the movements of the players.

Analysis of golf patents

	1844–1889	1890	1891	1892	1893	1894	1895	1896	1897	1898	1899	1900
UK												
Balls	6	2	3	2	3	—	3	5	5	4	1	1
Clubs	1	4	8	3	2	15	8	7	3	4	2	•8
Shafts	1	2	1	5	3	3	2	4	1	1	1	—
Bags, etc.	2	2	5	9	4	4	4	3	2	2	5	1
Grips	1	2	—	1	1	5	1	5	5	2	—	2
Misc.	3	—	2	3	3	3	7	6	7	7	4	3
Total	14	12	19	23	16	30	25	30	23	20	13	15
										Prior to 1898		
USA												
Balls										1	—	1
Clubs										9	3	4
Shafts										—	—	1
Bags, etc.												
Grips										—	2	—
Misc.										1	—	—
Total										11	5	6

1913

No. 23,899 Maher, D. A putting-practice device for use on carpets, etc. A similar contraption is still used today.

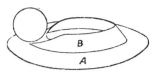

1914

No. 8341 Lovibond, J. L. A guide for teaching the correct golf swing with the help of a captive ball.

1914

No. 19,941 Gunzburg, R. A funnel-shaped structure into which the ball is driven and its velocity measured by the number of times it goes round the ball race.

US PATENT

1906

No. 815,649 Everett Smith, Schenectady, N.Y. A practice putting mat incorporating a golf hole and one or more inclined planes.

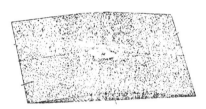

1901	1902	1903	1904	1905	1906	1907	1908	1909	1910	1911	1912	1913	1914	Total
6	46	27	12	12	14	14	11	6	8	17	10	3	6	227
7	11	12	7	7	14	5	8	9	4	14	—	9	7	179
4	—	1	2	1	3	2	1	1	2	5	—	4	3	53
2	2	—	1	5	1	3	5	2	1	2	—	5	8	80
—	1	2	3	2	3	3	3	2	1	1	—	3	—	49
2	5	4	4	9	3	2	6	6	4	3	10	3	11	120
21	65	46	29	36	38	29	34	26	20	42	20	27	35	708
—	75	25	5	5	3	—	6	1	—	1	—	—	—	124
5	7	10	5	3	4	2	2	2	2	1	2	2	8	71
1	2	1	—	1	1	—	—	—	1	—	—	—	1	9
—	—	1	—	—	1	—	—	—	—	2	1	—	—	7
—	—	—	—	—	1	—	1	—	1	—	—	1	—	5
6	84	37	10	9	10	2	9	3	4	4	3	3	9	216
												Grand	Total	924

Chapter 9

Golfiana

Apart from the origins, history, appearance and uses of golf clubs and balls there are some subjects which are indirectly concerned with golf clubs, balls and golfers which are both interesting and important. These are subjects on which the authors have acquired information in the course of research. They are not particularly related to one another but have in common a relation to golf and golfing implements and requisites. None of them warrants a lengthy discourse and they are simply included in order to draw them to the reader's attention and, hopefully, to stimulate interest and encourage further research into what might be termed 'para-golf' subjects.

Restoration, care and identification of antique golf clubs

Many people interested in the golfing past are collectors of golf clubs and golf balls. The purpose of this section is to give the collector some hints on the care of old clubs, on the way to restore them (and to suggest how much, if any, restoration is desirable) and on how to identify them.

Time was, when the only wooden clubs considered collectable were scared-head clubs. Now the older socket-headed clubs are becoming of interest: it will not be long before any club with a wooden shaft will be a collector's item. Already collectors are interested in early steel-shafted clubs – today's rubbish in the attic is tomorrow's antique.

Look in your own attic, your friend's lumber room and in the junk shops. At present the ordinary antique dealer knows little or nothing about golf clubs and does not regard them as of value; as a collector you may profit from this.

Examination of wooden clubs

First, dust the club off gently and then look at it in a good light. In particular, look for the maker's name on the head and look at the shaft immediately below the grip – there may be the same name or the original distributor's name on the shaft, in which case the club has its original shaft still present. If there is no name on the shaft it may still be the original shaft but you cannot prove it. Next, examine the head, the shaft and the grip for worm-holes. If they are present, tap the area gently. If much wood dust falls out the worm is probably active and you would do well to isolate this club from any other wooden objects without more ado. The active-worm areas will need treatment, but more of that anon: at present we are dealing with the preliminary assessment.

The next step is to examine the horn leading edge in the sole and/or the brass plate, if present. Is the horn much damaged, cracked, loose? Check if the wooden pegs holding the horn in place are present. Sometimes the horn is held in place by screws. Usually this indicates that, at some time, the pegs came out and were replaced by screws but occasionally, after 1900, screws were used to hold the horn in position, rather than wooden pegs. Such screws are usually neatly countersunk into the horn.

Then examine the lead. Is it smooth or much dented? Loose? Missing? Held in by screws in some way? The latter indicates bad workmanship originally, or amateur, bungled repairs later. If the lead or horn is missing, go back to the attic, ring up your friend or the junk shop. The missing piece may be there and will make an original piece for replacement rather than a new one. During these examinations it may have become evident that some wood is actually missing from the head. Probably the head has been dark-stained and has had, over the years, several coats of varnish, sometimes to such an extent that the maker's name is no longer legible, and, in any event, identification of the wood of which the head is made is not possible. There will, of course, be no varnish on the sole and you may be able to identify the wood by examination of this.

Next, the shaft: is it straight or warped? Is the wood stiff and brittle or has it still retained resilience and whip? Do not be too enthusiastic when making this test or you may have to start your restoration by joining two pieces of shaft.

Examine all the whipping. Is it tight? Is the thread brittle-looking? Often, the whipping is absent or hanging in festoons or loops, like an old sailing ship that has survived a hurricane. There should be $\frac{1}{4}-\frac{1}{2}$ inch of whipping at the top and at the bottom of the grip. The nature and thickness of the thread should be noted and it is as well to keep a length of it as a sample.

Lastly, the grip. Is it present? There will be an undergrip or rind which is of cloth or even, occasionally, cork. The rind will *never* be of leather. If it is leather, it is the grip proper. There may be a whole leather grip or no leather grip or any condition between these two extremes. The leather grip on an old scared-head club is usually soft with a slightly 'furry' surface, and is brown or sometimes 'off white' in colour. Later grips are often of hard, shiny leather and this leather is usually dark.

Restoration

The main problem with restoration is, how much? There can be no rules about this. We are aware that museums, in general, do not favour restoration and might, in fact, feel that clubs should be left as they are, unless they are so badly damaged as not to justify exhibition. We take the view that a club should be restored until it is in a usable state. All parts of clubs wear in use and the owner would regularly replace worn parts in the days when the club was working. Whipping would be renewed; the grip might be renewed. If the horn became loose it would be refixed – if it came off it would be replaced or a new one fitted. The same considerations would apply to the lead. It is reasonable to restore a club to a condition when it looks right and feels right. Of course, to carry this analogy to absurdity it could be that one might take a piece of horn – all that was left of some old club – and build the rest of the club round it.

Conservation and repair, rather than renewal, is the watchword. Nevertheless, it seems to us right to replace a grip of which only a few tatters remain, or to put lead in a clubhead which has only a gaping hole in the back, or to replace a horn edge if it is absent. We also feel that, if you have a good complete clubhead with no shaft, it is better to put a shaft and grip to it so that it is once more a club. But we are not at all sure that, if you have a shaft which is old, it is right to put on a grip and make a completely new head. In other words, it is probably the head which is the important part of the club and which gives character to it. A careful list of all repairs should be kept and there should be no attempt to conceal the fact that a club has been restored and to what degree.

Materials used in restoration

In this matter we feel on firmer ground and unequivocably state that materials used in the repair (and the method of repair) should be those materials (or methods) used in the original club.

The grip

This must be leather, in an old club, and preferably the 'split' leather with soft, slightly rough, external surface. It should be shaped, and attached at its upper and lower end by a small headed tack: the lower $\frac{1}{4}$–$\frac{1}{2}$ inch being further secured by thread whipping. The latter is treated with cobbler's wax and carefully varnished with a clear varnish after. The leather should be cowhide or sheepskin leather. If this material is not available and the grip cannot be put on in a proper manner, nothing should be done and the club should be left as it is.

And so it goes with the rest – the horn must be ram's horn and may require steaming to get it straight. The horn must be held in place by wooden pegs, inserted at an angle. To stick the horn on with glue only, would be quite wrong, as wrong as it would be to use a synthetic in place of horn.

The lead

This must be pure lead and any remains of old lead must be drilled out so that the new lead can be poured in and will be held in by the 'undercut' of the cavity and the holes drilled at angles at the bottom of it.

The whipping

Especially in the older clubs, the thread is thick at the scare (and, in fact, was often obtained by untwisting strands from a rope). It is for this reason that you will have kept what remains of the original thread, so that you may estimate the thickness of thread required to replace it. It should be cobbler's waxed and a clear coat of varnish applied over the whole whipping after. In socket-headed clubs, finer whipping can be used.

The varnish

This should be the original resin varnish and not modern patent plastic varnish. Resin varnish can be very difficult to find, and if none can be obtained, a plastic varnish or a 'French polish' may have to be used, but should never be left so that there is a highly polished mirror-like surface such as is seen in modern clubs; it can be 'taken down' with fine scouring powder, metal polish or fine wire wool and the surface then lightly wax-polished.

Treating for worm

If the worm is active it requires treating and a woodworm-killer fluid can be used. An alternative is to give the part a good soaking in paraffin and also to inject paraffin, using a fine hypodermic needle and syringe, into the individual worm-holes. More than one treatment may be needed. Inactive worm-holes are probably best left. Woodworm infiltrates into leather grips as well and is probably best treated there individually using a syringe and needle. Soaking a leather grip in paraffin may produce damaging side effects.

Old varnish and staining

We are of the opinion that clubheads are best light in colour, as a very dark head breeds a suspicion that there may be concealed defects and, in addition, a light, well-polished head shows the grain of the wood to advantage and makes it easier to see the maker's name. Very fine wire wool with 'white spirit' applied carefully by hand will get rid of old varnish and stain. The work must be done slowly, so that a minimum of stain is left: do not hurry the process and do not use mechanical tools for this job. 'Brasso' (and perhaps other metal polishes) applied with fine wire wool will achieve much the same effect. Lastly, and by no means least, a wood 'scraper', carefully used, will do the job also. After the head is a suitable colour, a clear varnish can be used, or a very light-coloured shoe polish. You will then have, after many subsequent 'polishes' and general care, a club-head of a light brown colour, which shows the grain of the wood and the maker's name well and, in time, develops the warm, mellow sheen such as is seen in old violins.

A shaft replacement should be of hickory and should be of the right length for the club. It should be shaped and sandpapered until the whip is right.

Continuing care of old wooden clubs

Probably old clubs are best kept in a glass-fronted case, but this arrangement can be expensive and also tends to take up more room. They can be laid horizontally across supports or they may be vertical or diagonal. They should never be held by tight metal bands and they must be easy of access, both for purposes of viewing and, more importantly, for maintenance. The latter really consists in giving the wooden parts a liberal application of linseed oil annually and an occasional dusting and polishing. If the whipping is in good order and well-varnished it will last a very long time indeed.

Care of iron clubs

As far as the shaft and grip are concerned, the care is similar to wooden clubs. There is only the head to be considered. This is unlikely to be greatly damaged but will usually be rusty. This rust should be cleaned off, by hand, using fine rather than coarse emery paper. Do not hurry this process and do not use mechanical methods or a fine 'mark' may disappear altogether. The maker's name, cleekmaker's mark, markings on the face will not be properly visible until all major rust is removed. The hose may be cleaned by placing emery paper around it and then rotating the club with the end of the shaft on the ground and the toe of the club in the palm of the disengaged hand. The face should be cleaned mainly from toe to heel and back again. It is useful, when most of the rust has gone, to use very fine emery paper with a little thin oil on it and, when the face is completed with longitudinal strokes, some vertical strokes down the middle of the face will show the centre up well and is the traditional way of cleaning these clubs. That is, you will be doing what thousands of caddies were doing many years ago, at the end of the round of golf. As the clubs are not going to be used it is as well, at the end, lightly to use an oily rag in order to prevent further rust.

Identification of wooden clubs and dating

Identification will not be too difficult if the descriptions in the earlier part of the book are followed closely. Some difficulty may be experienced with some wooden clubs, e.g. it is often not easy to distinguish between a baffing spoon and a short spoon. It is not easy to be certain, on occasions, whether a short-headed wooden club with a brass sole is an early brassie or a wooden niblick (see Chapter 6). The difference between a driver and a grassed driver is merely one of loft. To differentiate between a putter and a driving putter can be difficult. The bulger driver definitely has a short head and the face is bulged but may have been driven back to straight with use.

In the case of wooden clubs there are certain tell-tale factors which are useful in helping to date clubs, but there are only a few really good yardsticks: we give some indication of date, based on the examination and measurement of more than 500 golf clubs:

1   Knowledge of the date of birth and death of the clubmaker will be a clue to the date of the club, but may only be of help in dating it within the period of his working life.

2   Wooden clubs that were used to hit feathery golf balls were never more than 1 inch in depth of face: they were made before 1850.

3   The neck of a wooden club made to hit gutty balls is always more substantial than that of a club used to hit feathery balls, but this, in itself, is not sufficiently well marked to allow of certain identification.

4   Wooden clubs with extra 'facings' were used to hit gutta balls, i.e. such clubs are after 1850. It is possible, nevertheless, that a wooden club made before 1850 has been used with gutta balls and, the face having been damaged, has been re-faced. (See Chapter 6).

5   Wooden clubs used to hit feathery balls had exceptionally long shafts (but the shaft may have been shortened at some later date).

6   In the early clubs, the whipping at the scare is definitely thick and strong compared with the whipping on later clubs.

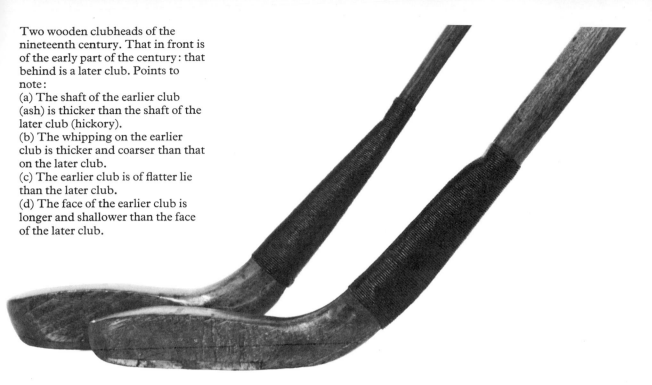

Two wooden clubheads of the nineteenth century. That in front is of the early part of the century: that behind is a later club. Points to note:
(a) The shaft of the earlier club (ash) is thicker than the shaft of the later club (hickory).
(b) The whipping on the earlier club is thicker and coarser than that on the later club.
(c) The earlier club is of flatter lie than the later club.
(d) The face of the earlier club is longer and shallower than the face of the later club.

7   Hickory first appeared in about 1852–55. Persimmon first appeared in 1896 but was not very common until about 1900. Persimmon did not take over completely as the wood for clubheads and beech heads were still advertised as late as 1913.

8   The baffing spoon became an unusual club after 1860–65.

9   Wooden putters were common up to 1860, but were uncommon after 1895 (but were, and are, still made).

10 The bulger driver came in in 1885–87 and was an instant success, but some of the long, narrow-headed drivers were made after that date. (See Chapter 6).

11 Before the bulger driver appeared, the long narrow-headed clubs had a very definite hook to the face in the early part of the nineteenth century, particularly those of McEwan and Philp. From 1850 onward the amount of hook became progressively less. (See Chapter 6.)

12 Socket-headed clubs became common after 1902–5. Not many were made before this date, but Anderson's Patent 1891 and the fact that Forrester of Elie advertised them in 1898, means that some existed before 1900.

13 Scared-head clubs at the turn of the century were small in the head and had a long and very fine scare. (See Chapter 6).

14 McEwan clubs are stamped as such and with no initial, so you will not know, generally, which McEwan made the club. As there were five generations, this covers a long time!

15 Hugh Philp handed over his clubmaking business to R. Forgan between 1852–56.

16 R. Forgan was made 'By Appointment' to HRH The Prince of Wales in 1863 and thereafter the Prince of Wales plumes are stamped on the club. When the Prince of Wales became King in 1901, Forgans stamped the Royal Crown on their clubs.

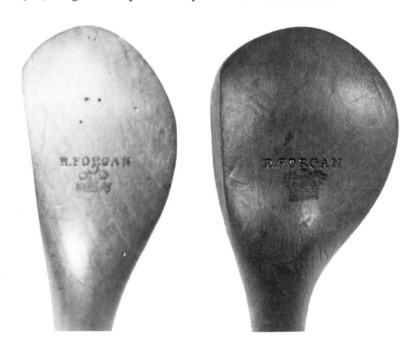

Right:
Bulger driver by Robert Forgan with Prince of Wales Feathers. Indicating 'By appointment clubmaker to HRH The Prince of Wales' (in 1901 to become King).

Far right:
Bulger driver by Robert Forgan with a crown. Indicating 'By appointment clubmaker to King Edward VII' (after 1901).

In addition, it must be pointed out that all the clubmakers had apprentices. The more clubs the clubmaker was asked to produce, the more he had to leave the apprentices to do the work. Thus, particularly among the better-known clubmakers, the maker's name on the wooden club may only mean that he supervised the making by others. It is probably because of the implication that the clubmaker did not necessarily make a club which had his stamp on it, that advertisements at the turn of the century contain statements such as 'All of my clubs are made by experienced clubmakers under my own supervision', 'Orders receive personal attention', etc. The most that can be said of the maker's name on a wooden club prior to 1900 is that the club is a product of his 'shop', and that the making of it was supervised by him. After 1900, the thousands of clubs 'in the rough' imported from the USA meant that a wooden club could be smoothed off, varnished, gripped, and the local professional's name stamped on it, in any Golf Club professional's shop.

The measurement of wooden clubs – length of shaft, weight,

Measurement of clubs as a means of identification

An instrument designed by the authors for measuring golf clubs and made by Mr Edward Davies of Northam, North Devon. The instrument will measure: length of club, angle of head to shaft, length of head, width of head (at widest) and depth of face.

Top:
The instrument folded, 24 inches long.

Centre:
Close-up of head end of instrument.

Bottom:
Instrument with club lying on it. Length 48 inches.

angle of head to shaft, length of head, width of head, depth of face, may all be of help toward making an identification of a club and also, occasionally, in estimating the date of origin. It must also be realised that, with all possible aids, it is not possible, except in unusual circumstances, to assess the date of a wooden club with 'pinpoint' accuracy.

Documentary clubs
Occasionally a collector obtains a club in which there is clear evidence from the possessor of the club (and preferably in writing) as to its date of origin. Such a piece of good fortune constitutes an 'unusual circumstance' and a documentary club is therefore of particular interest.

The authors and their research team have measured and weighed hundreds of old golf clubs, using an instrument of their own devising. Such measurements are of value in expressing, in scientific terms, what is, otherwise, a vague description of the general proportions of a club. The conclusion, based on this research, is that the differences in the shape of similar clubs made by different makers is so small that it is not possible to ascribe any wooden club to a particular maker based on measurement alone.

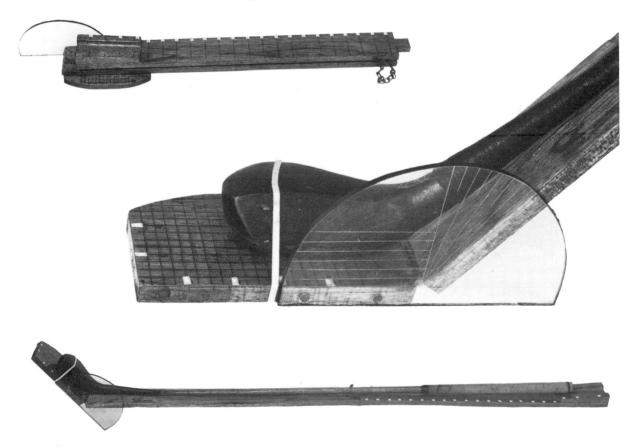

Dating of wooden clubs – A checklist

In making an estimate of the period during which a clubmaker, included in the checklist, would be likely to have been occupied in making long-headed clubs, two assumptions are made: first that he would be competent to make a club from the age of twenty or thereabouts and second that, by c.1888, long-headed clubs had been superseded by 'bulger-type' woods. It should not be assumed, however, that the maker was in a position to stamp his own name on the club during the whole of the period mentioned. Those making clubs in the feathery-ball era are marked with an asterisk.

		Period for which clubmaker could have been making clubs	
*Ballantyne, William (1793–1845)	Musselburgh	1813–45	34 years
*Ballantyne, William Jr. (1826–1851)	Musselburgh	1846–51	5 years
Butchart, J. (1854–)	Carnoustie	1874–88	14 years
*Cossar, Simon (1766–1811)	Leith	1786–1811	25 years
*Cossar, David (1788–1816)	Leith	1808–16	8 years
Crowley, James (1860–1937)	Elie	1880–88	8 years
*Davidson, Robert (1801–1875)	Montrose	1821–75	54 years
Day, W. D. (1837–)	Bruntsfield & Musselburgh	1857–88	33 years
Dickson, J. & Alexander (1861–1926)	Edinburgh	1881–88	7 years
Dow, Robert (Bob) (1832–1909)	Montrose & Dundee	1852–88	36 years
Dunn, W. (1821–1878)	North Berwick & Blackheath	1851–78	27 years
Jamie (1821–1871)	North Berwick & Blackheath	1851–71	20 years
Thomas (1849–1902)	Wimbledon	1869–88	19 years
W. (Jr.) (1865–1952)	Westward Ho! & Chingford	1885–88	3 years
Fernie, W. (1858–1924)	Troon	1878–88	10 years
Forrester, G. (1847–1930)	Elie	1867–88	21 years
Forgan, R. (1824–1900)	St Andrews	Philp/Forgan 1852–57	5 years
		R. Forgan 1857–63	6 years
		POW Feathers 1863–88	25 years
Forgan, Thomas B. (1853–1906)	St Andrews	R. Forgan & Son 1881–88	7 years
Gibson, C. (1864–1937)	Westward Ho!	1884–88	4 years
Greig, Alexander ( )	Leith 1866–72 Gen. Directory	1866–72	6 years
Hood, Thomas (1843–1909)	Musselburgh	1863–88	25 years
Hunter, Charles (1837–1921)	Royal Blackheath & Prestwick	1857–88	31 years
Hutchison, J. H. (1847–1912)	North Berwick	1867–88	21 years
*Jackson, John (1805–1878)	Perth	1825–78	53 years
Kirk, R. Jr. (1845–1886)	St Andrews & Royal Blackheath	1865–86	21 years
Lang, Bennet (1849–1913)	Perth	1869–88	19 years
*Manderson, Alexander B. (1813–1891)	Dunbar	1833–91	58 years
*McEwan – see family history	Bruntsfield & Musselburgh	1770–1888 (using same stamp after 1800)	118 years
Morris, Tom (1821–1906)	Prestwick & St Andrews	1851– 1865–88	37 years
*Munro, Alexander (1796–1847)	Aberdeen (golf club & fishing rod maker)	1816–47	31 years
Park, W. Senr. (1834–1903)	Musselburgh	1854–88	34 years
Mungo (1839–1904)	Musselburgh	1860–88	28 years
*Patrick, John (1820–1866)	Leven (cabinet maker & clubmaker)	1847–66	19 years
Alexander (1845–1932)	See family history	1865–88	23 years
Paxton, Peter (1859–)	Eastbourne 1888	1879–88	9 years
Philp, Hugh (1782–1856)	See also Forgan above	1820–52	32 years
*Sandison, L. (1825–1884)	Aberdeen	1847–84	37 years
Simpson, R. (1862–1923)	Carnoustie	est. 1885–88	3 years
Strath, A. (1836–1868)	Prestwick	1856–68	12 years
Wilson, James (1803–1866)	St Andrews	1852–66	14 years

Iron clubs – some indication of date

1   Iron clubs before 1830 are characterised by being heavy, with a long thick hose, rather crudely made and often with the blacksmith's hammer-marks visible. The hose is not only long and thick but it is large in diameter and the shaft will be exceptionally large and strong. The 'nicking' of the top of the hose is correspondingly large. The general impression is of an exceptionally tough club used for desperate situations only. There is usually no cleekmaker's mark and no face marking. The face is often hooked and is concave from upper to lower edge.

2   The characteristics of the rutter or rut iron are: a head only little larger than a golf ball, a round sole and a very substantial hose. We have seen some rutters with long hoses and some with short, but either way the club gives an impression of bullet-headed solidity and compact weight. Few rutters have face-markings and most do not have a cleekmaker's mark.

3   The date of birth and death of the cleekmaker may give an idea of the club's date but often only within the period of his working life. A knowledge of cleekmaker's marks is of great importance if the cleekmaker is to be identified.

4   Lofting irons began to appear in about 1830–40 and were on the way out in 1885. The mashie was coming in at about the same time.

5   After 1850 iron clubs became more refined and there was, progressively, a move towards smaller heads and lighter hoses.

6   The cleek began to appear in 1840–50 and continued in use in all its various forms until World War I.

7   Willie Park's wry-necked putter appeared in 1891.

8   The jigger and the sammy became popular in about 1906–08. Few were made after 1920.

9   At the risk of repetition, it cannot too often be stated that the professional's name and Golf Club stamped on the back of an iron club means *only* that he bought the head from a cleekmaker and had his name and Golf Club stamped on it by the cleekmaker, who had hundreds of different stamps in his shop and that he, the clubmaker or Golf Club professional, shafted the club and put a grip on it. The clubmaker's sole expertise was in working wood: the cleekmaker was expert only in metal. The only exceptions to this rule are iron clubs by the Parks of Musselburgh, and A. J. Ife of The Hague, all of whom were capable of making iron heads and wooden clubs.

Conclusion

Golf clubs, balls, etc. which may be termed antique and can be dated prior to 1890 are never likely to be readily available, especially to the new collector. As has already been pointed out, the period covering the great 'golf craze' of the 1890s is likely to prove of outstanding historical interest. All hickory-shafted clubs are already collectable but still freely available at reasonable prices. Examples of anything included in the chapter on patents will prove well worth collecting. With hickory-shafted clubs remaining in use well into the 1930s there are still plenty of opportunities for the building-up of worthwhile collections, not only of clubs but of other golfing artefacts.

Ladies' clubs

Not much has been said about ladies' clubs in this book because their form and general shape was the same as men's clubs; there were no particular specialists who made ladies' clubs to the exclusion of other clubs. The clubmaker simply made lighter and shorter clubs for ladies, because the ladies were shorter than men and less muscular. In wooden clubs these are the only differences and wooden clubs for ladies have no particular mark on them to signify that they are for ladies. The difference between a light man's club and a lady's club is not great: the great Harry Vardon, a long and accurate driver, for several years at the height of his fame used ladies' wooden clubs.

In iron clubs the differences of weight and length are the same but here it is usually possible to distinguish ladies' clubs because they are often marked on the back with an 'L'. Relatively few have no such marking and can only be identified by length and weight while an even smaller number, if made by Tom Stewart of St Andrews, have a snake as a mark instead of his usual pipemark. In putters, wooden putters are not marked. Simple blade putters and aluminium Mills putters are usually marked with an L: other various kinds of putter do not always carry a mark.

The back of a mashie iron shafted by Cann & Taylor; probably the head was made by Anderson of Anstruther. The capital L indicates that the club is a ladies club.

Children's clubs

Children's clubs from bygone days exist, but they are not common. They were passed from child to child until they became so worn and generally damaged that they were thrown away. Probably the earliest child's club in the world now, is a very fine spoon made by Simon Cossar, in the Collection of the Royal & Ancient Golf Club. Also in this collection is a child's putter made by Hugh Philp. A few examples exist in other collections.

In the matter of children's clubs from the past, it is necessary to be cautious; not every short club is a child's club. Many apparent children's clubs are men's or ladies' clubs with the shaft cut down. A child's club is short and the size and weight of the head should be in keeping with the length. There are no distinguishing marks on the heads of children's clubs, iron or wood, except in the case of some children's clubs made by Burke of Newark, USA which are marked 'Midget'.

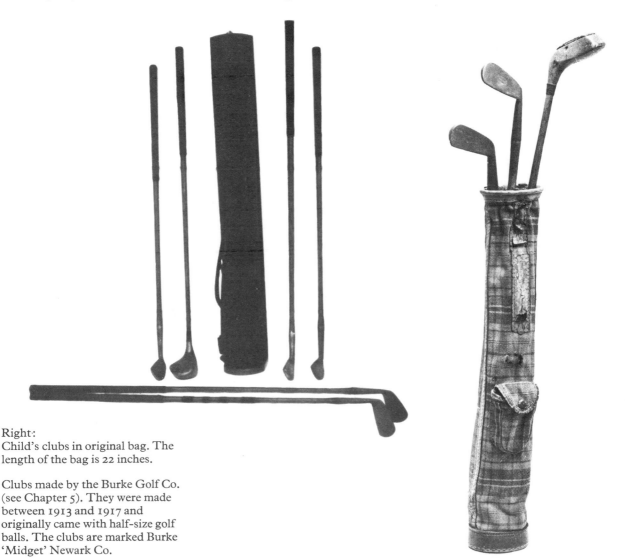

Below:
Some children's clubs and a (leather) children's bag. The length of the bag is 29 inches.

Right:
Child's clubs in original bag. The length of the bag is 22 inches.

Clubs made by the Burke Golf Co. (see Chapter 5). They were made between 1913 and 1917 and originally came with half-size golf balls. The clubs are marked Burke 'Midget' Newark Co.

Model and miniature clubs

The making of small-scale models and miniatures of golf clubs has interested clubmakers over many years and is probably motivated by pride in the craft and in the ability to make a small, perfectly executed image of the real thing, as much perhaps for their own satisfaction as for the satisfaction of others.

There is no evidence that model clubs were made by apprentices to demonstrate that they were worthy of promotion to full master craftsmen, such as occurred in the cabinet-maker's trade. In the course of research for this book quite a number of model and miniature clubs have been found. They include miniature clubs, about $3\frac{1}{4}$ inches long, the three woods made by Charles Gibson of Westward Ho! and three irons made by Ben Sayer of North Berwick. The bag for these is of leather and they were presented to the late Queen Mary for inclusion in the Doll's House at Windsor Castle where they can still be seen today. A set of six wooden clubs about 15–18 inches long made by William Auchterlonie can be seen in the Royal & Ancient Golf Club showcase at St Andrews.

Other miniature clubs seen are some fine clubs about 12 inches long, both woods and irons, very well arranged in a showcase at the

Above:
The miniature clubs in the Queen's Dolls House at Windsor Castle. The wooden clubs were made by Charles Gibson (right) and the iron clubs by Ben Sayer of North Berwick. The golf bag is made of leather – maker unknown. The clubs are said to be $3\frac{1}{4}$ inches long and the bag $2\frac{1}{2}$ inches high.

Royal Blackheath Golf Club. These were made by Robert Kirk when professional at Blackheath (1864–66).

Illustrated is a miniature driver about 10 inches long with a scared head made by J. Rowe of Royal Ashdown Forest Golf Club, probably about 1910. John Rowe was one of Charles Gibson's first apprentices at Westward Ho! He served as professional to Royal Ashdown Forest Golf Club for over fifty years and was at one time President of the Professional Golfers Association of Great Britain. Also illustrated are three wooden clubs made by 'Bert' Way. They are 'scared-head' clubs, amusing but somewhat out of proportion. Way was another apprentice of Charles Gibson, contemporary with John Rowe. He went to the United States and became President of the USPGA. He lived to a ripe old age and became the 'Grand Old Man' of golf in America.

A picture of James Walker of the Glasgow North Western Golf Club proudly proclaims him to be the maker of the smallest set of golf-clubs in the world. The clubs, eight in number, both woods and irons, are leaning against a book and appear to be about 4 inches in length (see overleaf).

Right: Miniature club made by John Rowe, Royal Ashdown Forest, c.1900. Three miniature clubs made by W. H. Way ('Bert' Way), one of Charles Gibson's apprentices who emigrated to America and became President of the USPGA.

283

Golfing costume

Above: Miniature clubs. Scale
models of, right to left: a driver by
Tom Morris; a long spoon by
H. Philp; a baffing spoon by Willie
Dunn Snr; a putter by W. Park Jnr.
Made by E. Davies and D. I.
Stirk, North Devon, 1977. The
longest club measures 11 inches.
Right: James Walker and miniature
clubs made by him. The caption to
this picture states: 'Maker of the
world's smallest set of golf clubs.
Each club is a replica of the
Standard Pattern'.

The types of dress worn by golfers for playing and the forms of club
uniform make an interesting study not only for golfers but also for
students of fashion and social change. Generally speaking, golf
costume has been little studied.

The men
In the early days of golf, men had no special clothes in which to play
golf. This meant a considerable variation in golfing dress. The
workaday clothes of, say, Sir David Blair, bore no similarity to those
of John Macrae, farm labourer. When the feathery was played, golf
was a rich man's game, partly because of expense and partly because
to have leisure you had to be rich. Thus, the commoner golfing
costume was that of the well-to-do gentleman of leisure. The
gentlemen wore tall silk hats, swallowtail coats of various
colours and tight trousers. The spectators were often similarly

attired. The caddies were not so well dressed, being clad in any old cast-off clothes and often no shoes.

Most of the formal pictures of golfers in red coats, sometimes with epaulettes, large hats and white silk trousers, were posed pictures for Club portraits. Nevertheless in the early part of the nineteenth century, many men golfers wore red coats, simply to let other people on the (common) land know that they were striking a golf ball. By 1857 'A Keen Hand' writes to say that the red coat is long outmoded.

A Grand match at St Andrews, 1850. The players are dressed in swallow tail coats and three of them wear top hats. They are wearing their usual 'everyday' dress of the 'landed gentry'. There are no golf bags, the caddies carry them under the arm or on the shoulder. Painting by Charles Lees, RA.

We do not know whether the soles of the shoes of the elegant gentry had studs in them, but probably not. The workaday clothes of the working man would probably consist of a cap or woollen hat or tam o'shanter, a rough shirt with no cravat or tie, and trousers with braces or tied up with string at the waist and made of rough baggy cloth or corduroy. In the matter of footwear he probably scored over his more elegant opponent by wearing boots with tacks or hobnails in the soles, 'tackety boots', which would give him a better grip of the ground and were his ordinary working boots.

With the advent of the gutta percha ball and the increased leisure of the 'working class', many lesser mortals took to golf, including the English. Dress became more varied. As the game had come from Scotland, those who were not Scottish sought to ape the Scots. Among the richer middle-class and professional people, tam o'shanters appeared as headgear, and the traditional dress of the

Above: members of Northam Artisans Golf Club, 1888. The working-man's dress for golf, 'Tackety boots' much in evidence.

Below: smart golfing costume, 1875. English type.

highland gillie became fashionable – knee-breeches, stockings, shoes or boots and a coat tailored for freedom of action around the shoulders – the 'knickerbocker' suit. Dress was, nevertheless, pretty varied and some played, in the better weather, in cricketing-type clothes, particularly (and understandably) those who were cricketers. Many wore ordinary suits and bowler hats. Advertisements for golfing dress in England at the time show considerable efforts by tailors, but a sad lack of golfing knowledge in the illustrations. The only constant dress feature was the caddy, still wearing cast-off clothing and no shoes. Vardon was the first professional to wear 'knickerbockers' for golf.

The ladies
The first picture showing ladies at golf is that reproduced on page 31 showing the Westward Ho! Ladies in 1873. The dress consisted of a long-skirted gown with a bustle which would make a true golf swing difficult. The only possible advantage of the ensemble is that the size of the bonnet would have kept the head fairly still! Although it would seem that putting, which the ladies in the foreground are engaged in, was as much as they would attempt, one of the ladies in the background is making a much more ambitious stroke – the club being at shoulder height. So it is clear that, despite the

Above:
English golfing dress, 1870. No golf bags, a shoeless caddie. One player wears a 'Tam o' Shanter'.

Above right:
English golfing scene, c. 1880. Golf bags, of a sort. One caddie shoeless. Contrast the well-dressed child spectator.

Centre left:
Circa 1895. *The man:* knickerbockers; spats and a 'Tam o' Shanter'. Grip and stance deplorable.
The lady: Daring show of the ankle. She wears gloves to protect her hands and appears to be about to wield an enormously long club.

Centre right:
Circa 1895. A knickerbocker suit. Tweed hat. The grip of the club and back swing abysmal; the position of the ball impossible. The caddie could well be in a dangerous position.

Bottom left:
Circa 1900. The knickerbockers are almost 'plus fours'. A coat which allows freedom of movement. The coat is almost certainly buttoned up; this was usual when playing.

Bottom right:
Circa 1914. Advertised as the 'free swing coat'. As usual, the coat appears to be buttoned up.

difficulties of the costume and the need to show no more than a toe, the ladies did, in fact, attempt a fairly healthy swipe. It must be remembered too, that there were such clubs as driving putters, and permission to use putters only may still have allowed the ladies quite a long shot.

Twenty years later a form of golfing dress appears in which the lady is making a real golf swing. Her costume is no great help to her but she swings superbly. She wears boots ('button-up', no doubt) a long full skirt, a blouse with leg o'mutton sleeves and a saucy straw boater (see page 208).

The problem of the long full skirt on a windy day was considerable, as, with the wind on one's back the skirt was blown forward, which at best disturbed the concentration and, at worst, might conceal the ball altogether. To prevent this the lady wore an elastic garter, which, worn on calm days round the waist, could be slipped down approximately to knee level on windy days, to control the skirt. On wet days, the wearer would lift the skirt *just* enough to clear the wet grass. Another lady's costume has a similarity, again with boots, in which, perhaps, some tack heads can be seen. She has a full long skirt (long enough even at the top of the backswing to show only the boots), a blouse with a collar and a generous sleeve – all topped with a straw boater. This woman player won the English Ladies Championship at Hoylake in 1898 and this picture was taken in that year (see page 209).

Above:
Circa 1875. Advertisement. Dress 'de rigueur' – golf unlikely!

Right:
Ladies golfing dress, 1911. The day is windy and this lady has a large elastic garter which has been slipped down from waist level to about knee level to stop her skirt blowing up.

In 1911 there were further changes. Ladies definitely had ankles! The lady in the illustration wears shoes. The skirt is generous, allowing a wide stance but not so generous that a restrainer would be needed on a windy day. She wears a tailored coat which allows her arms to swing freely. To complete the slightly male appearance of the coat she wears a blouse with a collar and a bow tie. She has a large hat with a wide brim. She has a fine, well balanced swing and, despite the hat, she manages very nicely.

In 1913 the lady wears an even more emancipated costume and copies the male even more closely. She wears shoes and spats: we are permitted to see well above the ankle. The skirt is practical and allows a wide stance; despite its width the player demonstrates that she has *knees*! The ensemble is completed by a shirt blouse and a long tie. The sleeves of the blouse are narrow. No hat is worn. The stroke is a beautiful example of how to play a 'run-up' approach shot.

Above: Lady Margaret Scott at the top of her swing.

Above right: Miss Grant Suttie, 1911.

Right: Miss Cecil Leitch, *c*.1913.

The children

No doubt children wore their ordinary clothes for golf, but, as with men's golfing dress, what they wore would depend on their station in life. From the working classes many small boys became caddies and played golf, when they were not caddying, with any old clubs or balls that they could lay their hands on. It was the caddy with some talent for hitting a golf ball who became a future professional player. Most had no shoes. Many wore the clothes they went to school in. Some, as they got larger, acquired various pieces of cast-off clothing from those for whom they caddied. Apart from pictures of caddies, there seem to be few pictures of children on the golf course. There are posed and rather artificial pictures of children of well-to-do families holding golf clubs and balls, dressed in finery which would make golf difficult. Some of these pictures are Dutch and some Scottish (see pages 11 and 14).

Collecting buttons
by Sheila Baird

A button collection has the following advantages over many other types of collection:

1 Buttons do not take up much space.

2 They are relatively cheap to buy and can still be found fairly easily.

3 They are decorative.

4 They are historically interesting.

Buttons are common and familiar objects. They first made their appearance about 4000 years ago, mainly in Egypt, Greece, Persia and China but at that time they were mainly ornamental as garments were loose and flowing. Utility became an important consideration as fashions changed and clothes became more fitted and required fasteners, though many were also extremely decorative.

The earliest metal buttons were flat one-piece discs without a raised rim, then slightly convex with a raised rim, though still one piece. A later development was a two-piece or shell button, sealed by stamping so that the rim enclosed the back. The one-piece buttons were either made of brass with a very thin coating of gold – the gilt button, or of a Sheffield-type silver-plating on a copper base – often called 'white metal'.

Dating of metal buttons is not easy though the type of shank and the back-mark, if any, can often give some indication of age. Silver buttons can be dated accurately if they have a hallmark. No button which bears a back-mark was made any earlier than the beginning of the nineteenth century as this was the period when back-marks first appeared. Sometimes back-marks enable a collector to determine the period of production, but only if the history of the firm has been accurately established. The back-mark is not necessarily the name of the maker but may be that of the wholesaler or tailor or it may establish the country of origin.

The earliest British button factory was set up in 1670 by Thomas Firmin of London, a business which is still in existence today. Another of the early makers was John Taylor of Birmingham. His factory was set up in the 1730s employing upwards of 500 people and achieving a weekly turnover of £800. Some of the buttons in the photograph were made by Armfield & Co., another famous Birmingham factory – founded in 1763 and eventually destroyed by the bombing during World War II in 1940. Nelson is said to have worn Armfield Buttons at the Battle of Trafalgar.

Many buttons during the early years of the nineteenth century were still cloth-covered and there is a minute dated 21st March 1828 that the Aberdeen Golf Club allowed their members to wear their new scarlet jackets with cloth-covered buttons until the metal buttons could be obtained.

A statute was passed by Queen Anne in March 1790 making the wearing of cloth-covered buttons illegal so presumably the Aberdeen members were breaking the law! The statute was printed in the *Caledonian Mercury* of March 1790 – 'Any tailor who uses cloth-covered buttons is liable to a penalty of £3 for each dozen used; and every person wearing such buttons is open to pay a penalty of £2 for each button so used'. The advertisement was inserted by The Incorporation of Button Makers and there seems to be some doubt as to whether this statute has in fact ever been revoked!

Golf buttons are not easily classified. They are sometimes loosely

Old golf buttons
Top row
1. Tantallon G.C. – gilt one piece – Armfield, Birmingham.
2. G.N.G.C. (Gullane Nine G.C.) – One piece Silver – 1934. No maker's name.
3. Not yet identified – Scottish Royal – 2-piece gilt shell.
Middle row
4. Gt. Yarmouth G.C. – gilt 2-piece shell. Later date than 1, 6, 7 & 9.
5. Newport Ladies G.C. – silver one piece 1907.
6. Guildford G.C. – as 1.
Bottom row
7. County Down G.C. – as 1.
8. R. & A. G.C. – gilt one piece – No back mark – Modern.
9. County G.C. – as 1.

described as livery buttons as people tend to think that 'livery' is synonymous with 'uniform'. This is incorrect. Livery buttons are strictly confined to those bearing family crests and coats of arms, though the construction of the button is similar and often the same makers would produce both types of buttons.

'Non-military' uniform buttons might be the best classification – they are made for occupational and ceremonial uniforms, often serving as a means of identification and they give the wearer a recognised position, usually in a select circle – this can be either aristocratic or menial. A good example of this is seen in the famous painting by Lemuel P. Abbott (1790) of 'The Golfers at Blackheath' where both the golfer and the caddy are arrayed in a fine collection of buttons – both for decoration and utility. These buttons were first made in the eighteenth century but few are found today that can pre-date 1800. The vast majority were made in the mid-nineteenth century and are now unfortunately almost obsolete. Possibly only a few Clubs have buttons for their members to wear – one being the Royal & Ancient Golf Club of St Andrews (see illustration).

Interesting references to golf buttons are made in *The History of the Royal and Ancient Golf Club* by H. S. C. Everard (1907). In a minute dated 4th August 1780 a reference is made to the disreputable state of the golfers' garments and they were asked 'to realise the nature of their shortcomings'. They therefore agreed to have new jackets, viz. red jackets with yellow (gilt) buttons. Four years later they changed their ideas as to what would be the most becoming raiment and declared that the uniform was to be 'a red coat with a

Modern golf buttons.
Assorted materials – pewter, gilt, plastic and leather.

dark blue velvet cape with white plain (silver) buttons, with an embroidered club and ball of silver on each side of the cape with two large buttons on the sleeves'.

In a minute of 1820 Col. R. T. Boothby tried to revive the custom (which had lapsed) of wearing a plain blue coat with Club buttons by providing himself with a garment of this description.

At this time several other Clubs also wore a Club uniform with their own buttons. The coat was not always red, as is often reported, 'as a protection to the general public', but sometimes green was chosen as at Aberdeen Golf Club and Crail Golf Club, or even grey (Glasgow GC) or blue (Kingston GC). Aberdeen GC did not keep their green coats for long. They were first worn on 31st March 1827 but only as a result of a majority vote, and they proved unpopular. They changed to scarlet coats with 'uniform gilt buttons with the words Aberdeen GC and a Scotch thistle raised thereon' just over a year later in March 1828, though it is uncertain when its use was discarded.

Crail GC decided on their original coat of red with plain yellow buttons on 5th September 1792 with a penalty of 'half a mutchkin of punch' for non-conformists – two of whom were Captain Aytone and Mr Ranken, both former Captains of the Club who appeared in green jackets. Just over one hundred years later on 29th February 1896 the colour was changed to 'green with yellow facings' – no mention being made of the buttons.

An interesting story is related in *The History of the Royal Perth Golfing Society* by Rev. T. D. Miller, MA about a disagreement over the design of the Club buttons.

In 1833, at the instigation of Lord Kinnaird, William IV became the Patron of the Society and was pleased to give his approval of a button to be worn by members – a one-piece button with crossed clubs – a crown between the handles and a tee'd ball between the heads with two large Scottish thistles on either side. Many dozens of these buttons were made. Eventually the mould showed signs of wear and the outline of the buttons became indistinct. It became necessary to procure a new mould and the feeling grew that a new design would be appropriate. At the general meeting in April 1841 a dispute ensued between two factions (Dr McFarlane for the old and Mr Archibald Turnbull for the new) and the new design was carried by a considerable majority. There was much ill-feeling and Lt-Col Belshes resigned as Councillor. Several months later fifty dozen new buttons for the coat and the same number for the vest were struck.

The subject was again brought up in 1842 and a vote taken (26–23) in favour of submitting the new button to the then Patroness, Queen Victoria, for her approval. Once more a protest ensued, and several reasons were given for retaining the old button, all to no avail. The new buttons had already been ordered on 10th September 1841.

The new button was of convex formation (two-piece shell) with the City of Perth arms and crown superimposed with initials of the

Club on a ribbon at the foot and a Scotch thistle at each side. This lasted fifty years and in April 1897 the original was again adopted – in our opinion a much more attractive button – but by then the coat was going out of fashion and the Rev. Miller declared in 1935 that 'Buttons are now and meanwhile as archaic as the top hat'.

Buttons are among the finest examples of design and metalwork. We find them attractive for their beauty and interesting for their historical associations. Charles Dickens wrote in *Household Words* in the mid-nineteenth century: 'There is surely something charming in seeing the smallest thing done so thoroughly, as if to remind the careless that whatever is worth doing is worth doing well. This is certainly true of buttons and buttonmakers.'

Golfing subjects depicted on ceramics

The earliest golfers or golfing scenes to appear on ceramics were used as decoration for Delft tiles in the seventeenth century. They were, however, stylistic and did not illustrate golf in action, although golf appears in some of the Dutch landscapes which were engraved, possibly at a later date, and the prints used on tiles. The illustration shown here is interesting because it was put on back to front.

Decorative tile, showing kilted figures playing golf (after Van de Velde 1668). See page 8.

From the 1880s onwards sporting subjects found increasing use as decoration for items such as mugs, bowls, tankards and even tea-sets. Some were offered as Golf Club prizes and many people must regret that this custom was not continued down to the present day in lieu of being encumbered by a wealth of silver items, all of which require cleaning. Those who are lucky enough to possess the china articles find them not only decorative but most collectable.

Insufficient information is at present available to enable any sort of checklist to be built up of the manufacturers, but the following potters are known to have produced golfing items:

*Doulton, London. c.*1900 they were producing a wide range of tankards, mugs, bowls, etc., some with art-nouveau borders and using embossed golfing white vignettes, some with coloured art-nouveau floral borders. Examples are also known of teapots and jugs with sprigged decoration, usually green, with figures in buff. There were small replicas of larger items – again as prizes. Doulton had a substantial business in this field.

Below: Morrissian Ware vase. Height 8¾ in. Doulton.

Right: Doulton tankard with silver rim, embossed white vignettes: 'The lost ball', 'putting and driving'. Height 5¼ in., *c.*1900. Pattern No. 8241.

Pale green vase with tinted print on each side of a golf scene by C. Dana Gibson (1867–1944), the American artist who immortalised the 'Gibson girls'. The sketch shown is entitled 'Is a caddy always necessary?' and on the reverse 'From 10 a.m. to 6.45 p.m. this dog has been kept out. Where is the S.P.C.A.?' (Society for Prevention of Cruelty to Animals). Height 3.6 in. (made at Royal Doulton, England). Note that the clubs are being carried upside down in the golf bag, which was at one time customary.

Copeland/Spode Pottery, Stoke on Trent. They produced jugs in blue and white and green/buff in stoneware with sprigged decorations of golfing groups *c.*1896. Teapots and tea services in dark blue with embossed golfing figures in white were also made. No evidence has yet come to hand indicating whether teasets were offered as prizes.

Grimwade Pottery, Stoke on Trent. Golfing cartoons appear on plates produced by this potter. They are now rare items.

Mintons Pottery, Stoke on Trent

Two dishes with transfer-printed golfing figures, in blue (diameter $7\frac{1}{4}$ in.). Minton mark for 1901. Signed W. S.

Souvenir items

These were popular before and after World War I. Some were crested and items such as tobacco jars were made. Some were made by W. H. Goss and marked with the Goss falcon mark; others by his imitators and marked Arcadian and Carlton ware, etc.

The Continental manufacturers were major suppliers of souvenir items before World War I – particularly ribbon-plates, sometimes with golfing scenes.

One of a pair of early nineteenth-century punch bowls (diameter 13¾ in.) and an enlargement of the golfing figures on the bowl. (Reproduced by courtesy of Royal Blackheath Golf Club).

Golfing Prints and Pictures
by Harry Langton

Above: Tea-caddy – Continental porcelain. Probably painted by a London decorator. Golfing figure taken from a print of 'The Blackheath Golfer': *c.*1825.

Above right: A 'daisy' plate, with transfer print of a kilted golfer. Mid-nineteenth century Scottish earthenware. Diameter 8¼ in.

There are few 'golfing' artists but a great many fine artists who once in a while painted, drew, or had printed a golfing picture. Many people are interested in golfing pictures and prints yet there is no work of reference which gives information about the artists in the context of their work on the sport. The following list has been compiled to give a short survey of those who are better-known, but there are many other artists who have been listed separately. The list is by no means complete and can be added to as the years go by and more information surfaces.

Collecting old prints, paintings and drawings or ephemera on golf is rewarding and difficult. 'Rewarding' means pleasing, enriching and educational, although a collection with, for example, just one rare print is certainly valuable not only in terms of enjoyment but also of money. Nevertheless, the collector is well advised to cling resolutely to the old-fashioned rule – buy for pleasure and not as an investment. For those seeking to possess a golfing picture of merit, it remains a fact that they are hard to find – increasingly so with growing worldwide interest. Many sets or individual prints of the 'hunting, shooting and fishing' type, mostly originating in the eighteenth and nineteenth centuries, pass through the London salerooms every year, yet only about a dozen golf prints of the first half of the nineteenth century have appeared since 1973.

List A below gives details of the more important artists, and List B provides a checklist of these and other artists.

List A

Abbott, Lemuel Francis
(1760–1803)
Portrait painter who taught, among others, the sporting artist Ben Marshall. His paintings of William Innes (painted in 1778 and often known as 'The Blackheath Golfer') and Henry Callender (painted in 1807) are probably the best-known pictures of golfers ever painted and have been reproduced in every thinkable method since then. See *Catalogue of British Engraved Portraits* (1908–1925) for further details of early prints. This records the first print of William Innes as '… walking on Blackheath, holding golf club and ball and followed by a caddie. Plate dedicated to the Society of Goffers at Blackheath. Published Abbott 1790. Mezzotint: 23¾ in × 17 in.' This print is black and white or sepia but may be seen with hand colouring. Over the past 200 years, this print and the following one were reprinted from about 1850 to 1950 in London, handpulled from

'The Blackheath Golfer'.

copper plates and coloured up or sold plain; mezzotints and lithographs similar in plate size to the originals, with added colour, were published about 1900; and countless cheap modern reproductions of all sizes are on offer today. The picture itself no longer exists and was probably destroyed with the Club's early records in an eighteenth-century fire. Abbott's painting of Henry Callender rests in the possession of the Blackheath Club. When a Mr. Henderson sent him £50 subscription arrears, Callender broke into this verse in gratitude:

'May your balls, as they fly and
    whiz through the air,
Knock down the blue devils, dull
    sorrow and care.
May your health be preserved,
    with strength active and bold
And may you long traverse the
    green, and forget to grow old.'

The *Catalogue of British Engraved Portraits* (above) describes the first print of Callender: 'standing in uniform of Blackheath Society of Golfers, resting club on ground. Published by W. Ward 1812. Mezzotint 23⅝ in × 16⅞ in. Engraved by W. Ward.' This seems to be a rarer print than Innes in its several issues, though a quantity of mid-nineteenth century reprints with slightly staring eyes have turned up in the 1970s.

Aldin, Cecil (1870–1935)
A most prolific commercial artist similar in style to Hassall. He illustrated many books on dogs and produced famous hunting prints and prints of English coaching inns, together with many comic illustrations on golf. In the early 1920s he had published (by Eyre & Spottiswoode) a large series of prints of British golf courses. Vast numbers of his prints, lithographs, woodblocks, etc. were signed with a florid pencil signature. Some of his work appears as decoration on ceramics in the late Victorian and Edwardian period.

Allen, G. (1800–1850)
Primitive English painter described as 'of Greenwich School'. His

painting of Alick Robertson (known as 'Old Alick'), caddie and hole-cutter, was given to the Blackheath Club in 1839. There are many reproductions and a nineteenth century print is recorded (see p. 22).

Ambrose, Charles (*c*.1905)
A magazine illustrator who drew long series of golf and tennis personalities for Edwardian publications, often white and grey on a green background.

Brock, Charles Edmund (1870–1938)
Member of the Royal Institute 1909. Lived at Cambridge and exhibited five works at the Royal Academy. Brock's work on golf is worthy of the highest ranking. It includes a series of sepia prints of golfers in action on the links reproduced by Leggatt Bros. of London in 1894 from engravings by Frank Paton (approx. size 9½ in. × 7 1/16 in.).

Browne, 'Tom' (1872–1910)
Born at Nottingham. Left school at 11 to work as errand boy, then printer's apprentice at 1s 0d a week. Sent sketches and cartoons to London newspapers and magazines and almost immediately was recognised as a genius in this field. A number of good golf cartoons are among his work, together with advertising and book illustrations. Many of his golf cartoons in colour were published as postcards, especially by Davidson Bros. of London *c*.1900–1910. (Some of these were reproduced in the 1970s but are easy to recognise).

Chalmers, Sir George (*c*.1720–1791)
Painted portrait of William St. Clair of Roslin, Captain of the Honourable Company of Edinburgh Golfers (1771, aged 71) (see page 198). Now in the Hall of the Royal Company of Archers. Coloured oleograph print (750 copies) was published in the 1970s.

Crombie, Charles (1885–1967)
Created the best-known series of golf cartoons 'The Rules of Golf',

published by Perrier (the sparkling table-water firm) as a book at the beginning of the twentieth century – together with similar cartoon series on cricket and motoring. The Rules of Golf, their titles printed in English and French and showing golfers dressed in nursery-rhyme medieval clothes in impossible situations, have been republished at least once in recent years. These reproductions are to be seen framed everywhere. The original lithographs are more difficult to recognise. Crombie's work on golf was quite prolific, including several Calendars where his highly-finished groups of Scotsmen playing can be a delight. His work was published in *The Bystander* 1904 and *Punch* 1902, 07, 08 and as coloured postcards.

Dollman, John Charles
(1851–1934)
Born at Hove. Painted 'domestic' subjects' – twenty-five exhibited at the Royal Academy. Painted the

Two cartoons from the sequence 'The Rules of Golf', by Charles Crombie.

famous picture 'The Sabbath Breakers' in 1896, a curious representation of the occasion in 1592 when John Henrie and Pat Rogie were prosecuted 'for playing Gowff on the links of Leith every Sabbath during the time of the Sermons'. This was published as a large black and white engraving ($26\frac{1}{4}$ in. $\times$ $18\frac{3}{4}$ in.) by the Fine Art Society in 1896. A highly-coloured modern reproduction of smaller size also exists.

Du Maurier, George Louis Palmella Busson (1834–1896)
Artist and novelist. Famous for stylish pen drawings of British social scene in *Punch* and other London magazines. Published several lively golf drawings, showing women playing golf seriously for the first time.

Furniss, Harry (1854–1925)
Cartoonist and illustrator from Wexford, Eire, who came to London in 1880 and worked on the staff of *Punch* from 1884 to 1894. Lively, ultra-happy style when dealing with golf. Helped illustrate the 'Golf' volumes in the Badminton series of sport edited by Horace G. Hutchinson, first produced in 1890.

Gordon, Sir John Watson, RA, PRSA (1788–1864)
Scotland's leading portrait painter after the death of his friend Raeburn. Exhibited 123 works at the Royal Academy. Best-known golf portrait that of John Taylor, Captain of the Honourable Company of Edinburgh Golfers in 1807/08, 1814/15, 1823, 1825. Recently reproduced as a colourful oleograph print in an edition of 750.

Grant, Sir Francis, PRA (1803–1878)
Fashionable Scottish portrait painter, mostly self-taught, he made his reputation with a picture of Queen Victoria and Melbourne riding in Windsor Park. Small sporting oils valued highly. Painted John Whyte Melville, nineteenth-century Captain of the Royal & Ancient Golf Club of St Andrews.

An oleograph print (750 only) issued recently.

Green, Valentine (1739–1813)
Celebrated mezzotint engraver including those from the portraits of W. Innes and H. Callender by L. F. Abbott.

Hassall, John (1868–1948)
Born at Walmer, educated at Newton Abbot College, Devon and Nevenheim College, Heidelberg. Failed Sandhurst, and went to Canada from where drawings accepted by the *Daily Graphic* and *Punch*. Produced several strongly-coloured sets of lithographs on golf around 1900. These included 'The Links at St Andrews' (exceptionally rare and perhaps the best set of golf prints of this era); 'Before' and 'After' (a pair showing young boy on the tee); 'Where Is It?' (pair showing plump golfer seeking lost ball on a beach); 'The Seven Ages of The Golfer' (from cradle to the grave, seven upright prints). There were also many posters, book and pottery illustrations, postcards and advertisements illustrating golf. Good sets of prints in unfaded condition are highly prized especially when signed in pencil; original works are seldom sold. His best work was of brilliant colour and simplicity.

Hodge, Thomas (fl.1880–1910)
Lived at St Andrews. Extremely important in the realm of golfing art, drawing famous early golfers (from life) at the forefront of the modern upsurge of the game (1880s–1890s). Sketches of Scottish characters, e.g. Tom Morris, have been worked up into paintings by other artists and into colourful, glossy modern prints, all of which fall far short of the character possessed by Hodge's pale, almost ghostly, originals. Illustrated Andrew Lang's *Golfing Papers* (1891), *A Golfing Handbook* (1887) (frontispiece of Tom Morris) and Robert Clarke's *Golf, a Royal and Ancient Game*. His portrait of George Glennie hangs in the Royal & Ancient Golf Club at St Andrews.

Then A Soldier. Full Of Strange Oaths ...

Seeking The Bubble Reputation Even In The Bunker's Mouth.

Then The Schoolboy With His Satchel   And Shining Morning Face.

Two of 'The Seven Ages of the Golfer' by John Hassall.

Lavery, Sir John, RSA, RA, RHA (1856–1941)
His early work was influenced by the Impressionists and he later became a society portrait painter. He painted a large, handsome oil of North Berwick Golf Course from the Ladies Tee (1918).

Lees, Charles, RSA (1800–1880)
Fifeshire artist, pupil of Raeburn. His many paintings of Scottish sporting life include 'The Golfers, St Andrews, 1847' (engraved Edinburgh, 20⅞ in. × 33¾ in.). The print has a key, which, as is often the case with this type of nineteenth-century British sporting print, can be more difficult to obtain than the picture. It shows a match at St Andrews between Sir David Baird and Sir Ralph Anstruther on one side and Major Playfair and John Campbell of Saddell on the other. The crowded scene is on the fifteenth green of the Old Course. William Mephibosheth Goddard of Leith (Captain of the Honourable

303

Company of Edinburgh Golfers 1852) is second from right. The picture seems to have been engraved first by Charles E. Wagstaffe and published in Edinburgh 1850 by Alexander Hill 'printseller to the Queen', with the title: 'The Golfers: A Grand Match Played Over St Andrews Links'. An outstanding reproduction was published in colour in 1973 to celebrate one hundred years of the British Open. Trial sketches and studies for the original painting, which hangs in Strathtyrum, are in the Royal & Ancient Golf Club, St Andrews.

May, P. W. (Phil) (1864–1903)
May's black and white drawings on golf are scarce. He was the recognised master of his art. (See *Punch* anthologies for his style).

Paton, Frank (1856–1909)
An artist and engraver who exhibited from 1872–1890. Among his work is a sporting series of etchings printed in sepia including the highly-regarded 'Royal and Ancient (St Andrews 1794)', published by Leggatt Bros., Cheapside, London 1894. This small print (the centrepiece is only 6 in. × 4 in.) shows four golfers in

William M. Goddard – a figure from Charles Lees' 'The Golfers: A Grand Match Played Over St Andrews Links'.

31.—THE DUFFER.

37.—A LONG PUTT.

16.—AN ANXIOUS
MOMENT.
"This for a Half."

Part of the set of Cope Bros. cigarette cards.

2.—TOM MORRIS.
The G.O.M. of Golf.

29.—THE "MASHIE."

32.—LADY MARGARET
SCOTT.
Lady Champion 1893·4·5·

imaginary eighteenth-century golf costume playing a hole at St Andrews, while four caddies, with bundles of clubs under their arms, look on. The borders of the print (plate size 10 in. × 8 in.) consist of cartoons illustrating golf phrases. Paton's centrepiece has been copied and enlarged to produce coloured prints in the twentieth century. He also engraved a series for C. E. Brock.

'Pipeshank, George'
(fl.1890–1900)
The signature on a set of four lithographs published by the British tobacco company, Cope Bros. & Co. Ltd. at the turn of the century. The illustrations, dated at various years in the 1890s, show

British Parliamentary figures such as the Hon. A. J. Balfour at play on the Scottish links with legendary golfers like Old Tom Morris. (Two of these prints were reproduced c.1972). Doubly interesting as they complement an extremely rare set of fifty cigarette cards sent out with their tobacco by Cope Bros. about 1900, with many of the illustrations by 'Pipeshank'. An interesting artistic note is that the originals are an identical size to the cards, which makes them unique as golfing miniatures.

Raeburn, Sir Henry, RA
(1756–1823)
Born in Edinburgh, he was Scotland's leading portrait painter during his lifetime. A keen golfer,

playing on the Leith Links, he drew portraits of two well-known golfers of that era, John Gray and James Balfour.

Reynolds, Frank (1876–1953) Born in London, he studied at Heatherley's of Newman Street, taught by John Crompton. He worked on magazines and illustrated editions of Dickens's works in colour. Some of his early golf designs were used on pottery and porcelain. He became art editor of *Punch*, and his many golf drawings give a remarkable view of the social impact of the game. Originals of this work are now difficult to obtain, but a few highly-finished watercolours on golf exist alongside many black and white sketches.

Rowntree, Harry (1880–1950) New Zealand artist and illustrator who made his career in England. He worked for *Punch* and produced many fine drawings and watercolours on golf, which was his pastime. He illustrated Bernard Darwin's book on British golf courses with a series of water-colours, many of which came on the market in the 1970s.

Sadler, W. Dendy (1854–1923) A prolific painter of sentimental genre oils, mostly in olde worlde costume, such as 'Stymied', a signed oil on canvas (22 in. × 32 in.). Sadler did a lot of golf paintings with Scottish settings which were often used as book illustrations. A set of large engravings exists which have been reprinted with facsimile signatures of Sadler and the engravers in recent years. Works by Sadler, who exhibited at the Royal Academy from 1873, are in the Tate Gallery, London, Liverpool, Manchester and Rochdale Galleries.

Sandby, Paul, RA (1730–1809) A highly-regarded English watercolour artist who specialised in topographical scenes. A draughtsman on the survey of the Highlands of Scotland after the rebellion of 1745. The British Museum has a watercolour entitled 'A View of Bruntsfield Links looking towards Edinburgh Castle' (overall size 18 in. × 11½ in.). This is possibly the earliest picture recorded not only of a golf links but of players using it and is of historical importance, (see page 14).

Thackerey, Lance (fl.1900–1916) A contemporary of Phil May and Tom Browne who also worked for *Punch*. He specialised in sets of lithographs in colour which included boy-and-girl flirtations linked amusingly to sporting terminology. There is also a set by him of golf course mixed foursomes, and he worked as a postcard artist (*c*.1900–10).

Wain, Louis (1860–1939) 'The cat artist', whose drawings and watercolours of cats behaving like human beings included scenes of feline activity on the golf course. (See illustration, page 27). There are a number of crude forgeries.

Ward, Sir Leslie, RP (1851–1922) Known principally as 'SPY', the cartoonist for the London society magazine *Vanity Fair*. Born in London, he was a grandson of the great English horse painter, James Ward, studied architecture under Sydney Smirke and at the Royal Academy (where he exhibited eleven works). Each week 1869–1914 *Vanity Fair* published a chromo-lithograph in colour as a magazine supplement and over the years some were of golfers, as follows:
  Horace G. Hutchinson 1890
  John Ball Junior 1892 (this was by 'LIB' but is included here as part of the series)
  'Muir' Samuel Muir Ferguson 1903
  'Hoylake' Horace Harold Hilton 1903
  'North Berwick' Robert Maxwell 1906
  'A Celebrated Oarsman' Mr George Duncan Rowe 1906
  'John Henry' John Henry Taylor 1906
  'Jimmy' James Braid 1907
  'The prince of Princes' H. Mallaby-Deeley 1909

'Dialectics' Rt. Hon. A. J. Balfour M.P. 1910 'Easton Hall' Marshall Roberts 1911

There is also a cartoon published by *The World* of Lloyd George when Prime Minister in barely recognisable golf dress – a rare item.

List B

Abbott, Lemuel Francis (1760–1803)	See List A.
Adams, Douglas (–1904)	Scottish landscape artist
Aikman, George, ARSA (1830–1905)	Oils and engravings
Aldin, Cecil (1870–1935)	See List A
Allan, David	Portrait of William Inglis (See Chap. 1)
Allen, G. (1800–1850)	See List A
Ambrose, Charles (c.1905)	See List A
Armour, G. D. (1864–1949)	Worked for *Punch*
Ayton, Symington J.	Illustrated for Sporting and Dramatic News, etc. c.1880
Bateman, H. M.	Worked for *Punch*
Baumer, Lewis (1870–1963)	Worked for *Punch*
Beardsley, Aubrey (fl.1872–98)	One golf picture known, for opening of Prince's Ladies' Golf Club, Mitcham, 1894
Birley, Oswald	Portrait of Horace G. Hutchinson, 1908
Blacklock, Thomas Bromley (1863–1903)	An amusing oil of a caddie
Boyd, A. S. (1854–1930)	Worked for *Punch*
Brock, Charles Edmund (1870–1938)	See List A
Brown, Michael (c.1890)	Life Association of Scotland calendars (1895 to 1916)
Browne, Tom (1872–1910)	See List A
Chalmers, Sir George (c.1720–1791)	See List A
Cleaver, Reginald	Worked for *Punch*
Crombie, Charles (1885–1967)	See List A
'Cynicus' (Anderson brothers)	Late nineteenth-century cartoons, postcards, etc.
Dadd, S. T. (–1892)	Illustrated for Sporting and Dramatic News, etc. 1880s
Davidson, Jeremiah (1745–1795)	Painted Alexander 1st Lord Macdonald (see page 14).
Dollman, John Charles (1851–1934)	See List A
Douglas, James, RSW	Exhibited 1861–1900, Edinburgh
Du Maurier, George (1834–1896)	See List A
Eliott, Harry	Woodcuts and lithographic series of prints; comic style similar to Crombie's
Ewing, Leckie	Pictures of St Andrews
Fish, Capt. G. Drummond	Watercolours of late Victorian golf groups
Flower, Clement (c.1900)	Portrait of 'The Triumvirate' (J. H. Taylor, James Braid and Harry Vardon)
Furniss, Harry (1854–1925)	See List A
Gibson, C. Dana (1867–1944)	Golf cartoons.
Green, Valentine (1739–1813)	See List A.

Woodblock print of the type used in late Victorian illustrated magazines; artist, F. Gilbert, 1869.

Gilbert, F.	Illustrated for Sporting and Dramatic News, etc. c.1880
Gillet, Frank, RA (1874–1927)	Sporting subjects and landscapes
Gordon, Sir John Watson, RA, PRSA (1788–1864)	See List A
Gruber, Jacques	Early twentieth-century decorative works (French)
Grant, Sir Francis, PRA (1803–1878)	See List A
Guthrie, Sir James. PRSA, HRA, RSW (1859–1930)	Glasgow. Portrait of Earl Haig of Bemersyde. Captain of the Royal & Ancient Golf Club 1920
Hardy, Dudley (1866–1922)	Worked for *Punch*
Hardy, Hayward, RA (1843–1933)	George Glennie at Blackheath c.1877 (see page 160).
Harrison, C.	Worked for *Punch*
Hassall, John (1868–1948)	See List A
Heard, H. Percy	Watercolour artist
Hindley, Godfrey C	Exhibited 1860–1910
Hodge, Thomas	See List A
Hutchinson, Sir William, PRSA	Portrait of Andrew Kirkaldy, Club professional 1910–1933 at St Andrews
Jelland, H. C.	Worked for *Punch*
Kay, John (c.1800)	A miniature painter – Edinburgh. See page 19, illustration of 'Cock o' the Green'
Kinsella, E.	Sets of postcards, c.1905
Lander, Edgar	Worked for *Punch*
Lavery, Sir John, RSA, RA, RHA (1856–1941)	See List A
Lees, Charles, RSA (1800–1880)	See List A
Lorimer, John Henry, RSA, RSW (1856–1936)	Portrait of Frederick Guthrie Tait, Amateur Champion 1896–98
Ludlow, H. S. (Hal) (1861–1903)	Early twentieth-century decorative works, including famous bronzes of Harry Vardon
Lunt, Wilmot	Worked for *Punch*
Mills, A. Wallis (c.1899)	Worked for *Punch*

May, P. W. (Phil) 1864–1903)	See List A
Neill, J. R. (c.1880–1920)	American illustrator working for *Sunday Magazine*, etc.
Nicholson, Sir William (1872–1949)	One golf picture is known in *Almanack of Sports*, Heinemann, 1898
Orpen, William	Portrait of the Prince of Wales, 1922
Owen, Will	Worked for *Punch*
Partridge, Bernard (1861–1945)	Worked for *Punch*
Paton, Frank (1856–1909)	See List A
Patrick, James (c.1891)	Portrait of Tom Morris (see page 196)
Pegram, F. (1870–1937)	Worked for *Punch*
Preiss, Frederick	Austrian artist whose work, including figures of golf girls, sold widely in UK and USA early twentieth century
Pettie, John, RA (1839–1893)	Portrait of H. A. Lamb, Captain of Royal Wimbledon Golf Club 1891
'Pipeshank, George'	See List A
Prance, Bertram	Worked for *Punch*
Raeburn, Sir Henry, RA (1756–1823)	See List A
Raven-Hill, L. (c.1890)	Worked for *Punch*
Reed, E. T. (c.1890)	Worked for *Punch*
Reid, Sir George, PRSA, HRSW (1841–1913)	Painted 'Old Tom' Morris 1903 in Royal & Ancient Golf Club
Reynolds, Frank (1876–1953)	See List A
Ridgewell, W. L.	Worked for *Punch*
Robinson, W. Heath	Worked for *Punch*
Rowntree, Harry (1880–1950)	See List A
Sadler, W. Dendy (1854–1923)	See List A
Sandby, Paul (1730–1809)	See List A
Shepard, Ernest H. (1879–1976)	Worked for *Punch*
Smart, John RSA (1838–1899)	Exhibited Edinburgh 1870–90
Smith, A. T.	Worked for *Punch*
Stampa, G. L. (1875–1951)	Worked for *Punch*
Stevenson, W. G., ARSA	'Golf' etching, 1892, of famous players (Tom Morris, etc.)
Studdy, George	Early twentieth-century prints, postcards of dogs 'playing' golf
Swinstead, George Hillyard (1860–1926)	Exhibited at Royal Academy 1880s. Works in Sheffield Museum
Temple, J. & G.	Illustrated for Sporting and Dramatic News, etc., c. 1880
Tennant, Dudley	Worked for *Punch*
Thackerey, Lance (fl.1900–1916)	See List A
Thomas, Bert	Worked for *Punch*
Thorpe, J. H.	Worked for *Punch*
Townsend, F. H. (1868–1920)	Worked for *Punch*
Wain, Louis (1860–1939)	See List A
Wallace, Hugh R.	Large watercolour drawings, Vanity Fair style
Ward, Sir Leslie, RP (1851–1922)	See List A
Wilson, David (1873–1934)	Worked for *Punch*
Wilson, James	Portrait of Sir Hugh Lyon Playfair, Captain of the Royal & Ancient Golf Club, 1856.
Wood, Frank W. (1862–1953)	Landscape and portrait prints
Wood, Starr	Worked for *Punch* (See page 256: Mr Punch's Caddie Car)

A Golf Library
by H. R. Grant

Over the last few years some fine golf libraries have been put together in the USA, the United Kingdom and South Africa, and until quite recently it was possible to obtain most of the golf books that have been published since the 1850s. Within the last five years the golf book collecting scene has developed enormously and it is now difficult to obtain golf books which appeared before 1900, particularly on a limited budget. This, however, should not discourage anyone from the gentle art of book collecting.

For anyone already collecting or intending to start, it is essential to be armed with *The Library of Golf 1743–1966* by Joseph S. F. Murdoch, published by Gale Research Company, 1968, together with the supplement now available, bringing in the period from 1967–1976.[1] This, the only comprehensive reference work on golf books, gives the information so useful in dating, classifying and collating publications. The next significant purchase should be a copy of *The Badminton Library – Golf*, edited by H. G. Hutchinson. First published in 1890, there are many subsequent editions and the seventh edition includes details of the evolution of the rubber-cored golf ball. Horace G. Hutchinson wrote many admirable books on golf including his biography *Fifty Years of Golf*, 1919. To obtain the true flavour of early golf, its difficulties and pleasures, it is best to look to the biographical books. Among those which can still be found on the dusty shelves of second-hand bookshops are: *F. G. Tait: A Record* by John L. Low, 1900; *My Golfing Reminiscences* by H. H. Hilton, 1907; *Fifty Years of Golf* by Andrew Kirkaldy, 1921; *Golfing Memories and Methods* by Joyce Wethered, 1933; *Thirty Years of Championship Golf* by Gene Sarazen, 1950; *The Bobby Jones Story* by Grantland Rice, 1953; *My Partner Ben Hogan* by J. Demaret, 1954; *Golfers Gold – An Inside View of the Pro Tour* by Tony Lema, 1964; *Come Swing With Me* by Doug Sanders, 1974. These biographies will give a firm base on which to build the biographical section of the library, and will also bring out the contrast between the days of Vardon and the days of Nicklaus.

There are many books which give some history of golf, but there are few which deal with it in detail. No library would be complete without some of the books which have been published on the history. One of the best publications in recent years is *A History of Golf in Great Britain* by Bernard Darwin and others, 1952. This deals with the history of the game from the earliest times and is well illustrated with colour and monochrome plates. *A History of Golf: The Royal and Ancient Game* by Robert Browning, 1955, is one of the best written histories of the game, and is still available to the assiduous searcher. *Fifty Years of American Golf* by H. B. Martin, 1936, is one of the outstanding American golf books; it covers in detail golf in America and contains some fine photographs.

The history of golf is also covered in the published histories of Golf Clubs. There are several which are currently in print and available from the secretary of the Golf Club concerned. Golf Club histories have always been keenly sought after by the collector and even the ones published within the last twenty years have now

[1] This book can be obtained from J. S. F. Murdoch, 638 Wagner Road, Lafayette Hill, Pa.19444, USA, or from Grant Books, Cutnall Green, Droitwich, Worcestershire, England.

become scarce. Recent histories cover *Troon, Formby, Muirfield, St Andrews, Elie, St Andrews* (New York), *Monterey Peninsular Country Golf Club* (Pebble Beach, California), *The Riviera Country Club* (Pacific Palisades, California), and *Golf at Merion 1896–1976* (Philadelphia).

There are more books published on the instructional side than any other, and though many of them are repetitive, a comprehensive library should have books of an instructional nature covering the last three-quarters of a century of golf, and the following are suggested as a base. The great triumvirate, Taylor, Braid and Vardon, all wrote instructional books, and *How to Play Golf* by Harry Vardon is readily available, first published in 1912, with many later editions. *Taylor on Golf*, 1902, is rather more difficult to acquire but there are still copies around, and Braid's *Advanced Golf – Hints and Instructions for Progressive Players,* 1908, can be obtained without much difficulty. These three should cover the first twenty years of golf instruction this century. The change from wooden-shafted clubs to steel-shafted clubs is not covered specifically by any book, although Henry Cotton wrote a pamphlet in 1934 called *Hints on Play with Steel Shafts.* In 1937, Pam Barton wrote *A Stroke a Hole.* This was the first book to incorporate 'flip sequence' photographs, and in 1938, Sam Snead produced *Sam Snead's Quick Way to Better Golf.* Forty years and six books later, he wrote *Sam Snead's Golf Book.*

After World War II, the deluge of golfing titles commenced. In 1946 E. M. Prain wrote one of the finest instructional books, *Live Hands – A Key to Better Golf.* Whilst still available, it is becoming increasingly difficult to obtain. In 1957, Ben Hogan wrote one of the classic instructional books on golf, *The Modern Fundamentals of Golf,* and, in 1959, Tommy Armour produced his second great instructional book – *A Round of Golf with Tommy Armour.* From 1960, nearly every pro who won a major title published an instructional book. Some of the better authors include Cary Middlecoff, Gary Player, Max Faulkner, Arnold Palmer, Jack Nicklaus, Johnny Miller and Lee Trevino.

For light entertainment and humour, there are many anthologies and fun books. Perhaps the greatest writer on golf, Bernard Darwin, published several books of his essays. Some of these are now very scarce, but *Out of The Rough,* 1932; *Playing the Like,* 1934; *Rubs of the Green,* 1936 are some which are still available. Henry Longhurst also published books which contain his essays, and his biography *My Life and Soft Times,* 1972, is a must for any library. George Houghton has written many books of humour and cartoons, and most of his titles are still to be found in your local bookshop. George Nash in his trilogy of letters to the Secretary of a Golf Club produced some really funny British humour. The illustrator, H. M. Bateman, collected together a number of his illustrations on golf and published them in 1923, and this has been reprinted in a smaller format in 1978. W. Heath Robinson's collection of humorous golf cartoons titled *The Humour of Golf* was reprinted in 1975. The caddie has not been missed by the humorist, and there are several books devoted specifically to him. Perhaps he is best typified in *Candid Caddies*, 1935, written by Charles Graves and Henry Longhurst.

All books mentioned are reasonably available to the collector or to those starting out on the trail of golf book collecting. Undoubtedly his appetite will be whetted, and he will start to seek out the more expensive and difficult books to obtain, but as anyone who has collected books knows, the treasures can be unearthed in the most unexpected places. Always try and obtain clean, bright copies, and check the contents before purchasing them. However, be satisfied with a tatty copy of the scarcer items. Never dither over the price of a book you want, because what is there today, may be scarce tomorrow and rare next week.

Appendices

Museum Locations of Pictures of Golf and Golfers prior to 1800

Belgium
Brussels, Kon. Bibliotheek
      Kon. Musea voor Schone
        Kunsten (2)

Canada
Ontario, Art Gallery of Ontario

England
Chichester, West Dean Park
Gloucester, Cathedral
London, British Museum (2)
      National Gallery (6)
      H.M. The Queen's
        Collection
Manchester, North Manchester
  Golf Club (tiles)
Polesden Lacey, Surrey

France
Paris, Bibliothèque Nationale
      Institut Néerlandais (4)
      Louvre

Germany
Cologne, Walraff-Richartz-
  Museum
Hamburg, Kunsthalle
Karlsruhe, Staatl. Kunsthalle (2)
Munich, Alte Pinakothek

Netherlands
Alkmaar, Stedelijk Museum
Amsterdam, Rijksmuseum (12)
      Rijksprentenkabinet
      (35)
      Amst. Historisch
      Museum (4)
      Gemeente Archief
Arnhem, Gemeente Museum
Delft, Stedelijk Museum 'Het
  Prinsenhof'
Dordrecht, Dordt's Museum
Enkhuizen, Gereformeerd
  Weeshuis
Enschede, Rijksmuseum Twenthe
Haarlem, Teylers Museum
The Hague, Mauritshuis (3)
      Gemeente Archief
Leeuwarden, Fries Museum
Rotterdam, Museum Boymans-van
  Beuningen (3)
Utrecht, Gemeente Archief
Wassenaar, Haagsche Golf &
  Country Club

Zandvoort, Kennemer Golf &
  Country Club (3)

Poland
Warsaw, Muzeum Narodowa

Scotland
St Andrews, Royal and Ancient
  Golf Club (2)
Edinburgh, National Gallery of
      Scotland
      National Portrait
      Gallery of Scotland

Spain
Madrid, Prado
Valencia, Museo del Patriarca

USA
Far Hills NJ, Golf House
Minneapolis, Institute of Arts
New York, The Metropolitan
  Museum
Washington DC, National Gallery
  of Art

Golf Club and Golf Ball Collections

Chapter 1   Appendix 1

Jeu de Mail

Extract from *Golfing Curios and the Like* by Harry B. Wood (London, Sherratt & Hughes 1911) p.44 (Translation of work by Lauthier, Paris, 1717)

'. . . It is suitable for all ages, from infancy to old age. Its beauty consists not in making great strokes, but in playing truly, neatly and without peculiarities, and when to that are added force and certainty in measuring the extent of the stroke, the player becomes perfect. To attain this degree of perfection, seek the most approved method of playing well, conforming to that of the best players. Place yourself easily by the ball, not too near it nor too far away. Do not stand with one foot too far in advance of the other. The knees should neither be relaxed nor too stiff but just firm enough to ensure a good stroke.

Attitude of the Body

The body should be neither too erect nor too inclined, but moderately bent, so that in striking one is sustained by the muscles remaining firm. Swing gently backwards, and from the waist upwards to the head, taking care at the same time not to lose sight of the ball. It is this last half-turn of the body which, describing a grand circular sweep with the club, produces the effect of force travelling from afar. The club should not be lifted too hastily, but in one movement without letting it run away from you. It should be held for an instant at its highest poise, in order to strike with vigour, and without altering the position of the body, wrist-force should be employed. The arms and legs should maintain the same easily-adjusted attitude which one learns to take at first glance before the ball.

Different Methods of Players

One sees some people who only play with the arms, i.e. who do not make that half-turn of the body which comes from the back. Not only do they harass the chest by the great effort thus made with the arms fore-shortened, but they will never become good players because they do not raise the club high enough.

   Others raise it too much over the shoulder, or again only use half their height, and strike the ball as if they were whipping it. Then there are those who, stretching wide their legs, balance themselves on tip-toes, and let themselves go so forcibly at the ball that they miss altogether, and nothing can prevent their falling 'nose to the ground'. Some others stick the left elbow in the air to measure the stroke, and they very rarely hit the ball fairly. All these habits are as bad as they are disagreeable, and should be got rid of. Every game has its own laws which must be followed: dancing, riding, and fencing have each attitudes and regulated movements, without cultivating which, one can be nothing but clumsy and ungraceful. Jeu de Mail is very much the same. It is a noble game played in public, and cannot be played before the public unless the correct methods are employed.

The Hands and Arms

The hands should be neither too close together nor too far apart; the arms neither too contracted nor too extended, but supple, so that the stroke may be free and easy. The left hand, which is higher, must have the thumb opposite the middle of the fingers, while the thumb of the right hand should cross the finger-tips rather obliquely, not to be above or level with the handle which spoils the stroke. If, in raising the hands to make the stroke the right thumb is not crossed, the club may shift itself in falling upon the ball, and fail to strike it fairly. The right hand must grasp the club as tennis-players hold the racket, for the thumb thus in contact with the finger-tips is much firmer, guides the stroke better in the desired direction, and gives more facility and force to the wrist, which should in both these games be actively employed.

The Feet
To place yourself properly before the ball, stand firm and assured upon your feet. Adopt an easy posture, and let the ball be opposite the left heel. Do not put the right foot too far behind, and neither stoop with the body or bend the knee too much in striking, as these things throw the swing out of gear, and often make the player miss the stroke. All these observations are important to those who wish to play well. Do not hesitate too long in measuring your stroke. A single calculation, after a little experience, is enough, and one notices how those who spend the most time in addressing the ball are those who often miss it, and become laughing-stocks, for spectators love to see prompt and smart play.

The Club
In order to acquire that exactness which is so necessary for this game, clubs of the same weight and length, duly proportioned to the strength and height of the player, should always be chosen. If the club be too long, or too heavy, it catches the ground, and if it be too short or too light, it does not give sufficient force, and the ball is struck on the top or 'by the hair' as they say. Each player, then, should choose a club which exactly suits him, of which he feels himself master, and of which the bulk is proportionate to the ball. It is wise to be careful in all these things.'

Chapter 1   Appendix 2

Registrum Secreti Sigilli
Lib. LXXXVIJ.169

Ane Letter maid makand mentioun that our Souerane Lord vnderstanding that thair is no small quantitie of gold and siluer transported zeirlie out of his Hienes kingdome of Scotland for bying of golf ballis, vsit in that kingdome for recreatioun of his Majesties subjectis, and his Hienes being earnestlie dealt with by James Melvill, in favors of Williame Bervick and his associate, who onlie makis, or can mak golf ballis within the said kingdome for the present, and were the inbringeris off the said trade thair: The said James Melvill vnderstanding by them and vther puir peopill (who now for laik of calling wantis mantenance), whome he sall adjoyne to the said Williame Bervick and his associate, to furnische the said kingdome with better golf ballis, and at ane moir easie rate then have beine sauld there these manie zeiris bypast: In consideratioun quhairof, his Majestie, bothe tendring the generall weill of his subjectis and increase of vertew within his said kingdome, geving and granting vnto the said James Melvill, with Williame Bervick and his associate, and sik vtheris as the said James Melvill sall adjoyne to them, onlie libertie to mak golf ballis within the said kingdome for the spaice of tuentie ane zeiris allanerlie, dischairging all vtheris alsweill of making as selling any golf ballis maid within the kingdome bot those that ar maid by the said James, his servantis, and William Bervick and his associate: Provyding allwayis, that the (said) merchandis sall not be restranit from importing and selling the said golfe ballis so brocht home or maid by the saidis patentis: Provyding lykwayis, that the saidis patentaris exceid not the pryce of four schillingis money of this realme for everie ane of the saidis golfe ballis as for the pryce thairof: And to the

effect the said James and his associates may have the benefits of his Majestie's grant, his Hienes by these presentis dothe expresslie prohibite and dischairge and forbid all and sindrie his Majesties subjectis, and vther persounes quhatsymever, that nane of them presume, nor tak vpone hand, to mak or sell anie golf ballis maid within the said kingdome, vtheris then the said James Melvill and his deputies, with the said Williame Bervick and his associate, for the spaice foirsaid, or to utter or sell the samyne to his Hienes subjectis vpone quhatsymever collour or pretence, vnder the paine of escheitting of all suche ballis so to be made or sauld; the ane half off the benefite aryssing thairby to come to our Souerane Lordis use, and the vther half to the use of the said James Melvill and his assignayis onlie: And that the said letter be extendit in the best form, with all clauses neidfull, with power in the samyn to the said James, by himself, his deputies, and servantis, in his name, to seirche, seik and apprehend all sik golf ballis as sall be maid or sauld within his Hienes said kingdome vtherways then according to the trew meaning of his Majesties grant, and to escheit the samyn in manner aboue specifeit. And for the better tryell heirof, his Majestie ordanes the said James Melvill to have ane particular stamp of his awin, and to cause mark and stamp all suche ballis maid be him and his foirsaidis thairwith; and that all ballis maid within the kingdome found to be vtherwayis stamped sall be escheated in maner foirsaid.

Gevin at our Court of Sallisbery the fyft day of August, the zeir of God IM.VIC. and auchteine zeiris.

Chapter 1 Appendix 3

The Register of the Privy Council of Scotland. 2nd Series
Vol.III   A.D.1629–30   p.174

Decreta. November 1627–January 1630.   fol.213b.
Complaint by William Dicksoun and Thomas Dicksoun, 'makers of gowffe ballis in Leith', as follows: James Melvill, quartermaster to the regiment of the Earl of Morton, pretends that he has a gift from his Majesty's late father, for exacting a 'certain impost aff everie gowffe ball made within this kingdome', which gift their Lordships had never ratified, and on 20th February last, he sent a number of 'lawlesse souldiours' to the complainers' dwelling houses in Leith, 'who after manie threatnings and execrable oathes uttered to take thair lyffes they violentlie reft and tooke from thame ane greate number of gowffe ballis quhilkis they had made for his Majesteis use at the desire of Arthure Naismith, indweller in Edinburgh', and the said James Melvill publicly avows that he will either take the complainers' lives or 'disappoint them of thair callings if they grant not unto him the said impost'. Charge having been given to the said James Melvill and pursuers and defender being personally present and heard, and also a number of witnesses examined, the Lords find that James Melvill and his servants took nineteen 'gowffe ballis' from the pursuers most unwarrantably, and ordain him to consign £5 as the price thereof in the hands of the Clerk of Council to be paid to the pursuers, and also to find caution in £100 acted in the Books of Secret Council for the indemnity of the pursuers.

Chapter 2 Appendix 1

Articles and Laws in Playing at Golf 1744
(The Rules of the Gentlemen Golfers)

1   You must Tee your Ball, within a Club's length of the Hole.
2   Your Tee must be upon the Ground.
3   You are not to change the Ball which you Strike off the Tee.
4   You are not to remove Stones, Bones or any Break Club, for the sake of playing your Ball, Except upon the fair Green, and that only within a Club's length of your Ball.
5   If your Ball comes among Watter, or any wattery filth, you are at liberty to take out your Ball and bringing it behind the hazard and Teeing it, you may play it with any Club and allow your Adversary a Stroke, for so getting out your Ball.
6   If your Balls be found anywhere touching one another you are to lift the first Ball, till you play the last.
7   At Holling, you are to play your Ball honestly for the Hole, and not to play upon your Adversary's Ball, not lying in your way to the Hole.
8   If you should lose your Ball, by its being taken up, or any other way you are to go back to the Spot, where you struck last, and drop another Ball, And allow your Adversary a Stroke for the Misfortune.
9   No man at Holling his Ball, is to be allowed, to mark his way to the Hole with his Club or any thing else.
10   If a Ball be stopp'd by any person, Horse, Dog, or any thing else, the Ball so stopp'd must be played where it lyes.
11   If you draw your Club, in order to Strike and proceed so far in the Stroke, as to be bringing down your Club; if then, your Club shall break, in any way, it is to be accounted a Stroke.
12   He whose Ball lyes farthest from the Hole is obliged to play first.
13   Neither Trench, Ditch or Dyke, made for the preservation of the Links, nor the Scholar's Holes or the Soldier's Lines, Shall be accounted a Hazard, But the Ball is

to be taken out Teed and play'd with any Iron Club.
John Rattray, Capt

One amendment was added later:

The 5th and 13th Articles of the foregoing Laws having occasioned frequent Disputes It is found Convenient That in all time Coming the Law shall be That in no case whatever a Ball shall be Lifted Without losing a Stroke Except it is in the Scholar's Holes When it may be taken and teed and played with any Iron Club without losing a Stroke And in all other Cases The Ball must be Played where it lyes Except it is at least half covered with Water or filth When it may if the Player chuses be taken out Teed and Played with any Club upon loosing a Stroke.
Thomas Boswell, Capt

Chapter 2 Appendix 2

Extract from
Customs Account Books
for the Port of Leith
                    Register House ref.
                        E.504 22/1
Entry for **10th May 1743**

In the Magdalen William Carse Ma^r for South Carolina[1]
(to shipped for) David Deas.

5 bundles q^t 20 pc containing 757 yards being 605$\frac{1}{2}$(?) British made sailcloth and fit to be made into sails p. affed: 2 Boxes q^t 8 dozen Golf Clubs, 3 Groce Golf Balls and 6 Shirls[2]: also 6 casks q^t 18 Bushells Scots Salt, which came here from Anstruther and per permit of the 11th May instant.

[1]A later entry shows that the Magdalen was bound for Charlestoun in South Carolina.

[2]This could be shirts – from other entries the writer very often missed the cross stroke on the t.

Chapter 3 Appendix 1

Song 'In Praise of Gutta Percha'

Sung at the meeting of the
Innerleven Golf Club, 1 September
1848, by W. Graham of Edinburgh

'Of a' the changes that of late
Have shaken Europe's social state,
Let wondering politicians prate,
   And 'bout them make a wark a'.
A subject mair congenial here,
And dearer to a Golfer's ear,
I sing – *the change brought round this year*
   By balls of GUTTA PERCHA!

Though Gouf be of our Games most rare,
Yet, truth to speak, the tear and wear
O' balls was felt to be severe,
   And source o' great vexation.
When Gourlay balls cost half-a-crown,
And Allan's not a farthing down,
The feck o's wad be harried soon
   In this era of taxation.

Right fain we were to be content
Wi' used up balls new lickt wi' paint,
That ill concealed baith scar and rent –
   Balls scarcely fit for younkers.
And though our best wi' them we tried,
And nicely every club applied,
They whirred and fuffed, and dooked and shied,
   And sklentit into bunkers.

But times are changed – we dinna care
Though we may ne'er drive leather mair,
Be't stuffed wi' feathers or wi' hair –
   For noo we're independent.
At last a substance we hae got
Frae which, for scarce mair than a groat,
A ba' comes that can row and stot –
   A ba' the most transcendent.

They say it comes frae yont the sea,
The concrete juice o' some rare tree –
And hard and horny though it be,
   Just steep it in het water –
As saft as potty soon 'twill grow,
   Then 'tween your loofs a portion row –
When cool, a ba' ye'll get, I trow,
   That ye for years may batter.

Hail, GUTTA PERCHA, precious gum!
O'er Scotland's links lang may ye bum –
Some purse-proud billies haw and hum,
   And say ye're douf at fleein'.
But let them try ye fairly out
Wi' ony balls for days about,
Your merits they will loudly tout,
   And own they hae been leein'.

'Tis true – at first ye seem to hing,
And try the air wi' timid wing –
But firmer grown, a sweep ye'll fling
   Wi' ony ba' o' leather.
Ye're keen and certain at a put –
Nae weet your sides e'er opens up –
And though for years your ribs they whup,
   Ye'll never moutt a feather.

And should ony wild unchancy whack
Or cleek-stroke e'er gie ye a chack,
As wi' some Indian tomahawk,
   Ye're mended unco easy.
How piteous e'er may be your plight,
The het bath puts you a' to right;
Again you grow right smooth, and tight,
   and fresh as ony daisy.

But Noo that a' your praise is spent,
Ye'll listen to a friend's comment,
And kindlier tak on the paint –
   Then ye wad be perfection.
And sure some scientific loon
On golfing will bestow a boon
And gie ye a cosmetic soon,
   And brighten your complexion.'

Chapter 5   Appendix 1

From *Practical Club-making* by
J. H. Taylor, a chapter in H.
Hutchinson, *Golf and Golfers*, 1899

The popularity gained by golf
within the last few years has made
the demand for golf clubs and balls
so great that hundreds of men are
now continually engaged in their
manufacture. The art of golf club
and ball making has long since
come to be considered a trade of
sufficient importance to guarantee
the apprenticing of lads to those
already adepts in the business, so
that the industry may be learned by
them the more perfectly with a view
to its becoming their means of
livelihood. Machinery also has been
invented to aid in the production of
clubs, but though a great deal of the
hard work has been saved in this
manner, the finishing has yet to be
done by skilled workmen, nor is it
likely that it will ever be otherwise.
In the manufacture of shafts even,
although they are sometimes turned
by machinery, yet in order to make
anything like a satisfactory job each
one has to be finished after the head
has been fixed on. The great
difficulty which golf club makers
have always experienced has been
the obtaining of good wood suitable
for the purpose of head-making.
Beech, which is more used than any
other wood, grows in great
abundance both in England and
Scotland, but, notwithstanding the
amount obtainable, it is exceedingly
difficult to get it really good. A great
deal depends on the manner in
which the tree has been grown; if in
some sheltered spot where plenty of
nourishment has been afforded, it
will generally be very soft, but if in
some exposed quarter, where the
growth has been slow and difficult
from the force of prevailing winds
and the lack of soil, it will then be
hard and durable. Under the latter
circumstances no wood can be
more suitable for making into golf
club heads, for while it is hard
enough to wear well, there is not
that stony hardness about it which
is sometimes found in holly,
hornbeam, rockwood, &c. To

inferior players this is a matter of
no importance; but to others, if a
yard or so can be added to the
length of the drive by the extra
spring in the wood, it is certainly
worth thinking about. Apple is
also often used, but being a more
brittle wood than beech it is not
easy to foretell what will happen to
it. If it stands for the first few
rounds it will probably last for
years, but with rough usage it is
very liable to break in the neck.
This is not so plentiful a wood as
beech, as the trees do not grow very
large. The hardness of apple-wood
does not depend so much on where
it has been grown as is the case with
beech; it is nearly always hard, but
the sour apple trees are the hardest.
There is a great deal of waste with
this wood in cutting it up, as the
trees are so small. It is also very
treacherous to work as there are
often little flaws in it which cannot
be seen at first, one of which may,
however, appear in the neck of the
club just when it is nearly finished,
and of course labour in that case
has been spent in vain. Thorn,
which is also sometimes used, is
very like apple in all respects.
Hornbeam also, although it may
turn out very well, being of a brittle
nature often breaks very quickly in
the neck. Nothing will so certainly
break a club as hitting the ball on
its neck. When a club has been
broken, it is quite customary for the
player to say: 'I did not strike the
ground, hence it ought not to have
broken,' whereas had he struck the
ground a hundred times, instead of
hitting the ball with the neck of his
club two or three times, it probably
would have remained whole. The
neck is the weakest part of a club,
and when it strikes the ball, there
being nothing to resist the forward
twist of the head, an unwonted
strain is put upon the neck which is
almost sure to end in a smash.
Because of the frequency with
which clubs are broken in this
manner bent woods have recently
been introduced in which the grain
runs straight up the neck of the
club, which is thereby wonderfully
strengthened. Hickory and beech
are mostly used in this way.

Although clubs made from this
kind of wood are rather more
expensive than the ordinary ones,
yet they are by far the more
economical in the end, as they last
much longer. Shafts are mostly
made of hickory, and for general
purposes it is by far the best wood.
It is also the cheapest. Greenheart
makes very good shafts, especially
for wooden clubs. Being stiff, it can
be reduced until it is very fine, and
it has a nice steely spring. It is not
very good for rough work, as it is
rather brittle and will break much
more easily than hickory. It does
not, however, become so easily bent
as hickory, but has greater power of
resistance. If pressed out of the
straight, it will readily regain its
former position as soon as the
pressure is removed. Lancewood
and lemon-wood, which are very
much alike, also make very good
shafts. They are neither quite so
stiff nor so brittle as greenheart, but
they possess much of its power for
keeping straight. Of texa wood I
can say but little, for,
notwithstanding the great things
claimed for it, I have not been able
to discover wherein lies the
advantage which it is supposed to
possess over other woods. There
are many woods which are
occasionally used both for heads
and shafts, besides those to which I
have referred, but I have not
mentioned them, as I thought it
best to confine myself to those only
which are most generally in use. All
wood must be thoroughly seasoned
before it is used. If heads were
made of wood that was not
seasoned, they would be more than
likely to come rapidly to pieces if
immediately played with, or would
shrink very badly out of shape if
kept, while shafts that were not
seasoned would soon become as
crooked as ram's horns. As shafts
are mostly made from foreign wood
the best way is to obtain them
already seasoned from timber
merchants, but as a beech or apple
tree may be cast in any one's way I
will explain briefly the treatment it
should receive preparatory to being
made into golf club heads. If the
tree has to be felled, late in the

autumn or mid-winter is the best time, as then the sap is not circulating. After it has been felled it should be sawn into plank $2\frac{3}{4}$ inches thick, care being taken to split the heart if possible, as a plank with the heart in the centre is next to useless. The next thing is to obtain from some club maker a block which has already been cut out for a head, and, taking this as a pattern, to draw on each plank the number of blocks it is calculated to produce. The simplest way is to cut the plank first into pieces the length of the block, which should be about eleven inches. In marking it off, the part of the block which is to form the neck of the club must have the grain running pretty straight up, and not across it. It was customary, a short time since, to cut blocks from the plank with the same amount of wood on each side of the angle, thus, so that either side might be used for the head or neck, as it was best suited for the purpose. The blocks were then sawn from the plank in this manner. This method was very useful, in so far as it always gave one or two chances of getting the grain right in the head, but the strength thus obtained in the neck was not sufficient to bear the strain put upon it, so another plan had to be adopted. Blocks are now usually sawn from the plank with one side of the angle already allotted for the neck and the other side for the head. The part which is to form the neck is therefore longer than that which is to form the head, thus. Instead, therefore, of cutting blocks from the plank in the manner shown above, they should be cut out thus. In this way the grain runs much straighter up the neck, which is consequently much stronger. The grain, however, must not be kept quite straight up the neck, as that could unduly weaken the head. The objection to cutting out blocks in this manner is that if the grain of the head is not right it cannot be altered, but the objection is small compared with its advantages. What I mean is this, the grain of the head should run in one of three ways, either straight across from

the face to the lead, longways from the toe to the heel, or curve from the face back towards the heel. With either of these three ways there is not much wrong, but if the grain runs from the face with an inclination towards the toe, the face will generally break up very soon after it is played with. The grain will usually be right if the block is sawn out so that the face of the club shall be formed of that part of the plank which was nearest the heart of the tree. This is also best for durability, as heart-wood, or duramen, is always the strongest. After the blocks are sawn out, they should be stacked in a well ventilated room to season. Plenty of space must be left between each block for the air to get through, but the sun must be kept from them or it will bake them to pieces. If the room is made hot by means of a fire they will also crack. The time they take to season depends on the degree of moisture in the wood when it was sawn up, but at the end of six months, if the room is well ventilated, they should be in pretty good working order. Of course blocks will season very much quicker than planks, and they are not so likely to split in drying as planks are. Wood is often seasoned artificially in a very short time, but it is not so good as when seasoned in the ordinary way. Before the blocks can be converted into golf club heads, a place must be found wherein to erect a bench, which must be strongly built, and should not be more than thirty-three inches high. Also the following implements must be obtained:

One vice, $3\frac{1}{2}$-inch jaw
One 14-inch bow saw
One 12-inch tenon saw
One 14-inch half-round wood rasp
One 14-inch half-round cabinet rasp
One 14-inch half-round cabinet file
One $\frac{3}{8}$-inch gouge
One 1-inch chisel
One medium hammer
One brace
One lead ladle
One $\frac{3}{16}$-inch twist drill
One small bit
One 12-inch screwdriver

One scraper
One screw for leads
One steel-bottom plane
One glue-pot
One oil-stone
One oil-can
One pair scales
Weights up to 8 ounces

A mould must be procured as a guide for the lie of the club and for the length, also one with which to mark out roughly the shape of the head. When all this is ready, and the vice has been firmly fixed to the bench, take one of the blocks and grip it in the vice, with the face upward and the part which is to form the neck pointing outward from the bench to your left. Mark off the lie of the club by placing the mould, which you have for that purpose, so that the angle and bottom of the mould comes flush with the angle and bottom of the block. Also mark on the block the length your head has to be. Then take it out of the vice and draw a line straight across the top, from the line which you drew on the face to denote its length. Place the mould, which gives you the shape of the head, with the point touching the line you have just drawn, and the front edge close to the face, and make a pencil mark round it. The head which we are about to produce is to be a bulger driver; and now that it is marked out, the first thing is to saw off the narrow strip from the front of the neck, that the bulge may be easily formed. Grip the block in the vice as before, and with the bow saw commence sawing where your line runs off to nothing, near the face, taking care to keep your hands a shade below, rather than above, the level. When that is sawn off, grip the block near the bend, on the left side of the vice, with the neck pointing straight up and down, and saw off the piece on the opposite side of the neck, working from the top down towards the head. Then put it into the vice on the right side, with the toe pointing upward and the neck toward yourself, and saw to your line around the toe—in this case keeping your hands rather above

319

the level. The lines drawn to show the lie were carried away when the piece was sawn from the front of the neck, so they must be drawn again in the same way as at first. Then put the head into the vice on the right side, with the face upward and the neck turned inward to the bench, and saw off the piece at the bottom of the neck with the tenon saw. Begin at the heel end of the line, and keep the saw leaning slightly towards the vice. The wood outside the line on the upper side of the neck must be left, in case it should be necessary to make the head more upright after it is finished. The head must now be put in the vice, with the face and back between the jaws and the neck upward to the right. The sharp edge on the upper side of the neck must be taken off with the bow saw, beginning at top and finishing near the face. You must stand rather to the right of the vice to do this. Then repeat the same operation on the opposite side of the neck, but instead of finishing as before—at the angle—continue right round the back and toe until the face is reached. To begin with, you must stand to the left of the vice, gradually moving to the right as the saw works round the head. The head is now ready for the rasp; but before we proceed any further, I had better define the names by which I shall refer to its various parts:

Bottom: the part which rests on the ground.

Top: the part with which the maker's name is stamped.

Face: the part with which the ball is struck.

Back: the part where the lead is inserted.

Toe: the point of the head furthest
from the neck.

Neck: that part as a whole which is attached to the shaft from the angle upwards.

Scare: the flat part on the under-side of the neck to which the shaft is glued.

Angle: the curve where the neck joins the head.

Heel: the part where the neck merges into the face.

It will be well now to procure, as a pattern, a head made by some club maker, which should be carefully studied during all the subsequent proceedings. This got, put your head into the vice, with the bottom upward and the neck downward, on the left side; then take the wood rasp and level all irregularities on the bottom. Alter the position of the head so that the face is upward and the neck outward on the left. Straighten up the front of the neck, and make the face slightly round, holding the rasp a little on the slant from right to left, and working it to and from you. Take off the sharp edge at the bottom of the heel, by moving the hands from right to left, and round up the neck a little at the top of the face by the same kind of stroke, with the round side of the rasp. Change the head to the right side of the vice, with the back upward and the neck still outward from the bench. Make the back of the neck to correspond with the front, working from the left of the vice, and if necessary, in order to get the neck small enough, reverse the head to its former position and take a little more off the front. The widening of the head should take place simultaneously on each side of the neck. When this is done, and the back also bears some resemblance to the pattern, turn the toe upward and execute the curve round from the back; then put the head in the left side of the vice, and make a curve to join the first from the face. This completes the outline of the head, and brings us to the top. Grip it by the face and back, with the neck upward on the right, and work back over from the toe, also further rounding up the neck while the head is in this position. The cabinet rasp must now be taken, and the head fined up by going over it in exactly the same order as with the wood rasp. Having done this, the next thing is to cut out the place for the lead, but care must be taken now that the vice does not damage the head; so it will be wise to get a straight piece of wood, about the same size as the jaw of the vice, to put between it and the head, and also a piece for

later use with one side hollowed out for the back of the head to fit into when cutting out the place for the horn. It will be well to draw the outline of the lead first with pencil; then put the head into the vice with the back upward and the neck outward on the right, and with the tenon saw, keeping as near as possible first to the bottom line, then to the top, without destroying them, cut the inside piece of wood quite or nearly out in the shape of a V, standing close to the bench on the right side of the vice. Then take the gouge and make the end of the lead-groove nearest you the right shape, after which run the chisel along the upper edge, then reverse the head and shape the opposite end with the gouge, and run the chisel along the bottom edge. All this has been done while standing in one position, and the lead-groove being now the right shape, the edges must not be again interfered with. Make the two ends deeper with the gouge, and with a chisel and hammer clear out the centre, keeping the inside V-shape throughout. The depth which you will have to go down must be left to your own judgment, as the amount of lead required depends on the weight of the wood, and also on the weight the head has to be when finished. The usual weight of a head is from $7\frac{1}{2}$ to 8 ounces. It is better, however, to make it rather too heavy than too light, as it can and must be made lighter when it is finished up. Having got it what you think to be the right depth, make three grooves on each side with the gouge, starting just below the edge, and continuing to the bottom with an inclination towards the heel. This is to prevent the lead from working backward, which it always has a tendency to do when the club is played with. The next thing is to get the twist drill and tie a piece of whipping around it, about an inch from the point, so that you may know when you have bored far enough, and having put it in the brace, make one hole at each end and one in the middle. Then insert the screw and turn it until it becomes fairly tight, being careful not to overdo it for fear it should split the head. When the three holes have been made in this manner, and their frayed edges, which might prevent the lead from running freely into them, have been cleaned off with the chisel, take a piece of clay about the size of a walnut, which should previously have been mixed with water until as pliable as putty, and, having made it a little longways, with one end square across, lay it in the palm of the left hand and flatten it out with the under edge of the right hand. Two pieces treated in this manner are to form a mould to keep the hot lead from running out at the ends of the cavity made to receive it, which it must otherwise do, as the centre has to be the highest part of it. First cover half of the cavity by placing the square end of one piece of clay across it near the middle, and pressing the edge tight against the wood all round it. Place the square end of the second piece of clay a quarter of an inch from the first piece, and cover the other half of the cavity in a similar manner to the first. The opening thus left between the two pieces of clay is for the lead to be poured into, but for fear it should flow over the sides of the opening little pieces of clay should be put to keep it back. Although nothing was said about it, I must presume that the ladle was put on the fire a few minutes ago, with some lead in it, and that the lead is now ready to pour into the head. Resting the bowl of the ladle on the jaws of the vice—which should be a little open—and having ascertained that the lead is not too hot, take the head by the neck with the left hand and pour the lead slowly into the opening, keeping it constantly running until the space is filled. If one part of the lead were allowed to become solid before the other part were poured in, the two lots would not knit together, and the upper piece would fly out when the club was being played with. If, however, when you begin to pour it in, the lead bubbles a good deal, which it will do if it is a little too hot, you may stop until the bubbling ceases somewhat, but do

not let the lead become solid. When the cavity is full, remove the clay, put the head into the vice, and knock the edges of the lead round with the hammer to make it fit firmly against the wood, and also fill, by knocking in its edges, the little hole which will probably be in the centre where the lead was poured in. Of course you must be careful not to knock it too hard, or the swelling of the lead will split the wood, especially at the toe. Cut off the superfluous lead with the chisel, which can be done all the better by wetting its edge, and the head will be ready for the horn. I advise that the horn should be obtained from a club-maker ready to put in, as it is difficult for one not accustomed to filing to work it straight, and unless this is done there is little hope of making a good fit. But if you are desirous of trying for yourself, cut off its ends with the tenon saw to the shape of the horn in your pattern head, then put it in the vice and make the bottom flat with the cabinet file. The back edge and end should be filed a little on the dovetail principle, so that it may not prise up when the ball is struck on it. Having done this, put your head into the vice with the bottom upward, the neck to the left and the back fitted into the hollow of the piece of wood which you have for that purpose. The top edge of the vice should be gripping about the middle of the face. Take the horn with the left hand, and place it on the head, keeping the thumb upon it to steady it, and the tips of the four fingers partly on its front edge and partly on the face of the club, to insure that a slight margin is projecting beyond the face, and mark it round with a pencil. Then saw along the back and end, keeping within the lines and not going very deep. The chisel must next be driven down all along the saw marks. A considerable amount of care is needed, especially at the end, as a piece of the heel may very soon be knocked out. Chip a little piece out at the heel end and let the head down in the vice until only about half the depth of the wood which has to be cut out is above its

upper edge, then, with the chisel and hammer, cut out the part which is above, beginning at the heel and working through to the toe. The grain from the toe runs downward into the head towards the heel, so that to begin cutting at the toe would be very dangerous. Next raise the head again, so that a little more may be cut out, using the edge of the vice as a guide to keep you straight. This must be repeated until you have gone down about the depth of your horn. Avoid cutting deeper at the back than at the front, and *vice versa*. It will be necessary to undermine the back edge a little, because of the bevel on the horn; this can be done by running the chisel along it from toe to heel, but the top edge should not be interfered with. When the horn is fitting, put the head in the vice as before, but grip the edge of the horn, with its front jaw, instead of the face of the club. Screw the vice up fairly tight, and tap the horn with the hammer until it has a firm bearing; then take the twist drill and bore three holes, each one inclining to the centre of the head. Care must be taken not to twist the drill or it will snap at once, and whether driving it in or pulling it out, the brace must be turned in the same way, the right hand doing the turning and the left hand either pressing on it or pulling outward. Chalk rubbed on the vice and pieces of wood will prevent any tendency the head may have to slip. Three pegs must now be made, about one and a half inches long, of hickory, to fit the holes, rather smaller at the bottom, but gradually widening toward the top. Glue in the horn, dip the points of the pegs in glue, insert them in the holes, replace the head in vice and drive the pegs home. Saw off the ends to within three-sixteenths of an inch of the horn, and then drive them further in by squeezing the horn and top of the head between the jaws of the vice. Now finish up the head by going over it in the same order as previously with the cabinet rasp. If it be necessary to file off some of the lead, use the wood rasp. When you have got it the right shape, fine it up with the cabinet file and it is then ready for the scraper. In using the scraper, work as much as possible with the grain, and proceed in much the same order as with the files, beginning at the front of the neck, working round the back and toe, and finishing with the top. The lead should be cleaned off with one end of the scraper, and not with a cutting edge. It will separate much more freely when wet. This done, our next business is with the shaft. Place it on the bench with its front against something to prevent its slipping, and taper it from top to bottom by planing the four sides equally. When it has been reduced to about half an inch square at the bottom end, round it up, keeping it as straight as possible. Before cutting the scare you must find out which way the grain runs, for the shaft will be made stronger or weaker by the manner in which it is glued to the head. Take a chisel and slice off one end, and you will see that the grain runs either straight across or up and down, just as you hold the shaft. If it were glued on with the grain running up and down, it would not be so strong by any means as if it ran through from side to side. Due regard having been paid to this, put the thin end of your shaft into the vice and cut the scare with the chisel, standing close to the shaft on the right of the vice. The scare should be about six inches long, and should be made very thin at the end. After you have cut it off roughly with the chisel, take the plane and make it smooth, keeping it if possible a little hollow in the middle, and then rough the surface with the cabinet rasp so that the glue may get a firm hold. Plane the scare of the head smooth, taking as little off it as possible at first, and tie it to the shaft to find out how it lies. If it is made too upright it cannot often be made flat again. To make it more upright the scare must be planed off at the end farthest from the angle. Having made it like the scare of the shaft, put some glue on each of them and tie them firmly together with an ordinary piece of string.

Having ascertained that the head is not turned in, nor lying back, the club must be left until the glue is dry. When it is fit to work, take off the string and grip the neck of the club in the vice, with the head on the right side and the toe upward. Take the cabinet rasp, and make the scare flat on the top, tapering from the angle down to nothing where it joins the shaft. Then take it out of the vice, leaving the jaws partly open, hold the head with the left hand, put the shaft across the bench, and, resting the neck slantwise between the jaws on the right side, file the neck and shaft at the joint into the customary shape. To guide you in this and what remains to be done, you had better keep a complete club by you. Now a piece of wood must be obtained about fourteen inches long, with a groove down the middle, which having been put in the vice, the shaft must be laid in the groove and planed up to the right feel. It should be set up a very little, and should be slightly oblong from the upper to the under side. When you have got enough spring in it, rub off any rough edges there may be with the fine file, and scrape it. Then give the head a good rubbing with No. 2 sandpaper, afterwards with No. 1, and varnish it with spirit varnish. Rub the shaft first with No. 3 sandpaper, then wet it to bring out the pithy substance from the grain. Allow it to dry, rub it with No. 2, and polish it by rubbing varnish and linseed oil upon it, with fine shavings. To assist in whipping the club, a hole should be made somewhere, in which to put the end of the shaft. Then start the whipping near the head, keeping the end underneath the string as you bind it round. Put the end of the shaft into the hole, and, standing with the club under the left arm, turn the head round with the left hand, letting the string slip through the right hand, but keeping it as tight as possible. When it is bound up to the top of the scare, cut the string, leaving about six inches for finishing it off. With this make two loops round the shaft, keeping the thumb

underneath them, then remove the thumb, pass the end of the string underneath, and pull the loops tight, keeping them so by drawing up the end, which may now be cut quite close. Gently tap the top and bottom edges round with the hammer, rub the whole of the whipping with the hammer handle to make it as smooth as possible, and give it a coat of varnish. Having now come to the grip, mark off eleven inches from the end of the shaft, and rough the surface with the cabinet rasp. Then put on plenty of pitch, and bind a piece of listing round to within three inches of the bottom. The listing should be overlapped at the top to prevent it slipping off. Pitch the first piece and bind another piece round in a similar manner, going to within two inches of the bottom. Pitch that, and carry another piece to within one inch. More pitch, and then put on the leather in just the same way as the listing, pulling it as tight as possible. Fasten it at the bottom with a small tin-tack, and cut the top and bottom edges round with the chisel. Then get a smooth piece of wood, and roll the grip between it and a clean part of the bench, afterwards taking off the rough edges with the cabinet file. Put the string on the top and bottom, making it secure in the same way that the whipping was secured. Tap it round with the hammer, and put varnish on the bottom piece. All that now remains to be done is to fine file the bottom and scrape it, clean up the face and rough it, make a chalk line over the top, on which to put the stamp if you have one, give the whipping and head two more coats of varnish, and the club is quite complete.

Horace Hutchinson comments on this description: 'It is a revelation that there is so much to be done in the making of a club – almost as difficult as playing golf itself – and **it seems to make the value of the four and sixpence that one pays for a club go up very considerably.'**

Chapter 7   Appendix 1

The Thoughts of Thomas Kincaid 1687–88

1687

'Jan 20 . . . After dinner I went out to the golve with Hen: Legatt. I found the only way of playing at the golve is—

1. To stand as you do at fencing with a small sword, bending your legs a little, and holding the muscles of your legs and back and armes exceeding bent or fixt or stiffe, and not at all slackening them in the time you are bringing down the stroak (which you readily doe).

2. The ball most be straight before your breast, a little towards the left foot.

3. Your left foot most stand but a little before the right, or rather it most be even with it, and a convenient distance from it.

4. Ye most lean most to the right foot.

5. But all the turning about of your body most be only upon your legs, holden together as stiff as ye can.

6. Then ye most incline your body a little forward from the small of the back and upwards; for seeing all the strenth of the stroake is from the swing of the body in turning about, then certainly the further forward you incline your body or shoulders, they most have the greater swing, and so consequently give the greater stroake; but you most not incline so fare forward as to make your stand the more unstedfastly and waver a little in bringing down the stroak.

7. You most keep your body in this posture all the time both in bringing back the club and forward, that is, you most nither raise your body straighter in bringing back the club nor incline it further in bringing down the club; but ye most bring back the club by turning your selfe about to the right hand, and that as it were upon a center without moveing your body out of the place of it, but only chainging the position of it in thrawing it about or turning it about upon that center, so that ye most cast the weight of your body off the on leg on the other in the time you are bringing about the club: neither most you in the least turn down your left shoulder and up your right in bringing back the club thinking thereby to give the club a larger swinge and so incresse its force or to raise the ball: for it is a verie unsetled motion that throw of the body whereby you turn down the left shoulder and up the right, so that thereby you will verie often misse the ball and allmost never hitt it exactly.

8. Your armes most move but verie little; all the motion most be performed with the turning of your body about. The armes serve only to guide the club and to second and carie on that motion imprest upon it by turning of your body: therefore ye most never begin to bring about the club with the motion of the armes first, but their motion most be only towards the end of the stroak.

9. All the motion of the armes most be at the shoulder and all the motion of the legs most be at the upmost joynt at the loins.

10. You most make no halt or rest, which is slakning of the muscles of the back, between the bringing-back of the club and the bringing it forward, but bring it about with that swiftness that the naturall swing of the club requires, holding it pretty fast in your hands. In every motion the muscles that concurr to the performing at golve keep bent and stayd, which in all motions of your armes you will be helped to do by contracting your fingers, and so if there be anything in your hand you most grip verie fast.

11. You most aim directly to hitt the ball it selfe and not aim to scum the ground or strick close to the ground, thinking that then you are sure to hitt it; for this is but ane indirect way of hitting the ball, neither is it sure when the ball lies inconveniently; neither 3dly is it exact, for you will butt seldome hitt the ball exactly and cleanly this way; and 4ly it is more difficult then the other way, whereas the other way is more easie. 2, sure, 3, better for hitting the ball exactly. The way to learn this is to tie your ball at first pretty high from the ground.

12. The shaft of your club most be of hazell. Your club most be allmost straight, that is, the head most make a verie obtuse angle with the shaft, and it most bend as much at the handle as it doth at the wooping (an exact description of what occurs when my great-grandfather's long-spoon by Philp is handled or swung), being very supple and both long and great.

13. Your ball most be of middle size neither too big nor too little, and then the heivier it is in respect to its bigness it is still the better. It most be of thick and hard leather not with pores or grains or that will let a pin easilly passe through it especially at the soft end.'

'Jan 21. I thought upon the way of playeing at golve . . . I found that the first point to be studied in playeing at the golve is to hitt the ball exactly; for if you hitt the ball exactly though the club have butt strenth yett the ball will fly verie farre. The way to attain this perfection is to play with little strenth at first but yet acuratly observing all the rules of poustaur and motion before sett down, and then when ye have acquired ane habit of hitting the ball exactly ye most learn to incresse your strenth to force in the stroak by degrees, staying still so long upon every degree till you have acquired ane habit of it; neither will the knowledge of these degrees be altogether uselese afterward, for they will serve for halfe chops, and quarter chops, and for holling the ball. But then in going through all these degrees of strenth you most be verie attentive and careful not to alter that poustaur of your body or [off in MS] way of moveing and bringing about the club which he observed when ye playd with little strenth: for only the reason why men readily miss the ball when they strick with more strenth then ordinaire is because their increasing their body and ordinare way of bringing about the club; as also it makes them stand much more unsetledly and waver in bringing about the club, and so they readily miss the ball. I found that in all motion the greatest and strongest motion most begin first.'

'Jan 24. I rose at 4 . . . and thought on severall things till 8, as of the way of standing at the Golve—that your feet most be both of ane equal distance from the ball, at least the ball most ly upon a line that is perpendicular to that line that passeth between the on foot and the other. These places will be found by drawing a circle round about the ball which most be in the center, and placeing your feet on that circle, that your feet most not stand parallel to the way you would have the ball fly, but upon a line declining towards the left-hand as it were 10 to 15 degrees . . .'.

'Jan 25. I glewed a club head. . . . After dinner I took out the plains and made a little skelpe to putt on the club. I took of the peice that was joynd to the old shaft. I glewed too that skelpe.'
'Golve' was still in his mind on the morrow, for:
'Jan 26. I thought on the playing at the golve. I found (1) that ye most rest most upon the right legg for the most part, but yet not too much so as to be exactly perpendicular upon it, which ye will know by the ballanceing of your body.
2. I found that the club most always move in a circle making an angle of 45 degrees with the horizon.
3. That the whole turning of your body about most be by thrawing the joynts of your right legg, and then when . . . [MS torn] you most thraw the small of your back so that the left shoulder will turn a little

down wards, because the body is inclined a little forward, but ye most beware of raising the on shoulder higher than the other as to their position in the body, for that motion is not convenient for this action.
4. I found in bringing down the club ye most turn your body as farr about towards the left following the swinge of the club as it had been turned before towards the right hand.
5. I found that seeing the swinge of your body by the turning it upon your legg is the largest and strongest motion, therefor it most begin first and the turning at the small of the back most only second it, and then most follow the motion at the shoulders. The other motions most be but verie little and imperceptible, neither most these motions at the small of the back and shoulders begin till the club have hitt the ball, or, at least, be verie near it.'

'Feb 9. I rose at 7. I thought upon the method of pathologie and in playing the golve. I found that in all motions of your armes ye most contract your fingers verie strait and grip fast anything that is in them, for that doth command the motion exactly and keeps all the muscles of armes verie bent, I digested the rules of playing the golve into verse thus:

> Gripe fast, stand with your
>   left leg first not farr;
> Incline your back and
>   shoulders, but beware
> You raise them not when back
>   the club you bring;
> Make all the motion with your
>   bodie's swinge
> And shoulders, holding still
>   the muscles bent;
> Play slowly first till you the
>   way have learnt.
> At such lenth hold the club as
>   fitts your strenth,
> The lighter head requires the
>   longer lenth.
> That circle wherein moves
>   your club and hands
> At forty five degrees from the
>   horizon stands

> What at on stroak to effectuat
>   your dispaire
> Seek only 'gainst the nixt it to
>   prepare.

I thought to digest the generall rules of motion into verse, which are these:

> All motions with the strongest
>   joynts performe
> Lett the weaker second and
>   perfect the same
> The stronger joynt its motion
>   first most end
> Before the nixt to move in the
>   least intend.
> The muscles most with touie
>   motion move
> For which the gripping fast
>   great helpe doth prove.'

Glossary

Approach	The stroke by which a player endeavours to play his ball on to the putting-green.
Back spin	See Bottom.
Baff (verb)	To strike the ground immediately behind the ball with the 'sole' of the wooden clubhead in playing. The object of so doing is to put undercut on the ball and send it high into the air, to make it fall dead when it lands. See also Sclaff.
Baffy-spoon or Baffy, Baffing spoon	A wooden club with a short shaft and very much lofted in the face, formerly used for playing approaches by the method of baffing.
Bap	A wooden club with a round head. So-called because the head was the same shape as a particular form of Scottish bun called a bap.
Bent	A coarse grass found on seaside links.
Bone or Horn	A piece of ram's horn, celluloid, wood fibre or other substance, inserted into the front edge of the sole of the wooden club to prevent the face from being injured at the bottom.
Bottom	Back-spin, or a spin which will theoretically have the effect of making the ball, after alighting, roll back towards the player, but which practically only tends to prevent its rolling forward any distance after alighting. Also called 'undercut'.
Brassey (ie)	A wooden club shod with brass on the sole.
Break-club	A stone or any other obstacle lying near the ball which might break or injure the club in the act of playing.
Bulger	A club with a convex face.
Bunker	A sand-hole in the golf course.
Caddie	The person who carried the golfer's clubs.
Carry	Used to express the distance between the spot from which a ball is driven to the place where it first alights, exclusive of the distance it may thereafter bound or roll. A long carry or a short carry are used to signify the distance a ball must be lofted usually over a hazard.
Cleek	A golf club with an iron head; also a form of shallow-faced iron.
Club	The implement with which the ball is struck in playing golf.
Course	A golf course is the ground upon which golf is played. See also Links.
Cup	A small, shallow hole in the course, frequently one made by the stroke of some previous player having removed turf.
Dead	This word is used in two senses; first, when a ball falls without rolling, it is said to fall 'dead'; and second, a ball is said to lie 'dead' when it lies so near

the hole that the player is certain to put it in with his next stroke. The term is also applied to putting, and a putt is said to be laid 'dead'.

Deep

Refers to the distance between the sole of the club and its upper edge. A club with a greater distance is deep, compared with a club with a lesser distance which is shallow.

Divot

A piece of turf. Frequently used to signify a piece of turf cut out of the links in the act of playing a stroke.

Draw

To play a ball so that it will travel with a curve towards the left hand. (Synonymous with Hook and Pull.)

Driver or Play-club

The wooden club with which the ball is usually driven from the tee, and with which the ball can be driven the furthest distance.

Driving

Used in two senses: first, playing tee-shots; and second, playing any full strokes.

Duff

To hit the ground behind the ball. With a duffed stroke the ground is hit so far behind that the ball will not be driven any distance; while in a sclaffed stroke, although the ground behind is also struck, the ball will usually be driven nearly as far as if clean hit.
See also Sclaff.

Face

This word is used in two senses: first, when one speaks of playing a ball over a 'face', it there signifies the rise of the hazard or ground over which the ball is to be played; second, it is applied to the front part of the club-head which strikes the ball.

Flat

A club is said to be 'flat' when its head is at a very obtuse angle to the shaft.

Fog

Moss; also thick, rank grass and small rushes.

Follow-through

The continuation of the swing of the club after the ball has been struck.

Foozle

A badly played stroke.

Fore

The warning cry which a golfer gives to any person apt to be struck by the ball which he has driven or is about to drive.

Fore-caddie

A person employed to go in advance of the players to watch where their balls alight.

Globe

Another term for a golf ball.

Gobble

A putt played with more than necessary force which goes into the hole, such that if the ball had not gone in it would have gone some distance past the hole.

Grassed

A club is said to be grassed when its face is spooned or sloped back so as to drive the ball high. Only used in connection with wooden clubs.

Green

First, the whole links or golf course; second, the putting-green or portion of the links devoid of hazards within twenty yards of a hole.

Grip

First, the part of the club shaft grasped by the golfer while playing; second, the grasp itself.

Gutta	A golf ball made of gutta percha only. It may be made by hand and may be 'hand hammered' or it may be made in a mould.
Gutty	A composite ball made of gutta percha mixed with other compounds and made in a mould. *Note*: These are the terms used by the Authors to distinguish between the two types of ball. In many books, no such distinction is made and the terms are freely interchangeable.
Half shot	A stroke of less distance than a full shot and played with a half swing; less than a three-quarter shot and more than a wrist or quarter shot.
Hanging ball	A hanging ball is one which lies on ground sloping downward in the direction in which it is to be driven.
Hazard	A general term for bunkers, water, sand, loose earth, mole-hills, paths, roads or railways, whins, bushes, rushes, rabbit-scrapes, fences, ditches, or anything which is not the green of the course, except sand blown on to the grass by wind, or sprinkled on grass for preservation of the links, or snow or ice, or bare patches on the course.
Head	The lowest part of a golf club.
Heel	First, that part of the clubhead nearest the shaft; second, to hit the ball with the heel of the club, which has the effect of driving the ball to the right hand.
Hole	First, the hole in the putting-green into which the ball is played; second, the whole space between any teeing-ground and the actual hole.
Hook	Hook on a club face refers to the fact that, when looking down on the head, the toe is in advance of the heel and the face therefore points to the left.
Horn	See Bone.
Hose or Hosel	The socket of iron-headed clubs into which the shaft is fitted.
Iron	A club with an iron head considerably lofted, to raise the ball.
Jerk	When a stroke is played with a 'jerk' the clubhead, after striking the ball, digs into the ground.
Lead	Name of the metal let into the head of a wooden club to give it weight.
Lie	First, the lie of a club refers to the angle of the head to the shaft. A club is said to have a flat lie when the angle is very obtuse, and to have an upright lie when the angle is less. Second, the lie of the ball refers to its position on the links, a good lie signifying that the ball lies clear so that it can easily be struck, and a bad lie signifying that the ball lies in a hole or in heavy grass, etc., and is difficult to play. The term 'cuppy lie' applies to a ball lying in a cup.
Links	Sandy ground at or near sea level covered with a special grass known as 'bent' grass and usually traversed by a stream ('burn' in Scotland). Most of the early golf courses were 'links courses'. The actual derivation of the word is unknown but it is Scottish in origin. Some have said that the term 'links' refers to the connecting links of the burn or stream as it twists and turns.
Listings	See Rind.

Loft	To drive the ball into the air in playing a stroke. Also used to refer to the degree or angle to which a club face is set back. A 'lofted club' has a definite angle of loft. A 'straight-faced' club has a small degree of loft.
Lofter	A lofting iron, that is, an iron club with a long face like a cleek but deeper and with more loft.
Long game	Driving and play through the green.
Mashie	An iron club with a deep, short blade. Well lofted.
Match	First, the sides playing against each other; second, the game itself.
Miss the Globe	To fail to strike the ball, as by swinging the club over the top of it, or by hitting the ground behind. This counts a stroke.
Mussel backed	Refers to those irons which had the weight in the head, concentrated in the centre, i.e. they were often round backed, the general appearance being rather like a mussel shell.
Neck	The neck of the club is the bent part of the head where it is connected with the shaft.
Niblick – Iron	An iron club with a small, heavy round head, used to play the ball out of bunkers, hazards and bad lies.
Niblick – Wooden	A small-headed club with a fair degree of loft, used to get the ball out of cuppy lies, in the days when the long-headed clubs were in fashion. Later versions of the wooden niblick had a brass sole.
Nose	The nose of the club is the pointed part of the head opposite the neck.
Play-club	See Driver.
Pull	See Draw.
Putt	To play strokes near the hole on the putting-green.
Putter (wooden or iron)	An upright club used for putting.
Putter, approaching	A putter with more loft than the one used on a putting green. Used for approaching the green from any distance under about 100 yards. Usually wooden.
Putter, Cleek	An iron putter with rather more loft than the usual iron putter.
Putter, Driving	A straight-faced wooden club with a short, stiff shaft, used for driving the ball low into the wind.
Putter, Wry–necked	An iron putter with a bent neck. Invented by W. Park, Jr.
Putty	A nickname for the Eclipse golf ball, a rather soft gutty.
Quarter or wrist shot	A stroke less than a half stroke. Generally played from an iron from the wrists. Sometimes referred to as 'off the wrist'.
Rind	Strips of coarse cloth ('listings') wrapped around the shaft under the leather grip to give it thickness.

Run	First, to run the ball along the ground instead of lofting it; second, the run of a shot is the distance the ball runs after alighting on the ground.
Rutter	A particular (and early) form of iron niblick. The head, little larger than a golf ball and heavy, was specially suited to get the ball out of small cups and cartruts – hence the name.
Scare or Scarff (less common)	The part of the club where the head and shaft are spliced together. Clubs with this method of fixing the head to the shaft are sometimes referred to as 'scared-head clubs' to distinguish them from the (later) socket-headed clubs.
Sclaff	See Baff. The distinction between the two words is somewhat subtle. In baffing a ball the stroke is played with the intention of lofting it high in the air, whereas a sclaffed ball is not necessarily lofted high. See also Duff.
Screamer	A very long stroke, so called from the whistling noise made by the ball.
Screw	To put spin on a ball either by 'pulling' it or 'slicing' it.
Set of clubs	The complement of clubs carried by a player.
Shaft	The stick or handle of the club.
Shaft, bowed	In many wooden putters and in some baffing spoons, the shaft was deliberately bent just below the grip, in a gradual curve in the plane of the head, so that the grip, on looking down the shaft, was pointing, not at the heel of the club but at the centre of the face or just on the heel side of it.
Shallow	See Deep.
Shank	The part of an iron clubhead into which the shaft is fitted. See Socket.
Shank (verb)	To hit the ball with the shank.
Short game	Approaching and putting.
Slice	To draw the face of the club across the ball from right to left in the act of hitting it, the result being that it will travel with a curve towards the right.
Socket (noun)	The part of the head of iron clubs into which the shaft is fitted.
Socket (verb)	To hit the ball with the socket.
Sole	The flat-bottom part of the clubhead which rests on the ground.
Sole (verb)	To sole the club is to set it on the ground so that the sole is in contact with the ground throughout its length.
Spoons	Clubs having wooden heads, lofted or grassed, so as to loft the ball.
Spring	The degree of suppleness of the club shaft.
Stance	The position of the player's feet when addressing himself to the ball.
Steal	To hole a long unlikely putt by a stroke which rolls the ball up to the hole so that it just drops in.

Stroke	Any movement of the club which is intended to strike the ball.
Swing	The mode in which the club is swung when in the act of hitting the ball.
Swipe	A full stroke.
Tee	The elevation, generally a small pinch of sand, on which the ball is placed for the first stroke to each hole.
Teeing-ground	The space marked out within the limits of which the ball must be teed.
Three-quarter stroke	A stroke of less distance than a full stroke, but more than a half stroke.
Toe	See Nose.
Top	To top the ball is to hit it above its centre.
Undercut	To hit the ball, by baffing or otherwise, so that it rises high in the air, and will not, owing to the spin on the ball, roll far after alighting. See Bottom.
Upright	See Lie.
Whins	Furze or gorse.
Whipping	The twine with which the clubhead and shaft are bound together.
Wrist shot	See Quarter shot.

Bibliography

Advanced Golf – Hints and Instructions for Progressive Players,
James Braid, London (Methuen) 1908
The Art of Golf,
Sir Walter Simpson, Edinburgh (David Douglas) 1887
The Art of Putting,
W. Park Jnr, Edinburgh (J. & J. Gray) 1920
The Badminton Library – Golf,
Horace Hutchinson, London (Longmans Green) 1892
The Book of Golf and Golfers,
Horace Hutchinson, London (Longmans Green) 1899
*The Chronicle of the Royal Burgess Golfing Society of Edinburgh
1735–1935,*
J. Cameron Robbie, Edinburgh (Morrison & Gibbs) 1936
The Complete Golfer,
Harry Vardon, London (Methuen) 1905
Concerning Golf,
John Low, London (Hodder & Stoughton) 1903
*The Curious History of the Golf Ball:
Mankind's Most Fascinating Sphere,*
John S. Martin, New York (Horizon Press) 1968
Early Golf: History and Development,
Steven van Hengel, 1972
Fifty Years of American Golf,
H. B. Martin, New York (Dodd Mead) 1936
Fifty Years of Golf,
Horace Hutchinson, London (Country Life) 1919
Fifty Years of Golf: My Memories,
Andrew Kirkaldy, London (Unwin Bros.) 1921
A Game of Golf: A Book of Reminiscences,
Francis Ouimet, New York (Houghton Mifflin) & London
(Hutchinson) 1932
The Game of Golf,
W. Park Jnr, London (Longmans Green) 1896
Golf: A Royal and Ancient Game,
Robert Clark, Edinburgh (R. & R. Clark) 1875
Golf and Golfers – Past and Present,
J. Gordon McPherson, Edinburgh (William Blackwood) 1891
The Golf Book of East Lothian,
John Kerr, Edinburgh (T. & A. Constable) 1896
The Golf House Club, Elie,
Alasdair M. Drysdale, 1975
Golf in America: A Practical Manual,
James P. Lee, New York (Dodd Mead) 1895
Golf on a New Principle: Iron Clubs Superseded,
L. Everage, London (Simpkin Marshall) 1897
The Golfer's Handbook,
Robert Forgan Jnr, Edinburgh (John Menzies) & London (Marcus
Ward) 1881
The Golfer's Manual,
'A Keen Hand' (H. B. Farnie), Cupar (Whitehead and Orr) 1857

The Golfer's Yearbook (for 1866),
Robert Howie Smith, Ayr (Smith & Grant) 1867
Golfing Curios and the Like,
Harry B. Wood, London (Sherratt & Hughes) 1911
Historical Gossip about Golf and Golfers,
'A Golfer' (George Robb), Edinburgh 1863
A History of Golf: The Royal and Ancient Game,
Robert Browning, London (Dent) 1955
A History of Golf in Britain,
Bernard Darwin, Sir Guy Campbell and others, 1952
A History of the Royal and Ancient Golf Club, St Andrews, from 1754–1900,
H. S. C. Everard, Edinburgh (William Blackwood) 1907
History of the Royal Perth Golfing Society,
T. D. Miller, Perth (Munro Press) 1935
The Library of Golf 1743–1966,
Joseph S. F. Murdoch, Detroit (Gale Research) 1968 (Supplement 1967–1976 now available)
The Life of Tom Morris,
W. W. Tulloch, London (T. Werner Laurie) 1908
Old Leith at Leisure,
J. S. Marshall, Edinburgh (Edina Press) 1976
'Old Memories of Westward Ho!',
H. G. Hutchinson in *The Midland Golfer* 1914
Prestwick St Nicholas Golf Club,
William Galbraith, 1950
Reminiscences of Golf and Golfers,
H. Thomas Peter, Edinburgh (James Thin) 1890
Reminiscences of Golf on St Andrews Links,
James Balfour, Edinburgh (David Douglas) 1887
Scotland's Gift: Golf; Reminiscences 1872–1927,
Charles B. Macdonald, New York (Scribner's) 1928
Shell International Encyclopaedia of Golf,
Donald Steel and Peter Ryde, London (Ebury Press & Pelham Books) 1975
Sixty Years of Golf,
Robert Harris, London (Batchworth Press) 1953
St Andrews Home of Golf,
James Robertson, (J. & G. Innes) 1967
Taylor on Golf: Impressions, Comments and Hints,
J. H. Taylor, London (Hutchinson) 1902

Supplement to

GOLF
IN THE MAKING

Revised edition

Sean Arnold's Gallery in London's Mayfair

Golf, polo and tennis. Antiques for collectors and interior decorators. The finest collection presented by experts.

Sean Arnold
Golf and Polo Antiques
Grays Antique Market
58 Davies Street
London W1Y 1AR
Tel: 071 409 7358
Fax: 071 499 5890

Historical note

Since the first edition of *Golf in the Making* appeared in 1979, we have published *Royal Blackheath* (Henderson & Stirk 1981). This is the history of the first Golf Club ever to be established outside Scotland, and the arrival of golf in England is attributed to James VI of Scotland becoming James I of England and bringing a large Scottish Court with him to London in 1604. Thus golf arrived at Blackheath as the result of a predominantly Scottish Court being in residence at Greenwich Palace, on the Thames near London.

An examination of the Blackheath records, however, revealed an entirely new explanation as to how organised golf was started both in Scotland and at Blackheath. The feature of all early Golfing Societies was their commitment to dining and conviviality. This can be understood now that we know that it was groups of Freemasons who had the happy idea of adding golf as a healthy form of exercise prior to their dining. They had Club uniforms, ceremonies, fines in the form of drink for absence or other offences; toasts, including the Masonic 'three times three'. New membership was controlled with the use of the 'Black Ball' when necessary. Attendance at dinners and guests were recorded, as were often the details of the meals. There was never a great deal in those days to mention about golf, except the bets on the matches, which were usually entered in a separate book, and were by no means all related to golf matches. An officer called the Registrar also frequently appears.

The way in which these societies were organised on similar lines could have been no accident, and once the Grand Master Mason of Scotland, Sinclair of Roslin, and his fellow Freemasons had been observed laying the foundation stone of a new golfing house at Leith in 1767 there can hardly be any doubt that the attractive concept of playing golf before banqueting was organised by them. Golf historians up to now have never been able to explain why there was the obligation to dine after playing golf; nor have they looked at the activities of the early Scots as a whole. We believe that the explanations now offered permit the history of these early societies to be examined on a far more logical basis.

'This day William St. Clair of Roslin Esquire, the Undoubted representative of the honourable and heritable G.M.M. of SCOTLAND In the presence of Alexander Keith Esquire Captain of the honourable Company of Golfers and other worthy members of the Golfing Company, all Masons, the G: (sic) now in his GRAND CLIMAX of Golfing laid the foundation stone of the Golfing House in the S.E. Corner thereof by THREE STROKES with the MALLETT

Alexr Peacocke M.M. Alexr Keith Capt.
                     Wm. ST: Clair G.M.M.
                     Robert Henderson

Alexr Duncan M.M.
  Capt Blackheath &
  Old Capt. of St Andrews
James Cheape
William Hogart
Alexr Orme M.M.
Robert Beatson M.M.
Henry Bethune G.M.
Richard Tod Sub. G.M.
Henry Seton 2 Capt. M.M.
Ben Gordon

Freemasons shared a secret, and as time went on, they played golf with non-Masons, who were not admitted to their ceremonies, or mysteries, as they were referred to. It will have been noticed that the Burgess, Bruntsfield, Musselburgh and Blackheath Societies all have foundation dates earlier than their first Minutes, and that considerable parts of the Edinburgh Company's Minutes are missing. We believe that the explanation for these missing minutes lies in the admission of non-Masons to the Societies, owing to the decline in the number of Masons who were golfers. Once this process reached a certain stage, the Societies decided to destroy any evidence which might reveal their secrets. By this means they were remarkably successful in covering their tracks for so many years, and this was done in accordance with masonic practice. Nevertheless, some of the original Societies have been left with a strong sense of tradition, the origins of which present members are unlikely to be aware of. This explains why the majority of the original Societies still have no lady membership. All that we can say with certainty is that these early Societies had similar customs not related to golf; they shared a secret – again not related to golf – and they were not formed with the primary object of playing golf. What was originally offered was, in today's terminology, a 'package deal' – golf, dinner and the mysteries.

At all events, they succeeded in keeping the game alive, when it might so easily have suffered the same fate as golf in Holland, and disappeared. Dining and conviviality belonged to that age, and golf was a most useful associate: simple and straightforward to play, 'the very healthful exercise of the golf', as it was called.

The foregoing now explains the activities of these early Societies, but it nullifies the basis on which all claims were previously made as to when each Society was formed as a Golf Club, because they were not Golf Clubs in the accepted sense, and their members were playing together as groups of Freemasons long before they decided to incorporate themselves into a society or club. We give as examples the Edinburgh Company of Golfers, who incorporated themselves in 1767, and St Andrews, in the same year; and with this consider the evidence already mentioned taken from the Edinburgh Company's Minutes, who in the same year 1767 as they incorporated laid the foundation stone of their Club House. Ten years later the same William St Clair of Roslin was laying the foundation stone of the

Archers Hall, Edinburgh which still stands today. The Royal Company of Archers was formed in 1676, and used Leith Links in Edinburgh to shoot on. In 1709 they obtained a Silver Prize from the City of Edinburgh to shoot for, and in 1744 the Edinburgh Company of Golfers obtained a Silver Putter from the same source to play for and inaugurated the idea of prizes for golf. The idea of prizes was already well established by the archers, many of whom at that period were also golfers. We may well wonder if the inspiration for the first unincorporated Society of Golfers did not stem from the activities of the archers.

In *Curling – An Illustrated History* by David B. Smith (John Donald Publishers Ltd, Edinburgh 1981) there is evidence that there was an almost Masonic feeling of brotherhood amongst curlers, and the author elaborates on the Curlers' Word and Grip and the ultimate formation of Curlers' Courts; undoubtedly the Brotherhood of the Rink had a deeper significance than the words suggest.

Once more it presupposes that the social activities of groups of Masons in the eighteenth century provided the original initiative for the formation of Sporting Societies.

The arrival of golf in America

Research into the Port of Leith records disclosed a large shipment of 96 clubs and 432 balls to Charleston, South Carolina in 1743. This was at a time when the first Societies or Clubs were being formed in Scotland. In due course, the South Carolina Golf Club was formed in 1786, followed by the Savannah Golf Club in 1795. To the shipments already mentioned must be added the following further information which has recently come to light:

> *Extract from Customer Accounts Book, Port of Leith*
> 10.5.1743 in Magdalen William Course for David Deas, South Carolina (Charlston): 8 doz golf clubs, 3 gross golf balls.

> *Extract from Greenock (Glasgow) Customs Accounts*
> 23.10.1750 in the William Irvine, John McLean, Master, for Virginia – 1 doz golf clubs, 12 doz. golf balls
> 27.2.1751 for Virginia – 4 doz. golf clubs, 2 groce golf balls
> 23.4.1751 in the Jean of Glasgow, John Modervell, Master; for Virginia – 1 doz golf clubs and balls.
> (In 1753 there was even a shipment to St Petersburgh in Russia).

> *Extract from Glasgow Customs Accounts*
> 26th February 1765 a shipment to Maryland of 1½ doz. golf clubs and 1 groce golf balls.

To the quite considerable amount of further information which has appeared in the last few years, must be added facts in the publication *The Carolina Low Country – Birthplace of American Golf, 1786* by Charles Price and George C. Rogers Jr (Sea Pines Company, Hilton Head Island, USA, 1980).

We can now look at all these facts in the light of the way in which golf was being played and organised in Scotland in the second half of the nineteenth century by Scottish Freemasons. We might expect that the customs would be similar in America, and that golf was the healthy prerequisite to dining. All the facts so far known appear to fall into place.

The first golf shipment of all to Carolina in 1743 was to David Deas, who was in partnership with his brother John as merchants certainly by 1748; and according to Colonel Alston Deas, a direct descendant, the family tradition has always maintained that the family introduced golf to America and, furthermore, that John Deas, a member of the Kilwinnig Lodge of Charleston, was the first Provincial Grand Master in America. (The Grand Lodge of Charleston was formed in 1772.) John Deas died in 1790. The golf tradition is now supported by fact, and the Masonic tradition is hardly surprising, but needs verifying by a Masonic historian. It is understood that the Charleston Grand Lodge records are now held in Columbia.

We note that there was a Club in Savannah (so they must have had shipments of equipment) and that golf was evidently played in Virginia and Maryland; and from the notice in the *Rivington Royal Gazette*, New York, in April 1779, they must have been playing in New York as well. The advertisement inserted reads: 'The reason for the pleasant and HEALTHY Exercise now advancing, Gentlemen may be furnished with excellent clubs and the veritable Caledonian balls by enquiring at the Printers'. Numerous advertisements appeared in Charleston and Savannah relating to meetings of the respective Golf Clubs, but it is perhaps not surprising that there is no mention of playing golf. It would have been part of the healthy exercise before dining; and there is no evidence of a prize, such as a Silver Club, being played for. The advertisements also bring to light the importance of the Anniversary Dinners, as with British Societies, such as Blackheath, and much in the Masonic tradition at the time.

So we have an authentic picture of golf in America being played in New York, Maryland, Virginia, South Carolina and Georgia between 1743 and 1811 – and then, maybe, dying a natural death. Golf was in the doldrums anyway until the first half of the nineteenth century. With the help of Masonic historians and port and customs records on both sides of the Atlantic, a more definitive picture may well emerge.

**Further information on
wooden clubmakers and
cleekmakers**

We have information on Thomas Nicholson of Pittenweem, b. 1864.
Listed in *Slaters* as cleekmaker in 1893. In 1891 he was listed as a
blacksmith. In 1893 he won the Gold Medal at the Edinburgh Golf
Exhibition. David Nicholson, probably a son, is listed in *Slaters* as a
cleekmaker 1903, 1907, 1911. The picture of the back of an iron club
shows that D. Nicholson was succeeded by T. Galloway but we do
not know on what date. All three men worked in Pittenweem.

Illustration shows a Carrick cleek mark which is different from the
usual Carrick mark.

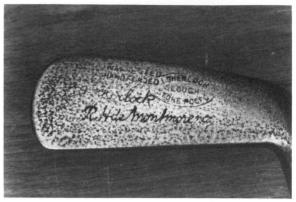

Two photographs of an R.H. de Montmorency 'Push Cleek'. A cleek specially designed for the 'push' shot, c. 1911.

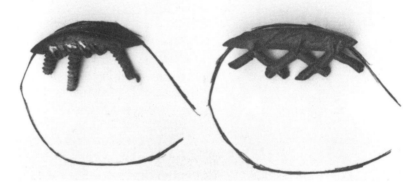

Two methods of fixing the lead in a wooden club are shown here. Right: the more usual method of drilling oblique holes in the wood. Left: an alternative method in which the holes, after drilling straight, were given a screw thread; the tongues of lead appear to be screws, which they are not.

On the back of some Stewart irons there is a small round dot near the toe. This dot was placed there when a clubhead had been personally inspected and finished off by Tom Stewart himself.

The Urquhart adjustable club
There is also a number, but it is not clear whether this is a patent number or, more likely, a serial number for each club. The name Urquhart is also stamped on the face. For information on Urquhart clubs, see page 249.

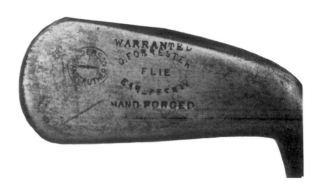

Robert Wilson (1845-1906)
See page 193. We have managed to obtain a good picture of his mark, taken from an old rutter. The two bent nail marks can easily ben seen at the heel of the club.

Note on Forrester of Elie irons
Nearly all his irons are stamped thus, with no cleekmakers' mark. We have found an iron which suggests that Anderson of Anstruther certainly made some of his iron heads, and quite possibly all (see page 120).

Mashie

In *The Golfers Handbook* (1881) by John Forgan, the 'Mashy' is described on page 15. It is said to be 'one of those fanciful clubs that have been invented in recent years, and is entirely unnecessary in the golfer's set'.

We do not think that John Henry Taylor would have agreed with this statement, but it certainly suggests that the mashie was in existence in 1880, or before, and not as we previously stated, introduced in 1885 (see page 179).

Hickory shafts

We are indebted to Mr Morton W. Olman of Cincinnati, for drawing our attention to the letter in *The Sporting Magazine*, August 1828, concerning hickory shafts. It is addressed to the Editor from 'D.A.', is dated June 1828 and headed 'The Game of Golf'. In the course of an attempt to describe the game and its implements the writer states: 'The upper part (i.e. the shaft) is generally of some very pliant tough wood, as hickory, and is joined slantingly to the head by strong glue, and strengthened by well resined cord'.

This account confirms that hickory was being used before 1828 and explains why we have seen several Philp clubs with hickory shafts.

The tales of hickory arriving from Russia and of Forgan being the first to use hickory wood for shafts must be relegated to the realms of fairy tales; what is far more likely is that Philp was the first to discover the value of hickory (and, possibly the early McEwans, also) and that it was he who taught his nephew, Robert Forgan, to use it (see pages 143, 144).

Nuts from a hickory tree.

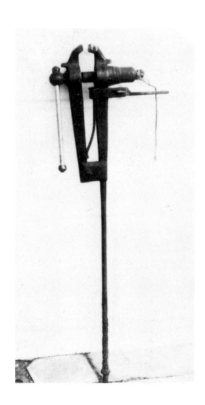

A 'one-leg' vice, originally used by gunsmiths and metal engravers, but much used by clubmakers: the horizontal projection on the right was the fitting for the bench and the end of the leg was embedded in the floor. The particular advantages of the vice were: narrow jaws, the fact that the vice was well above the level of the bench so that it was possible to work from all sides, and the fact that the jaws were well sloped down from the gripping edge, allowing filing, etc. to be done down to the vice edge.

An iron clubhead in which the head and upper hose have been made in two parts and joined by a braised brass joint.

Top surface of an anvil, showing the coned end and, at the near end, the hardie, a square hole used to fit on various accessory pieces but which was also used in making iron clubs (see page 171).

Other additional information (including paintings)

A gutty mould with square mesh markings, a 'bar' of pure gutta percha, a clay pipe mounted on a stand.

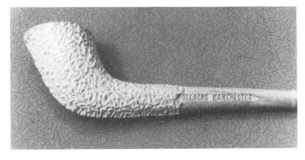

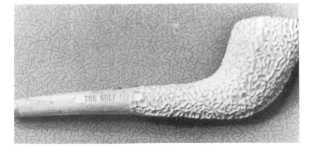

Two views of a clay pipe, 'The Golf Pipe', made by Pollocks of Manchester, probably around 1900.

A heap of sand, a ball on a sand tee, the sand tee maker which made the former (see Patents Section page 260).

Wallet containing patent 'Goffix'. Two brass plates, with studs, which could be fixed to the sole of boots (which must have had a slot into which the rear tongue fitted) to convert a smooth-soled boot into a 'tackety' boot. The price was 5/6d and there was a small tool provided to help take them on and off. Patent c. 1900.

Heard, Percy H. We have seen a number of oil paintings of golf scenes by this artist (see page 308).

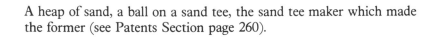

Hopkins, F.P. This painter is the outstanding depicter of early English golf. He painted the picture of Blackheath, which forms the dust cover of this book, and also painted members and scenes of Westward Ho! in oils. He depicted many golfers and scenes at both Westward Ho! and Hoylake in watercolour also, using the name Major Shortspoon or Major S. Research into this painter and his work continues.

Corrigendum

We are indebted to Roy Sollars of Bedford, England, a Golf Collectors' Society member and a Lecturer in Metallurgy, for both drawing our attention to this error and, also, for giving us the necessary information to correct it.

On page 175, lines 15 and 16, the description of the drop forging process is incorrect. 'Pouring molten steel into metal moulds' really describes a casting process.

Drop forging, probably using mild steel, in the early days, is a process in which highly malleable hot steel is placed in a dye fixed to a massive anvil; a slight excess of steel is placed in the dye. A large hammer, accurately positioned by guides, drops on to the dye, and, in doing so, forces the steel into all the cavities in the dye, thus accurately reproducing the dye shape in steel.

List of Prominent Professionals in the UK in 1906

Adwick, James b. 1882 at Turnerwood, Shireoaks, Notts. Club Barnsley.

Anderson, David b. 1874 St Andrews. Club Bromley and Bickley.

Anderson, James Henry b. 1881 Edinburgh. Club Ballater.

Auchterlonie, William b. 1872 St. Andrews. Professional at St Andrews. Open Champion 1893. A noted clubmaker.

Aveston, Willie b. 1873 Holyhead. Club Royal Cromer G.C. Professional at Littlestone G.C. 1899.

Ayton, David b. 1857 St Andrews. Club Great Yarmouth. Has been Professional at Warwick and Lincoln.

Ball, Thomas b. 1882 Hoylake. Club West Lancs. Formerly at Disley G.C.

Batley, James, B. b. 1876 London. Club Bushey Hall G.C. Formerly at Caister-on-Sea.

Beck, Alfred, Ward b. 1883 Jersey, C.I. Club Shirley, Southampton. Formerly at Romsey and Filey, Yorks.

Beck, Thomas, Helier b. ? Jersey, C.I. Club Filey G.C. Formerly at Dinard G.C., France.

Beverley, Ernest Edwin b. 1887 Hunstanton, Norfolk. Club Royston G.C.

Booth, Ernest Edwin b. 1868 Twyning. Club Swansea G.C.

Bradbeer, James b.1880 Berrow, Somerset. Club Porters Park G.C.

Braid, James b.1870 Earlsferry, Fife. Club Walton Heath G.C. Formerly at Romford G.C. (8 yrs.) before that employed at Army & Navy Stores, London as senior clubmaker. Open Champion 1901, 1905.

Bremner, Donald b. ?. Club Glenburn, Rothesay.

Brien, James b. 1882 Tramore, Ireland. Club Chertsey G.C.

Brooks, Charles b. 1876 Knaresborough. Club Hest Bank G.C. Nr. Lancaster.

Brown, Alex Wallace b. 1873 St Andrews. Club Worsley G.C. Manchester.

Brown, Daniel b. 1869 Musselburgh. Club Fairhaven G.C. Lytham.

Brown, David b. 1869 Musselburgh. Club 'in U.S.A.' Formerly at Malvern. Tied with W. Anderson for Open Championship of America in 1903.

Bryant, Albert b.1879 Ascot. Club Reading G.C.

Burns, Jack b. ? St Andrews. Club probably 'unattached'. He worked on the railway. Open champion 1888.

Butchard, Charles S. b. 1876 Carnoustie. Club 'unattached'. He ran a golf factory at 71 Archway Road, N. London. Patentee of v-joint clubs.

Butler, William b. 1866 Athy, Ireland. Club Bache G.C. Chester.

Cahill, Michael Andrew b. 1881 Dublin. Club Atlantic Golf Links, Co. Cork, Ireland.

Callaway, Christopher Edward b. 1869 Isle of Wight. Club United Services Club, Gosport, Hants (since 1885).

Castle, John b. 1879 Littlestone-on-Sea. Club Royal Blackheath.

Cawkwell, George b. 1882 Woodsetts. Club Hallamshire G.C.

Cawsey, George Henry b. 1863 Westward Ho! Club Worcester G.C., Malvern.

Cawsey, Harry b. 1875 Westward Ho! Club Manor G.C., Ashford, Kent.

Chenery, Alfred b. ? Felixstowe. Appears to be 'unattached' but is engaged at present, with Capt. The Hon. R. Greville M.P. at The Priory, Reigate.

Clay, William b. 1875 Yorkshire. Club Foxrock G.C.

Clucas, J. b. 1878 Douglas, Isle of Man. Club Sicklehome G.C., Bamford.

Coburn, George b. 1876 Garvald, Haddingtonshire. Club Portmarnock.

Collins, James Frederick b. 1879 Dunham Woodhouses. Club N. Wales G.C. Llandudno.

Collins, Richard, Senr b. 1852 Leith. Club Tyneside G.C. Ryton-on-Tyne.

Collins, Richard, Jun. b. 1874. Club Cleveland G.C., Redcar.

Coltart, Frank b. 1883 Kinross. Club King James 6th Club, Moncrieffe Island, Perth.

Coper, Sidney John b. 1872. Club Surrey G.C., Leatherhead.

Currie, Thomas Denholm b. 1878 Colinsburgh, Fife. Club Dornoch G.C. (Emigrated to USA – Pittsburgh – after World War I.)

Cuthbert, John b. 1872 St Andrews. Club Wellington G.C. Formerly Stanmore G.C.

Curtis, Herbert Lewis b. 1878 Northam, N. Devon. Club ?

Dalgleish, Joseph b. 1860 Aberlady. Club Nairn G.C.

Davey, Ashley b. 1876 Caister-on-Sea. Club Thanet G.C., Kent.

Day, Arthur b. 1878 Burham-on-Sea, Somerset. Club Town G.C., Scarborough.

Duncan, George b. 1883 Aberdeen. Club Timperley G.C. (later to become Open Champion, etc.)

Duncan, John b. 1861 Earlsferry. Club Stirling G.C.

Edgar, J. Douglas b. 1884 Newcastle-on-Tyne. Club Northumberland G.C.

Fairbrother, Walter Charles b. 1878 Richmond, Surrey. Club Redhill and Reigate.

Ferguson, Bob b. 1846 Musselburgh. Club Musselburgh (caddie & greenkeeper). Open Champion 1880, 1881, 1882.

Fernie, Thomas R. b. 1858 St Andrews. Club Troon.

Fernie, William b. 1863 St Andrews. Club Glamorganshire G.C. Open Champion 1883.

Fletcher, Walter b. 1879 Watford. Club Harpenden G.C.

Foord, Ernest b. 1884 Berrow, Somerset. Club Burnham G.C.

Freemantle, Sam b. 1874 Upham, Hants. Club Summer: Ostend. Winster: Cannes.

Fulford, John b. 1879 Northam. Club Birstall G.C. Formerly at Helouan, Egypt.

Fulford, T. Henry b. 1877 Northam. Club Bradford G.C. Yorks. (Formerly at Helouan, Egypt.)

Gaudin, Phillip John b. 1879 Jersey. Club Trafford Park, Manchester.

Gaudin, W C b. 1874 Jersey. Club Royal Portrush G.C.

Gibson, Charles H. b. 1860 Musselburgh. Club Westward Ho! A noted clubmaker.

Gow, Allan Grant b. 1885 Lochton. Club Gog Magog G.C., Cambridge. Formerly at Gullane.

Gowans, James Jun. b. 1880 Edinburgh. Club Flimpton & Bury St Edmunds.

Gray, Arthur George b. 1879 Climping, Sussex. Club Port Elizabeth G.C., S. Africa. (Formerly Chichester, Surbiton and Gravesend.)

Gray, Reginald b. 1886 Littlehampton. Club Summersdale G.C., Chichester.

Green, J.W. b. 1870 Coatham. Club High Coniscliffe, Darlington.

Hallam, W. b. 1877 Southport. Club Ormskirk G.C., Lancashire. (Formerly Newquay)

Hamlet, W.R. b. ? Sunninghill. Club Atherstone G.C. (Formerly, Ascot and Hyères)

Harris, G.T. b. 1874 Sandwich. Club (Private Professional to Duke and Duchess of Fife)

Harris, Harry James b. 1877 Sandwich. Club Sandwich G.C. (Royal St Georges)

Haskins, Albert b. 1875 Woburn. Club West Derby G.C.

Heath, William Richard b. 1874 Isle of Wight. Club St Margarets-at-Cliffe, Kent.

Hepburn, James b. 1876 Carnoustie. Club Home Park, Surbiton.

Herd, Alexander b. 1868 St Andrews. Club Huddersfield G.C., Fixby, Yorks. Open Champion 1902 (Later at Moor Park G.C.)

Herd, David b. 1872 St Andrews. Club Littlestone-on-Sea.

Hills, Percy b. 1880 Ashford, Kent. Club North Manchester G.C.

Hocking, Fred b. 1875 Northam, N. Devon. Club Copthorne G.C., Sussex.

Hogg, John b. 1872 North Berwick. Club Sandown.

Hooker, Ernest James b. 1874 Epsom. Club Enfield.

Howlett, Albert James b. 1876 Haslemere. Club Puttenham.

Hugh, Henry b. 1877 Portrush. Club Rye.

Hughes, R. Osbert b. 1881. Club Coventry.

Humble, George b. 1875. Club Llandrindod Wells G.C.

Hunter, John b. 1871 Prestwick. Club Prestwick. (Two years with Tom Morris)

Hunter, William b. 1878 Perth. Club Richmond G.C., Surrey. Formerly at Australian G.C., Sydney & Shelter Island G.C., USA.

Hutcheson, J.G. b. 1873 Glasgow. Club Porthcawl G.C., Wales.

Hutchison, Jack b. 1885 St Andrews. Club 'engaged at St Andrews'.

Jacobs, John Charles b. 1878 Ryde, Isle of Wight. Club Royal Isle of Wight G.C.

Jacobs, Robert b. 1883 Brancaster. Club Waveney Valley G.C., Bungay.

Jeffery, William J. Kellaway b. 1876 Newport, Monmouthshire. Club Saunton G.C., North Devon

Job, Leonard Charles b. 1883 Deal. Club Dover. Formerly Deal.

Jones, Rowland b. 1872 St Helens, Isle of Wight. Club Wimbledon Park G.C.

Kennet, Charles b. 1877 Eastbourne. Club Hampstead G.C.

Kenny, Daniel b. 1882 North Berwick. Club Kirkcudbrightshire G.C.

Kenyon, Ernest b. 1877 Eastbourne. Club Exmouth, Devon.

Kinnell, David b. 1879 Leven, Fife. Club Prestwick St Nicholas.

Kinnell, James b. 1876 Leven, Fife. Club Purley Downs G.C. Surrey.

Kirk, Walter b. 1868 Blackheath. Club Wallasey G.C.

Kirkaldy, Andrew b. 1860 Denhead, Fife. Club R & A.

Kirkaldy, Jack b. 1858 Denhead, Fife. Club 'unattached'. Worked for R. Forgan.

Larke, Frank Arthur b. 1879 Great Yarmouth. Club Mid-Norfolk G.C. Scoulton.

Larkin, Richard b. 1877 Meath, Ireland. Club Bray G.C.

Lawrence, Charles H. b. 1878 Sandwich. Club Charnwood G.C., Loughborough.

Leaver, Thomas N. b. 1872 Liverpool. Club Conwey G.C. Formerly Aberdovey.

Leaver, William John b. 1879 Liverpool. Club Harlech.

Leigh, Charles Henry b. 1878 Redmire. Club Windermere G.C.

Lewis, Leonard b. 1879 Gt Malvern. Club Dudley, Worcester.

Lewis, William Price b. 1874 Gt Malvern. Club Kings Norton. Formerly Stinchcombe.

Lloyd, Charles b. 1867 Presteigne, Wales. Club Newport, Mon.

Logan, Hugh b. 1880 Prestwick. Club London Scottish G.C., Wimbledon. Formerly at Prestwick. Also cleekmaker with Gibsons of Kinghorn (Genii irons).

Longhurst, Joseph George b. 1863 Ascot. Club Royal Ascot G.C. and at Homberg, Germany.

Lonie, William Roy b. 1863 St. Andrews. Club Warlingham G.C. Formerly Rye.

Loveridge, Henry Alexander b. ? Shipley. Club Shipley G.C.

Lowe, George b. ? Carnoustie. Club Old Links G.C., St Annes-on-Sea. Formerly Hoylake 12 years; Lytham and St Annes 17 years. Apprenticed at St Andrews and Carnoustie. Captain Leven Thistle G.C. 1876.

Lowe, William b. ? Carnoustie. Club Buxton and High Peak G.C.

MacDonald, William Thomas b. ? St. Andrews. Club Sheringham.

MacNamara, William b. 1883 Lahinch. Club Lahinch, Ireland.

Magee, H.J. b. 1875 Portrush. Club Greenore. Formerly Portrush.

Matthews, Alfred b. 1882 Streetly. Club Rhyl G.C.

Martin, Robert b. 1853 Cupar, Fife. Club 'unattached', clubmaker to Tom Morris at St Andrews. Open Champion 1876, 1885. Formerly at Cambridge and Felixstowe.

Martin, Robert Bell b. 1871 Club Kirkaldy, Balwearie G.C.

May, George Henry b. 1875. Club Ashstead G.C. Epsom.

Mayd, Charles Henry b. 1884 Dudley. Club Bridgnorth G.C.

McDonald, Edward b. ? Montrose. Club Whitby G.C.

McEwan, Douglas b. 1869 Musselburgh. Club Musselburgh (The clubmaking family).

McEwan, Peter b. 1874 Musselburg. Club Hesketh G.C., Lancs (The clubmaking family).

McKenna, John Joseph b. 1879 Dollymount. Club Malahide G.C., Ireland.

Monk, Arthur Charles b. 1867 Cobham, Surrey. Club Roehampton G.C.

Moore, John William b. 1867 Greenwich. Club North Hants G.C., Fleet. (Formerly Blackheath).

Morris, John b. 1847 St Andrews. Club Hoylake (since formation in 1869). Nephew of Tom Morris, Senr.

Morris, Thomas b. 1821 St Andrews. Club St. Andrews (retd 1904). Formerly at Prestwick 12 years. Open Champion 1861, 1862, 1864, 1867.

Mundy, Herbert Rupert b. 1878 Winchester. Club Churston G.C., S. Devon. Formerly Winchester.

Munro, Robert b. 1871 Arbroath. Club Royal Wimbledon G.C. Formerly Mid-Surrey. Apprenticed to Simpson of Carnoustie.

Neaves, Charles b. 1871 Leven, Fife. Club Lossiemouth.

Nelson, James b. 1872 Elie, Fife. Club Peebles, G.C.

O'Brien, James b. 1882 Tramore, Ireland. Club Chertsey G.C.

Padgham, Alfred b. 1876 Forest Row. Club Caterham and Kenley G.C.

Park, William b. 1864 Musselburgh. Club Huntercombe G.C. Open Champion 1887, 1889. A noted clubmaker.

Parr, Joseph b. 1872 Hoylake. Club Bromborough G.C. Formerly W. Lancs G.C.

Parr, Simon b. 1869 Hoylake. Club Seacroft G.C. Skegness. Formerly Exmouth and N. Manchester.

Parr, Thomas Ernest b. 1882 Hoylake. Club Heswell G.C.

Paxton, James b. 1874 Musselburgh. Club Littlestone G.C. Formerly Bray, Guernsey.

Paxton, Peter b. 1859 Musselburgh. Club Leeds G.C. (A man of invention. Later at R. Eastbourne.) A noted clubmaker.

Powell, A.W. b. 1880 Gt Malvern. Club Leominster G.C.

Randall, John b. 1880 London. Club Sundridge Park G.C.

Randall, Robert D. b. ? Barnet. Club South Bedfordshire G.C. Formerly at Ghent G.C., Belgium and Weintorf-Reinbek G.C., Germany. St. Petersburg G.C. Russia 'in their seasons'.

Ray, Edward b. 1879 Jersey. Club Ganton G.C. Formerly at Churston. (Open Champion 1912 and later at Oxhey G.C., Herts.)

Reid, Arthur E. b. 1882 Bulwell, Notts. Club Blackpool N. Shore G.C. Formerly engaged at Boston, Lucerne and Paris. Open Champion of Switzerland 1905.

Renouf, T. George b. 1878 Jersey. Club Silloth G.C.

Richards, Vivian Stephen b. 1880 Ludgvan, Cornwall. Club Burton-on-Trent G.C.

Riseborough, Ernest H. b. 1878 Sheringham, Norfolk. Club Royal Norwich.

Roberts, Charles b. 1881 Hoylake. Club Woolton G.C.

Roberts, Ernest Charles b. 1882 London. Club Surbiton G.C.

Robinson, John E.P. b. 1879 Cambridge. Club Rochdale G.C.

Robinson, William b. 1882 Baildon. Club Baildon G.C.

Rolland, Douglas Stewart b. 1860 Earlsferry. Club Bexhill G.C. A great amateur golfer, before he turned pro.

Ross, John b. 1879 St Andrews. Club 'unattached'. Formerly at Seaford and Banstead Downs.

Rowe, Arthur John b. 1870 Westward Ho! Club Royal Ashdown Forest G.C. Was at R. Ashdown for over 50 years. Later President P.G.A.

Sargent, George b. ? Brookham, Surrey. Club Dewsbury and District G.C.

Saunders, Fred b. 1876 Northam, Devon. Club Highgate G.C.

Savage, George Robert b. 1882 Ascot. Club Redhill and Reigate G.C.

Sayers, Bernard b. 1866 Earlsferry. Club North Berwick.

Scott, Andrew Herd b. 1875 Elie. Club Elie G.C. A noted clubmaker.

Sellers, Robert John b. 1876 Roehampton. A clubmaker with Spalding Bros. Formerly clubmaker at Wimbledon, Leven and Bournemouth.

Sherlock, James George b. 1875 High Wycombe. Club University G.C., Oxford.

Simpson, Archie b. 1866 Earlsferry. Club Aberdeen. Formerly Carnoustie.

Simpson, Robert b. 1862 Earlsferry. Club Carnoustie. A noted clubmaker.

Simpson, Thomas William b. 1877 Cayton. Club Lytham and St Annes.

Smith, Charles Ralph b. ? Quebec, Canada. Club West Middlesex G.C.

Smith, George Reginald b. 1872 Malvern. Club Leicester G.C.

Smyth, Fred b. 1882 Carnalea, County Down. Club Newcastle, County Down.

Spraggs, George Owen b. 1870 Hayling Island. Club Hayling Island G.C.

Stephenson, George Henry b. 1884 Nottingham. Club Tunbridge Wells.

Stephens, James b. 1885 West Derby. Club Huyton G.C.

Strong, Herbert b. 1880 Ramsgate. Club Cambridge.

Taylor, John Henry b. 1871 Northam, N. Devon. Club Royal Mid-Surrey. Formerly Burnham and Berrow, Winchester and Wimbledon. Open Champion 1894, 1895, 1900, 1909, 1913.

Taylor, John William b. 1870 Seaton Carew. Club Late of the Cleveland G.C. Redcar.

Taylor, Joshua b. 1881 Northam, N. Devon. Club Aldeburgh G.C.

Toogood, Alfred Harry b. 1872 St Helens, Isle of Wight. Club West Essex G.C. Formerly at Eltham and Minchinhampton.

Toogood, Walter G. b. 1874 St Helens, Isle of Wight. Club Ilkley G.C., Yorks. Formerly at Eltham.

Tribble, Alan b. 1877 Romsey, Hants. Club Bicester G.C.

Trineman, Charles Frederick b. 1881 Exeter, Devon. Club Axe Cliff G.C.

Tuck, Harry Hobart b. 1879 Brancaster. Club Hull G.C.

Turner, John Henry b. 1880 Lincoln. Club Wycombe and Bourne End G.C.

Vardon, Harry W. b. 1870 Jersey. Club South Herts G.C. Formerly Ganton. Open Champion 1896, 1898, 1899, 1903, 1911, 1914. US Open 1900.

Vardon, Thomas Alfred b. 1872 Jersey. Club Royal St George's Sandwich.

Wade, Harry Benjamin b. 1881 Gt Yarmouth. Club Lowestoft G.C.

Warburton, William b. ? Dunham Town. Club Grimsby and Cleethorpes G.C.

Walker, Maitland James b. 1882 Kingston, Surrey. Club Barton-on-Sea, Hants.

Walker, Robert F. b. 1861 Earlsferry, Fife. Club Rochester G.C. Kent.

Weir, Alex Naish b. 1874 Arbroath. Club Cruden Bay G.C.

Weston, Frederick William b. 1869 Wimbledon. Club Wimbledon (6 years).

White, Jack b. 1873 Pefferside, N. Berwick. Club Sunningdale. Open Champion 1904. Notable putter and clubmaker. Ben Sayers' nephew.

White, Samuel b. 1879 Carnoustie. Club Culcrieff G.C. Crieff.

Whiting, Frederick b. 1874 Worcester. Club West Cornwall G.C. Lelant.

Whiting, Samuel b. 1879 Malvern. Club Rotheram and District G.C.

Whiting, Walter b. 1870 Worcester. Club Edgebaston G.C. Birmingham.

Williamson, Tom b. 1880 Grantham. Club Hollinwell.

Wilson, Reginald R. b. 1886 New Bushey. Club Berkhamsted G.C.

Wingate, Charles Henry b. 1875 Hoylake. Club Olton G.C.

Alterations and Additions to the 1906 List of Prominent Professionals, in 1912

Baggs, A.E. b. 1887 Westbury-on-Trim, Bristol. Club Willingdon G.C. Eastbourne.

Ball, Sidney b. 1878 Hoylake. Club Wrexham G.C.

Barker, H.H. b. 1883 Kirkburton. Club Garden City G.C., New York. Irish Open Amateur Champion 1906.

Binnie, William b. 1876 Kinghorn, Fife. Club Burntisland G.C.

Brace, T.J. b. 1884 Camarthen. Club Brecon G.C., Wales.

Cawsey, Harry See 1906 List – now at Skegness G.C.

Coltart, Frank See 1906 List – now at Clacton-on-Sea G.C.

Duncan, George See 1906 List – now at Hanger Hill G.C., Ealing.

Edmundson, James b. 1886 Portrush. Club Bromborough G.C., Chester.

Fernie, William See 1906 List – now at Troon G.C.

Gaudin, Phillip See 1906 List – now at Fulwell G.C., Middlesex.

Harris, G.T. See 1906 List – now also Professional at Royal Craggon G.C.

Herd, Alexander See 1906 List – now at Coombe Hill G.C.

Hills, Percy See 1906 List – now at Harrogate G.C.

Horne, W.H. b. 1881 Dover. Club Chertsey G.C.

Hughes, Cyril b. 1890 Hoylake. Club Chester G.C.

Irving, John A. b. 1876 Eastbourne. Club Eastbourne Downs G.C.

Kay, James b. 1855 Leith. Club Seaton Carew G.C. (since 1886).

Leach, Fred b. 1885 Baildon. Club Northwood G.C., Middlesex.

Leaver, W.J. See 1906 List – now at Worsley G.C. Manchester. (8 years at Hoylake).

McEwan, David b. 1867 Musselburgh. Club Birkdale G.C. (Formby 6 years).

McEwan, Douglas See 1906 List – now at Leasowe G.C., Cheshire.

Mayo, Charles See 1906 List – now at Burhill G.C., Walton-on-Thames.

Moran, Michael b. 1886 Dollymount. Club Royal Dublin G.C. Dollymount.

Nicholls, Bernard b. 1877 Dover. Club Seaford G.C., Sussex. Formerly at Aix-les-Bains and Cannes, France. Lennox G.C. Massachusetts. Philadelphia Country Club; Hollywood Club; Nashville Golf and Country Club, USA. (In all 18 years abroad)

Oke, J.H. b. 1880 Northam, N. Devon. Club Streetly G.C. Sutton Coldfield. Formerly at Ottawa G.C. Canada (2 years). Canadian Open Champion 1904.

Park, W. See 1906 List – now Judge at the International Golf Exhibition of 1910. 'Well known as a golf green architect'. Unattached. Address, Edinburgh.

Rainford, Peter b. 1878 Club Llangammarch G.C., Wales.

Randall, Robert D. See 1906 List – now at Herne Bay G.C., Kent.

Reid, Arthur E. See 1906 List – now at Castle Bromwich G.C., Birmingham.

Reid, Wilfred E. b. 1884 Bulwell, Notts. Club Banstead Downs G.C. Formerly Skegness and La Boulie.

Renouf, Thomas G. See 1906 List – now at Trafford Park G.C., Manchester.

Robson, Frederick b. 1885 Shotten. Club West Surrey G.C., Godalming. 7 years assistant to Jack Hughes at Chester. (Later he went to Addington G.C. and became noted for teaching and clubmaking.)

Sherlock, James George See 1906 List – now at Stoke Poges G.C.

Thomson, Robert b. ? N. Berwick. Club North Berwick.

Toogood, Alfred Henry See 1906 List – now at Beckenham G.C.

Toogood, Walter G. See 1906 List – now at Alwoodley G.C. Leeds.

Vardon, Thomas Alfred See 1906 List – now at Owentsia G.C. Lake Forrest, USA.

Watt, Tom b. 1881 Bridge of Weir. Club Timperley G.C.

Wynne, Phillip b. 1875 Haddington. Club Addington Court G.C., East Croydon.

Index

We are much indebted to John Marsh of Chapel Hill, North Carolina, a Golf Collectors Society member, who compiled this Index and kindly allowed us to use it in our Revised Edition.